6 LANGUAGE
VISUAL DICTIONARY

Thunder Bay Press
An imprint of Printers Row Publishing Group
9717 Pacific Heights Blvd, San Diego, CA 92121
www.thunderbaybooks.com • mail@thunderbaybooks.com

Thunder Bay Press
Publisher: Peter Norton • Associate Publisher: Ana Parker
Art Director: Charles McStravick
Acquisitions Editor: Kathryn C. Dalby
Editor: Angela Garcia
Production Team: Beno Chan, Mimi Oey, Rusty von Dyl

Produced by Moseley Road Inc.
1780 Chemin Queens Park, Gatineau, QC, J9J 1V1, Canada
www.moseleyroad.com
President: Sean Moore • Art and Editorial Director: Lisa Purcell
Production Director: Adam Moore
Translations Editor: Finn Moore
Translators: Maria Müller (German), Estefania Angueyra (Spanish), Max Delphin (French),
Fabio Massarenti (Italian), Fernando Micael Pinto and Mónica Cabral (Portuguese)
Photo Research: Elizabeth Bressanelli, Lisa Purcell, Grace Moore
Images © Dreamstime.com and Shutterstock.com.
For specific credits, please contact Moseley Road Inc. (info@moseleyroad.com).

Library of Congress Control Number: 2021953283
ISBN: 978-1-6672-0047-7

Printed in China
26 25 24 23 22   1 2 3 4 5

À PROPOS DE
CE DICTIONNAIRE

Le dictionnaire visuel en 6 langues offre un moyen efficace d'apprendre et de mémoriser des milliers de mots couramment utilisés via l'association de mots et d'images des six langages européens les plus populaires.

Ce dictionnaire abondamment illustré est subdivisé par thème en douze sections qui couvrent un large éventail de sujets, allant du corps à la maison en passant par les affaires, les sports, les loisirs, les sciences et beaucoup d'autres. Il renferme également des mots et des expressions supplémentaires, que ce soit pour les voyages, les conversations ou simplement pour élargir votre vocabulaire dans une nouvelle langue.

Pour simplifier votre apprentissage, le dictionnaire restitue les termes dans le même ordre—anglais, allemand, espagnol, français, italien et portugais—et leur attribue un code couleur pour faciliter le repérage visuel, par exemple:

house / das Haus / la casa
la maison / la casa / a casa

Hormis l'anglais, les noms incluent leurs articles définis pour indiquer le genre (masculin, féminin ou neutre) et s'ils sont masculins ou pluriels. Les verbes sont désignés par un *(v)* suivant le terme anglais, par exemple:

sing (v) / singen / cantar
chanter / cantare / cantar

Tout au long du livre, vous trouverez aussi des cases grises avec des mots ou phrases supplémentaires qui reflètent le thème de la page. Chaque langue dispose aussi de son propre index à votre disposition.

INFORMAZIONI
SUL DIZIONARIO

Abbinando parole e immagini, *il Dizionario visivo delle 6 lingue* ti offre un modo efficace per imparare e memorizzare migliaia di termini comuni in sei lingue europee ampiamente parlate.

Questo compendio altamente illustrato è diviso tematicamente in dodici sezioni che coprono una vasta gamma di argomenti, dal corpo alla casa agli affari, sport, tempo libero, scienza e molti altri. Sono incluse anche parole e frasi aggiuntive, sia per i viaggi, la conversazione o semplicemente per ampliare il tuo vocabolario in una nuova lingua.

Per facilità d'uso, il dizionario presenta i termini nello stesso ordine—inglese, tedesco, spagnolo, francese, italiano e portoghese—e li codifica a colori per una facile individuazione visiva, per esempio:

house / das Haus / la casa
la maison / la casa / a casa

A parte l'inglese, i sostantivi includono i loro articoli definiti per indicare il genere (maschile, femminile o neutro) e se sono singolari o plurali. I verbi sono indicati con una *(v)* dopo il termine inglese, per esempio:

sing (v) / singen / cantar
chanter / cantare / cantar

In tutto il libro, troverete anche caselle grigie con ulteriori parole o frasi che riflettono il tema della pagina. Ogni lingua ha anche un proprio indice per una rapida consultazione.

SOBRE O DICIONÁRIO

Emparelhando palavras e imagens, *o visual Dicionário de 6 línguas* oferece-lhe uma forma eficiente de aprender e memorizar milhares de termos comuns em seis línguas europeias amplamente faladas.

Este compêndio altamente ilustrado está dividido tematicamente em doze secções que cobrem uma vasta gama de tópicos, desde o corpo a casa, o negócio, o desporto, o lazer, a ciência, e muitos outros. Também estão incluídas palavras e frases adicionais, seja para viagens, conversação, ou simplesmente para alargar o seu vocabulário numa nova língua.

Para facilitar a sua utilização, o dicionário apresenta consistentemente os termos na mesma ordem—inglês, alemão, espanhol, francês, italiano e português—e codifica-os para um fácil seguimento visual, por exemplo:

house / das Haus / la casa
la maison / la casa / a casa

Para além do inglês, os substantivos incluem os seus artigos definidos para indicar o género (masculino, feminino ou neutro) e se são singulares ou plurais. Os verbos são indicados com um *(v)* seguindo o termo inglês, por exemplo:

sing (v) / singen / cantar
chanter / cantare / cantar

Ao longo do livro, também encontrarás caixas cinzentas com palavras ou frases adicionais que refletem o tema da página. Cada língua também tem o seu próprio índice para uma referência rápida.

THE BODY
AND HEALTH

DER KÖRPER UND
DIE GESUNDHEIT

EL CUERPO
Y LA SALUD

LE CORPS HUMAIN
ET LA SANTÉ

IL CORPO
E LA SALUTE

O CORPO
E A SAÚDE

PARTS OF THE BODY / DIE TEILE DES KÖRPERS / LAS PARTES DEL CUERPO
LES PARTIES DU CORPS HUMAIN / LE PARTI DEL CORPO / AS PARTES DO CORPO

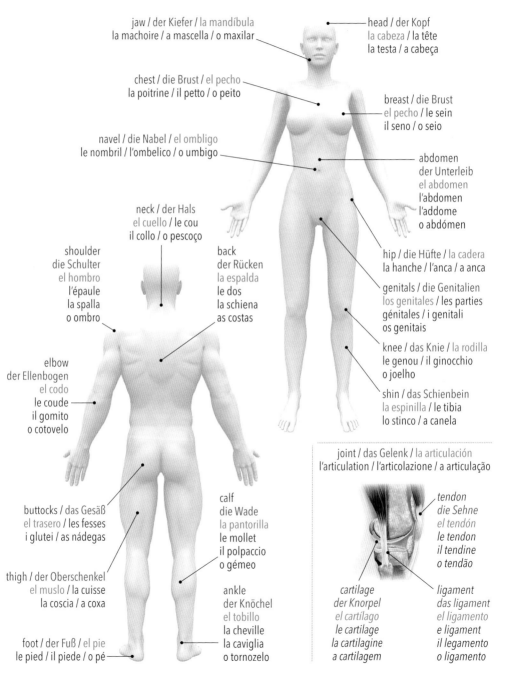

jaw / der Kiefer / la mandíbula
la machoire / a mascella / o maxilar

head / der Kopf
la cabeza / la tête
la testa / a cabeça

chest / die Brust / el pecho
la poitrine / il petto / o peito

breast / die Brust
el pecho / le sein
il seno / o seio

navel / die Nabel / el ombligo
le nombril / l'ombelico / o umbigo

abdomen
der Unterleib
el abdomen
l'abdomen
l'addome
o abdómen

neck / der Hals
el cuello / le cou
il collo / o pescoço

back
der Rücken
la espalda
le dos
la schiena
as costas

hip / die Hüfte / la cadera
la hanche / l'anca / a anca

shoulder
die Schulter
el hombro
l'épaule
la spalla
o ombro

genitals / die Genitalien
los genitales / les parties
génitales / i genitali
os genitais

knee / das Knie / la rodilla
le genou / il ginocchio
o joelho

elbow
der Ellenbogen
el codo
le coude
il gomito
o cotovelo

shin / das Schienbein
la espinilla / le tibia
lo stinco / a canela

joint / das Gelenk / la articulación
l'articulation / l'articolazione / a articulação

buttocks / das Gesäß
el trasero / les fesses
i glutei / as nádegas

calf
die Wade
la pantorilla
le mollet
il polpaccio
o gémeo

tendon
die Sehne
el tendón
le tendon
il tendine
o tendão

thigh / der Oberschenkel
el muslo / la cuisse
la coscia / a coxa

ankle
der Knöchel
el tobillo
la cheville
la caviglia
o tornozelo

cartilage
der Knorpel
el cartílago
le cartilage
la cartilagine
a cartilagem

ligament
das ligament
el ligamento
e ligament
il legamento
o ligamento

foot / der Fuß / el pie
le pied / il piede / o pé

BODY STRUCTURE / DIE STRUKTUR DES KÖRPERS LA ESTRUCTURA DEL CUERPO / LA STRUCTURE DU CORPS HUMAIN / LA STRUTTURA CORPOREA A ESTRUTURA CORPORAL

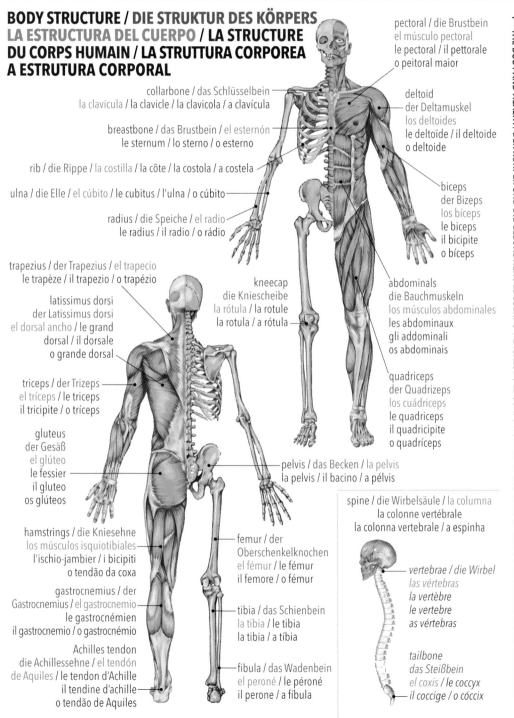

pectoral / die Brustbein
el músculo pectoral
le pectoral / il pettorale
o peitoral maior

collarbone / das Schlüsselbein
la clavicula / la clavicle / la clavicola / a clavícula

deltoid
der Deltamuskel
los deltoides
le deltoïde / il deltoide
o deltoide

breastbone / das Brustbein / el esternón
le sternum / lo sterno / o esterno

rib / die Rippe / la costilla / la côte / la costola / a costela

ulna / die Elle / el cúbito / le cubitus / l'ulna / o cúbito

biceps
der Bizeps
los bíceps
le biceps
il bicipite
o bíceps

radius / die Speiche / el radio
le radius / il radio / o rádio

trapezius / der Trapezius / el trapecio
le trapèze / il trapezio / o trapézio

kneecap
die Kniescheibe
la rótula / la rotule
la rotula / a rótula

abdominals
die Bauchmuskeln
los músculos abdominales
les abdominaux
gli addominali
os abdominais

latissimus dorsi
der Latissimus dorsi
el dorsal ancho / le grand
dorsal / il dorsale
o grande dorsal

triceps / der Trizeps
el tríceps / le triceps
il tricipite / o tríceps

quadriceps
der Quadrizeps
los cuádriceps
le quadriceps
il quadricipite
o quadríceps

gluteus
der Gesäß
el glúteo
le fessier
il gluteo
os glúteos

pelvis / das Becken / la pelvis
la pelvis / il bacino / a pélvis

spine / die Wirbelsäule / la columna
la colonne vertébrale
la colonna vertebrale / a espinha

hamstrings / die Kniesehne
los músculos isquiotibiales
l'ischio-jambier / i bicipiti
o tendão da coxa

femur / der
Oberschenkelknochen
el fémur / le fémur
il femore / o fémur

vertebrae / die Wirbel
las vértebras
la vertèbre
le vertebre
as vértebras

gastrocnemius / der
Gastrocnemius / el gastrocnemio
le gastrocnémien
il gastrocnemio / o gastrocnémio

tibia / das Schienbein
la tibia / le tibia
la tibia / a tíbia

Achilles tendon
die Achillessehne / el tendón
de Aquiles / le tendon d'Achille
il tendine d'achille
o tendão de Aquiles

tailbone
das Steißbein
el coxis / le coccyx
il coccige / o cóccix

fibula / das Wadenbein
el peroné / le péroné
il perone / a fíbula

BODY SYSTEMS / DIE KÖRPER-SYSTEME / LOS SISTEMAS DEL CUERPO
LES SYSTÈMES DU CORPS / SISTEMI DEL CORPO / OS SISTEMAS DO CORPO

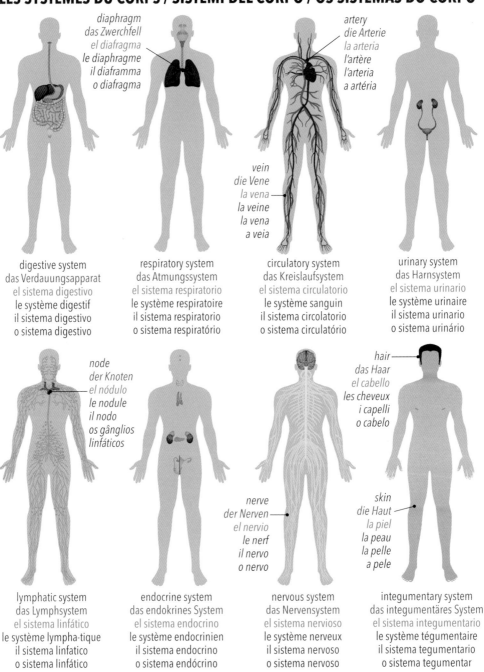

diaphragm
das Zwerchfell
el diafragma
le diaphragme
il diaframma
o diafragma

artery
die Arterie
la arteria
l'artère
l'arteria
a artéria

vein
die Vene
la vena
la veine
la vena
a veia

digestive system
das Verdauungsapparat
el sistema digestivo
le système digestif
il sistema digestivo
o sistema digestivo

respiratory system
das Atmungssystem
el sistema respiratorio
le système respiratoire
il sistema respiratorio
o sistema respiratório

circulatory system
das Kreislaufsystem
el sistema circulatorio
le système sanguin
il sistema circolatorio
o sistema circulatório

urinary system
das Harnsystem
el sistema urinario
le système urinaire
il sistema urinario
o sistema urinário

node
der Knoten
el nódulo
le nodule
il nodo
os gânglios
linfáticos

hair
das Haar
el cabello
les cheveux
i capelli
o cabelo

nerve
der Nerven
el nervio
le nerf
il nervo
o nervo

skin
die Haut
la piel
la peau
la pelle
a pele

lymphatic system
das Lymphsystem
el sistema linfático
le système lympha-tique
il sistema linfatico
o sistema linfático

endocrine system
das endokrines System
el sistema endocrino
le système endocrinien
il sistema endocrino
o sistema endócrino

nervous system
das Nervensystem
el sistema nervioso
le système nerveux
il sistema nervoso
o sistema nervoso

integumentary system
das integumentäres System
el sistema integumentario
le système tégumentaire
il sistema tegumentario
o sistema tegumentar

INTERNAL ORGANS / INNERE ORGANE / LOS ÓRGANOS INTERNOS
LES ORGANES INTERNES / ORGANI INTERNI / OS ÓRGÃOS INTERNOS

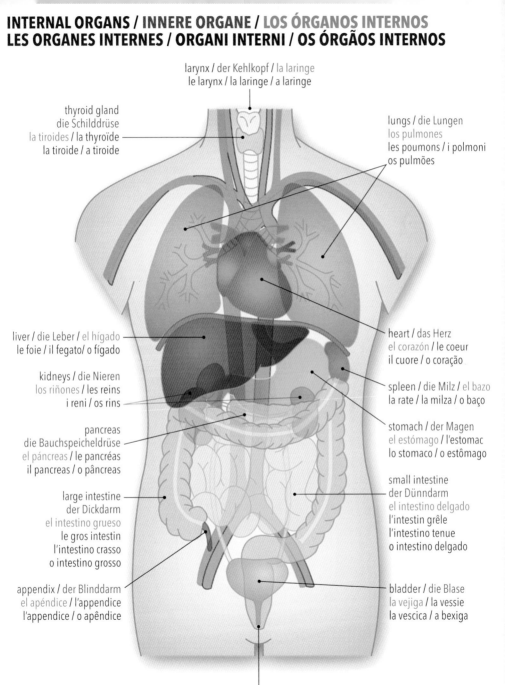

larynx / der Kehlkopf / la laringe
le larynx / la laringe / a laringe

thyroid gland
die Schilddrüse
la tiroides / la thyroïde
la tiroide / a tiroide

lungs / die Lungen
los pulmones
les poumons / i polmoni
os pulmões

liver / die Leber / el hígado
le foie / il fegato / o fígado

kidneys / die Nieren
los riñones / les reins
i reni / os rins

pancreas
die Bauchspeicheldrüse
el páncreas / le pancréas
il pancreas / o pâncreas

large intestine
der Dickdarm
el intestino grueso
le gros intestin
l'intestino crasso
o intestino grosso

appendix / der Blinddarm
el apéndice / l'appendice
l'appendice / o apêndice

heart / das Herz
el corazón / le coeur
il cuore / o coração

spleen / die Milz / el bazo
la rate / la milza / o baço

stomach / der Magen
el estómago / l'estomac
lo stomaco / o estômago

small intestine
der Dünndarm
el intestino delgado
l'intestin grêle
l'intestino tenue
o intestino delgado

bladder / die Blase
la vejiga / la vessie
la vescica / a bexiga

rectum / der Enddarm /el recto
le rectum / il retto / o reto

head and throat / der Kopf und Rachen / la cabeza y la garganta / la tête et la gorge
testa e gola / a cabeça e a garganta

sinus / die Nasennebenhöhlen
el seno / le sinus / il sinus
os seios nasais

nasal cavity / die Nasenhöhle
la cavidad nasal / la fosse nasale
la cavità nasale / a cavidade nasal

tongue / die Zunge / la lengua
la langue / la lingua / a língua

mandible / der Unterkiefer
a mandíbula / la mandibule
la mandibola / a mandíbula

larynx / der Kehlkopf / la laringe
le larynx / la laringe / a laringe

Adam's apple / der Adamsapfel
la manzana de Adán / la pomme d'Adam
il pomo d'Adamo / a maçã de Adão

brain / das Gehirn / el cerebro
le cerveau / il cervello / o cérebro

olfactory bulb / der Riechkolben
el bulbo olfatorio/ le bulbe olfactif
il bulbo olfattivo / o bulbo olfatório

palate / der Gaumen / el paladar
le palais / il palato / o palato

epiglottis / der Kehldecke
la epiglotis / l'épiglotte
l'epiglottide / a epiglote

pharynx / der Pharynx / la faringe
le pharynx / la faringe / a faringe

esophagus / die Speiseröhre
el esófago / l'oesophage
l'esofago / o esófago

trachea / die Luftröhre / a tráquea
la trachée / la trachea / a traqueia

male reproductive organs / die männlichen Fortpflanzungsorgane
el sistema reproductor masculino / les organes reproducteurs masculins
organi riproduttivi maschili / órgãos reprodutores masculinos

ureter / der Harnleiter / el ureter
l'uretère / l'uretere / o ureter

seminal vesicle / die Samenleiter
la vesícula seminal / la vésicule séminale
la vescicola seminale / a vesícula seminal

prostate / die Prostata / la próstata
la prostate / la prostata / a próstata

vas deferens / der Samenleiter
los conductos deferentes / le canal déférent
il vaso deferente / o canal deferente

epididymis / die Nebenhoden
el epidídimo / l'épididyme
l'epididimo / o epidídimo

testicle / der Hoden / el testículo
le testicule / il testicolo / o testículo

bladder / die Blase / la vejiga
la vessie / la vescica/ a bexiga

penis / der Penis / el pene
le pénis / il pene / o pênis

hormone / das Hormon
la hormona / l'hormone
l'ormone / a hormona

testosterone / das Testosteron
la testosterona / la testostérone
il testosterone / a testosterona

impotent / impotent
impotente / impuissant
impotente / a impotência

sexually transmitted disease
die sexuell übertragbare
Krankheit / la enfermedad de
transmisión sexual / la maladie
sexuellement transmissible
la malattia sessualmente
trasmissibile / a doença
sexualmente transmissível

female reproductive organs / die Weibliche Fortpflanzung-sorgane / el sistema reproductor femenino / les organes reproducteurs féminins / organi riproduttivi femminili órgãos reprodutores femininos

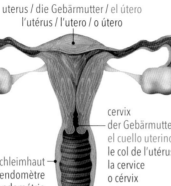

uterus / die Gebärmutter / el útero
l'utérus / l'utero / o útero

fallopian tube
der Eileiter
las trompas de Falopio
la trompe de Fallope
le tube di Falloppio
a trompa de Falópio

ovary / der Eierstock
el ovario / l'ovaire
l'ovaio / o ovário

cervix
der Gebärmutterhals
el cuello uterino
le col de l'utérus
la cervice
o cérvix

endometrium / die Gebärmutterschleimhaut
el endometrio / l'endomètre
l'endometrio / o endométrio

fertilization / die Befruchtung
la fertilización / la fécondation
la fecondazione / a fertilidade

egg
das Eizelle
el óvulo
l'œuf
l'uovo
o óvulo

sperm / die Spermien
el esperma / le spermatozoïde
lo sperma / o esperma

---

menstruation / die Menstruation / la menstruación la menstruation / le mestruazioni / a menstruação

feminine hygeine products / die Damenhygieneprodukte / los productos de higiene femenina / les produits d'hygiène féminins i prodotti per l'igiene femminile / os produtos de higiene feminina

menstrual cup
die Menstruationstasse
la copa menstrual
la coupe menstruelle
la coppetta mestruale
o copo menstrual

tampon / der Tampon / el tampón
le tampon / il tampone / o tampão

sanitary pad / die Damenbinde
la toalla sanitaria / la serviette hygiénique
l'assorbente / o penso higiénico

birth control injection
die Verhütungsspritze / la inyección
anticonceptiva / l'injection
contraceptive / l'iniezione
anticoncezionale / a injeção
anticoncecional

diaphragm / das Diaphragma
el diafragma / le diaphragme
il diaframma / o diafragma

vaginal ring / der Vaginalring
el anillo vaginal / l'anneau vaginal
l'anello vaginale / o anel vaginal

contraceptive patch
das Verhütungspflaster / el parche
anticonceptivo / le patch contraceptif
il cerotto contraccettivo / o adesivo
contracetivo

cervical cap / die Portiokappe
el capuchón cervical / la cape
cervicale / il cappuccio cervicale
o capuz cervical

gynecologist / der Gynäkologe
el ginecólogo / e gynécologue
il ginecologo / a ginecologista

---

contraception / die Verhütung los anticonceptivos la contraception la contraccezione a contraceção

pill / die Pille / la púldora
la pillule / la pillola / a pílula

condom / das Kondom
el condón / le préservatif
il preservativo / o preservativo

IUD / die Spirale / el dispositivo
intrauterino / DIU / la spirale
intrauterina / o DIU

pregnancy / die Schwangerschaft / el embarazo / la grossesse / gravidanza / a gravidez

pregnancy test
der Schwangerschaftstest
la prueba de embarazo
le test de grossesse
il test di gravidanza
o teste de gravidez

umbilical cord
die Nabelschnur
el cordón umbilical
le cordon ombilical
il cordone ombelicale
o cordão umbilical

placenta
die Plazenta
la placenta
le placenta
la placenta
a placenta

fetus / der Fötus / el feto
le foetus / il feto / o feto

amniotic fluid
das Fruchtwasser
el líquido
amniótico
le liquide
amniotique
il liquido
amniotico
o líquido
amniótico

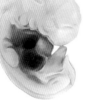

embryo
der Embryo
el embrión
l'embryon
l'embrione
o embrião

vagina / die Scheide
la vagina / le vagin
la vagina / a vagina

pregnancy stages / die
Schwangerschaftsstadien
las etapas del embarazo / les étapes
de la grossesse / le fasi della gravidanza
as fases da gravidez

first trimester / das erstes
Trimester / el primer trimestre
le premier trimestre
il primo trimestre
o primeiro trimestre

second trimester
das zweites Trimester
el segundo trimestre
le deuxième trimestre
il secondo trimestre
o segundo trimestre

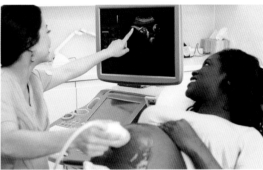

ultrasound / der Ultraschall / la ecografía
les ultrasons / l'ecografia / o ultrassom

third trimester
das drittes Trimester
el tercer trimestre
le troisième trimestre
il terzo trimestre
o terceiro trimestre

birth / die Geburt
el nacimiento
la naissance / la nascita
o nascimento

conceive (v) / schwanger werden
embarazarse / tomber enceinte
rimanere incinta / engravidar

pregnant / schwanger
embarazada / enceinte
incinta / grávida

ovulation / der Eisprung
la ovulación / l'ovulation
l'ovulazione / a ovulação

intercourse / der Geschlechtsverkehr
el coito / le rapport sexuel
il rapporto sessuale / a relação sexual

fertile / fruchtbar / fértil / fertile
fertile / fértil

infertile / unfruchtbar / estéril
stérile / infertile / infértil

prenatal / pränatal / prenatal
prénatal / prenatale / pré-natal

womb / die Gebärmutter / el útero
l'utérus / l'utero / o ventre

adoption / die Adoption
la adopción / l'adoption
l'adozione / a adoção

childbirth / die Geburt / el nacimiento / l'accouchement / parto / o nascimento

labor / die Wehen
el parto / le travail
il travaglio
o trabalho de parto

midwife
die Hebamme
la partera
la sage-femme
l'ostetrica / a parteira

delivery room / der Kreißsaal
la sala de partos / la salle d'accouchement
la sala parto / a sala de parto

fetal monitor
der Wehenschreiber
el monitor fetal / le moniteur
foetal / il monitor fetale
o monitor fetal

contraction / die Wehe
las contracciones / la contraction
la contrazione / a contração

amniocentesis / die
Amniozentese / la amniocentesis
l'amniocentèse / l'amniocentesi
a amniocentese

epidural / die Epiduralanästhesie / la epidural
la péridurale / l'epidurale / a epidural

dilation / die Dilatation
la dilatación / la dilatation
la dilatazione / a dilatação

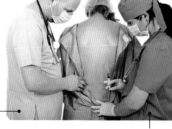

episiotomy / die Dammschnitt
la episiotomía / l'épisiotomie
l'episiotomia / a episiotomia

breech birth / die Steißgeburt
el parto de nalgas
l'accouchement par le siège
a nascita podalica
o nascimento de culatra

obstetrician
der Geburtshelfer
el obstetra / l'obstrécien
l'ostetrica / o obstetra

anesthetist
der Anästhesist
el anestesista
l'anesthésiste
l'anestesista
a anestesista

cesarean section / der
Kaiserschnitt / la cesárea
la césarienne / il taglio cesareo
a cesariana

premature birth / die Frühgeburt / el nacimiento
prematuro / la naissance prématurée
la nascita prematura / o nascimento prematuro

forceps / die Zange / los fórceps
le forceps / il forcipe / o fórceps

miscarriage / die Fehlgeburt
el aborto espontáneo / la fausse
couche / l'aborto spontaneo
o aborto espontâneo

newborn baby
das neugeborenes Baby
el recién nacido
le nouveau-né
il neonato
o recém-nascido

abortion / die Abtreibung
el aborto / l'avortement
l'aborto / o aborto

incubator / der Inkubator / la incubadora
l'incubateur / l'incubatrice / a incubadora

FACE / DAS GESICHT / LA CARA / LE VISAGE / FACCIA / O ROSTO

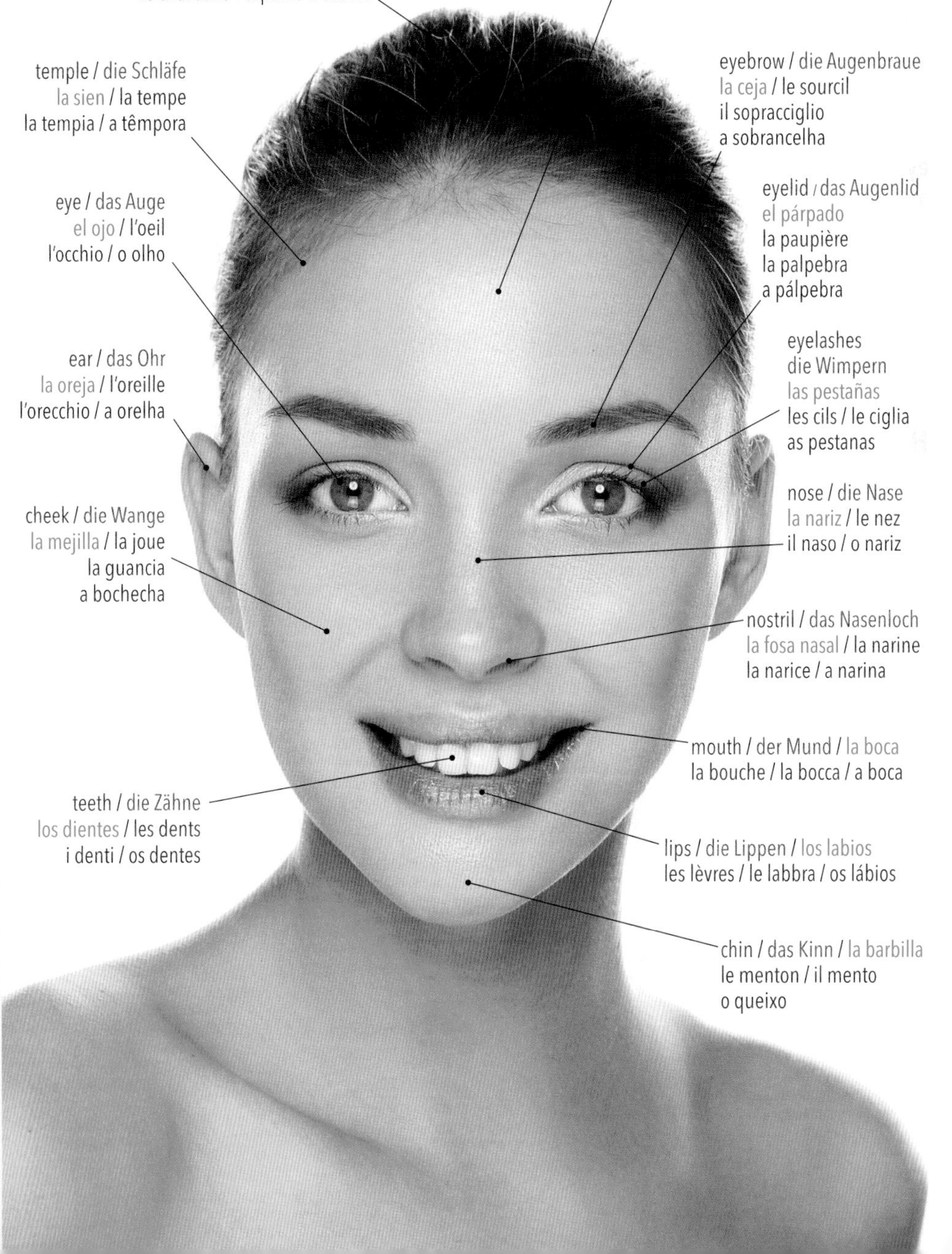

hair / das Haar / el cabello
le cheveux / i capelli / o cabelo

forehead / die Stirn / la frente
le front / la fronte / a testa

temple / die Schläfe
la sien / la tempe
la tempia / a têmpora

eyebrow / die Augenbraue
la ceja / le sourcil
il sopracciglio
a sobrancelha

eye / das Auge
el ojo / l'oeil
l'occhio / o olho

eyelid / das Augenlid
el párpado
la paupière
la palpebra
a pálpebra

ear / das Ohr
la oreja / l'oreille
l'orecchio / a orelha

eyelashes
die Wimpern
las pestañas
les cils / le ciglia
as pestanas

nose / die Nase
la nariz / le nez
il naso / o nariz

cheek / die Wange
la mejilla / la joue
la guancia
a bochecha

nostril / das Nasenloch
la fosa nasal / la narine
la narice / a narina

mouth / der Mund / la boca
la bouche / la bocca / a boca

teeth / die Zähne
los dientes / les dents
i denti / os dentes

lips / die Lippen / los labios
les lèvres / le labbra / os lábios

chin / das Kinn / la barbilla
le menton / il mento
o queixo

mole / das Muttermal
el lunar / le grain de
beauté / il neo / a verruga

dimple / das Grübchen
los hoyuelos / la fossette
le fossette / as covinhas

freckles / die
Sommersprossen
las pecas / les tâches de
rousseur / le lentiggini
as sardas

birthmark / das Mutterma
la marca de nacimiento
la tâche de naissance
la voglia / a marca
de nascença

eye color / die Augenfarbe / el color de ojos / la couleur des yeux / il colore degli occhi
a cor dos olhos

brown / braun / marrones
marron / marrone
castanho

hazel / haselnussbraun
color avellana / noisette
nocciola / avelã

blue / blau / azules
bleu / blu / azul

green / grün / verdes
vert / verde / verde

HANDS / DIE HÄNDE / LAS MANOS / LES MAINS / MANI / AS MÃOS

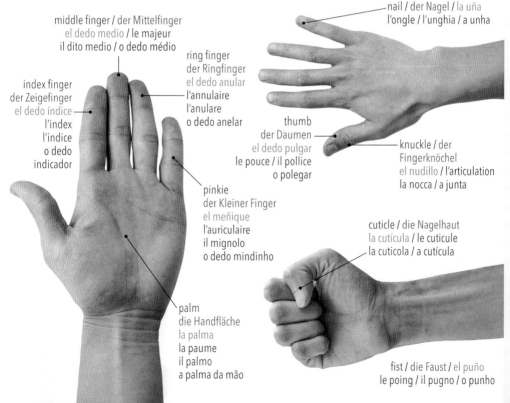

nail / der Nagel / la uña
l'ongle / l'unghia / a unha

middle finger / der Mittelfinger
el dedo medio / le majeur
il dito medio / o dedo médio

ring finger
der Ringfinger
el dedo anular
l'annulaire
l'anulare
o dedo anelar

index finger
der Zeigefinger
el dedo índice
l'index
l'indice
o dedo
indicador

thumb
der Daumen
el dedo pulgar
le pouce / il pollice
o polegar

knuckle / der
Fingerknöchel
el nudillo / l'articulation
la nocca / a junta

pinkie
der Kleiner Finger
el meñique
l'auriculaire
il mignolo
o dedo mindinho

cuticle / die Nagelhaut
la cutícula / le cuticule
la cuticola / a cutícula

palm
die Handfläche
la palma
la paume
il palmo
a palma da mão

fist / die Faust / el puño
le poing / il pugno / o punho

FEET / DIE FÜßE / LOS PIES / LES PIEDS / PIEDI / OS PÉS

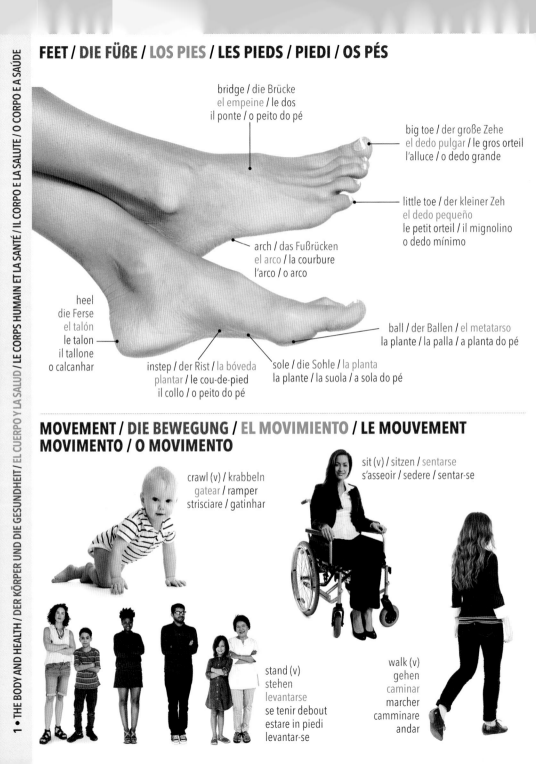

bridge / die Brücke
el empeine / le dos
il ponte / o peito do pé

big toe / der große Zehe
el dedo pulgar / le gros orteil
l'alluce / o dedo grande

little toe / der kleiner Zeh
el dedo pequeño
le petit orteil / il mignolino
o dedo mínimo

arch / das Fußrücken
el arco / la courbure
l'arco / o arco

heel
die Ferse
el talón
le talon
il tallone
o calcanhar

ball / der Ballen / el metatarso
la plante / la palla / a planta do pé

instep / der Rist / la bóveda
plantar / le cou-de-pied
il collo / o peito do pé

sole / die Sohle / la planta
la plante / la suola / a sola do pé

MOVEMENT / DIE BEWEGUNG / EL MOVIMIENTO / LE MOUVEMENT
MOVIMENTO / O MOVIMENTO

crawl (v) / krabbeln
gatear / ramper
strisciare / gatinhar

sit (v) / sitzen / sentarse
s'asseoir / sedere / sentar-se

stand (v)
stehen
levantarse
se tenir debout
estare in piedi
levantar-se

walk (v)
gehen
caminar
marcher
camminare
andar

run (v) / rennen / correr / courir / correre / correr

hop (v) / hüpfen
saltar / sautiller
saltellare / pular

kick (v) / treten
patear / frapper
calciare / pontapear

lie down (v) / hinlegen
acostarse / s'allonger
sdraiare / deitar-se

jump (v) / springen
saltar / sauter
saltare / saltar

kneel (v)
knien
arrodillarse
s'agenouiller
inginocchiare
ajoelhar-se

bend (v) / sich bücken
agacharse / se pencher
piegarsi / inclinar-se

squat (v) / hocken
ponerse en cuclillas
s'accroupir / abbassarsi
agachar-se

lift (v) / heben
levantar / soulever
sollevare / levantar

ILLNESS / DIE KRANKNEIT / LAS ENFERMEDADES
LA MALADIE / MALATTIA / AS DOENÇAS

fever / das Fieber
la fiebre / la fièvre
la febbre / a febre

thermometer / das Thermometer
el termómetro / le thermomètre
il termometro / o termómetro

headache / die Kopfschmerzen
I dolor de cabeza / le mal
de tête / il mal di testa
a dor de cabeça

sore throat / die
Halsentzündung / el dolor
de garganta / le mal à la
gorge / il mal di gola
a dor de garganta

inhaler / der Inhalator
el inhalador / l'inhalateur
l'inalatore / o inalador

influenza / die Grippe
la influenza / la grippe
l'influenza / a gripe

nausea
die Übelkeit
las náuseas
la nausée
la nausea
as náuseas

allergy / die Allergie
la alergia / l'allergie
l'allergia / a alergia

asthma / das Asthma
el asma / l'asthme
l'asma / a asma

diabetes / der Diabetes
la diabetes / le diabète
il diabete / a diabetes

stomach ache / der
Magenschmerzen / el dolor
de estómago / le mal
d'estomac / il mal di stomaco
a dor de estômago

cancer / der Krebs
el cáncer / le cancer
il cancro / o cancro

infection / die Infektion
la infección / l'infection
l'infezione / a infeção

cough / der Husten
la tos / la toux
la tosse / a tosse

sneeze / das Niesen
el estornudo / l'éternuement
lo starnuto / os arrepios

heart attack / der
Herzinfarkt / el infarto
l'attaque cardiaque
l'attacco di cuore
o ataque cardíaco

faint (v) / in Ohnmacht
fallen / desmayarse
s'évanouir / svenire
desmaiar

hives / die Nesselsucht
la urticaria / l'urticaire
l'orticaria / a urticária

epilepsy / die Epilepsie
la epilepsia / l'épilepsie
l'epilessia / a epilepsia

chills
der Schüttelfrost
los escalofríos
les frissons
i brividi
os arrepios

hay fever / der
Heuschnupfen
la alergia al polen
le rhume des foins
la febbre da fieno
a febre dos fenos

migraine / die Migräne
la migraña / la migraine
l'emicrania / a enxaqueca

virus / der Virus
el virus / le virus
il virus / o vírus

nosebleed / das Nasenbluten
la hemorragia nasal
le saignement du nez / il sangue
dal naso / a hemorragia nasal

cold / die Erkältung
el resfriado / le rhume
il raffreddore
a constipação

vomit (v) / erbrechen
vomitar / vomir
vomitare / vomitar

diarrhea / die Diarrhöe
la diarrea / la diarrhée
la diarrea / a diarreia

rash
der Ausschlag
el sarpullido
les éruptions cuta-nées
l'eruzione cutanea
a erupção cutânea

measles / die Masern
el sarampión
la rougeole / il morbillo
o sarampo

eczema / das Ekzem
el eczema / l'eczéma
l'eczema / a eczema

back pain / die
Rückenschmerzen / el dolor de
espalda / le mal de dos / il mal
di schiena / a dor de costas

chicken pox / die
Windpocken / la varicela
la varicelle / la varicella
a varicela

mumps / die Mumps
las paperas / les oreillons
gli orecchioni / a papeira

stroke / der Schlaganfall
el accidente
cerebrovascular
l'accident vasculaire
cérébral / l'ictus / o AVC

INJURY / DIE VERLETZUNG / LAS LESIONES
LES BLESSURES / INFORTUNIO / AS LESÃOS

fracture / die Fraktur / las fracturas
la fracture / la frattura / a fratura

sling / die Schlinge / el cabestrillo
l'écharpe / la fasciatura / a faixa

cast / der Gips / el yeso / le plâtre / il gesso / o gesso

compress / die Kompresse
la compresa / la compresse
la compressione / a compressa

sprain / die Verstauchung
el esguince / l'entorse
la distorsione / a entorse

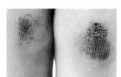

abrasion / die Abschürfung
la raspadura / l'éraflure
l'abrasione / a abrasão

cut / die Schnittwunde
el corte / l'entaille
il taglio / o corte

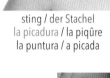

sting / der Stachel
la picadura / la piqûre
la puntura / a picada

splinter / der Splitter
la astilla / l'écharde
la scheggia / a farpa

bite / der Biss
la mordedura / la morsure
il morso / a mordidela

blister / die Blase
la ampolla / l'ampoule
la vescica / a bolha

sunburn / der Sonnenbrand
la insolación / le coup de soleil
la scottatura / o escaldão

bruise / der Bluterguss
el moretón / l'hématome
il livido / o hematoma

break / der Bruch
la ruptura / la cassure
la rottura / a ruptura

crutches
die Krücken
las muletas
les béquilles
le stampelle
as muletas

splint
die Schiene
la férula
l'attelle
la stecca
a tala

accident / der Unfall / el accidente
l'accident / l'incidente / o acidente

hemorrhage / die Blutung
la hemorragia / l'hémorragie
l'emorragia / a hemorragia

wound / die Wunde / la herida
la blessure / la ferita / a ferida

concussion / die
Gehirnerschütterung / la concusión
la commotion cérébrale
la commozione cerebrale
a concussão

head injury / die Kopfverletzung
la lesión cerebral / la blessure
à la tête / il trauma cranico
a lesão na cabeça

electric shock / der elektrischer
Schock / la descarga eléctrica
le choc électrique / lo shock
elettrico / o choque elétrico

whiplash / das Schleudertrauma
el latigazo / le traumatisme cervical
il colpo di frusta / o esticão

neck brace / die Halskrause
el cuello ortopédico / la minerve
il collare / o colar cervical

stitches / die Stiche / las suturas
les points de suture
i punti di sutura / os pontos

burn / die Verbrennung
la quemadura / la brûlure
l'ustione / a queimadura

first aid kit / das Erste-Hilfe-Kasten
el kit de primeros auxilios
le kit de premiers soins
il kit di primo soccorso
o kit de primeiros socorros

tweezers
die Pinzette
las pinzas
la pince à épiler
le pinzette
a pinça

adhesive tape
das Klebeband
la cinta adhesiva
le ruban adhésif
il nastro adesivo
a fita adesiva

sterile gauze / die sterile
Gaze / la gasa esterilizada
la gaze stérile / la garza
sterile / a gaze esterilizada

Band-Aids
die Heftpflaster
las curitas / les pansements
i cerotti / os pensos rápidos

non-latex gloves / die
Nicht-Latex-Handschuhe
los guantos sin látex
les gants sans latex
i guanti non in lat-tice
as luvas sem látex

elastic bandage
der elastische Binde
el vendaje elástico
le bandage élastique
la benda elastica
a faixa elástica

hydrogen peroxide
das Wasserstoffperoxyd
el agua oxigenada
le peroxyde
d'hydrogène
il perossido
di idrogeno
a água oxigenada

wound pad
die Wundauflage
la compresa para heridas
la compresse / il tampone
per ferite / a compressa

antiseptic wipes / die
antiseptische Tücher
las toallitas anti-sépticas
les lingettes antiseptiques
le salviette anti-settiche
as toalhitas desinfetantes

antibiotic ointment
die antibiotische Salbe
el ungüento anti-biótico
la pommade antibiotique
a pomata antibi-otica
a pomada antibiótica

scissors / die Schere
las tijeras / les ciseaux
le forbici / a tesoura

pain killer
das Schmerztablette
el analgésico / l'anti-douleurs
l'antidolorifico / o analgésico

safety pins / die
Sicherheitsnadeln
los imperdibles
les épingles à nourrice
le spille da balia
os alfinetes

oral antihistamine / das
orale Antihistaminikum
el antihistamínico oral
l'antihistaminique à avaler
l'antistaminico orale
o anti-histamínico oral

flashlight / die
Taschenlampe / la linterna
la lampe torche / la torcia
elettrica / a lanterna

instant cold pack / das
Kühlakku / la compresa
fría instantánea / la poche
de froid / il ghiaccio
istantaneo / a bolsa de
frio instantâneo

alcohol pad
das Alkoholtupfer
la toallita con alcohol
les compresses imbibées
il tampone di alcool
toalhitas humedecidas
com álcool

saline solution
die Kochsalzlösung
la solución salina
la solution saline
la soluzione salina
o soro fisiológico

anesthetic spray
der Anästhesiespray
el aerosol
anestésico
l'aérosol
d'anesthésique
lo spray anestetico
o spray anestésico

nasal spray
das Nasenspray
el aerosol nasal
le spray nasal
lo spray nasale
o spray nasal

hand sanitizer / das
Handdesinfektionsmittel
el gel antiséptico
le gel hydroalcoolique
il disinfettante
per le mani
o desinfetante
para as mãos

mask / die Maske
la mascarilla / le masque
la maschera / a máscara

cigarette lighter / der
Zigarettenanzünder
el encendedor / le briquet
l'accendino / o isqueiro

resealable bags
die wiederverschließbare
Beutel / las bolsas resellables
les sacs refermables
i sacchetti richiudibili
os sacos reutilizáveis

blanket / die Decke
la manta / la couverture
la coperta / o cobertor

EMERGENCY SERVICES / DIE NOTFALLDIENSTE / LOS SERVICIOS DE EMERGENCIA / LES SERVICES D'URGENCE / I SERVIZI DI EMER-GENZA OS SERVIÇOS DE URGÊNCIA

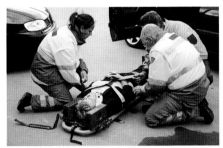

emergency room / die Notaufnahme
la sala de emergencias / les urgences
il pronto soccorso / o pronto-socorro

ambulance / der Krankenwagen
la ambulancia / l'ambulance
l'ambulanza / a ambulância

air rescue
die Luftrettung
el rescate aéreo
l'intervention
par les airs
il soccorso aereo
o resgate aéreo

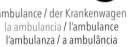

stretcher / die Bahre / la camilla
le brancard / la barella / a maca

paramedic
der Rettungssanitäter
el paramédico / le médecin
du SAMU / il paramedico
o paramédico

PHARMACY / DIE APOTHEKE / LA FARMACIA
LA PHARMACIE / FARMACIA / A FARMÁCIA

prescription
die Verschreibung
a prescripción
la prescription
la prescrizione
a receita médica

tablet / die Tablette
la pastilla / le comprimé
la compressa / o comprimido

medication
das Medikament
el medicamento
le médicament
il farmaco
a medicação

dosage
die Dosierung
la dosis
la posologie
il dosaggio
a dose

drops / die Tropfen
las gotas / les gouttes
le gocce / as gotas

dropper / der Tropfer
el cuentagotas
le compte-gouttes
il contagocce
o conta-gotas

pharmacist / der Apotheker
la farmacéutica / le pharmacien
il farmacista / o farmacêutico

pill box / die Pillendose / el pastillero
le pillulier / la scatola di pillole
a caixa de comprimidos

blister pack / die Blisterpackung
el paquete de medicamentos
l'emballage blister / il blister
a embalagem blíster

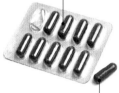

suppository / das Zäpfchen
el supositorio
le suppositoire / la supposta
o supositório

cough syrup / der Hustensaft
el jarabe para la tos
le sirop antitussif
lo sciroppo per la tosse
o xarope contra tosse

gel cap / die Gelkappe
la cápsula de gel
des gélules de gel / la capsula
in gel / a cápsula mole

capsule / die Kapsel
la cápsula de gel
la gélule / la capsula
a cápsula

aisles / den Gängen / los pasillos / les rayons / le corsie / os corredores

beauty / die Schönheit
belleza / la beauté
la bellezza / a beleza

skin care / die Hautpflege
protección de la piel
les soins pour la peau
i prodotti per la cura della
pelle / os cuidados de pele

vitamins / die Vitamine
vitaminas / les vitamines
le vitamine / as vitaminas

pain relief / die
Schmerzlinderung / alivio
del dolor / soulager les
douleurs / l'antidolorifico
os analgésicos

baby / das Baby
bebé / les bébés
il bambino / o bebé

dental care / die
Zahnpflege / cuidado
dental / les soins dentaires
i prodotti per la cura
dei denti / os cuidados
dentários

cough and cold / der
Husten und die Erkältung
tos y resfriado / la toux et
le rhume / la tosse
e il raffreddore / a tosse
e constipação

hair care / die Haarpflege
cuidado del cabello
les soins capillaire
i prodotti per la cura dei capelli
os cuidados de cabelo

ABOUT THE DICTIONARY

Pairing words and pictures, the *6-Language Visual Dictionary* offers you an efficient way to learn and memorize thousands of terms common in six widely spoken European languages.

This highly illustrated compendium is divided thematically into twelve sections that cover a broad range of topics, from the body to the home to business, sports, leisure, science, and many others. Also included are additional words and phrases, whether for travel, conversation, or simply to widen your vocabulary in a new language.

For ease of use, the dictionary consistently presents the terms in the same order–English, German, Spanish, French, Italian, and Portuguese–and color-codes them for easy visual tracking, for example:

house / das Haus / la casa
la maison / la casa / a casa

Other than English, nouns include their definite articles to indicate gender (masculine, feminine, or neutral) and whether they are singular or plural. Verbs are denoted with a *(v)* following the English term, for example:

sing (v) / singen / cantar
chanter / cantare / cantar

Throughout the book, you will also find gray boxes with additional words or phrases that reflect the theme of the page. Each language also has its own index for quick reference.

ÜBER DAS WÖRTERBUCH

Durch die Kombination von Wörtern und Bildern bietet Ihnen dieses *6-sprachige visuelles Wörterbuch* eine effiziente Methode, tausende gängige Begriffe in sechs weit verbreiteten europäischen Sprachen zu lernen.

Dieses stark illustrierte Handbuch ist zwölf Abschnitte untergliedert, die eine breite Palette an Themen abdecken - vom menschlichen Körper und dem Zuhause bis hin zu Business, Sport, Freizeit, Wissenschaft und vielem mehr. Es sind ebenfalls zusätzliche Wörter und Ausdrücke enthalten, beispielsweise für Reisen und Unterhaltungen oder einfach nur, um Ihren Wortschatz in einer neuen Sprache zu erweitern.

Für die leichtere Verwendung bildet das Wörterbuch die Begriffe fortlaufend in derselben Reihenfolge ab–Englisch, Deutsch, Spanisch, Französisch, Italienisch und Portugiesisch– und kodiert sie farblich, damit sie leichter erkannt werden können. Zum Beispiel:

house / das Haus / la casa
la maison / la casa / a casa

Substantive werden zudem mit ihrem bestimmten Artikel aufgeführt, um das Geschlecht zu markieren (männlich, weiblich oder neutral) und ob sie in der Ein- oder Mehrzahl sind. Verben werden mit einem *(v)* nach dem englischen Begriff gekennzeichnet, zum Beispiel:

sing (v) / singen / cantar
chanter / cantare / cantar

Im gesamten Buch finden Sie schließlich noch graue Kästen mit weiteren Wörtern oder Ausdrücken, die den Themenbereich der Seite widerspiegeln. Jede Sprache hat außerdem ihren eigenen Index zum schnellen Nachschlagen.

ACERCA DEL DICCIONARIO

Combinando palabras e imágenes, el *Diccionario visual de 6 Idiomas* te ofrece una forma eficaz de aprender y memorizar miles de términos comunes en seis lenguas europeas muy habladas.

Este compendio altamente ilustrado está dividido temáticamente en doce secciones que abarcan una amplia gama de temas, desde el cuerpo hasta el hogar, pasando por los negocios, los deportes, el ocio, la ciencia y mucho más. También se incluyen palabras y frases adicionales, ya sea para viajar, conversar o simplemente para ampliar tu vocabulario en un nuevo idioma.

Para facilitar su uso, el diccionario presenta los términos siempre en el mismo orden– inglés, alemán, español, francés, italiano y portugués–y los codifica por colores para facilitar su seguimiento visual, por ejemplo:

house / das Haus / la casa
la maison / la casa / a casa

Aparte del inglés, los sustantivos incluyen sus artículos definidos para indicar el género (masculino, femenino o neutro) y si son singulares o plurales. Los verbos se indican con una *(v)* tras el término inglés, por ejemplo

sing (v) / singen / cantar
chanter / cantare / cantar

A lo largo del libro, también encontrarás cuadros grises con palabras o frases adicionales que reflejan el tema de la página. Cada idioma tiene también su propio índice para una rápida referencia.

DOCTOR / DIE ÄRZTE / EL DOCTOR / LE MÉDECIN / MEDICO / O MÉDICO

doctor's office / die Arztpraxis / el consultorio / le cabinet du médecin
l'ufficio del medico / o consultório médico

vaccination
die Impfung
la vacunación
la vaccination
la vaccinazione
a vacinação

nurse
die Krankenschwester
la enfermera
l'infirmière
l'infermiera
a enfermeira

appointment
der Termin / la cita
le rendez-vous
l'appuntamento
a marcação

consultation
die Sprechstunde
la consulta
la consultation
la consultazione
a consulta

exam room / der Untersuchungszimmer / el cuarto de examen / la salle d'examen
la sala esami / a sala de exames

I need a doctor.
Ich brauche einen Arzt.
Necesito un médico.
J'ai besoin d'un
médecin. / Ho bisogno
di un medico. / Preciso
de um médico.

syringe
die Spritze
la jeringe
la seringue
la siringa
a seringa

It hurts here. / Es tut
hier weh. / Me duele
aquí. / J'ai mal ici.
Mi fa male qui.
Dói-me aqui.

telemedicine / die Telemedizin
la telemedicina
la télémédecine
la telemedicina
a telemedicina

electronic blood pressure monitor
das Elektronisches Blutdruckmessgerät
el tensiómetro electrónico
l'appareil de surveil-lance
de la pression sanguine
il monitor elettronico
della pressione sanguigna
o medidor de tensão arterial eletrónico

needle / die Nadel / la aguja
l'aiguille / l'ago / a agulha

medical exam / die medizinische Untersuchung / el examen médico
l'examen médical / l'esame medico / o exame médico

blood pressure cuff / die Blutdruckmanschette
el esfigmomanómetro / le tensiomètre / il bracciale per
la pressione sanguigna / a braçadeira de tensão arterial

patient / der Patient
el paciente / le patient
il paziente / o doente

waiting room / das
Wartezimmer / la sala
de espera / la salle d'attente
la sala d'attesa / a sala
de espera

exam table
der Untersuchungstisch
la camilla
la table d'examen
il tavolo d'esame
a mesa de exame

stethoscope / das Stethoskop
el estetoscopio
le stétoscope / lo stetoscopio
o estetoscópio

HOSPITAL / DAS KRANKENHAUS / EL HOSPITAL / L'HÔPITAL
OSPEDALE / O HOSPITAL

surgeon / der Chirurg / el cirujano
le chirurgien / il chirurgo / o cirurgião

IV drip / der IV-Tropf
el goteo intravenoso / la perfusion
intraveineuse / la flebo
o gotejamento IV

surgical technician
der Operationstechniker
el técnico quirúrgico
l'assistant
il tecnico chirurgico
o médico-cirúrgico

anesthetist / der Anästhesist
el anestesista / l'anesthésiste
l'anestesista / a anestesista

gown / der Kittel
la bata / la blouse
il camice / a bata

scrubs / der Kittel / la ropa quirúrgica
la blouse / il camice / o pijama cirúrgico

operating room / der Operationssaal / el quirófano / la salle d'opération / la sala operatoria / o bloco operatório

ICU / die Intensivstation
la UCI / l'USI / la terapia
intensiva / a UCI

injection / die Injektion
la inyección / l'injection
l'iniezione / a injeção

blood test / der Bluttest
la prueba de sangre
le test sanguin / l'esame
del sangue / as análises

X-ray / das Röntgenbild
la radiografía / la radio
i raggi x / o raio X

children's ward / die
Kinderstation / la sala
de niños / le service
pédiatrique / la pediatria /
a ala infantil

maternity ward
die Wöchnerinnenstation
la sala de partos
le service obstétrique
il reparto maternità
a ala de maternidade

visiting hours
die Besuchszeiten
las horas de visita
les horaires de visite
l'orario di visita
o horário de visita

emergency room
die Notaufnahme / la sala
de urgencias / les urgences
il pronto soccorso / a sala
de emergência

outpatient clinic / die
Ambulanz / la clínica de
consulta externa / l'hôpital
de jour / l'ambulatorio
o ambulatório

chart / das Krankenblatt
el gráfico / le dossier
médical / la cartella
a prancheta

gurney / die Trage
la camilla / le lit d'hôpital
la barella / a maca

wheelchair / der Rollstuhl
la silla de ruedas
le fauteuil roulant
la sedia a rotelle
a cadeira de rodas

departments / die Abteilungen / los departamentos
les services / dipartimenti / as especialidades

cardiology
die Kardiologie
cardiología / la cardiologie
la cardiologia / a cardiologia

obstetrics
die Geburtshilfe
obstetricia / l'obstétrique
l'ostetricia / a obstetrícia

ENT / die HNO
otorrinolaringología
l'ORL / l'otorinolaringoiatra
a otorrinolaringologia

pediatrics / die Pädiatrie
pediatría / la pédiatrie
la pediatria / a pediatria

orthopedics
die Orthopädie
ortopedía
l'orthopédie
l'ortopedia
a ortopedia

gynecology
die Gynäkologie
ginecología
la gynécologie
la ginecologia
a ginecologia

dermatology
die Dermatologie
dermatología
la dermatologie
la dermatologia
a dermatologia

plastic surgery
die Plastische Chirurgie
cirugía plástica
la chirurgie plastique
la chirurgia plastica
a cirurgia plástica

urology / die Urologie
urología / l'urologie
l'urologia / a urologia

radiology / die Radiologie
radiología / la radiologie
la radiologia / a radiologia

oncology / die Onkologie
oncología / l'oncologie
l'oncologia / a oncologia

podiatry / die Podologie
podología / la podologie
la podologia / a podologia

---

admitted / aufgenommen / aceptado
admis / ammesso / o internado

discharged / entlassen
dado de alta / autorisé à sortir
dimesso / ter alta

result / das Ergebnis / el resultado
les résultats / il risultato / o resultado

surgery / die Operation / la cirugía
la chirurgie / la chirurgia / a cirurgia

operation / die Operation
la operación / l'opération
l'operazione / a operação

call button / die Ruftaste / el botón
de llamada / le bouton d'appel
il pulsante per chiamare
a campainha de aviso

specialist / der Facharzt
el especialista / le spécialiste
lo specialista / o especialista

referral / die Überweisung
la remisión / le patient
il rinvio / o encaminhamento

endocrinology / die Endokrinologie
endocrinología / l'endocrinologie
l'endocrinologia / a endocrinologia

pathology / die Pathologie
patología / la pathologie
la patologia / a patologia

DENTIST / DER ZAHNARZT / EL DENTISTA
LE DENTISTE / DENTISTA / O DENTISTA

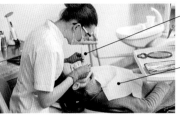

probe / die Sonde / la sonda
la sonde / la sonda / a sonda

bib / das Lätzchen
el babero / la bavette
il bavaglino / a babete

dental exam / die Zahnärztliche
Untersuchung / el examen dental
l'examen dentaire / l'esame dentale
o exame dentário

reflector / der Reflektor / el reflector
le réflecteur / il riflettore / o refletor

dentist's chair
der Zahnarztsessel
la silla de dentista
la chaise de dentiste
la sedia del dentista
a cadeira dentária

X-ray
das
Röntgenbild
la radiografía
la radio
i raggi x
o raio X

drills
die Bohrer
el torno
les fraises
i trapani
a broca

brush teeth (v) / Zähne
putzen / cepillarse los dientes
se brosser les dents / lavarsi
i denti / escovar os dentes

floss (v) / Zahnseide
verwenden / usar hilo dental
utiliser du fil dentaire
passare il filo interdentale
passar fio dental

dentures / der Zahnersatz / la dentadura
postiza / les dentiers / le dentiere
a dentadura

braces / die Zahnspange
los frenos / les bagues
gli apparecchi / o aparelho

teeth / die Zähne / los dientes
les dents / i denti / os dentes

incisor / der Schneidezahn / el incisivo
l'incisive / l'incisivo / o incisivo

premolar
der Prämolar
el premolar
la prémolaire
il premolare
o pré-molar

molar / der
Backenzahn
el molar
la molaire
il molare
o molar

canine / der Eckzahn
el canino / la canine
il canino / o canino

enamel / der Zahnschmelz / el esmalte
l'émail / lo smalto / o esmalte

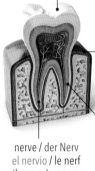

gum / das
Zahnfleisch
la encía
la gencive
la gengiva
a gengiva

root
die Wurzel
la raíz
la racine
la radice
a raiz

nerve / der Nerv
el nervio / le nerf
il nervo / o nervo

toothache / die
Zahnschmerzen / el dolor
de dientes / le mal
de dents / il mal di denti
a dor de dente

plaque / der Zahnbelag
la placa / la plaque
dentaire / la placca
a placa

decay / die Karies
el deterioro / la carie
la carie / a cárie

cavity / der Hohlraum
la caries / la carie
le cavità / a cavidade

filling / die Füllung
las calzas / le plombage
l'otturazione / a obturação

extraction / die Extraktion
la extracción / l'extraction
l'estrazione / a extração

crown / die Krone
la corona / la couronne
la corona / a coroa

implant / das Implantat
el implante / l'implant
l'impianto / o implante

6 LANGUAGE
VISUAL DICTIONARY

THUNDER BAY
P·R·E·S·S
San Diego, California

CONTENTS

OPTOMETRIST / DER AUGENOPTIKER / EL OPTÓMETRA / L'OPTOMÉTRISTE
OPTOMETRISTA / O OPTOMETRISTA

eye exam / die Augenuntersuchung / el examen de la vista
l'examen de la vue / l'esame della vista / o exame oftalmológico

eye chart
die Augendiagramm
la tabla optométrica
la table optométrique
l'ottotipo a tabela
oftalmológica

phoropter
die Phoropter
el foróptero
le réfracteur
il forottero
o feróptero

eye doctor
die Augenarzt
el especialista en ojos
l'ophtalmologiste
il medico oculista
o médico dos olhos

eyeglasses / die Brillen / los anteojos
les lunettes de vue / gli occhiali da vista / os óculos

sunglasses / die Sonnenbrille / las gafas de sol
les lunettes de soleil / gli occhiali da sole
os óculos de sol

bifocal lens
die Bifokalglas
el lente bifocal
les verres à
double-foyers
la lente bifocale
a lente bifocal

frame
die Rahmen
el cuadro
la monture
la montatura
a armação

cleaning cloth / das Putztuch / el paño
limpiador / la lingette nettoyante / il panno
per la pulizia / o pano de limpeza

optician / der Optiker
el oculista / l'opticien
l'ottico / o oculista

lens case
die Linsenetui
el estuche para lentes
l'étui à lentilles
la custodia per lenti
a caixa de lentes

ophthalmologist / der Opthamologe
el oftalmólogo / l'ophalmologiste / l'oculista
o oftalmologista

vision / die Sehkraft / la visión / la vision
la visione / a visão

farsightedness / die Weitsichtigkeit
la hipermetropía / la vision de loin
la lungimiranza / a hiperopia

contact lens / die Kontaktlinse / los lentes de contacto
la lentille de contact / la lente a contatto / as lentes de contacto

nearsightedness / die Kurzsichtigkeit / la miopía
la vision de près / la miopia / a miopia

astigmatism / der Astigmatismus / el astigmatismo
l'astigmatisme / l'astigmatismo / o astigmatismo

tear / die Tränenflüssigkeit / la lágrima / la larme
la lacrima / a lágrima

cataract / der grauer Star / la catarata / la cataracte
la cataratta / a catarata

glaucoma / der Glaukom / el glaucoma
le glaucome / il glaucoma / o glaucoma

eye / das Auge / el ojo / l'oeil / l'occhio / o olho

cornea
die Hornhaut
la córnea
la cornée
la cornea
a córnea

retina / die Netzhaut
la retina / la rétine
la retina / a retina

optic nerve
der Sehnerv
el nervio óptico
le nerf optique
il nervo ottico
o nervo óptico

pupil
die Pupille
la pupila
la pupille
la pupilla
a pupila

lens / die Augenlinse
el lente / la lentille
la lente / a lente

OTHER THERAPY / DIE ANDERE THERAPIE / OTRAS TERAPIAS
LES AUTRES TRAITEMENTS / GLI ALTRA TERAPIA / AS OUTRAS TERAPIAS

group therapy / die Gruppentherapie / la terapia grupal
la thérapie de groupe / la terapia di gruppo / a terapia de grupo

reiki / der Reiki / el reiki
le reiki / il reiki / o reiki

reflexology
die Reflexzonenmassage
la reflexología
la réflexologie
la riflessologia
a reflexologia

acupressure
die Akupressur
la acupresión
la digipuncture
l'agopressione / a acupressão

hypnotherapy
die Hypnotherapie
la hipnoterapia
l'hypnothérapie
l'ipnoterapia
a hipnoterapia

chiropractic
die Chiropraktik
la quiropráctica
la chiropractie
la chiropratica
a quiroprática

homeopathy
die Homöopathie
la homeopatía
l'homéopathie
l' omeopatia / a homeopatia

meditation
die Meditation
la meditación
la méditation
la meditazione / a meditação

shiatsu / das Shiatsu
el shiatsu / le shiatsu
lo shiatsu / o shiatsu

mat / die Matte
la estera / le tapis
il tappetino
/ o tapete

pose
die Pose
la pose
la pose
la posa
a pose

yoga / das Yoga / el yoga / le yoga
lo yoga / o yoga

stress / der Stress
el estrés / le stress
lo stress / o stress

relaxation
die Entspannung
la relajación / la relaxation
il rilassamento
o relaxamento

feng shui / das Feng
Shui / el feng shui
le feng shui / il feng shui
o feng shui

naturopathy
die Naturheilkunde
la naturopatía
la naturopathie
la naturopatia
a naturopatia

hydrotherapy
die Hydrotherapie
la hidroterapia
l'hydrothérapie
l'idroterapia
a hidroterapia

essential oil
das ätherische Öl
el aceite esencial
l'huile essentielle
l'olio essenziale
o óleo essencial

aromatherapy
die Aromatherapie
la aromaterapia
l'aromathérapie
l'aromaterapia
a aromaterapia

psychotherapy
die Psychotherapie
la psicoterapia
la psychothérapie
la psicoterapia
a psicoterapia

massage / die Massage
el masaje / le massage
il massaggio
a massagem

osteopathy
die Osteopathie
la osteopatía
l'osthéopathie
l'osteopatia / a osteopatia

acupuncture
die Akupunktur
la acupuntura
l'acupuncture / l'agopuntura
a acupuntura

supplement
die Ergänzung
el suplemento
les compléments
alimentaires
l'integratore
o suplemento

ayurveda / der Ayurveda
el ayurveda / l'ayurveda
l'ayurveda / o aiurveda

counselor / der Berater
el consejero / le thérapeute
il consulente / o terapeuta

art therapy
die Kunsttherapie
el arteterapia
l'art-thérapie
la terapia dell'arte
a arteterapia

herbalism
die Kräuterkunde
la herbolaria
la phytothérapie
l'erboristeria / o herbalismo

PEOPLE
DIE MENSCHEN
LAS PERSONAS
LES GENS
LE PERSONE
AS PESSOAS

FAMILY / DIE FAMILIE / LA FAMILIA / LA FAMILLE / LA FAMIGLIA / A FAMÍLIA

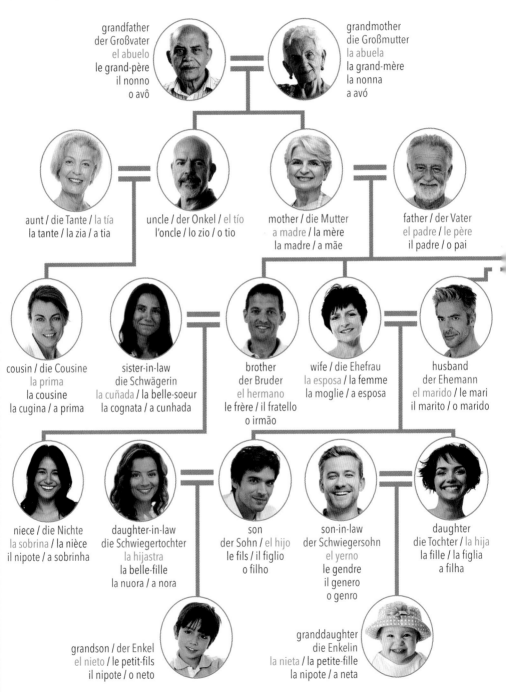

grandfather
der Großvater
el abuelo
le grand-père
il nonno
o avô

grandmother
die Großmutter
la abuela
la grand-mère
la nonna
a avó

aunt / die Tante / la tía
la tante / la zia / a tia

uncle / der Onkel / el tío
l'oncle / lo zio / o tio

mother / die Mutter
a madre / la mère
la madre / a mãe

father / der Vater
el padre / le père
il padre / o pai

cousin / die Cousine
la prima
la cousine
la cugina / a prima

sister-in-law
die Schwägerin
la cuñada / la belle-soeur
la cognata / a cunhada

brother
der Bruder
el hermano
le frère / il fratello
o irmão

wife / die Ehefrau
la esposa / la femme
la moglie / a esposa

husband
der Ehemann
el marido / le mari
il marito / o marido

niece / die Nichte
la sobrina / la nièce
il nipote / a sobrinha

daughter-in-law
die Schwiegertochter
la hijastra
la belle-fille
la nuora / a nora

son
der Sohn / el hijo
le fils / il figlio
o filho

son-in-law
der Schwiegersohn
el yerno
le gendre
il genero
o genro

daughter
die Tochter / la hija
la fille / la figlia
a filha

grandson / der Enkel
el nieto / le petit-fils
il nipote / o neto

granddaughter
die Enkelin
la nieta / la petite-fille
la nipote / a neta

stepmother / die Stiefmutter
la madrastra / la belle-mère
la matrigna / a madrasta

stepfather / der Stiefvater
el padrastro / le beau-père
il patrigno / o padrasto

stepdaughter / die Stieftochter
la hijastra / la belle-fille
la figliastra / a enteada

stepson / der Stiefsohn
el hijastro / le beau-fils
il figliastro / o enteado

stepsister / die Stiefschwester
la hermanastra / la belle-soeur
la sorellastra / a meia-irmã

stepbrother / der Stiefbruder
el hermanastro / le beau-frère
il fratellastro / o meio-irmão

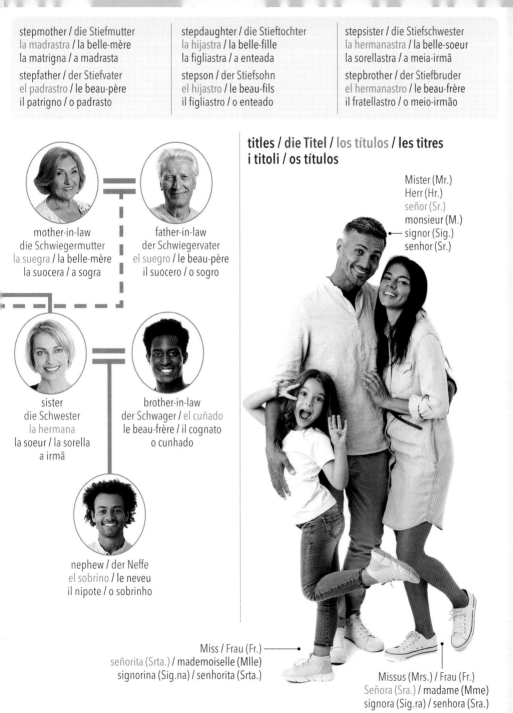

mother-in-law
die Schwiegermutter
la suegra / la belle-mère
la suocera / a sogra

father-in-law
der Schwiegervater
el suegro / le beau-père
il suocero / o sogro

sister
die Schwester
la hermana
la soeur / la sorella
a irmã

brother-in-law
der Schwager / el cuñado
le beau-frère / il cognato
o cunhado

nephew / der Neffe
el sobrino / le neveu
il nipote / o sobrinho

titles / die Titel / los títulos / les titres
i titoli / os títulos

Mister (Mr.)
Herr (Hr.)
señor (Sr.)
monsieur (M.)
signor (Sig.)
senhor (Sr.)

Miss / Frau (Fr.)
señorita (Srta.) / mademoiselle (Mlle)
signorina (Sig.na) / senhorita (Srta.)

Missus (Mrs.) / Frau (Fr.)
Señora (Sra.) / madame (Mme)
signora (Sig.ra) / senhora (Sra.)

STAGES OF LIFE / DIE LEBENSABSCHNITTE / LAS ETAPAS DE LA VIDA
LES ÉTAPES DE LA VIE / LE FASI DELLA VITA / AS ETAPAS DA VIDA

infant / der Säugling
el recién nacido / le nourisson
il neonato / o recém-nascido

girl / die Mädchen / la niña
la fille / la ragazza / a rapariga

woman / die Frau / la mujer
la femme / la donna / a mulher

baby / das Baby / el bebé
le bébé / il bambino / o bebé

boy / der Junge / el niño
le garçon / il ragazzo / o rapaz

man / der Mann / el hombre
l'homme / l'uomo / o homem

toddler / das Kleinkind
el niño pequeño / le tout-petit
l'infante / a criança pequena

teenager / der Teenager
el adolescente / l'adolescent
l'adolescente / o adolescente

senior / der Senior
la persona mayor / le senior
l'anziano / o idoso

child / das Kind / el niño / l'enfant
il bambino / a criança

adult / der Erwachsener / el adulto
l'adulte / l'adulto / o adulto

RELATIONSHIPS / DIE BEZIEHUNGEN / LAS RELACIONES / LES RELATIONS
LE RELAZIONI / AS RELAÇÕES

friend / der Freund
el amigo / l'ami
l'amico / o amigo

neighbor / der Nachbar
el vecino / le voisin
il vicino di casa / o vizinho

boyfriend — der Freund — el novio — le petit-ami — il ragazzo — o namorado

girlfriend — die Freundin — la novia — la petite-amie — la ragazza — a namorada

couple / das Paar / la pareja / le couple / la coppia / o casal

sibling / das Geschwister
el hermano
le frère/la soeur
il fratello / o irmão

acquaintance
die Bekannte / el conocido
la connaissance
il conoscente / o conhecido

fiancé — der Verlobter — el prometido — le fiancé — il fidanzato — o noivo

fiancée — die Verlobte — la prometida — la fiancée — la fidanzata — a noiva

engaged couple / das verlobtes Paar
la pareja comprometida
le couple fiancé / la coppia di fidanzati / os noivos

twins / die Zwillinge
los mellizos / les jumeaux
i gemelli / os gémeos

teammates
die Arbeitskollegen
los compañeros de equipo
les coéquipiers
i compagni di squadra
os companheiros
de equipa

business partner
der Geschäftspartner
el socio de negocios
le partenaire commercial
il partner commerciale
o sócio

employer / der Arbeitgeber
el empleador / l'employeur
il datore di lavoro / o patrão

employee
der Arbeitnehmer
el empleado
l'employé
il dipendente
o empregado

manager
der Geschäftsführer
el gerente
le manager
il manager
o gestor

assistant
der Assistent
el asistente
l'assistant
l'assistente
o assistente

colleagues / die Kollegen
los colegas / les collègues
i colleghi / os colegas

at work / bei der Arbeit / en el trabajo
au travail / al lavoro / no trabalho

LIFE EVENTS / DIE LEBENSEREIGNISSE
LOS ACONTECIMIENTOS DE LA VIDA / LES ÉVÈNEMENTS DE LA VIE
GLI EVENTI DELLA VITA / ACONTECIMENTOS DA VIDA

christening / die Taufe
el bautizo / le baptème
il battesimo / o batismo

get a job (v) / einen Job
bekommen / conseguir
un trabajo / trouver un
travail / ottenere un lavoro
arranjar um emprego

have a baby (v)
ein Baby bekommen
tener un bebé
avoir un bébé / avere
un bambino / ter um filho

move (v) / umziehen
mudarse / déménager
trasferirsi / mudar-se

start school (v) / Schule
beginnen / empezar la
escuela / commencer
l'école / cominciare la
scuola / começar a escola

fall in love (v) / sich
verlieben / enamorarse
tomber amoureux
innamorarsi / apaixonar-se

divorce / die Scheidung
el divorcio / le divorce
il divorzio / o divórcio

funeral / die Beerdigung
el funeral / les obsèques
il funerale / o funeral

make friends (v) / Freunde
finde / hacer amigos
se faire des amis / fare
amicizia / fazer amigos

get married (v) / heiraten
casarse / se marier
sposarsi / casar

birth / die Geburt / el nacimiento / la naissance
la nascita / o nascimento

birth certificate / die Geburtsurkunde / el certificado
de nacimiento / le certificat de naissance / il certificato
di nascita / a certidão de nascimento

bar mitzvah / die Bar Mitzvah / el bar mitzvah
la bar mitzvah / il bar mitzvah / o bar mitzvah

wedding reception / die Hochzeitsempfang
la fiesta nupcial / la réception de mariage
il ricevimento di nozze / a festa de casamento

marriage / das Heirat / el matrimonio / le mariage
il matrimonio / o casamento

emigrate / auswandern / emigrar / émigrer
emigrare / emigrar

retire (v) / sich zur Ruhe set-zen / jubilarse
prendre sa retraite / andare in pensione / reformar-se

make a will (v) / ein Testament ma-chen
hacer un testamento / faire un testament
lasciare un testamento / fazer um testamento

graduate (v)
Schulabschluss / graduarse
/ obtenir un diplôme
laurearsi / formar-se

honeymoon
die Flitterwochen
la luna de miel / la lune
de miel / la luna di miele
a lua-de-mel

die (v) / sterben / morir / mourir / morire / morrer

death / der Tod / la muerte / la mort / la morte / a morte

holidays / die Feiertage / las vacaciones / les fêtes / le vacanze / as festividades

New Year / das Neujahr
el año nuevo / le Nouvel An
il Capodanno / o Ano Novo

carnival / der Karneval
el carnaval / le carnaval
il carnevale / o Carnaval

Thanksgiving / das Erntedankfest
el día de acción de gracias
le Thanksgiving / il giorno
del ringraziamento / o dia de
ação de graças

Christmas
Weihnachten
la Navidad
Noël
il Natale
o Natal

presents
die Geschenke
los regalos
les cadeaux
i regali
as prendas

Easter / Ostern
la Semana Santa / Pâques
Pasqua / a Páscoa

Passover / Pessach
la pascual / Pessah
Pasqua / a Páscoa Judaica

special occasions / die Besondere Anlässe las ocasiones especiales / les occasions spéciales / occasioni speciali as ocasiões especiais

party
die Party
la fiesta
la fête
la festa
a festa

birthday / der Geburtstag / el cumpleaños
l'anniversaire / il compleanno / o aniversário

Ramadan / Ramadan
el ramadán / Ramadan
il Ramadan / o Ramadão

Yom Kippur / Jom Kippur
el Yom Kippur
Yom Kippur / lo Yom
Kippur / o Yom Kippur

gift bag / die Geschenktüte
la bolsa de regalos
le paquet cadeau / la borsa regalo
o saco de prendas

card / die Karte / la tarjeta
la carte / la carta / o cartão

balloon / der Luftballon
el globo / le ballon
il palloncino / o balão

Halloween / Halloween
el día de brujas
Halloween / Halloween
o Dia das Bruxas

Diwali / Diwali
el Diwali / Dipavali
Diwali / o Diwali

anniversary
der Jahrestag
el aniversario
l'anniversaire
l'anniversario
o aniversário

EMOTIONS / DIE GEFÜHLE / LAS EMOCIONES / LES ÉMOTIONS
LE EMOZIONI / AS EMOÇÕES

frown (v)
die Stirn runzeln
fruncir el ceño
froncer les sourcils
aggrottare le ciglia
fazer cara feia

calm / ruhig / tranquilo
calme / calmo / calmo

angry / wütend / enfadado
en colère / arrabbiato / zangado

excited / aufgeregt / emocionado
excité / emozionato / entusiasmado

smile (v)
lächeln
sonreír
sourire
sorridere
sorrir

happy / glücklich / contento
heureux / felice / feliz

scared / verängstigt / asustado
effrayé / spaventato / assustado

annoyed / verärgert / molesto
contrarié / irritato / chateado

sad / traurig / triste
triste / triste / triste

confused / verwirrt / confundido
désorienté / confuso / confuso

surprised / überrascht / sorprendido
surpris / sorpreso / surpreso

shout (v) / schreien
gritar / crier
gridare / gritar

boisterous / ausgelassen / bullicioso
bruyant / chiassoso / turbulento

nervous / nervös / nervioso
nerveux / nervoso / nervoso

upset / aufgeregt / disgustado
déçu / sconvolto / incomodado

confident / vertrauensvoll / confiado
confiant / confidente / confidente

shocked / schockiert / conmocionado
choqué / scioccato / chocado

content / zufrieden / contenido
satisfait / contento / satisfeito

proud / stolz / orgulloso
fier / orgoglioso / orgulhoso

yawn (v)
gähnend
bostezar
bâiller
sbadigliare
bocejar

tired / müde / cansado
fatigué / stanco / cansado

grateful / dankbar / agradecido
reconnaissant / grato / grato

blush (v)
erröten
ruborizarse
rougir
arrossire
corar

embarrassed / peinlich berührt
avergonzado / embarassé
imbarazzato / constrangido

suspicious / misstrauisch / suspicaz
méfiant / sospettoso / desconfiado

cry (v)
weinen
llorar
pleurer
piangere
chorar

miserable / miserabel / miserable
misérable / miserabile / miserável

ashamed / beschämt
avergonzado / honteux
imbarazzato / envergonhado

bored / gelangweilt / aburrido
ennuyé / annoiato / aborrecido

laugh (v)
lachen
reír / rire
ridere / rir

amused / amüsiert / divertido
amusé / divertito / divertido

APPEARANCE / DIE ERSCHEINUNGSBILD / LA APARIENCIA
L'APPARENCE / L'ASPETTO / A APARÊNCIA

HAIR / DAS HAAR / EL CABELLO / LES CHEVEUX / I CAPELLI / O CABELO

comb (v) / kämmen
peinar / peigner
pettinare / pentear

brush (v) / bürsten
cepillar / brosser
spazzolare / escovar

blow-dry (v) / föhnen
secar con blower
sécher / asciugare
secar

rinse (v) / ausspülen
enjuagar / rincer
risciacquare
enxaguar

set (v) / einstellen
fijar / placer
fissare / arranjar

brush
die Bürste
el cepillo
la brosse
la spazzola
a escova

curler
der Lockenwickler
el rulo
le bigoudi
il bigodino
o rolo de cabelo

curling iron
der Lockenstab / el rizador
le fer à friser / l'arricciacapelli
o modelador

blow-dryer / der Föhn / el secador
le sèche-cheveux / l'asciugacapelli / o secador

wash (v) / waschen / lavar
laver / lavare / lavar

hairdresser
der Friseur
el peluquero
le coiffeur
il parrucchiere
o cabeleireiro

comb / der Kamm
el peine / le peigne
il pettine / o pente

highlights / die Strähnchen
los reflejos / les mèches
i colpi di sole / as madeixas

scissors / die Schere
las tijeras / les ciseaux
le forbici / a tesoura

cut (v) / schneiden
cortar / couper
tagliare / cortar

permanent / die dauerhaft
la permanente / la permanent
la permanente / a permanente

dandruff / die Schuppen
la caspa / les pellicules
la forfora / a caspa

---

colors / die Farben / los colores / les couleurs / i colori / as cores

blond / blond / rubio
blonde / biondo / loiro

brunette / brünett
castaño / brune
bruno / moreno

auburn / kastanienbraun
caoba / auburn / ramato
castanho-avermelhado

red / rot / rojo / rouge
rosso / ruivo

black / schwarz / negro
noir / nero / preto

gray / grau / gris / gris
grigio / cinzento

white / weiß / blanco
blanc / bianco / branco

dyed / gefärbt / teñido
teints / tinto / pintado

hairstyles / die Frisuren / las peinadas / les coiffures / acconciature / os penteados

straight / gerade / liso
lisse / dritto / liso

wavy / gewellt / ondulado
ondulé / ondulato
ondulado

curly / lockig / rizado
bouclé / ricci
encaracolado

ponytail / die Pferdeschwanz
la cola de caballo / la queue
de cheval / la coda di cavallo
o rabo de cavalo

braid / der Zopf
la trenza / la tresse
la treccia / a trança

buzz cut / der Kurzhaarschnitt
el rapado / la boule à zéro
il taglio a spazzola / o rapado

wig / die Perücke
la peluca / la perruque
la parrucca / a peruca

bangs / der Pony
el flequillo / la frange
la frangia / a franja

pigtails / die Zöpfe
las coletas / les nattes
le trecce / os puxos

bald / glatze / calvo
chauve / calvo / careca

bun / der Dutt / el moño
le chignon / lo chignon
o coque

bob / der Bob
el bob / la coupe au carré
il bob / o cabelo curto

---

haircare products / die Haarpflegeprodukte / los productos para el cuidado del cabello / les produits capillaires prodotti per capelli / os produtos decabelo

barrette / die Haarspange
la hebilla / la barrette
la barrette / a mola

shampoo
das Shampoo
el champú
le shampooing
lo shampoo
o champô

conditioner
der Spülung
el acondicionador
l'après-shampooing
il balsamo
o condicionador

gel / das Gel / el gel
le gel / il gel / o gel

hair dye / das Haarfärbemittel
el tinte para el cabello
la coloration capillaire
la tintura per capelli
a tinta de cabelo

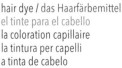
bobby pins / die
Haarklemmen / las horquillas
les pinces à cheveux
le forcine / os ganchos

hair spray
das Haarspray
a laca / la laque
la lacca per capelli
a laca

updo
die Hochfrisur
el recogido
le updo
il capelli raccolti
o updo

BEAUTY / DIE BEAUTY / LA BELLEZA / LA BEAUTÉ / LA BELLEZZA / A BELEZA

makeup / das Make-Up / el maquillaje / le maquillage / il trucco / a maquiagem

mascara / das Mascara
la máscara de pestañas
le mascara
il mascara / o rímel

eyebrow pencil
der Augenbrauenstift
el lápiz de cejas / le crayon
à sourcils / la matita per
sopracciglia / o lápis
de sobrancelha

eyeliner / der Eyeliner
el delineador de ojos / e eyeliner
l'eyeliner / o delineador de olhos

brush / die Pinsel
l cepillo /le pinceau
il pennello / o pincel

highlighter / der Highlighter
el iluminador / le highlighter
l'evidenziatore / o iluminador

lip gloss / das Lipgloss
el brillo de labios / le gloss
il lucidalabbra / o brilho labial

lipstick
der Lippenstift
la barra de labios
le rouge à lèvre
il rossetto
o batom

lip brush / der Lippenpinsel
el pincel para labios
le pinceau à lèvres
il pennello per labbra
o pincel labial

eyebrow brush
die Augenbrauenbürste
el cepillo de cejas
la brosse à sourcils
il pennello per sopracciglia
o pincel de sobrancelhas

blush / das Rouge
el colorete / le fard à joues
il fard / o blush

false eyelashes
die falschen Wimpern
las pestañas postizas
les faux-cils / le ciglia finte
a pestanas falsas

lip liner / der Lippenkonturenstift
el delineador de labios
le rayon à lèvres / il liner per labbra
o delineador labial

concealer / der Concealer
el corrector / le anti-cernes
il correttore / o corretivo

compact / die Puderdose
el polvo compacto / le compact
il compatto / o pó compacto

foundation / die Grundierung
la base de maquillaje / le fond
de teint / la fondotinta / a base

face powder
das Gesichtspuder
el polvo facial
le fond de teint en poudre
la cipria
o pó facial

powder puff
das Puderkissen
la borla de maquillaje
la houpette à poudre
la cipria in polvere
o aplicador de pó

eyelash curler
der Wimpernformer
el rizador de pestañas
le recourbe-cils
il piegaciglia
o revirador de
pestanas

complexion / die Gesichtsfarbe / la tez
le teint / la carnagione / a compleição

oily / fettig / aceitoso / huileux / oleoso
oleoso

fair / hell / limpio / simple / chiara / feira

sensitive / empfindlich / sensible
sensible / sensibile / sensível

eye shadow / der Lidschatten
la sombra de ojos / la ombre
à pau-pières / l'ombretto
a sombra de olhos

dark / dunkel / oscuro / sombre / scuro
escuro

dry / trocken / seco / sec / secco / seco

GROOMING / DIE KÖRPERPFLEGE / EL ASEO / LE TOILETTE
LA TOELETTATURA / A PROMOÇÃO

barber / der Frisör / el barbero
le coiffeur / il barbiere / o barbeiro

mustache
der Oberlippenbart
el bigote / la moustache
i baffi / o bigode

beard / der Bart / la barba
la barbe / la barba / a barba

manicure / die Maniküre
la manicura / la manucure
la manicure / a manicura

pedicure / die Pediküre / la pedicura
la pédicure / la pedicure / a pedicure

nail file / die Nagelfeile
la lima de uñas / une lime
à ongles / la lima per unghie
a lixa de unhas

nail clippers
die Nagelknipser
el cortaúñas / le coupe-
ongles / il tagliaunghie
o corta-unhas

facial / die kosmetische
Gesichtsbehandlung
el facial / le visage
il viso / o facial

face mask / die Gesichtsmaske
la mascarilla facial / le masque
visage / la maschera per il viso
a máscara facial

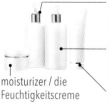

moisturizer / die
Feuchtigkeitscreme
la crema hidratante
une crème hydratante
l'idratante / o hidratante

cleanser / der Gesichtsreiniger
el limpiador / le nettoyant
il detergente / o limpador

toner / das Gesichtswasser
el tónico / une lotion tonifiante
il tonico / o toner

body lotion / die Bodylotion
la loción corporal / une lotion
pour le corps / la lozione per
il corpo / a loção corporal

shaving cream / die Rasiercreme
a crema de afeitar / la crème
de rasage / la crema da barba
o creme de barbear

razor / der Rasierer
a maquinilla de afeitar
le rasoir / il rasoio
a lâmina de barbear

wax / das Wachs / la cera
la cire / la cera / a cera

nail polish / der Nagellack
el esmalte de uñas
le vernis à ongles / lo smalto
per unghie
o verniz de unhas

cologne / das Rasierwasser
la colonia / une eau
de cologne / la colonia
a água-de-colónia

makeup remover
der Make-up-Entferner
el desmaquillante
le démaquillant
lo struccante
o removedor de maquilhagem

shaving / die Rasur
el afeitado / le rasage
a rasatura / o barbeação

electric razor
der Elektrorasierer
la maquinilla
de afeitar eléctrica
le rasoir électrique
il rasoio elettrico
a máquina
de barbear eléctrica

pumice / der Bimsstein
la piedra pómez / une
pierre ponce / la pomice
a pedra-pomes

perfume / das Parfüm
el perfume / le parfum
il profumo / o perfume

nail polish remover
der Nagellackentferner
el quitaesmalte
le dissolvant pour vernis
à ongles / il solvente
per unghie / o removedor
de esmaltes

APPAREL / DIE KLEIDUNG / LA PRENDAS DE VESTIR
LES VÊTEMENTS / L'ABBIGLIAMENTO / A ROUPA
BABY / DAS BABY / EL BEBE / LE BÉBÉ / IL BAMBINO / O BEBÊ

bib
das Lätzchen
el babero
le bavoir
il bavaglino
o babador

onesie
der Einteiler
la pijama
la combinaison
enfan
la tutina
o macacão

beanie
die Mütze
el gorro
le bonnet
il berretto
o gorro

cloth diaper / die Stoffwindeln
el pañal de tela / la couche
lavable / il pannolino di stoffa
a fralda de pano

disposable diaper
die Wegwerfwindel
el pañal desechable
la couche jetable
il pannolino usa e getta
a fralda descartável

socks
die Socken
las medias
les chaussettes
i calzini
as meias

snowsuit
der Schneeanzug
el traje para la nieve
la combinaison de neige
la tuta da neve
o fato de neve

booties / die Babystiefelchen
los botines / les chaussons
gli stivaletti / as botas

romper / der Spielanzug
el mameluco / la
grenouillère
la tutina / o romper

sleeper / der Schlafanzug
la babucha / le pyjama
la traversina / o sleeper

TODDLER / DAS KLEINKIND / EL NIÑO PEQUEÑO
LE PETIT ENFANT / IL BAMBINO PICCOLO / A CRIANÇA PEQUENA

overalls
der Overall
el sobretodo
la salopette
la tuta da lavoro
o macacão

umbrella / der Regenschirm
la sombrilla / le parapluie
l'ombrello / o guarda-chuva

rain poncho / der Regenponcho
el poncho para la lluvia
le imperméable
il poncho per la pioggia
o poncho de chuva

Crocs / die Crocs
las crocs / les crocs
le crocs / os crocs

T-shirt
das T-Shirt
la camiseta
le t-shirt
la maglietta
a t-shirt

duffel coat / der Dufflecoat
el abrigo de lana
le duffle-coat
la pelliccia di montgomery
o casaco de lona

rain boots
die Regenstiefel
as botas para la lluvia
les bottes de pluie
gli stivali da pioggia
as botas de chuva

sunhat / der Sonnenhut
el gorro para el sol
le chapeau de soleil
il cappello da sole
o chapéu de sol

shorts / die kurze Hose
los pantaloncillos
les shorts / i pantaloncini
os calções

CHILD / DAS KIND / EL NIÑO / L'ENFANT / IL BAMBINO / A CRIANÇA

wool cap
die Wollmütze
el gorro de lana
le bonnet
de laine
il berretto di lana
o boné de lã

mittens / die Fäustlinge
los guantes / les moufles
i guanti / os mitenes

wool scarf / der Wollschal
la bufanda de lana
l'écharpe en laine
la sciarpa di lana
o lenço de lã

down jacket
die Daunenjacke
la chaqueta
de plumón
la veste en duvet
il piumino
o casaco
de inverno

cargo pants
die Cargohose
los pantalones
de montaña
le pantalon cargo
i pantaloni cargo
as calças cargo

tunic / die Tunika / la túnica
il tunique / la tunica / il túnica

leggings
die Leggings
los leggins
les leggings
i leggings
os leggings

sandals / die Sandalen
las sandalias / les sandales
i sandali / as sandálias

sundress
das Sonnenkleid
el vestido de verano
la robe d'été
il parasole
o vestido de verão

sneakers / die Turnschuhe
las zapatillas de deporte / les baskets
le scarpe da ginnastica / as sapatilhas

blouse / die Bluse
la blusa / le chemisier
la camicetta / a blusa

jogging suit
der Jogginganzug
el conjunto para trotar
le jogging
la tuta da jogging
o fato de corrida

tights / die Strumpfhose
las mallas / les collants
i collant / os collants

jumper / das Trägerkleid
el vestido del delantal
la robe chasuble / l'abito
scamiciato / o vestido maiô

sweater / der Pullover
el sweater / le chandail
il maglione / a camisola

beret / die Baskenmütze
a boina / le béret
il berretto / a boina

maryjanes / der Spangenschuh
los mary-janes
les chaussures de bebé
i sandali maryjanes
o sapato boneca

jeans / die Jeans
los vaqueros / les jeans
i jeans / as calças de ganga

skirt / der Rock
la falda / la jupe
la gonna / a boina

pajamas / die Schlafanzüge
la pijama / le pyjama
il pigiama / a pijama

WOMEN'S CLOTHING / DIE DAMENKLEIDUNG / LA ROPA PARA MUJERES
LES VÊTEMENTS POUR FEMMES / L'ABBIGLIAMENTO DONNA / A ROUPA DE MULHER

casual wear / die legere Kleidung
a vestimenta casual
les vêtements décontractés
l'abbigliamento casual / a roupa casual

sweatshirt / das Sweatshirt
la sudadera / le sweat-shirt
la felpa / a camisola

yoga pants / die Yogahose
los pantalones de yoga
le pantalon de yoga
i pantaloni yoga
as calças de yoga

turtleneck
der Rollkragenpullover
la camisa cuello de tortuga
le col roulé
la dolcevita
a gola alta

trench coat / der Trenchcoat
la gabardina / le trench-coat
il trench / a gabardine

halter neck / das Nackenband
el escote halter/ le col bénitier
il collo alto / o pescoço de
cabresto

ruffle / die Rüschen
el cuello alto / le volant
i volant / o ruffle

denim shorts / die Jeanshose
los pantaloncillos de
mezclilla / le short en denim
i pantaloncini in denim
os calções de ganga

tank top / das Tanktop
las camiseta de tirantes
le débardeur
la canotta
a camiseta

minidress / das Minikleid
el minivestido / la minirobe
il miniabito / o minivestido

work attire / die Arbeitskleidung / a vestimenta de trabajo / la tenue de travail
l'abbigliamento da lavoro / o traje de trabalho

blazer / der Blazer
la chaqueta / le blazer
il blazer / o blazer

pantsuit
der Hosenanzug
el traje de pantalón
le tailleur pantalon
il tailleur pantalone
o fato de calças

pants / die Hose
los pantalones
le pantalon
i pantaloni / as calças

knee-length skirt
der knielange Rock
la falda hasta la rodilla
la jupe aux genoux
la gonna al ginocchio
a saia à altura dos joelhos

tote
die Tragetasche
la cartera / le cabas
la tote / o tote

cardigan
der Cardigan
la chaqueta
de punto
le cardigan
il cardigan
o cardigã

shift dress
das Etuikleid
el vestido
de enagua
une robe
coupe droite
l'abito mutevole
o vestido reto

lingerie / die Unterwäsche / la lencería / la lingerie / la lingerie / a roupa íntima

slippers
die Hausschuhe
las zapatillas
des pantoufles
le pantofole
os chinelos

dressing gown / der Bademantel
la bata / une robe de chambre
la vestaglia / o roupão

pantyhose / die Strumpfhose
as pantimedias
le collant / i collant
a meia-calça

tap pants / die Tap-Pants
los pantalones de claqué / le pantalon
i pantaloni da tip tap / os shorts de dança

camisole / das Leibchen
la camisola / le caraco
la canotta / a camisola

nightgown / das Nachthemd
el camisón / une chemise
de nuit / la camicia da notte
o vestido de noite

stockings
die Strümpfe
las medias
les bas / le calze
as meias

panties / das Höschen
las bragas / les culottes
le mutandine
as cuecas

bra / der BH / el sujetador
le soutien-gorge
il reggiseno / o sutiã

sports bra / der Sport-BH
el sujetador deportivo
le soutien-gorge de sport
il reggiseno sportivo
o sutiã esportivo

size / die Größe
la talla / la taille
la taglia / o tamanho

corset / das Korsett
el corsé / le corset
il corsetto / o espartilho

shapewear
die Formwäsche
la ropa moldeadora
la lingerie
lo shapewear
o modelador

garter / das Strumpfband
el liguero
le porte-jarretelles
la giarrettiera / a liga

underwire / der Bügel
el sujetador con aro
l'armature / il ferretto
o sutiã com aro

slip / der Slip
el vestido de lencería
le slip / gli slip
o vestido slip

formal wear / die formelle Kleidung / la ropa formal / une tenue de soirée
l'abbigliamento formale / a roupa formal

sleeveless
ärmellos
sin mangas
sans manches
senza maniche
sem mangas

beading
die Perlenstickerei
la pedrería
le perlage
il ricamo
a miçanga

slit / der Schlitz
la falda abierta
la fente / la fessura
o vestido slit

evening dress / das Abendkleid / el vestido de noche
la robe de soirée / l'abito da sera / o vestido de noite

bridal veil
der Brautschleier
el velo de novia
le voile de mariée
il velo da sposa
o véu nupcial

lace
die Spitze
el encaje
la dentelle
il pizzo
a renda

train
die Schleppe
la cola
la traîne
il treno
o treino

strapless / trägerlos
sin tirantes / sans bretelles
senza spalline / sem alças

wedding gown
das Hochzeitskleid
el vestido de novia
la robe de mariage
l'abito da sposa
o vestido de noiva

MEN'S CLOTHING / DIE HERRENBEKLEIDUNG / LA ROPA PARA HOMBRES
LES VÊTEMENTS POUR HOMMES / L'ABBIGLIAMENTO UOMO / O VESTUÁRIO HOMEM

work attire / die Arbeitskleidung la ropa de trabajo / les vêtements de travail / l'abbigliamento da lavoro o traje de trabalho

tie / die Krawatte
la corbata / la cravate
la cravatta / a gravata

pocket square
das Einstecktuch
el pañuelo de bolsillo
le carré de poche
il fazzoletto da taschino
o lenço de bolso

lapel / das Revers
la solapa / la boutonnière
il bavero / a lapela

jacket / das Jackett
la chaqueta / la veste
la giacca / o casaco

trousers / die Hose
el pantalón / le pantalon
i pantaloni / as calças

business suit / der Anzug / el traje de negocios
le costume d'affaires / l'abito d'affari / o fato de trabalho

button
der Knopf
el botón
le bouton
il bottone
o botão

collar
der Kragen
el cuello
le col
il colletto
o colarinho

placket
der Schlitz
la tapeta
la patte de boutonnage
l'abbottonatura
a carcela

cuff
die Manschette
el puño
la manchette
il polsino
o punho

shirt / das Hemd / la camisa
la chemise / la camicia / a camisa

formal wear / die formelle Kleidung la ropa formal / la tenue de soirée l'abbigliamento formale / a roupa formal

bow tie / die Fliege
la pajarita / le nœud papillon
la cravatta a farfalla
a gravata-borboleta

satin lapel / das Satin-Revers
la solapa satinada / le revers en satin
il risvolto di raso / a lapela de cetim

dinner jacket / das Dinnerjacket
el chaleco formal / la veste de soirée
la giacca da sera / o smoking

tuxedo / der Smoking / el esmoquin
le smoking / lo smoking / o tuxedo

outerwear / die Oberbekleidung / la ropa para exteriores / les vêtements de sport l'abbigliamento esterno / o agasalho

double-breasted / zweireihig
doble abotonado
à double boutonnage
doppiopetto
abas sobrepostas

overcoat / der Mantel / el
abrigo / le manteau / il
cappotto / o sobretudo

peacoat / der Caban
el chaquetón
le imperméable
la peacoat / o casaco peacoat

bomber jacket
die Bomberjacke
la chaqueta bomber
une veste bomber
il bomber
o casaco bomber

windbreaker
die Windjacke / la cazadora
le coupe-vent / la giacca
a vento / o quebra-vento

casual wear / die legere Kleidung / la vestimenta casual / des vêtements de détente
l'abbigliamento casual / a roupa casual

khaki shorts
die Khakihose
os pantalones
cortos caqui
le short kaki
i pantaloncini kaki
os calções cáqui

polo shirt
das Polohemd
la camiseta
polo
le polo
la polo
a camisa polo

hoodie
der Kapuzenpullover
a sudadera con capucha
le sweat à capuche
la felpa con cappuccio
o capuz

flannel
der Flanell
la franela
le flanelle
la flanella
a flanela

zipper
der Reißverschluss
la cremallera
la fermeture éclair
la cerniera / o zíper

plaid shirt / das Karohemd
la camisa a cuadros / la chemise
à carreaux / la camicia a quadri
a camisa xadrez

vest / die Weste
el chaleco / le gilet
il gilet / o colete

jeans / die Jeans
los vaqueros
des jeans
i jeans
as calças de ganga

tailored / maßgeschneidert
a la medida / sur mesure
su misura / à medida

bespoke / maßangefertigt
personalizado / sur mesure
su misura / sob medida

fitting room / die Ankleidekabine
el probador / la cabine d'essayage
il camerino / a sala de prova

Do you have this in a larger/
smaller size? / Haben Sie das in
einer größeren/kleineren Grö-ße?
¿Tienes esto en una talla más grande/
pequeña? / Auriez-vous ce modèle
dans une taille plus grande/plus
petite ? / Avete questo in una taglia
più grande/piccola? / Tens isto num
tamanho maio/pequeno?

sleepwear
die Schlafkleidung
la ropa para dormir
les vêtements de nuit
gli sleepwear
a roupa de dormir

underwear
die Unterwäsche
la ropa interior
les sous-vêtements
la biancheria intima
a roupa interior

undershirt / das Unterhemd / la camiseta interior
le maillot de corps / la maglietta intima / a camisola interior

bathrobe / der Bademantel
el albornoz / le peignoir
l'accappatoio
o roupão

briefs / die Unterhose
los calzoncillos / les lips
gli slip / a cueca
de homem

boxer briefs
die Retropants
el bóxer / les caleçons
i boxer / a cueca boxer

boxer shorts
die Boxershorts / el bóxer
les boxers / i boxer
os calções de boxer

pajamas
die Schlafanzüge
la pijama / les pyjamas
il pigiama / a pijama

SHOES / DIE SCHUHE / LOS ZAPATOS / LES CHAUSSURES
LE SCARPE / OS SAPATOS

pumps / die Pumps / los tacones
les escarpins / le decolleté / os pumps

leather / das Leder
el cuero / le cuir
la pelle / o couro

high heel
die Highheels
los tacones altos
les talons-hauts
i tacchi alti
os sapatos de
calcanhar alto

sole
die Sohle
la suela
la semelle
la suola
a sola

wing-tips / der Wingtip-Schuh
la costura inglesa / les mocassins
la punta alare / o executivo

sandals / die Sandale / las sandalias
les sandales / i sandali / as sandálias

clogs / die Pantoffeln / los zuecos
les sabots / gli zoccoli / los zuecos

flats / die Ballerinas
los planos / les chaussures plates
le ballerine / os flats

stilettos
die Stöckelschuhe
los tacones de aguja
les talons aiguilles
i tacchi a spillo
os stilettos

patent leather / das Lackleder
el charol / le cuir verni / la pelle
verniciata / o couro envernizado

platform
das Plateau
la plataforma
l'emelle plateforme
la piattaforma
a plataforma

ankle boots / die Stiefelette
los botines / les bottines courtes
gli stivaletti / as botas de tornozelo

moccasins / die Mokassins
os mocasines / les mocassins
i mocassini / os mocassim

boots / die Stiefel / las botas
les bottes / gli stivali / as botas

rubber boots
die Gummistiefel
las botas de goma
les bottes souples en caoutchouc
gli stivali di gomma
as botas de borracha

cowboy boots
die Cowboystiefel
las botas de vaquero
les bottes style cow-boy
gli stivali da cowboy
as botas de cowboy

high-tops
die Knöchelturnschuhe
los botas altos
les chaussures montantes
gli stivali alti / os high-top

desert boots / die Desert
Boots / las botas del
desierto / les bottes
cavalières / gli stivali del
deserto / as botas deserto

open-toe
zehenfreie
punta abierta
à bout ouvert
open-toe
abertos nos dedoso

sling-backs
die Slingbacks
la punta
cerrada
les escarpins
le sling-back
os sapatos
de calcanhar
aberto

wedges / die Keilabsätze / las cuñas
less talon compensés / le zeppe /as cunhas

espadrilles
die Espadrilles
las alpargatas / les espadrilles
le espadrillas / os espadrilhes

boaters / die Bootsschuhe
los náuticos
les chaussures bateau
le pagliette
os sapatos de barco

T-straps / die T-Strap Pumps
las correas en t
les escarpins en t
le t-strap / as correias em t

flip-flops / die Flipflops
las chancletas / les tongs
gli infradito
os chinelo de dedo

ankle straps / die
Fesselriemen / las correas
en el tobillo / les chaussures
à lanière tour de cheville
i cinturini alla caviglia
as correias no tornozelo

work boots / die
Arbeitsschuhe / las botas
de trabajo / les chaussures
de travail / gli stivali da
lavoro / as botas
de trabalho

loafers / der Slipper
los mocasines / les mocassins
i mocassini / os loafer

brogues
die Herrenhalbschuhe
los brogues / les derbies
le brogues / os brogues

shoelace
der Schnürsenkel
el cordón / le lacet
il laccio da scarpa
a atacador

tongue / die Lasche
la lengüeta / la languette
la lingua / a língua

dress boots / die
Schnürschuhe / las botas
de vestir / les bottes de
ville / gli stivali da lavoro
as botas de vestir

hiking boots / die
Wanderstiefel / las botas
de montaña/ les bottes de
randonnée / gli scarponi
as botas para caminhadas

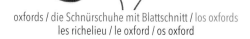

oxfords / die Schnürschuhe mit Blattschnitt / los oxfords
les richelieu / le oxford / os oxford

ACCESSORIES / DIE ACCESSOIRES / LOS ACCESORIOS / LES ACCESSOIRES
GLI ACCESSORI / OS ACESSÓRIOS

hat / der Hut
el sombrero / le chapeau
il cappello / o chapéu

cap / die Mütze
la gorra / la casquette
il berretto / o boné

kerchief / das Halstuch
la pañoleta / le foulard
il fazzoletto / o lenço

silk scarf / der Seidenschal
el pañuelo de seda
le foulard en soie
la sciarpa di seta
o lenço de seda

ear muffs
die Ohrenschützer
las orejeras
le cache-oreilles
il paraorecchie
os abafadores

headband / das Kopfband
la diadema / le bandeau
la fascia per capelli
a faixa de cabeça

handkerchief
das Taschentuch / el pañuelo
le mouchoir de poche
il fazzoletto / o lenço

*buckle / die Schnalle / la hebilla
la boucle de ceinture / la fibbia / a fivela*

gloves / die Handschuhe
los guantes / les gants
i guanti / as luvas

belt / der Gürtel / el cinturón
la ceinture / la cintura / o cinto

shawl / der Schal / el chal
le châle / lo scialle / o xaile

jewelry / der Schmuck / la joyas / les bijoux / i gioielli / as joias

jewelry box
das Schmuckkästchen
la caja de joyería
la boîte à bijoux
la scatola di gioielli
a caixa de joias

wedding band
der Ehering
la alianza de boda
l'alliance
la fede nuziale
a aliança de casamento

watch / die Armbanduhr
el reloj / la montre
l'orologio / o relógio

engagement ring
der Verlobungsring
el anillo de compromiso
la bague de fiançailles
l'anello di fidanzamento
o anel de noivado

rings / die Ringe / los anillos
les bagues / gli anelli / os anéis

bags / die Taschen / las bolsas / les sacs / le borse / as malas

wallet / die Geldbörse
la billetera / le portefeuille
il portafoglio / as carteira

purse / das Portemonnaie
el bolso / le porte-monnaie
la borsa / a bolsa

handbag / die Handtasche
el bolso de mano
le sac à main / la borsa
a mala de mão

shoulder-strap bag
die Tasche mit Tragegurt
el bolso con correa
para el hombro
le sac à ban-doulière
la borsa a tracolla
a mala tiracolo

strap
der Tragegurt
la correa
le sac à dos
la cinghia
a alça

duffel / die Reisetasche
el bolso de viaje
le polochon / il borsone
a bolsa marinheira

backpack / der Rucksack / la mochila
le sac à dos / lo zaino / a mochila

briefcase / der Aktenkoffer
el maletón / une mallette
la valigetta / a pasta

waist pack
die Bauchtasche
el riñonera / le sac banane
il marsupio / a mochila
para a cintura

earrings / die Ohrringe
los pendientes
des boucles d'oreilles
gli orecchini / os brincos

chain
die Kette
la cadena
la chaine
la catena
a corrente

bracelet / das Armband
el brazalete / le bracelet
il bracciale / o bracelete

necklace / die Halskette
el collar / le collier
la collana / o colar

pendant / der Anhänger
el colgante / le pendentif
il ciondolo / o pingente

cufflinks
die Manschettenknöpfe
los gemelos / les boutons
de manchette / i gemelli
os botões de punho

cameo
der geschnittene Stein
el camafeo
le camée
il cameo
o cameo

tie pin / die Krawattennadel
el alfiler de corbata
l'épingle de cravate
la spilla da cravatta
o alfinete de gravata

strand of pearls / die Perlen
el collar de perlas / le collier de perles
il filo di perle / o fio de pérolas

brooch / die Brosche
la broche / la broche
la spilla / o broche

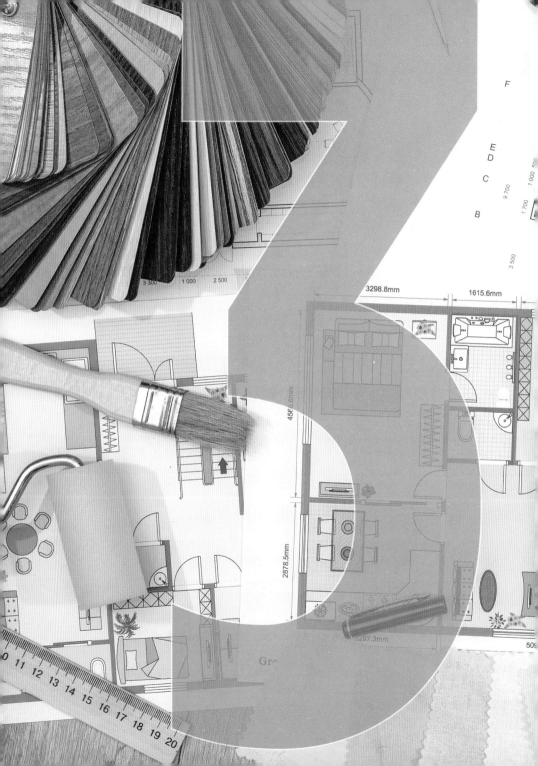

THE HOME
DAS HAUS
EL HOGAR
LA MAISON
LA CASA
O LAR

HOUSE / DAS HAUS / LA CASA
LA MAISON / LA CASA / A CASA

skylight
das Dachfenster
la claraboya
le velux
il lucernario
a clarabóia

chimney / der Schornstein
la chimenea / la cheminée
il camino / a chaminé

window / das Fenster
la ventana / la fenêtre
la finestra / a janela

garage
die Garage / el garaje
le garage / il garage
a garagem

steps / die Treppe
las escaleras / les marches
i gradini / os degraus

front door / die Haustür / la puerta principal
la porte d'entrée / la porta d'ingresso / a porta de entrada

roof / das Dach
el techo / le toit
il tetto / o telhado

shingle / die Schindel / la teja
la tuile / la tegola / a telha

eave
die Traufe
el alero
l'avant-toit
la grondaia
a cornija

gutter
die Dachrinne
la alcantarilla
la gouttière
la grondaia
a caleira

balcony
der Balkon
el balcón
le balcon
il balcone
a varanda

post
den Pfosten
el poste
le poteau
il paletto
o poste

railing / das Geländer / la barandilla
la balustrade / la ringhiera / a grade

veranda/covered porch / die Veranda/die überdachte Veranda
la veranda/el porche cubierto / la véranda/la ter-rasse couverte
a varanda/il portico coperto / o alpendre/pátio coberto

column / die Säule / la columna
le pilier / la colonna / a coluna

types / die Typen / los tipos / les genres / i tipi / os tipos

single-family / das Einfamilienhaus
el hogar unifamiliar / la maison
individuelle / la casa monofamiliare
a casa unifamiliar

bungalow / der Bungalow
el bungaló / le bungalow
il bungalow / o bangalô

duplex / das Doppelhaushälfte
el dúplex / le duplex
bifamiliare / o duplex

row house / das Reihenhaus / la casa
adosada / la maison mitoyenne
la casa a schiera / a casa geminada

townhouse / das Stadthaus
el piso / la maison de ville
la villetta a schiera / a moradia

condo / die Eigentumswohnung
el condominio / l'immeuble
il condominio / o condomínio

levels / die Ebenen
los niveles / les niveaux
livelli / os andares

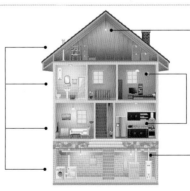

stories
die Stockwerke
los pisos
les étages
i piani
os andares

attic / das Dachgeschoss / el ático
le grenier / la soffitta / o sótão

rooms / die Räume
las habitaciones / les chambres
le camere / as divisões

basement / das Untergeschoss
el sótano / le sous-sol
il seminterrato / a cave

entrance / der Eingang / la entrada / l'entrée / l'ingresso / a entrada

door knocker / der Türklopfer / la aldaba
/ l'heurtoir / battente / a aldraba

doorbell / die Türklingel / el timbre
la sonnette / il campanello / a campainha

mail slot / der Briefschlitz
el buzón / la fente à courrier
la buchetta della posta / a ranhura do correio

doormat / die Fußmatte / la felpudo
le paillasson / lo zerbino / o tapete de entrada

mailbox / der Briefkasten / el buzón
la boite aux lettres / la cassetta postale
a caixa de correio

porch light
das Verandaleuchte
la luz del porche
le lampadaire
la luce del portico
a luz do alpendre

ceiling / die Decke / el techo
le plafond / il soffitto / o teto

banister / das Geländer / el pasamanos
la rampe / la ringhiera / o corrimão

wall
die Wand
la pared
le mur
il muro
a parede

staircase
die Treppe
la escalera
les escaliers
la scala
a escadaria

landing
der Treppenabsatz
el rellano
le palier
il pianerottolo
o patamar

floor
der Boden
el suelo
le sol
il pavimento
o chão

entrance hallway / der Eingangsflur / el hall de entrada / l'entrée
il corridoio d'ingresso / o hall de entrada

security / die Sicherheit
la seguridad / la sécurité
la sicurezza / a segurança

door chain / die Türkette / la cadena
de seguridad / la chaine de porte
la catena della porta / a corrente

door bolt / der Türriegel / el cerrojo
le verrou / il chiavistello
o trinco da porta

doorknob / der Türknauf
la perilla / la poignée
la maniglia / a maçaneta da porta

key
der Schlüssel
la llave
la clé
la chiave
a chave

lock / das Schloss
el seguro
la serrure / la serratura
a fechadura

apartment / die Wohnung / el apartamento / l'appartement
l'appartamento / o apartamento

landlord / der Vermieter
el propietario / le propriétaire
il padrone di casa / o senhorio

tenant / der Mieter / el inquilino
le locataire / l'inquilino / o inquilino

lease / der Mietvertrag
el arrendamiento / le bail
l'affitto / o arrendamento

rent / die Miete / la renta
la location / l'affitto / a renda

intercom / die Gegensprechanlage
el intercomunicador / l'interphone
il citofono / o intercomunicador

apartment building / das Wohnhaus
el edificio de aparta-mentos
l'immeuble / il condominio
o prédio

stairwell
das Treppenhaus
las escaleras
la cage d'escalier
la scala
a escadaria

elevator
der Aufzug
el ascensor
l'ascenseur
l'ascensore
o elevador

lobby / die Lobby / el recibidor / le hall / l'atrio / o átrio

UTILITIES / DIE UTILITÄTEN / LAS UTILIDADES
LES COMMODITÉS / LE UTENZE / OS SERVIÇOS

plumbing / die Klempnerarbeiten / la plomería / la plomberie
l'impianto idraulico / a canalização

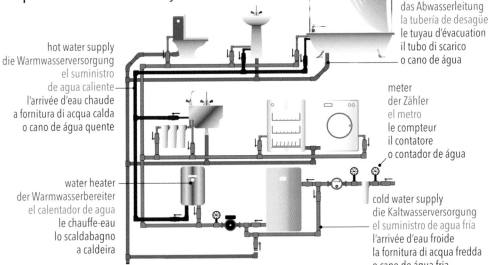

waste pipe
das Abwasserleitung
la tubería de desagüe
le tuyau d'évacuation
il tubo di scarico
o cano de água

hot water supply
die Warmwasserversorgung
el suministro
de agua caliente
l'arrivée d'eau chaude
a fornitura di acqua calda
o cano de água quente

meter
der Zähler
el metro
le compteur
il contatore
o contador de água

water heater
der Warmwasserbereiter
el calentador de agua
le chauffe-eau
lo scaldabagno
a caldeira

cold water supply
die Kaltwasserversorgung
el suministro de agua fría
l'arrivée d'eau froide
la fornitura di acqua fredda
o cano de água fria

temperature control / das Temperaturregelung / el control de temperatura
le thermostat / il termostato / o controlo de temperatura

air conditioner
das Klimagerät
el aire acondicionado
la climatisation
il condizionatore
o ar condicionado

fan / der Ventilator
el ventilador / le ventilateur
il ventilatore / a ventoinha

ceiling fan
der Deckenventilator
el ventilador de techo
le ventilateur de plafond
il ventilatore a soffitto
a ventoinha de teto

furnace / der Ofen
la caldera / la chaudière
il forno / a caldeira
de aquecimento

space heater
die Raumheizung
el calefactor / le chauffage
d'appoint / la stufetta
o aquecedor elétrico

convector heater
der Konvektorheizung
la estufa de convección
le radiateur à convection
il termoconvettore
o aquecedor de convetores

radiator / der Heizkörper
el radiador / le radiateur
il termosifone / o radiador

thermostat
das Thermostat
el termostato / le thermostat
il termostato / o termostato

electricity / der Elektrizität / la electricidad / l'électricité / l'elettricità / a eletricidade

wire / das Kabel
el alambre/ le fil
il filo / o fio

cable / das Kabel / el cable
/ le câble / il cavo / o cabo

light bulb
die Glühbirne
la bombilla
l'ampoule
la lampadina
a lâmpada

fuse box / der
Sicherungskasten / la caja
de fusibles / le tableau
électrique / la scatola dei
fusibili / a caixa de fusíveis

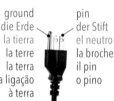

surge protector
der Überspannungsschutz
el protector de sobretensión
le parasurtenseur
il limitatore di sovratensione
o descarregador
de sobretensão

cord
das Kabel
el cordón / le câble
il cavo
o cabo elétrico

outlet / die Steckdose
el enchufe / la prise
la presa / a tomada

ground
die Erde
la tierra
la terre
la terra
a ligação
à terra

pin
der Stift
el neutro
la broche
il pin
o pino

light switch / der Lichtschalter
el interruptor de luz
l'interrupteur / l'interruttore
della luce / o interruptor

plug / der Stecker
la clavija / la prise
la spina / a tomada

AC adapter / das AC-Adapter
el adaptador de CA
l'adaptateur / l'adattatore
o adaptador AC

alternating current
der Wechselstrom
la corriente alterna
le courant alternatif
la corrente alternata
a corrente alternada

direct current
der Gleichstrom
la corriente continua
le courant continu
la corrente continua
a corrente contínua

waste disposal / die Abfallentsorgung / la gestión de residuos
le traitement des déchets / lo scarico dei rifiuti
a eliminação de resíduos

trash can
der Mülleimer
el bote de
basura
la poubelle
il bidone della
spazzatura
a lata do lixo

recycling bin / die Wertstofftonne
la papelera de reciclaje
le bac de recyclage
il cestino per il riciclaggio
o caixote de reciclagem

trash bag
der Müllsack
la bolsa de basura
le sac poubelle
il sacco della spazzatura
o saco do lixo

garbage bin
der Mülleimer / el cubo
de basura / la poubelle
de déchets ménagers
il bidone della spazzatura
o caixote do lixo

voltage / die Spannung
el voltaje / la tension
la tensione / a voltagem

power / die Leistung
la potencia
la puissance
la potenza / a energia

amp / das Ampere
el amperio / l'ampli
l'amplificatore
o ampere

fuse / die Sicherung
el fusible / le fusible
il fusibile / o fusível

security camera / die
Überwachungskamera
la cámara
de seguridad
la caméra de sécurité
la telecamera
di sicurezza
a câmara de vigilância

home security / die Haussicherheit / la seguridad para el hogar
la sécurité du domicile / l'antifurto / a segurança interna

burglar alarm
der Einbruchsalarm
la alarma antirrobo
l'alarme anti-effraction
l'allarme antifurto
o alarme antirroubo

control panel
die Schalttafel
el panel de control
le panneau de contrôle
il pannello di controllo
o painel de controlo

smoke detector
der Rauchmelder
el detector de humo
le détecteur de fumée
il rilevatore di fumo
o detetor de fumo

LIVING ROOM / DAS WOHNZIMMER / LA SALA / LE SALON
IL SOGGIORNO / A SALA DE ESTAR

built-in shelves / die Einbauregale
las estanterías integradas
les étagères intégrées
le mensole a incasso
as prateleiras embutidas

mantle / der Kaminsims
la repisa / le manteau
la cornice del camino / a verga

vase / die Vase / el florero / le vase / il
vaso / o vasos

fireplace / der Kamin / la chimenea
la cheminée / il camino / a lareira

armchair / der Sessel / el sillón
le fauteuil / la poltrona / o cadeirão

throw pillow / das Kopfkissen
el cojín / le coussin décoratif
il cuscino / a almofada

lamp / die Lampe
la lámpara / la lampe
la lampada / o candeeiro

draperies / die Vorhänge
las cortinas / les rideaux
le tende / os cortinados

side table / der Beistelltisch
la mesa auxiliar
la table d'appoint
il tavolino / a mesa de apoio

Venetian blinds / die
Jalousien / las persianas
venecianas / le store vénitien
le tende veneziane
os estores venezianos

sheer curtain / der durchsichtiger
Vorhang / la cortina transparente
le rideau fin / la tenda trasparente
a cortina translúcida

ottoman
die Ottomane
la otomanaa
l'ottomane
l'ottomana
o otomano

ceiling lamp / die Deckenlampe
la lámpara de techo / le plafonnier
la lampada da soffitto
o candeeiro de teto

hall / der Flur / el corredor
le hall d'entrée / la sala / o hall

foyer / das Foyer / el vestíbulo
le vestibule / il foyer / o saguão

coffee table / der Couchtisch
la mesa de café / la table basse
il tavolino / a mesa de centro

sofa / das Sofa / el sofá
le canapé / il divano / o sofá

entertainment center / das Unterhaltungszentrum
el centro de entretenimiento / la chaîne hi-fi
il centro d'intrattenimento / a combinação de arrumação

area rug / der Vorleger
la alfombra
le tapis décoratif
il tappeto / o tapete

recliner / der Liegesessel
el sillón reclinable
le siège inclinable
la poltrona reclinabile
a poltrona reclinável

DINING ROOM / DER ESSZIMMER / EL COMEDOR / LA SALLE À MANGER
LA SALA DA PRANZO / A SALA DE JANTAR

table / der Tisch / la mesa
la table / il tavolo / a mesa

centerpiece / das Mittelstück
el centro de mesa
la décoration de table
il centrotavola / o centro de mesa

back
die Rückseite
el respaldo
le dossier
il retro
o encosto

chair
der Stuhl
la silla
la chaise
la sedia
a cadeira

seat
der Sitz
el asiento
le siège
il sedile
o assento

leg
das Bein
la pata
le pied
la gamba
a perna

tablecloth / das Tischtuch
el mantel / la nappe
la tovaglia / a toalha de mesa

serving cart
der Servierwagen
el carrito de servicio
le chariot de service
il carrello di servizio
o carrinho de servir

hutch / das Büffetschrank
el gabinete / le buffet
la credenza / a cristaleira

sideboard / die Anrichte
el aparador / la commode
la credenza / o aparador

placemat
das Platzdeckchen
el salvamantel / le set
de table / la tovaglietta
o individual

eat (v) / essen
/ comer / manger
mangiare / comer

drink (v) / trinken
beber / boire
bere / beber

hungry / hungrig
hambriento / affamé
/ affamato / faminto

full / voll / lleno
plein / pieno
satisfeito

serve (v) / servieren
servir / servir
servire / servir

host / der Gastgeber
el anfitrión / l'hôte
il padrone di casa
o anfitrião

hostess / die
Gastgeberin
la anfitriona
l'hôtesse / la padrona
di casa / a anfitriã

guest / der Gast
el invitado / l'invité
l'ospite / o convidado

set the table (v)
den Tisch decken
poner la mesa
mettre la table
apparecchiare
la tavola
pôr a mes

May I have some more, please?
Darf es noch etwas mehr sein, bitte?
¿Me puede dar un poco más, por favor?
Pourrais-je en avoir un petit peu plus
s'il vous plaît ?
Posso averne ancora, per favore?
Posso comer mais, por favor?

I've had enough, thank you.
Ich hatte schon genug, danke.
Ya comí suficiente, gracias.
J'ai assez mangé merci.
Sono a posto così, grazie.
Estou satisfeito, obrigado.

crockery / das Geschirr / la vajilla / la vaisselle / le stoviglie / a louça

teapot / die Teekanne
la teteta / la théière
la teiera / o bule

creamer
das Milchkännchen
la crema / le pot à crème
la lattiera / a leiteira

sugar bowl
die Zuckerdose
el azucarero / le sucrier
la zuccheriera
o açucareiro

cup and saucer
die Tasse und Untertasse
la taza y el platillo
la tasse et la soucoupe
la tazza e il piattino
a chávena e o pires

soup tureen
die Suppenterrine / la
sopera / la soupière
la zuppiera / a terrina

mug / der Becher
el pocillo / le mug
la tazza / a caneca

gravy boat / die Sauciere
la salsera / la saucière
la salsiera / a molheira

bowl / die Schüssel
el tazón / le bol
la ciotola / a taça

silverware / das Silberbesteck / los cubiertos / l'argenterie / l'argenteria / os talheres

serving knife / die Serviergabel
el tenedor para servir / la fourchette
de service / la forchetta da portata
o garfo de servir

serving spoon / der Servierlöffel
la cuchara para servir / la cuillère
de service / il cucchiaio da portata
a colher de servir

cake knife / das Kuchenmesser
el cuchillo de pastel / le couteau
à gâteau / il coltello da torta
a espátula

place setting / das Gedeck / el servicio de mesa / le couvert / il posto a sedere
a organização da mesa

butter knife
das Buttermesser
el cuchillo para untar
le couteau à beurre
il coltello da burro
a faca de manteiga

side plate / der Beilagenteller
el plato de pan / la petite
assiette / il piattino
o prato do pão

spoon / der Löffel
la cuchara / la cuillère
il cucchiaio / a colher

knife
das Messer
el cuchillo
le couteau
il coltello
a faca

napkin ring
der Serviettenring
el servilletero
le rond de serviette
il portatovaglioli
o anel de
guardanapo

salad fork / die Salatgabel
el tenedor de ensalada
la fourchette à salade
la forchetta da insalata
o garfo de salada

napkin
die Serviette
la servilleta
la serviette
il tovagliolo
o guardanapo

fork
die Gabel
el tenedor
la fourchette
la forchetta / o garfo

soup bowl / der Suppenteller
el plato sopero / l'assiette
à soupe / la ciotola per zuppa
a tigela de sopa

dinner plate / der Essteller
el plato llano / la grande
assiette / il piatto da
portata / o prato de jantar

soup spoon / der Suppenlöffel
la cuchara sopera
la cuillère à soupe / il cucchiaio
da minestra / a colher de sopa

KITCHEN / DIE KÜCHE / LA COCINA / LA CUISINE / LA CUCINA / A COZINHA

backsplash
die Aufkantung
la pared posterior
la crédance
il paraschizzi
o backsplash

stovetop
die Herdplatte
la estufa
la table de cuisson
il piano cottura
o fogão

oven
der Backofen
el horno / le four
il forno / o forno

cabinet
der Schrank
la alacena
le rangement
l'armadio
o armários

microwave
die Mikrowelle
el horno microondas
le micro-onde
il microonde
o micro-ondas

countertop
die Arbeitsplatte
la encimera
le plan de travail
il bancone
a bancadao

drawers / die Schubladen
los cajones / les tiroirs
i cassetti / as gavetas

faucet / der Wasserhahn
el grifo / le robinet
il rubinetto / a torneira

faucet lever
der Wasserhahnhebel
la palanca del grifo
la poignée du robinet
la leva del rubinetto
a manete para torneira

drain / der Abfluss / el desagüe
l'évacuation / lo scarico / o ralo

spray head
der Brausekopf
el cabezal rociador
la douchette
lo spruzzino
o pulverizador

basin
das Waschbecken
el fregadero
l'évier / il catino
a bacia

dishwasher tablet
die Spülmaschinentablette
la pastilla detergente
la tablette pour lave-vaisselle
le pastiglie di detersivo
per lavastoviglie
a pastilha detergente para
máquina de lavar

dish detergent
das Geschirrspülmittel
el detergente para platos
le liquide vaisselle
il detersivo per piatti
o detergente da louça

dish drainer / der Geschirrabtropfer
el escurridor / l'égouttoir
lo scolapiatti / o escorredor de louça

dishwasher / der Geschirrspüler
el lavavajillas / le lave-vaisselle
la lavastoviglie / a máquina de lavar louça

appliances / die Geräte / los electrodomésticos / l'électroménager
gli elettrodomestici / os eletrodomésticos

coffee machine
die Kaffeemaschine
la máquina de café
la machine à café
la macchina del caffè
a máquina de café

food processor
die Küchenmaschine
el procesador de alimentos
le robot ménager
il robot da cucina
o processador de alimentos

mixer / der Mixer
la batidora / le mixeur
il mixer / a batedeira

blender / der Mixer
la licuadora / le blender
il frullatore
a liquidificadora

slow cooker / der
Langsamkocher / la olla de
cocción lenta / la mijoteuse
la pentola a cottura lenta
a panela de cozedura lenta

rice cooker / der Reiskocher
la olla arrocera
l'autocuiseur de riz
il cuociriso / a arrozeira

air fryer / die
Heißluftfritteuse
la freidora de aire
la friteuse à air
la friggitrice ad aria / a air fryer

electric kettle
die Wasserkocher
el hervidor eléctrico
la bouilloire électrique
il bollitore elettrico
a chaleira elétrica

refrigerator / die Kühlschrank / el refrigerador / le réfrigérateur
il frigorifero / o congelador

freezer
der Gefrierschrank
el congelador
le congélateur
il congelatore
o frigorífico

shelf / das Regal
el estante / la tablette
il ripiano / a prateleira

crisper / das Gemüsefach
el cajón de verduras
le bac à légumes
la teglia / a gaveta
de legumes

multicooker / der
Multikocheri / la multiolla
le multicuiseur
il multifunzione
o robô de cozinha

toaster / der Toaster
la tostadora
le grille-pain / il tostapane
/ a torradeira

KITCHENWARE / DIE KÜCHENWARE / LOS UTENSILIOS DE COCINA
L'EQUIPEMENT POUR LA CUISINE / A CUCINA / OS ARTIGOS DE COZINHA

cookware / das Kochgeschirr / los utensilios para cocinar
la batterie de cuisine / le pentole / as panelas

soup pot / der Suppentopf
la olla sopera / la cocotte
la pentola per zuppa
a panela de sopa

lid / der Deckel
la tapa / le couvercle
coperchio / a tampa

oven mitt
der Topflappen
el guante de cocina
les maniques
il guanto da forno
a luva de forno

pot holder
der Topflappen
la agarradera
les manipules
il portapentole
a base para tachos

saucepan
der Kochtopf
la cacerola
la casserole
il pentola
a caçarola

dish towel
das Geschirrhandtuch
el paño de cocina
le torchon
il canovaccio
o pano de cozinha

handle / der Griff
la manija / la poignée
il manico / a pega

grater / die Reibe / el rallador
la râpe / la grattugia / o ralador

frying pan / die Bratpfanne
la sartén / la poêle
la padella / a frigideira

griddle / der Grillplatte
la plancha / le grill
la piastra / a chapa

cooking / das Kochen / cocinar / cuisiner / la cottura / cozinhar

grill (v) / grillen
asar a la parrilla
griller / grigliare
grelhar

poach (v) / pochieren
escalfar / pocher
cucinare alla brace
escalfar

bake (v) / backen
hornear / cuire
cuocere al forno
cozer

peel (v) / schälen
pelar / éplucher
sbucciare
descascar

slice (v) / in Scheiben
schneiden / rebanar
découper / affettare
fatiar

saute (v) / sautieren
saltear / faire sauter
saltare / saltear

fry (v) / braten / freír
frire / friggere / fritar

grate (v) / reiben
rallar / râper
grattugiare / ralar

mix (v) / mischen
mezclar / mélanger
mescolare / misturar

stir (v) / rühren
revolver / remuer
mescolare / mexer

chop (v) / hacken
picar / hâcher
tritare / cortar

roast (v) / braten
asado / rôti
arrostire / assar

whisk (v) / quirlen
batir / battre
frullare / bater

broil (v) / grillen
asar / griller
grigliare / grelhar

boil (v) / kochen
hervir / bouillir
bollire / ferver

roasting pan / der Bratentopf
la asadera
la plaque du four / la teglia
o tabuleiro de assar

cutting board
das Schneidebrett
la tabla de cortar
la planche
à découper
il tagliere
a tábua de cortar

colander / der Seiher / el colador
la passoire / lo scolapasta / o coador

garlic press / die Knoblauchpresse
el triturador de ajo / le presse-ail
la pressa per l'aglio / a prensa de alho

whisk / der Schneebesen
el batidor / le fouet
la frusta / a batedeira

ladle / die Schöpfkelle / el cucharón
la louche / il mestolo / a concha

spatula / der Spatel
la espátula / la spatule
la spatola / a espátula
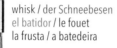

wooden spoon / der Holzlöffel
la cuchara de madera
la cuillère en bois
il cucchiaio di legno
a colher de pau

baking dish / die Auflaufform
la refractaria / le plat à four
teglia da forno / a assadeira

baking equipment / die Backausrüstung / el equipo para hornear / le matériel de cuisson l'attrezzatura per la cottura / o equipamento de panificação

mixing bowl / die
Rührschüssel / el tazón
para mezclar / le saladier
la scodella / a tigela
de mistura

rolling pin / die Nudelholz
el rodillo / le rouleau
à pâtisserie / il mattarello
o rolo da massa

measuring spoons
die Messlöffel / las cucharas
medidoras / la cuillère à mesure
i cucchiai di misura
as colheres de medida

cookie sheet
das Backblech
la bandeja para galletas
la plaque de cuisson
la teglia per biscotti
o tabuleiro para bolachas

loaf pan / die Laibform
el molde para pan
le moule cake
la teglia per pane
a forma para pão

cake tin / die Kuchenform
el molde de pastel
le moule à gâteau
la tortiera / a forma para bolos

muffin tin / die Muffinform
los moldes para muffin
le moule à muffin
la teglia per muffin
a forma para queques

pie tin / die Kuchenform
el molde para tarta
le moule à tarte / la tortiera
a forma para tarte

cutlery / das Besteck / los cuchillos / les couverts / le posate / os talheres

kitchen knives / die
Küchenmesser / los cuchillos
de cocina / les couteaux
de cuisine / i coltelli da cucina
as facas de cozinha

carving knife and fork
das Tranchiermesser und Gabeln
el cuchillo y tenedor
para trinchar
le couteau et la
fourchette à découper
il coltello e
la forchetta da carne
a faca o garfo
de entalhe

knife block / der Messerblock
el bloque portacuchillos / le bloc
à couteaux / il ceppo di coltelli
o bloco de facas

sharpener / das Schärfgerät
el afilador / l'aiguiseur
l'affilatrice / o afiador

cleaver / das Hackmesser
el cuchillo de carnicero
le fendoir / la mannaia
o cutelo

BEDROOM / DAS SCHLAFZIMMER / LA HABITACIÓN / LA CHAMBRE
LA CAMERA DA LETTO / O QUARTO

furniture / die Möbel / los muebles / les meubles / i mobili / a mobília

headboard
das Kopfteil
la cabecera
la tête de lit
la testiera
a cabeceira

bedside lamp
die Nachttischlampe
la lámpara de noche
la lampe de chevet
l'abatjour
a luz de cabeceira

closet
der Kleiderschrank
el clóset
le placard
l'armadio
o roupeiro

wardrobe
der Kleiderschrank
el armario
la garde-robe
l'armadio
o guarda-roupa

nightstand / der Nachttisch / la mesa de noche
la table de nuit / il comodino / a mesa de cabeceira

footboard / der Fußteil / el pie de cama
le pied de lit / la pedana / os pés da cama

mirror / der Spiegel / el espejo
le miroir / lo specchio / o espelho

stool / der Hocker / el taburete
le tabouret / lo sgabello / o banco

vanity / der Frisiertisch / el tocador / la coiffeuse
la toletta / o toucador

chest of drawers / die Kommode
mit Schubladen / la cajonera
le semainier / la cassettiera
a cómoda

full-length mirror
der Ganzkörperspiegel
el espejo de cuerpo entero
le miroir pleine longueur
lo specchio a figura intera
o espelho de corpo inteiro

bed / das Bett / la cama
le lit / il letto / a cama

double bed
das Doppelbett
la cama doble
le lit de 140
il letto intero
a cama de casal

daybed / das Tagesbett
el diván / le canapé-lit
il lettino / o sofá-cama

dresser / die Kommode
la cómoda / la commode
il comò / a cómoda

platform bed / das Podestbett
la cama de plataforma / le lit
à coffrage / il letto a piattaforma
a cama plataforma

mattress / die Matratze
el colchón / le matelas
il materasso / o colchão

trundle / das Rollbett / la cama nido
le lit gigogne / il letto estraibile
a cama deslizante

four-poster
das Himmelbett
la cama con dosel
le lit à baldaquin
il baldacchino
a cama de quatro colunas

sofa bed / das Bettsofa / el sofa cama
le canapé convertible
il divano letto / o sofá-cama

bunk bed / das Etagenbett
el camarote / le lit superposé
il letto a castello / o beliche

bedpost
der Bettpfosten
la columna de
la cama
la colonne de lit
la rete del letto
a coluna

twin bed / das Einzelbett
la cama sencilla
les lits jumeaux
il letto matrimoniale
a cama de casal

bed frame / der Bettrahmen
el marco de la cama
le cadre de lit / la struttura
del letto / o estrado

slat / die Latte
la tablilla / la latte
la doga / a ripa

futon / der Futon / el futón
le futon / il futon / o futon

bed linen / die Bettwäsche / la ropa de cama
le linge de lit / la biancheria da letto / a roupa de cama

sleep mask / die Schlafmaske
el antifaz para dormir
le masque de nuit
la maschera per il sonno
a máscara para dormir

sheet / das Laken
la sábana / les draps
il lenzuolo / o lençol

pillow / das Kopfkissen
la almohada / l'oreiller
il cuscino / a almofada

comforter / der Tröster
el edredón / la couette
il piumino / o edredão

pillow case
der Kissenbezug
la almohada
l'oreiller
il cuscino
a almofada

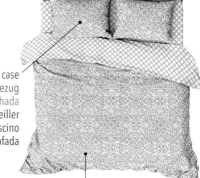

duvet cover / der Bettbezug / la funda de edredón
la housse de couette / il copripiumino / a capa de edredão

go to bed (v) / zu Bett gehen
ir a la cama / aller au lit
andare a letto / ir para a cama

go to sleep (v) / schlafen gehen
ir a dormir / aller se coucher
andare a dormire / ir dormir

bedspring / die Bettfeder
el somier / le sommier
la rete del letto / a mola

king-size bed / das Kingsize-Bett
la cama tamaño king / un lit king size
il letto matrimoniale / a cama king size

dust ruffle
die Staubrüsche
el plumero
le cache sommier
il soffietto
a capa de sommier

NURSERY / DAS KINDERZIMMER / LA HABITACIÓN DEL BEBÉ
LA CHAMBRE D'ENFANT / LA NURSERY / O QUARTO DO BEBÊ

bedtime / die Schlafenszeit / la hora de dormir / le coucher / dormire / a hora de dormir

bumper / die Stoßstange
la almohadilla de cuna
le tour de lit / il girello
o amortecedor

crib sheet / das Betttuch
la sábana de cuna / le drap
il lenzuolo da culla
o lençol de berço

crib / das Kinderbett / la cuna
le lit à barreaux / la culla / o berço

mobile / das Mobile
el móvil / le mobile
il mobile / o móbil

rocking chair
der Schaukelstuhl
la mecedora / le rocking-chair
la sedia a dondolo
a cadeira de baloiço

bassinet / der Stubenwagen
el moisés / le couffin
la culla / a alcofa

blanket / die Decke
la manta / la couverture
la coperta / o cobertor

---

baby care / die Babypflege / el cuidado de bebé / pour s'occuper de bébé
la cura del bambino / os cuidados de bebé

teething ring
der Beißring
el mordedor
l'anneau de
dentition
l'anello da
dentizione
o anel mordedor

diaper pail / der Windeleimer
el cubo de pañales / la poubelle
à couches / il bidone per pannolini
o caixote para fraldas

potty / das Töpfchen
la bacinilla / le pot
il vasino / o penico

baby bath
die Baby-Badewanne
el baño de bebé
la baignoire
pour bébé
la vaschetta
per bambini
a banheira
de bebé

changing table / der Wickeltisch
el cambiador / la table à langer
il fasciatoio / a mesa muda-fraldas

rattle / die Rassel
la sonaja / le hochet
il sonaglio / a roca

playpen / der Laufstall / el corral
le parc / il box / o parque para bebé

pacifier
der Schnuller
el chupete
la tétine
il ciuccio
o chupeta

bath toy / das Badespielzeug
el juguete de baño / le jouet de bain
il giocattolo da bagno / o brinquedo de banho

feeding / die Fütterung le repas / l'alimentation l'allattamento a alimentação

high chair
der Hochstuhl
el comedor de bebé
la chaise haute
il seggiolone
a cadeira alta

nipple / die Brustwarze / la tetina
la tétine / il capezzolo / a tetina

bottle / die Babyflasche
el biberón / le biberon
il biberon / o biberão

baby food / die Babynahrung
la comida para bebé / la nourriture
pour bébé / il cibo per bambini
a comida de bebé

safety / die Sicherheit la seguridad / la sécurité la sicurezza / a segurança

child lock / die
Kindersicherung
el seguro para niños
le verrou pour enfants
il blocco per bambini
o bloqueio de crianças

stair gate / das Treppengitter
la reja de seguridad / la barrière
de sécurité / il cancello per scale
a barreira para escadas

baby monitor / das Babyphon
el monitor para bebés
le babyphone / il monitor per
bambini / o monitor de bebé

playing / das Spielen / el juego / le jeu / il gioco / o jogo

teddy bear / der Teddybär / el oso
de peluche / l'ours en peluche
l'orsacchiotto / o ursinho de peluche

toy chest / die
Spielzeugtruhe / la caja
de juguetes / le coffre
à jouets / il baule
dei giocattoli / o cesto
de brinquedos

toys / die Spielzeug
los juguetes / les jouets
i giocattoli / os brinquedos

blocks / die Blöcke
los bloques / les cubes
i blocchi / os blocos

rocking horse
das Schaukelpferd
el caballito
le cheval à bascule
il cavallo a dondolo
o cavalo de baloiço

stuffed toy / das Plüschtier
el peluche / la peluche
il giocattolo di peluche
o peluche

doll / die Puppe
la muñeca / la poupée
la bambola / a boneca

going out / das Ausgehen / la salida / la sortie / l'uscita / a saída

stroller
der Kinderwagen
el coche / la poussette
/ il passeggino
o carrinho de bebé

carriage / der Kinderwagen
el carruaje / le landau
la carrozzina
o carrinho de bebé

carrier / der Träger
el portabebés
le porte-bébé
il trasportino / a alcofa

car seat / der Autositz / la silla
de bebé / le siège auto
il seggiolino auto / a cadeirinha

diaper bag
die Wickeltasche
la bolsa de pañales
le sac de couches
la borsa per pannolini
a bolsa de fraldas

baby sling
das Babytragetuch
la canguera
le porte-bébé
la fascia per bambini
o marsúpio

BATHROOM / DAS BADEZIMMER / EL BAÑO
LA SALLE DE BAIN / IL BAGNO / A CASA DE BANHO

shower head / der Duschkopf
el cabezal rociador
le pommeau de douche
il soffione della doccia
o chuveiro

tile / die Fliese
la baldosa / le carreau
le piastrelle / o azulejo

cold faucet / der kalter
Wasserhahn / el grifo frío
le robinet d'eau froide
il rubinetto dell'acqua fredda
a torneira de água fria

towel rack
der Handtuchhalter
el toallero
le porte serviette
il porta asciugamani
o toalheiro

hot faucet / der heißer
Wasserhahn / el grifo caliente
le robinet d'eau chaude
il rubinetto dell'acqua calda
a torneira de água quente

shower door / die Duschtür
la puerta de la ducha
la paroi de douche
la porta della doccia
a porta do chuveiro

drain / der Abfluss / el desagüe
l'évacuation / lo scarico / o ralo

bath mat / die Badematte
la alfombra de baño / le tapis
de bain / il tappetino da bagno
o tapete de banho

shower stall / die Duschkabine / la cabina de ducha
la cabine de douche / il box doccia / o poliban

handle
der Griff
la palanca
la poignée
la maniglia
o manípulo

tank / der Tank
el tanque / le réservoir
la caldaia / o tanque

seat / der Sitz
el asiento / le siège
la seduta / o assento

bathtub / die Badewanne / la bañera
a baignoire / la vasca da bagno / a banheira

toilet / die Toilette
el inodoro / les toilettes
la toilette / a sanita

urinal
das Urinal
el orinal
l'urinoir
l'orinatoio
o urinol

toilet paper / das Toilettenpapier
el papel higiénico / le papier
toilette / la carta igienica
o papel higiénico

toilet bowl brush
die Toilettenbürste
el cepillo de baño
la brosse à toilettes
lo scopino del wate
o piaçaba

sink
das Waschbecken
el lavabo
l'évier
il lavandino
o lavatório

toilet paper holder / der
toilettenpapierhalter / el soporte
para papel higiénico / le porte
papier toilette / il porta carta
igienica / o porta-rolos

bidet / das Bidet / el bidé
le bidet / il bidet / o bidé

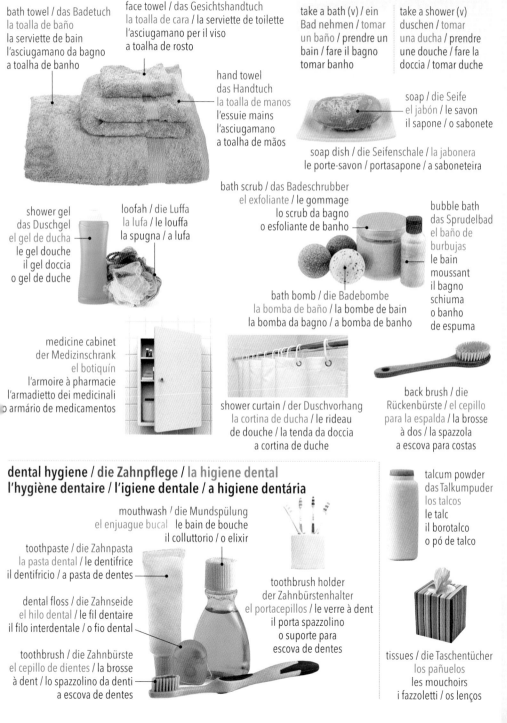

bath towel / das Badetuch
la toalla de baño
la serviette de bain
l'asciugamano da bagno
a toalha de banho

face towel / das Gesichtshandtuch
la toalla de cara / la serviette de toilette
l'asciugamano per il viso
a toalha de rosto

take a bath (v) / ein
Bad nehmen / tomar
un baño / prendre un
bain / fare il bagno
tomar banho

take a shower (v)
duschen / tomar
una ducha / prendre
une douche / fare la
doccia / tomar duche

hand towel
das Handtuch
la toalla de manos
l'essuie mains
l'asciugamano
a toalha de mãos

soap / die Seife
el jabón / le savon
il sapone / o sabonete

soap dish / die Seifenschale / la jabonera
le porte-savon / portasapone / a saboneteira

bath scrub / das Badeschrubber
el exfoliante / le gommage
lo scrub da bagno
o esfoliante de banho

shower gel
das Duschgel
el gel de ducha
le gel douche
il gel doccia
o gel de duche

loofah / die Luffa
la lufa / le louffa
la spugna / a lufa

bubble bath
das Sprudelbad
el baño de
burbujas
le bain
moussant
il bagno
schiuma
o banho
de espuma

bath bomb / die Badebombe
la bomba de baño / la bombe de bain
la bomba da bagno / a bomba de banho

medicine cabinet
der Medizinschrank
el botiquín
l'armoire à pharmacie
l'armadietto dei medicinali
o armário de medicamentos

shower curtain / der Duschvorhang
la cortina de ducha / le rideau
de douche / la tenda da doccia
a cortina de duche

back brush / die
Rückenbürste / el cepillo
para la espalda / la brosse
à dos / la spazzola
a escova para costas

dental hygiene / die Zahnpflege / la higiene dental
l'hygiène dentaire / l'igiene dentale / a higiene dentária

mouthwash / die Mundspülung
el enjuague bucal   le bain de bouche
il colluttorio / o elixir

talcum powder
das Talkumpuder
los talcos
le talc
il borotalco
o pó de talco

toothpaste / die Zahnpasta
la pasta dental / le dentifrice
il dentifricio / a pasta de dentes

toothbrush holder
der Zahnbürstenhalter
el portacepillos / le verre à dent
il porta spazzolino
o suporte para
escova de dentes

dental floss / die Zahnseide
el hilo dental / le fil dentaire
il filo interdentale / o fio dental

toothbrush / die Zahnbürste
el cepillo de dientes / la brosse
à dent / lo spazzolino da denti
a escova de dentes

tissues / die Taschentücher
los pañuelos
les mouchoirs
i fazzoletti / os lenços

UTILITY ROOM / DER HAUSHALTSRAUM / EL LAVADERO
LA BUANDERIE / LA LAVANDERIA / A DESPENSA

laundry / die Wäsche / la lavanderia / la lessive / la lavanderia / a lavanderia

laundry basket / der Wäschekorb
el cesto de la ropa / le panier à linge
il cesto per il bucato
o cesto de roupa suja

laundry detergent
das Waschmittel
el detergente
de lavandería
la lessive
il detersivo
per il bucato
o detergente
para a roupa

washing machine
die Waschmaschine
la lavadora
le lave-linge
la lavatrice
a máquina de lavar

fill (v) / füllung / llenar / remplir / riempire / encher

fabric softener / der Weichspüler
el suavizante / l'assouplissant
l'ammorbidente
o amaciador para a roupa

soap powder / das Seifenpulver
el jabón en polvo / la lessive
en poudre / il sapone in polvere
o detergente em pó

dryer sheet
das Trocknerblatt
las hojas suavizantes
les feuilles
assouplissantes
le salviette / as toalhitas
para máquina de secar

laundry pod / die Wäschepad
el detergente en cápsula
la capsule de lessive
la capsula per il bucato
as pastilhas para máquina de lavar

bleach
das Bleichmittel
el blanqueador
la javel
la candeggina
a lixívia

dryer / der Trockner
la secadora / le sèche-linge
l'asciugatrice
a máquina de secar

ironing board / das Bügelbrett
la mesa de planchar
la table à repasser
l'asse da stiro / a tábua de passar

clothespin / die Wäscheklammer
el gancho de ropa / la pince à linge
a molletta / a mola de roupa

iron / das Bügeleisen
la plancha / le fer à repasser
il ferro da stiro / o ferro

clothesline
die Wäscheleine
el tendedero
la corde à linge
lo stendibiancheria
o varal

rinse cycle / der
Klarspülgang
el ciclo de enjuague
le cycle de rinçage
il ciclo di risciacquo
o ciclo de levagem

spin (v) / schleudern
girar / tourner
centrifugare
centrifugar

iron (v) / bügeln / planchar
repasser / stirare / passar a ferro

dry (v) / trocknen / secar
faire sécher / asciugare / secar

cleaning / die Reinigung / la limpieza / le lavage / la pulizia / a limpeza

apron
die Schürze
el delantal
le tablier
il grembiule
o avental

dustpan
die Kehrschaufel
el recogedor
la pelle à
poussière
la paletta
a pá de lixo

vacuum cleaner
der Staubsauger
la aspiradora
l'aspirateur
l'aspirapolvere
o aspirador

brush / die Bürste
el cepillo / la balayette
la spazzola / a escova

broom / der Besen
la escoba / le balai
la scopa / a vassoura

feather duster
der Staubwedel
el plumero
le plumeau
lo spolverino
o espanador

sweep (v) / kehrer / barrer
balayer / spazzare / varrer

plunger
der Stößel
el destapador
la ventouse
lo sturalavandini
o desentupidor

mop
der Mopp
el trapero
la serpillière
il mocio
a esfregona

spray cleaner
der Sprühreiniger
el spray limpiador
le spray
il detergente spray
o produto de
limpeza em spray

bucket
der Eimer
la cubeta
le seau
il secchio
o balde

rubber gloves / die Gummihandschuhe
los guantes de caucho / les gants
de caoutchouc / i guanti di gomma
as luvas de borracha

sponge / der Schwamm
la esponja / l'éponge
la spugna / a esponja

dust cloth / das Staubtuch
el trapo para polvo
le chiffon
il panno per la polvere
o pano do pó

wipe (v) / wischen / limpia
essuyer / pulire / limpar

polish (v) / polieren / pulir
astiquer / lucidare / polir

scrub (v) / schrubben / fregar
frotter / strofinare / esfregar

dust (v) / abstauben / desempolvar
épousseter / spolverare / limpar o pó

wash (v) / waschen / lavar
laver / lavare / lavar

WORKSHOP / DIE WERKSTATT / EL TALLER
L'ATELIER / L'OFFICINA / A OFICINA

tool bench / die Werkbank / la mesa de herramientas / l'établi / il banco degli attrezzi a bancada de ferramentas

duct tape / das Klebeband
la cinta adhesiva / le ruban adhésif
il nastro adesivo / a fita adesiva

electrical tape / das Isolierband
la cinta aislante / l'adhésif d'électricien
il nastro isolante / a fita isoladora

rasp / die Raspel
la escofina / la râpe
la raspa / o raspador

file / die Feile
la lima / la lime
la lima / a lima

combination wrench
der Ringmaulschlüssel
la llave de
combinación
la clé mixte
la chiave universale
a chave inglesa

monkey wrench
der Rollgabelschlüssel
la llave inglesa
la clé à molette
la chiave a pappagallo
a chave grifo

vise
der Schraubstock
la prensa de banco
l'étau
la morsa
a pega

storage box
die Aufbewahrungsbox
la caja de
almacenamiento
la boite de rangement
la cassetta
a caixa de
armazenamento

cordless drill / die Akkubohrmaschine / el taladro inalámbrico
la perceuse sans fil / il trapano senza fili / o berbequim sem fios

materials / die Werkstoffe / los materiales / les matériaux / i materiali / os materiais

MDF / die MDF / el MDF
le medium / l'MDF / o MDF

hardwood / das Hartholz / la madera dura
le bois dur / il legno massiccio / a madeira dura

particle board / die Spanplatte
la madera aglomerada / l'aggloméré
il truciolato / o contraplacado

stainless steel
der rostfreier Stahl
el acero inoxidable
l'acier inoxydable
l'acciaio inossidabile
o aço inoxidável

hardboard / die Hartfaserplatten
la madera prensada / le panneau dur
il cartongesso / o HDF

plywood / das Sperrholz / la madera
contrachapada / le contreplaqué
il compensato / o contraplacado

galvanized steel
der verzinkter Stahl
el galvanizado
l'acier galvanisé
il acciaio zincato
o aço galvanizado

softwood / das Weichholz
la madera blanda / le bois
tendre / il legno tenero
a madeira macia

sheet metal / das Metallblech / la hoja
de metal / la tôle / la lamiera / a chapa metálica

power tools / die Elektrowerkzeuge / las herramientas eléctricas / les outils électriques
gli utensili elettrici / as ferramentas eléctricas

electric drill
die elektrische
Bohrmaschine
el taladro eléctrico
la perceuse électrique
il trapano elettrico
o berbequim elétrica

drill bits / die Bohrer
las brocas
les forets
le punte
del trapano
a broca

circular saw
die Kreissäge
la sierra circular
la scie circulaire
la sega circolare
a serra circular

jigsaw / die Stichsäge
la sierra de vaivén
la scie sauteuse
il seghetto alternativo
a serra de vaivém

table saw
die Tischsäge
la sierra de mesa
la scie d'établi
la sega da banco
a serra de mesa

blade / das Blatt / la cuchilla
la lame / la lama / a lâmina

sandpaper / das Schleifpapier
el papel de lija / le papier de verre
la carta vetrata / a lixa

orbital sander / der Exzenterschleifer
la lijadora orbital / la ponceuse excentrique
la levigatrice orbitale / a lixadeira orbital

shop-vac
der Nass-Trockensauger
la aspiradora
en seco y húmedo
l'aspirateur de chantier
il bidone aspiratutto
o aspirador de
pó seco e úmido

miter saw
die Gehrungssäge
la sierra de inglete
la scie à onglet
la sega circolare
a serra meia-esquadria

nail gun
die Nagelpistole
la pistola de clavos
le pistolet à clous
lo sparachiodi
a pistola de pregos

extension cord
die Verlängerungskabel
el cable de extensión
la rallonge
la prolunga
o cabo de extensão

nail / der Nagel / el clavo
le clou / il chiodo / o prego

---

techniques / die Techniken / las técnicas / les techniques / le tecniche / as técnicas

cut (v) / schneiden
cortar / découper
tagliare / cortar

plane (v) / hobeln
cepillar la madera / raboter
piallare / aplainar

hammer (v) / hammer
martillar / marteler
martellare / martelar

drill (v) / bohren
taladrar / percer
trapanare / perfurar

saw (v) / säge / serruchar
scier / segare / serrar

turn (v) / drehen / girar
faire tourner / girare / virar

solder (v) / löten / soldar
souder / saldare / soldar

carve (v) / schnitzen / tallar
graver / intagliare / talhar

TOOLS / DIE WERKZEUGE / LAS HERRAMIENTAS / LES OUTILS
GLI ATTREZZI / AS FERRAMENTAS

toolbox
der Werkzeugkasten
la caja de herramientas
la boite à outils
la cassetta degli attrezzi
a caixa de ferramentas

claw hammer
der Klauenhammer
el martillo sacalavos
le marteau arrache-clou
il martello tira chiodi
o martelo

tool belt / der Werkzeuggürtel
el cinturón para herramientas
la ceinture à outils / la cintura
degli attrezzi / o cinto
de ferramentas

plane / die Hobel
la garlopa / le rabot
la pialla / a plaina

clamp / die Zwinge
la abrazadera / la pince
il morsetto / a abraçadeira

miter box / die Gehrungslade
la caja de ingletes
la boite à onglets
la cassetta per cornici
a caixa de esquadriass

tenon saw
die Zapfensäge
la sierra de espiga
la scie à tenon
la sega per tenoni
serrote de costas

Phillips screwdriver
der Kreuzschlitzschraubendreher
el destornillador Phillips
le tournevis Phillips / il cacciavite
a croce / a chave-de-fenda Phillips

flathead screwdriver
der Schlitzschraubendreher
el destornillador de cabeza plana
le tournevis plat
il cacciavite a testa piatta
a chave-de-fenda de ponta chata

head
der Kopf
la cabeza
la tête
la testa
a cabeça

screw / die Schraube / el tornillo
la vis / la vite / o parafuso

nut
die Mutter
la tuerca
l'écrou
il dado
a porca

bolt
die Schraube
el perno
le boulon
il bullone
o parafuso

washer
die Unterlegscheibe
la junta / la rondelle
la rondella / a anilha

square / der Vierkant
la escuadra / le carré
la squadra / o esquadro

ball-peen hammer
der Kugelhammer
el martillo de bola
le marteau à panne ronde
il martello a sfera
o martelo de bola

sledgehammer
der Vorschlaghammer
el mazo / la masse
la mazza / a marreta

level / die Wasserwaage
la plana / le niveau
la livella / o nível

handsaw / die Handsäge
la sierra de mano
la scie à main / il seghetto
o serrote

hacksaw / das Bügelsäge
la sierra para metales
la scie à métaux
il seghetto / a serra de arco

fretsaw / die Laubsäge
la segueta
la scie à découper
il seghetto
a serra tico-tico

kneepads / die Knieschoner
las rodilleras / les genouillères
le ginocchiere / as joelheiras

goggles / die Schutzbrille
las gafas de protección
les lunettes de sécurité
gli occhiali di protezione
os óculos de proteção

work gloves / die
Arbeitshandschuhe
los guantes de trabajo
les gants de travail
i guanti da lavoro
as luvas de trabalho

solder / das Lötzinn
la soldadura / le fil à souder
il saldatore / a solda

stepladder / die Trittleiter
la escalera plegable
l'escabeau / la scaletta
o escadote

ladder / die Leiter
la escalera / l'échelle
la scala / a escada

socket wrench / der Steckschlüssel
la llave de tubo / la clé à douille
la chiave a bussola
a chave de caixa

soldering iron
der Lötkolben
el soldador
le fer à souder
il saldatore
o ferro de solda

vice-grip pliers
die Schraubstockzange
los alicates de sujeció
la pince étau
la pinza a morsa
o alicate de pressão

needle-nose pliers
die Spitzzange
los alicates de punta
la pince à becs fins
la pinza ad ago
o alicate de ponta

adjustable wrench
der verstellbarer
Schraubenschlüssel
la llave ajustable
la clé à molette
la chiave regolabile
a chave ajustável

caliper / die Schieblehre
la pinza / le pied à coulisse
la pinza / o calibrador

putty knife / der Spachtel
la espátula / le couteau
à mastic / la spatola
a espátula

steel wool / die Stahlwolle
el estropajo de acero
la paille de fer / la lana
d'acciaio / a lã de aço

workbench / die Werkbank
la mesa de trabajo
l'établi / il banco da lavoro
a bancada de trabalho

caulking gun
die Abdichtungspistole
la pistola de calafateo
le pistolet à silicone
la pistola per calafataggio
a pistola de calafetagem

Allen key
der Inbusschlüssel
la llave Allen / la clé Allen
la chiave a brugola
a chave Allen

hand drill
die Handbohrmaschine
el taladro de mano
la chignole
il trapano a mano
o berbequim manual

DECORATING / DAS DEKORIEREN / LA DECORACIÓN / LA DECORATION DECORARE / A DECORAÇÃO

wall / die Wand / la pared / le mur / il muro / a parede

roller / das Walze
el rodillo / le rouleau
il rullo / o rolo

paint can / die Farbdose
la lata de pintura / le pot de peinture
il secchio di vernice / a lata de tinta

paint tray / die Farbwanne
la bandeja de pintura
le bac à peinture
il vassoio di vernice
a bandeja de tinta

paint
die Farbe
la pintura
la peinture
la vernice
a pintura

brush / die Bürste / el pincel
la brosse / il pennello / o pincel

samples / die Muster
las muestras / les échantillons
i campioni / as amostras

paint (v) / streichen / pintar /
peindre / verniciare / pintar

drywall / der Trockenbau
el panel de yeso / la cloison sèche
il muro a secco / a parede de gesso

masking tape / das Abdeckband
la cinta de enmascarar
le ruban de masquage
il nastro adesivo
a fita crepe

molding / die Leiste / la moldura
la moulure / la modanatura
o ornamento da cornija

exposed brick / die Sichtziegel
el ladrillo visto / la brique apparente
il mattone a vista / o tijolo exposto

scraper
der Spachtel
el raspador
le grattoir
il raschietto
o raspador

patch (v) / flicken / parchear
réparer / rattoppare / corrigir

artwork / das Kunstwerk
la obra de arte / le tableau
l'opera d'arte / a obra de arte

scrape (v) / kratzen / raspar
gratter / raschiare / raspar

floor / der Fußboden / el piso / le sol / il pavimento / o chão

skirting
die Sockelleiste
el rodapié
la plinthe
il battiscopa
o rodapé

linoleum / das Linoleum / el linóleo
le linoléum / il linoleum / o linóleo

laminate
das Laminat
el laminado / le stratifié
il laminato / o laminado

hardwood floor / der Hartholzbohlen
el piso de madera / le parquet
il pavimento in legno massicco
o assoalho em madeira

ceramic tile / die Keramikfliesen / la baldosa
de cerámica / la plaque de céramique
le piastrelle di ceramica / o azulejo

glue brush / der Klebepinsel
el cepillo de pegamento
la brosse à colle / la spazzola
per colla / o pincel de cola

smoothing brush
die Glättungsbürste / el cepillo
suavizador / la brosse à lisser
la spazzola per lisciare
a escova de parede

smoothing tool
die Glättwerkzeug
la herramienta
de suavizado
l'outil de lissage
lo strumento per
lisciare / a espátula
para alisar

pasting table
die Leimtisch
la mesa de pegar
la table à encoller
il tavolo da lavoro
a bancada de colagem

wallpaper (v) / tapezieren
empapelar / tapisser
applica lo sfondo
aplicar papel de parede

plumb bob
das Lot
la plomada
le niveau
il filo a piombo
o prumo

utility knife / das Universalmesser
el cuchillo multiuso / le cutter
il coltello multiuso / o x-ato

wallpaper / die Tapete
el papel tapiz / le papier-peint
la carta da parati
o papel de parede

sander / der Schleifer / la lijadora
la ponçeuse / la levigatrice / a lixadora

respirator
die Atemschutzmaske
el respirador
le masque filtrant
il respiratore
o respirador

strip (v) / abziehen / quitar
décaper / togliere / descascar

sand (v) / sand / lijar
poncer / sabbiare / lixar

tile (v) / fliese / embaldosa
carreler / piastrellare / adrilhar

trowel / der Kelle / la paleta
la truelle / la cazzuola / a talocha

varnish (v) / lackieren / barnizar
vernir / smaltare / envernizar

tile adhesive / der Fliesenkleber
el adhesivo para baldosas / la colle
à carrelage / l'adesivo per piastrelle
o adesivo para azulejo

stain (v) / beize / manchar
lasurer / tingere / tingir

lacquer / der Lack / la laca
le vernis / la lacca / o verniz

GARDENING / DIE GARTENARBEIT / LA JARDINERÍA / LE JARDINAGE
IL GIARDINAGGIO / A JARDINAGEM

courtyard
der Hof
el patio
la cour
il cortile
o quintal

greenhouse
das Gewächshaus
el invernadero
la serre / la serra
a estufa

flowerbed
das Blumenbeet
el macizo de flores
le parterre
l'aiuola
o canteiro

lawn
der Rasen
el césped
la pelouse
il prato
o relvado

path / der Weg / el camino / l'allée / il sentiero / o caminho

shade tree / der schattenspendender Baum
el árbol de sombra / l'arbre d'ombrage
l'albero da ombra / a árvore de sombra

bush
der Strauch
el arbusto
le buisson
il cespuglio
o arbusto

hedge / die Hecke
el seto / la haie
la siepe / a sebe

ground cover / die Bodendecker / la cubierta del suelo
la couverture végétale / la copertura del terreno / a cobertura de solo

flowering shrub / der blühender Strauch
el arbusto floreciente / l'arbuste en fleur
l'arbusto da fiore / o arbusto com flores

potted plant / die Topfpflanze
la planta en maceta / la plante
en pot / la pianta in vaso
a planta de vaso

creeper
die Schlingpflanze
la enredadera
la plante grimpante
la liana
a planta rasteira

herbaceous border / das Staudenbeet / el arriate herbáceo
la bordure / il confine erbaceo / a divisória de plantas

garden styles / die Gartenstile
los estilos de jardín / les styles de jardin
gli stili di giardino / os estilos de jardinagem

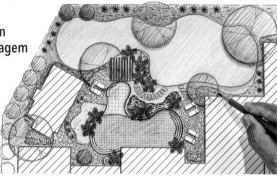

formal garden / der formaler Garten
el jardín formal / le jardin classique
il giardino formale / o jardim formal

landscape architect / der Landschaftsarchitekt / el arquitecto paisajista
le paysagiste / l'architetto paesaggista / o arquiteto paisagista

cottage garden / das Cottage-Garten
el jardín de casa de campo
le jardin à l'anglaise / il giardino di casa
o jardim rural

water garden / der Wassergarten
el jardín de agua / le jardin aquatique
il giardino acquatico
o jardim aquático

herb garden / der Kräutergarten
el jardín de hierbas / le jardin de
fines herbes / il giardino delle erbe
o jardim de ervas

roof garden / der Dachgarten
el jardín de azotea / le jardin sur toit
il giardino pensile / o jardim no terraço

community garden
der Gemeinschaftsgarten / el jardín
comunitario / le jardin partagé
il giardino comunitario
o jardim comunitário

rock garden / der Steingarten
el jardín de rocas / le jardin de pierres
il giardino roccioso / o jardim de pedras

raised-bed garden
der Hochbeetgarten / el jardín
de camas elevadas / le jardin de
plate-bandes surélevées / il giardino
rialzato / o jardim sobrelevado

vegetable garden
der Gemüsegarten / el huerto
le jardin potager / l'orto / a horta

knot garden / der Knüpfgarten
el jardín del nudo / le jardin de noeuds
il giardino a nodi / o jardim knot

garden features / die Gartenelemente / las características del jardín / les éléments du jardin / le caratteristiche del giardino / os elementos do jardim

windowbox
der Blumenkasten
el macetero / la jardinière
il vaso da finestra
a floreira de janela

arbor / die Laube
la cenador / la tonnelle
la pergola / o arco

trellis / das Spalier / el enrejado
le treillis / il traliccio / a treliça

climber / die Kletterpflanze
los trepadores
la plante grimpante
il rampicante / a trepadeira

picket fence / der Lattenzaun
la valla de estacas / la palissade
il recinto di legno / a cerca

hanging basket / der Hängekorb
la cesta colgante
le panier suspendu
il cesto appeso / o cesto suspenso

fountain / der Springbrunnen
la fuente / la fontaine
la fontana / a fonte

water feature / das Wasserspiel
la fuente de agua / le bassin
l'elemento d'acqua
o elemento aquático

---

backyard / der Hinterhof / el patio / l'arrière-cour / il cortile / o pátio

deck / die Terrasse / la terraza
la terrasse / il ponte / o terraço

gazebo / die Gartenlaube / el mirador
le belvédère / il gazebo / o gazebo

pergola / die Pergola / la pérgola
la pergola / la pergola / a pérgula

barbecue grill
der Barbecue-Grill
la parrilla
de barbacoa
le barbecue
la griglia
per il barbecue
a churrasqueira

covered patio
die überdachte Veranda
el patio cubierto
le patio couvert
il patio coperto
o pátio coberto

firepit / die Feuerstelle
la hoguera / le foyer
il focolare / a fogueira

plants / die Pflanzen / las plantas / les plantes / le piante / as plantas

annual / die
einjährige Pflanze /
la anual / l'annuelle /
l'annuale / o anual

perennial / die
mehrjährige Pflanze
la perenne / la vivace
la perenne / o perene

biennial / die
zweijährige Pflanze
la bienal / a bisannuelle
la biennale / a bienal

bulb / die Zwiebel
el bulbo / le bulbe
il bulbo / o bulbo

weed / das Unkraut
las malas hierbas
la mauvaise herbe
l'erbaccia
a erva daninha

herb / das Kraut
la hierba
l'herbe de cuisine
l'erba / a erva

aquatic plant
die Wasserpflanze
el acuático / l'aquatique
l'acquatico / a aquática

succulent
die Sukkulente
la suculenta
la succulente
la pianta grassa
a suculenta

cattail / der Rohrkolben
la espadaña
la massette-quenouille
la coda di gatto
a tabua

cactus / die Kaktus
el cactus / le cactus
il cactus / o cato

fern / der Farn
el helecho
la fougère / la felce
o feto

alpine plant
die Alpenpflanze
el alpino / la fleur des
Alpes / l'alpino / a alpina

grass / das Gras
el césped / l'herbe
l'erba / a relva

moss / das Moos
el musgo
la mousse / il muschio
o musgo

vine
der Weinstock / la vid
la plante grimpante
la vite / a videira

---

trees / die Bäume / los árboles / les arbres / gli alberi / as árvores

evergreen tree
der immergrüner Baum
el árbol de
hoja perenne
l'arbre à feuilles
persistantes
l'albero sempreverde
a árvore perene

cone
der Zapfen
el cono
la pomme de pin
la pigna
a pinha

conifer / der Nadelbaum
la conifera / le conifère
la conifera / a conífera

deciduous tree
der laubabwerfender
Baum
el árbol de
hoja caduca
l'arbre à feuilles
caduques
l'albero deciduo
a árvore caduca

palm
die Palme
la palma
le palmier
la palma
a palmeira

topiary / die Formschnitt
el topiario / la topiaire
la topiaria / a topiaria

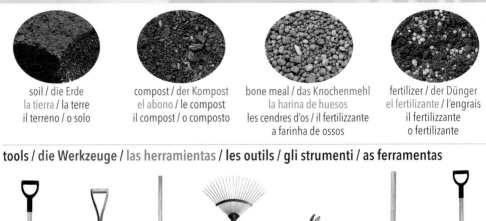

soil / die Erde
la tierra / la terre
il terreno / o solo

compost / der Kompost
el abono / le compost
il compost / o composto

bone meal / das Knochenmehl
la harina de huesos
les cendres d'os / il fertilizzante
a farinha de ossos

fertilizer / der Dünger
el fertilizante / l'engrais
il fertilizzante
o fertilizante

tools / die Werkzeuge / las herramientas / les outils / gli strumenti / as ferramentas

shovel
die Schaufel
la pala
la pelle
la pala
a pá

spade
der Spaten
la pica
la bêche
la vanga
a pá de
ponta reta

rake
die Harke
el rastrillo
le râteau
il rastrello
o ancinho

lawn rake
die Rasenharke
el rastrillo
de césped
la râteau à feuilles
il rastrello da prato
a vassoura
para relva

lopper
die Astschere
el cortarramas
le sécateur
il troncarami
a tesoura
de poda

hoe
die Hacke
la azada
la houe
la zappa
o sacho

pitchfork
die Mistgabel
la horquilla
la fourche
il forcone
a forquilha

hedge trimmer / die Heckenschere
el cortasetos / le taille-haie
la tagliasiepi / o aparador de sebe

trimmer / der Trimmer
la recortadora / le coupe-bordures
la tagliasiepi / o podador

chainsaw
die Kettensäge
la motosierra
la tronçonneuse
la motosega
o motosserra

grass bag
der Grasfangsack
la bolsa de hierba
le réservoir d'herbe
il sacco per l'erba
o saco de recolha

leaf blower / der Laubbläser / el soplador de hojas
le souffleur à feuilles / il soffiatore / o aspirador de folhas

lawn mower / die Rasenmäher / el cortacesped
la tondeuse / il tosaerba / o corta-relvas

hose reel / der *Schlauchhaspel*
el carrete de manguera
le dévidoir / l'avvolgitubo
o enrolador de mangueira

nozzle / die *Düse*
la boquilla / l'embout
il beccuccio / a ponteira

garden hose / der Gartenschlauch
la manguera de jardín
le tuyau d'arrosage
il tubo dell'irrigazione
a mangueira de jardim

rubber boots
die Gummistiefel
las botas de goma
les bottes en
caoutchouc
gli stivali di gomma
as galochas

watering can
die Gießkanne
la regadera
l'arrosoir
l'annaffiatoio
o regador

pot / der Topf / la maceta
le pot / il vaso / o vaso

peat pot / der Torf-Topf
la maceta de turba / le pot en tourbeil
vaso di torba / o vaso de turfa

sprinkler / der Sprinkler
el aspersor / l'arroseur
l'irrigatore / o aspersor

trug / der Gartenkorb
la cesta / le panier
il cesto trug / o cesto

pruning clippers / die Gartenschere
las tijeras de podar / le sécateur
le cesoie / a tesoura de podar

gardening gloves / die Gartenhandschuhe
los guantes de jardinería / les gants
de jardinage / i guanti da giardinaggio
as luvas de jardinagem

shears / die Schere
las tijeras / la cisaille
le cesoie / a cisalha

stake (v) / pfahl / plantar
tuteurer / picchettare / estacar

saw / die Säge / la sierra
a scie / la sega / o serrote

seed tray / die Saatschale
la bandeja de semillas
le plateau de semis
il contenitore per i semi
a bandeja de sementeira

label
das Etikett
la etiqueta
le panneau
l'etichetta
a etiqueta

hand trowel
die Handkelle
la paleta de mano
la truelle à main
la cazzuola
a pá de jardim

garden fork
die Gartengabel
la horquilla de jardín
la bêche à dents
la forca da giardino
a forquilha de jardim

seed packet
das Samenpaket
el paquete de semillas
le paquet de graines
la bustina di semi
o pacote de sementes

wheelbarrow / die Schubkarre
la carretilla / la brouette
la carriola / o carrinho de mão

kneepad / der Knieschoner
la rodillera / la genouillère
la ginocchiera / a joelheira

seeds / die Saatgut / las semillas
les graines / i semi / as sementes

CITIES
DIE STÄDTE
LAS CIUDADES
LES VILLES
LE CITTÀ
AS CIDADES

THE CITY / DIE STADT / LA CIUDAD / LA VILLE / LA CITTÀ / A CIDADE

office building / das Bürogebäude
el edificio de oficinas / l' immeuble de bureaux
l'edificio per uffici / o edifício de escritórios

street / die Straße / la calle
la rue / la strada / a rua

apartment building
das Wohnhaus
la casa de pisos / l'immeuble
il condominio / o prédio

sidewalk / der Bürgersteig
la acera / le trottoir
il marciapiede / o passeio

traffic light / die Ampel
el semáforo / le feu
il semaforo / o semáforo

intersection / die Kreuzung
la intersección / l'intersection
l'incrocio / o cruzamento

street sign / das Straßenschild
placa de la calle / la plaque
de rue / il cartello stradale
a placa de rua

crosswalk / der Zebrastreifen
el paso de peatones / le passage piéton
le strisce pedonali / a passadeira

street corner / die Straßenecke
la esquina de la calle / le coin de la rue
l'angolo di strada / a esquina

curb / der Bordstein
la acera / le trottoir
il cordolo / a calçada

city / die Stadt
la ciudad / la ville
la città / a cidade

town / die Stadt
la ciudad / la ville
la città / a cidade

village / das Dorf
la aldea / le village
il villaggio / a aldeia

suburb / der Vorort
el suburbio / la banlieue
il sobborgo / o subúrbio

parking lot / der Parkplatz
el estacionamiento
le parking / il parcheggio
o parque de
estacionamento

avenue / die Allee
la avenida / l'avenue
il viale / a avenida

plaza / der Platz
la plaza / la place
la piazza / a praça

park / der Park
el parque / le jardin public
il parco / o parque

infrastructure / die Infrastruktur / la infraestructura
l'infrastructure / l'infrastruttura / as infraestruturas

bridge / die Brücke
el puente / le pont / il
ponte / a ponte

dam / der Damm
la presa / le barrage
la diga / a barragem

aqueduct / der Aquädukt
el acueducto / l'aqueduc
l'acquedotto / o aqueduto

viaduct / das Viadukt
el viaducto / le viaduc
il viadotto / o viaduto

BUILDINGS / DIE GEBÄUDE / LOS EDIFICIOS / LES BÂTIMENTS
GLI EDIFICI / OS EDIFÍCIOS

town hall / das Rathaus
el ayuntamiento / la mairie
il municipio
a câmara municipal

court house
das Gerichtsgebäude
el juzgado / le palais de justic
il tribunale / o tribunal

jail / das Gefängnis
la cárcel / la prison
la prigione / a prisão

post office / das Postamt
el correo / la poste
l'ufficio postale
os correios

library / die Bibliothek
la biblioteca
la bibliothèque
la biblioteca / a biblioteca

museum / das Museum
el museo / le musée
il museo / o museu

theater / das Theater
el teatro / le théâtre
il teatro / o teatro

movie theater
das Filmtheater / el cine
le cinéma / il cinema
o cinema

school / die Schule
la escuela / l'école
la scuola / a escola

university / die Universität
la universidad
l'université / l'università
a universidade

bank / die Bank
el banco / la banque
la banca / o banco

hospital / das Krankenhaus
el hospital / l'hôpital
l'ospedale / o hospital

skyscraper / der Wolkenkratzer / el rascacielos
le gratte-ciel / il grattacielo / o arranha-céus

industrial park / das Gewerbegebiet
el parque industrial / la zone industrielle
il parco industriale / a zona industrial

factory / die Fabrik
la fábrica / l'usine
la fabbrica / a fábrica

headquarters
der Hauptsitz / la sede
le siège social
la sede centrale / a sede

warehouse / das Lagerhaus
el almacén / l'entrepôt
il magazzino / o armazém

ARCHITECTURE / DIE ARCHITEKTUR / LA ARQUITECTURA / L'ARCHITECTURE L'ARCHITETTURA / A ARQUITETURA

architect / der Architekt
el arquitecto / l'architecte
l'architetto / o arquiteto

blueprint / der Bauplan
el plano / le plan
la cianografia / a planta

religious structures / die religiöse Strukturen / las estructuras religiosas les bâtiments religieux / le strutture religiose / as estruturas religiosas

mosque / die Moschee
la mezquita / la mosquée
la moschea / a mesquita

synagogue / die Synagoge
la sinagoga / la synagogue
la sinagoga / a sinagoga

church / die Kirche
la iglesia / l'église
la chiesa / a igreja

temple / der Tempel
el templo / le temple
il tempio / o templo

cathedral / die Kathedrale / la catedral
la cathédrale / la cattedrale / a catedral

abbey / die Abtei
la abadía / l'abbaye
l'abbazia / a abadia

chapel / die Kapelle
la capilla / la chapelle
la cappella / a capela

monastery / das Kloster
el monasterio
le monastère
il monastero
o mosteiro

castle / die Burg
el castillo / le château
il castello / o castelo

architectural styles / die Architekturstile / los estilos arquitectónicos
les styles architecturaux / gli stili architettonici / os estilos arquitetónicos

Renaissance / der Renaissancestil
el estilo renacentista / le style
Renaissance / lo stile rinascimentale
o estilo renascentista

Gothic / der Gotikstil
el estilo gótico / le style gothique
lo stile gotico / o estilo gótico

Victorian / der viktorianischer Stil
el estilo victoriano / le style victorien
lo stile vittoriano / o estilo vitoriano

Baroque / der Barockstil
el stilo barroco / le style baroque
lo stile barocco / o estilo barroco

Art Deco / Art-Deco-Stil
el estilo Art Deco / le style Art-déco
l' Art Déco / o estilo Art Déco

Art Nouveau / Jugendstil
el estilo Art Nouveau / l'Art Nouveau
l'Art Nouveau / a Arte Nova

Classical / der klassische Stil
el estilo clásico / le style classique
lo stile classico / o estilo clássico

Modern / der moderner Stil
el estilo moderno / le style moderne
lo stile moderno / o estilo moderno

Neoclassical / der neoklassischen
Stil / el estilo neoclásico / le style
néoclassique / lo stile neoclassico
o estilo neoclássico

Postmodern / der postmoderne Stil
el estilo postmoderno
le style postmoderne
lo stile postmoderna
o estilo pós-moderna

Neofuturist / der neofuturistisch
Stil / el estilo neofuturista
le style néofuturiste / lo stile
neofuturista / o estilo neofuturista

COMMUNICATION / DIE KOMMUNIKATION / LA COMUNICACIÓN
LES TÉLÉCOMMUNICATIONS / LA COMUNICAZIONE / A COMUNICAÇÃO

cell phone / das Mobiltelefon / el celular / le cellulaire / il telefonino / o celular

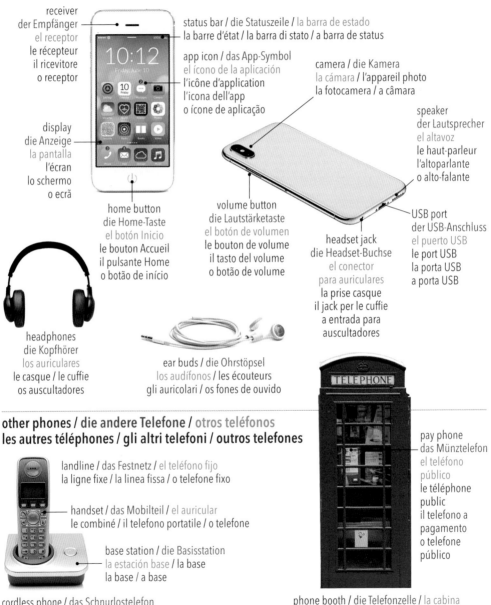

receiver
der Empfänger
el receptor
le récepteur
il ricevitore
o receptor

status bar / die Statuszeile / la barra de estado
la barre d'état / la barra di stato / a barra de status

app icon / das App-Symbol
el ícono de la aplicación
l'icône d'application
l'icona dell'app
o ícone de aplicação

camera / die Kamera
la cámara / l'appareil photo
la fotocamera / a câmara

display
die Anzeige
la pantalla
l'écran
lo schermo
o ecrã

speaker
der Lautsprecher
el altavoz
le haut-parleur
l'altoparlante
o alto-falante

home button
die Home-Taste
el botón Inicio
le bouton Accueil
il pulsante Home
o botão de início

volume button
die Lautstärketaste
el botón de volumen
le bouton de volume
il tasto del volume
o botão de volume

headset jack
die Headset-Buchse
el conector
para auriculares
la prise casque
il jack per le cuffie
a entrada para
auscultadores

USB port
der USB-Anschluss
el puerto USB
le port USB
la porta USB
a porta USB

headphones
die Kopfhörer
los auriculares
le casque / le cuffie
os auscultadores

ear buds / die Ohrstöpsel
los audífonos / les écouteurs
gli auricolari / os fones de ouvido

other phones / die andere Telefone / otros teléfonos
les autres téléphones / gli altri telefoni / outros telefones

landline / das Festnetz / el teléfono fijo
la ligne fixe / la linea fissa / o telefone fixo

handset / das Mobilteil / el auricular
le combiné / il telefono portatile / o telefone

base station / die Basisstation
la estación base / la base
la base / a base

cordless phone / das Schnurlostelefon
el teléfono inalámbrico / le téléphone sans fil
il telefono cordless / o telefone sem fios

pay phone
das Münztelefon
el teléfono
público
le téléphone
public
il telefono a
pagamento
o telefone
público

TELEPHONE

phone booth / die Telefonzelle / la cabina
telefónica / la cabine téléphonique / la
cabina telefonica / a cabine telefónica

postal service / der Postdienst / el servicio postal / les services postaux
il servizio postale / o serviço de correios

mailbag
der Postsack
la bolsa de correo
le sac postal
io sacchetto
della posta
a mala postal

stamp vending machine
der Briefmarken-Automat
la máquina
expendedora de sellos
le distributeur
automatique de timbres
il distributore
automatico di francobolli
a máquina automática
de venda de selos

postal worker
der Postbeamte
el trabajador postal
l'employé de la poste
l'impiegato della posta
o trabalhador dos correios

mail carrier
der Briefträger
el cartero
le postier
il postino
o carteiro

mailbox / der Briefkasten
el buzón / la boite aux lettres
la cassetta postale
a caixa de correio

postmark / der Poststempel / el matasellos
le cachet de la poste / il timbro postale / o carimbo

return address
die Rücksendeadresse
la dirección de devolución
l'adresse de l'expéditeur
l'indirizzo di ritorno
o endereço do remetente

Maria Jones
45 E 51st Street
NY NY XXXXX

Jean Smith
123 South Elm Boulevard
Anytown, OR 10000

stamp / die Briefmarke
el sello / le timbre
il francobollo / o selo

envelope / der Umschlag
el sobre / l'enveloppe
la busta / o envelope

address / die Adresse
la dirección / l'adresse
l'indirizzo / o endereço

letter / der Brief / la carta
la lettre / la lettera / a carta

zip code / die Postleitzahl
el código postal / le code postal
il codice postale / o código postal

courier / der Kurier
el servicio de mensajería / le coursier
il corriere / a transportadora

package / das Paket / el paquete
le paquet / il pacchetto / a encomenda

airmail / die Luftpost
el correo aéreo / la poste
aérienne / la posta aerea
o correio aéreo

letter slot / der Briefschlitz
la ranura de correo / la fente
à lettres / la fessura per le lettere
a ranhura para cartas

FREE
SHIPPING

free shipping / der kostenloser
Versand / el envío gratuito
l'expédition gratuite / la spedizione
gratuita / o frete grátis

fragile / zerbrechlich / frágil / fragile
fragile / frágil

do not bend / nicht biegen
no doblar / ne pas plier
non piegare / não dobrar

bluetooth / das Bluetooth
el bluetooth / le bluetooth
il bluetooth / o bluetooth

service plan / der Serviceplan
el plan de servicio / le plan de service
il piano / o plano de serviços

answer (v) / antworten / responder
répondre / rispondere / atender

hang up (v) / auflegen / colgar
raccrocher / riagganciare / desligar

call (v) / anrufen / llamar
appeler / chiamare / ligar

voicemail / die Voicemail / el correo
de voz / la boite vocale / la segreteria
telefonica / o correio de voz

busy signal / das Besetztzeichen
la señal de ocupado / le son occupé
il segnale di occupato
o sinal de ocupado

BANK / DIE BANK / EL BANCO / LA BANQUE / LA BANCA / O BANCO

window / das Fenster
la ventana / la fenêtre
lo sportello / a janela

teller / der Kassierer
el cajero / le guichetier
il bancario / o caixa

counter / der Schalter
el contador / le comptoir
lo sportello / o balcão

customer / der Kunde
el cliente / le client
il cliente / o cliente

deposit slip
der Einzahlungsschein
el recibo de depósito
le bordereau de dépôt
la distinta di versamento
o comprovativo
de depósito

bank lobby / die Banklobby / el lobby del banco
le hall de la banque / l'atrio della banca / o átrio do banco

check / der Scheck / el cheque / le chèque / l'assegno / o cheque

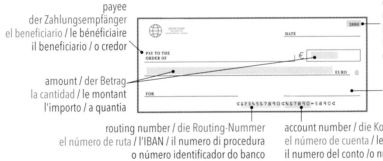

check number
die Schecknummer
el número de cheque
le numéro de chèque
il numero dell'assegno
o número de cheque

payee
der Zahlungsempfänger
el beneficiario / le bénéficiaire
il beneficiario / o credor

signature / die Unterschrift
la firma / la signature
la firma / a assinatura

amount / der Betrag
la cantidad / le montant
l'importo / a quantia

routing number / die Routing-Nummer
el número de ruta / l'IBAN / il numero di procedura
o número identificador do banco

account number / die Kontonummer
el número de cuenta / le numéro de compte
il numero del conto /o número de conta

bank card / die Bankkarte / la tarjeta bancaria / la carte bancaire
la carta di credito / o cartão bancário

magnetic strip
der Magnetstreifen
la banda magnética
la bande magnétique / la banda
magnetica / a faixa magnética

account number / die Kontonummer / el número de cuenta
le numéro de compte / il numero del conto / o número de conta

smart chip
der Chip
el chip inteligente
la puce
il chip intelligente
o chip inteligente

signature box
das Unterschriftsfeld
el espacio para firma
la zone de signature
la casella della firma
o espaço de assinatura

security code / der
Sicherheitscode / el código de
seguridad / le code de sécurité
il codice di sicurezza
o código de segurança

cardholder / der Karteninhaber
el titular de la tarjeta / le titulaire de
la carte / il titolare della carta / o titular

expiration date / das Verfallsdatum
a fecha de expiración / la date d'expiration
la data di scadenza / a data de validade

screen / der Bildschirm
la pantalla / l'écran
la schermo / o ecrã

card reader / der Kartenleser
/ el lector de tarjetas
le lecteur de cartes
il lettore di schede
o leitor de cartões

keypad / die Tastatur
el teclado / le clavier
la tastiera / o teclado

cash dispenser
der Geldautomat / el cajero
automático / le distributeur
de billets / il distributore
automatico / a caixa
automática

ATM / der Geldautomat
el cajero automático
le DAB / il bancomat
o multibanco

foreign currency / die Fremdwährung
la moneda extranjera / la monnaie étrangère
la valuta estera / a moeda estrangeira

exchange rate
der Devisenkurs / la tasa
de cambio / le taux de
change / il tasso di cambio
a taxa de câmbio

currency exchange / die Wechselstube / il cambio valuta
le bureau de change / il cambio valuta / a casa de câmbio

bill
die Banknote
la factura
le billet
la banconota
la nota

coin / die Münze
la moneda / la pièce
la moneta / a moeda

money / das Geld / el dinero / l'argent / i soldi / o dinheiro

finance / die Finanzen / las finanzas / la finance / la finanza / as finanças

stockbroker / der Börsenmakler
el corredor de bolsa / l'agent
de change / l'agente di cambio
o corretor

stock exchange / die Börse
la bolsa de valores / la bourse
la borsa valori / a bolsa de valores

financial advisor / der Finanzberater
el asesor financiero / le conseiller
financier / il consulente finanziario
o consultor financeiro

checkbook / das Scheckbuch
el corredor de bolsa / l'agent
de change / l'agente di cambio
o corretor

investment / die Anlage
la inversión / l'investissement
l'investimento / o investimento

share / die Aktie / la cuota / l'action
l'azione / a ação

commission / die Provision
la comisión / la commission
la commissione / a comissão

dividend / der Dividende
el dividendo / le dividende
il dividendo / o dividendo

PIN / das PIN / el pin / le code PIN
il PIN / o código PIN

mortgage / die Hypothek
la hipoteca / le prêt immobilier
il mutuo / o financiamento

lender / der Darlehensgeber
el prestamista / le prêteur
il prestatore / o credor

tax / die Steuer / el impuesto
la taxe / la tassa / o imposto

overdraft / der Überziehungskredit
el sobregiro / le découvert
lo scoperto / o saque a descoberto

interest rate / der Zinssatz / la tasa
de interés / le taux d'intérêt
il tasso di interesse / a taxa de juro

payment / die Zahlung / el pago
le versement / il pagamento
o pagamento

auto payment / die automatische
Zahlung / el pago automático
le versement automatique
il pagamento automatico
o pagamento automático

deposit / die Einzahlung / el depósito
le dépôt / il deposito / o depósito

withdrawal / die Abhebung / el retiro
le retrait / il ritiro / a rescisão

transfer / die Überweisung
la transferencia / le virement
il trasferimento / a transferência

bank fee / die Bankgebühr / la tarifa
del banco / les frais bancaires
la commissione bancaria
a comissão bancária
credit / der Kredit / el crédito
le crédit / il credito / o crédito

HOTEL / DAS HOTEL / EL HOTEL / L'HÔTEL / L'HOTEL / O HOTEL

receptionist
der Rezeptionist
el recepcionista
le réceptionniste
il receptionist
o rececionista

reception
die Rezeption
la recepción
la réception
la reception
a receção

concierge
der Concierge
el conserje
le concierge
il concierge
o porteiro

lobby
die Lobby
el lobby / le hall
la lobby / o átrio

front desk
die Rezeption
el escritorio delantero
la réception / la reception
o balcão de informações

check in (v) / einchecken
hacer check-in / enregistrer
fare il check-in
fazer o check-in

guest / der Gast
el invitado / le client
l'ospite / o convidado

service bell / die Dienstklingel
la campana de servicio
la cloche de service
il campanello di servizio
a campainha de serviço

key / der Schlüssel
la llave / la clé
la chiave / a chave

bellhop / der Page
el botones / le groom
il campanello
o carregador de malas

doorman / der Pförtner
el portero / le portier
il portiere / o porteiro

porter / der Pförtner
el mozo / le baggagiste
il portiere
o carregador de malas

key card / die Schlüsselkarte
la tarjeta de acceso
la carte d'accès / la chiave
elettronica / o cartão-chave

single room / das Einzelzimmer
la habitación individual
la chambre simple / la camera
singola / o quarto individual

double room / das Zweibettzimmer
la habitacion doble
la chambre double
la camera doppia / o quarto duplo

suite / die Suite / la suite
la suite / la suite / a suite

services / die Dienstleistungen / los servicios / les services / i servizi / os serviços

maid service / die Zimmermädchen
el servicio de limpieza
le ménage / il servizio di pulizia
o serviço de limpeza

laundry service / der Wäscheservice
el servicio de lavandería
la lessive / il servizio lavanderia
o serviço de lavandaria

room service / der Zimmerservice
el servicio de habitaciones / le service
de chambre / il servizio in camera
o serviço de quarto

room safe / der Zimmersafe
la caja fuerte de la habitación
le coffre de chambre
la cassaforte in camera / o cofre

breakfast buffet / das Frühstücksbuffet
el desayuno buffet / le buffet de
petit-déjeuner / la colazione a buffet
o bufê de pequeno-almoço

minibar / die Minibar
el minibar / le minibar
il minibar / o minibar

restaurant / das Restaurant
el restaurante / le restaurant
il ristorante / o restaurante

pool / das Schwimmbad
la piscina / la piscine
la piscina / a piscina

gym / der Fitnessraum
el gimnasio / la salle de sport
la palestra / o ginásio

I have a reservation. / Ich habe eine
Reservierung. / Tengo una reserva.
J'ai une réservation / Ho effettuato una
prenotazione. / Tenho uma reserva.

Do you have a vacancy? / Haben
Sie noch ein Zimmer frei? / ¿Tiene
habitaciones libres? / Avez-vous une
chambre disponible ? / Avete un
posto libero? / Tem alguma vaga?

I would like a room for two nights,
please. / Ich hätte gerne ein Zimmer
für zwei Nächte, bitte. / Me gustaría
una habitación por dos noches, por
favor. / Je souhaiterais réserver une
chambre pour deux nuits, s'il vous
plait. / Vorrei una camera per due
notti, per favore. / Queria um quarto
para duas noites, por favor.

When is check-out time? / Wann ist
die Check-out-Zeit? / ¿Cuándo es
la hora de salida? / A quelle heure
faut-il libérer la chambre ?
Quando è il momento del check-out?
A que horas é o check-out?

check-out (v) / auschecken / hacer
check-out / libérer la chambre
check-out / fazer o check-out

motel / das Motel
el motel / le motel
il motel / o motel

bed-and-breakfast
das Bed-and-Breakfast
la cama y desayuno
le bed and breakfast
il bed-and-breakfast
o alojamento e pequeno-almoço

inn / das Gasthaus
la posada / l'auberge
la locanda / a pousada

youth hostel
die Jugendherberge
el hostal para jóvenes
l'auberge de jeunesse
l'ostello della gioventù
a pousada da juventude

TOURISM / DER TOURISMUS / EL TURISMO / LE TOURISME
EL TURISMO / O TURISMO

tourist attraction / die Touristenattraktion / la atracción turística
l'attraction touristique / l'attrazione turistica / a atração turística

tourists
die Touristen
los turistas
les touristes
i turisti
os turistas

suitcase
der Koffer
la maleta
la valise
la valigia
a mala de viagem

fountain
der Springbrunnen
la fuente
la fontaine
la fontana / a fonte

ART EXHIBITION
CITY ART MUSEUM
12 MAR €5⁰⁰
No 012345
ADMIT ONE
12 MAR
No 012345

entrance fee / der Eintrittspreis
la tarifa de entrada / le droit d'entrée
il biglietto d'ingresso
a taxa de entrada

exhibit / das Exponat
la exposición / l'exposition
la mostra / a exibição

guided tour / die Führung
la visita guiada / la visite
guidée / a visita guidata
a visita guiada

tour guide / der Reiseleiter
el guía turístico / le guide
touristique / la guida turistica
o guia turístico

map / die Karte
el mapa / la carte
la mappa / o mapa

Baedeker
Cologne

currency / die Währung
la moneda / la devise
la valuta / a moeda

guide book / der Reiseführer
la guía / le guide papier
il libro guida / o guia

passport / der Reisepass
el pasaporte / le passeport
il passaporto / o passaporte

10 EURO

UNIÃO EUROPEIA
PORTUGAL
PASSAPORTE

points of interest / die Sehenswürdigkeiten / los puntos de interés
les points d'intérêt / i punti di interesse / os pontos de interesse

historic site
die historische Stätte
el sitio histórico
le site historique
il sito storico
o local histórico

monument
das Denkmal
el monumento
le monument
il monumento
o monumento

national park
der Nationalpark
el parque nacional
le parc national
il parco nazionale
o parque nacional

ancient ruin
die alte Ruine
la ruina antigua
la ruine antique
l'antica rovina
as ruínas antigas

museum / das Museum
el museo / le musée
il museo / o museu

garden / der Garten
el jardín / le jardin
il giardino / o jardim

casino / das Kasino
el casino / le casino
il casinò / o casino

festival / die Festspiele
el festival / le festival
il festival / a festa

statue
das Statue
la estatua
la statue
la statua
a estátua

postcards / die Postkarten / las postales
les cartes postales / le cartoline / os postais

landmark
das Wahrzeichen
el lugar
emblemático
le monument
il punto
d'interesse
o ponto de
referência

souvenir / das souvenir / el souvenir
le souvenir / il souvenir / a lembrança

TRANSPORTATION
DER VERKEHR
EL TRANSPORTE
LE TRANSPORT
I TRASPORTI
O TRANSPORTE

ROADS / DIE STRAßEN / LOS CAMINOS / LES ROUTES / LE STRADE / AS ESTRADAS

highway interchange / das Autobahndreieck / el intercambio de la autopista
l'échangeur d'autoroute / lo svincolo autostradale
o entroncamento rodoviário

median strip
der Mittelstreifen
la franja mediana / la ligne
médiane / la striscia di
mezzeria / a mediana

overpass / die Überführung
el paso elevado / le pont
il cavalcavia / o viaduto

guardrail / die Leitplanke
la barandilla / la glissière
il guardrail / a balaustrada

shoulder / der Seitenstreifen
el hombro / la bande d'arrêt
d'urgence / la sponda
a berma

lane / die Fahrspur
el carril / la voie
la corsia / a via

divider / der Fahrbahnteiler
el divisor / le terre-plein central
il divisorio / a faixa divisória

off-ramp / die Abfahrtsrampe
la rampa de salida
la bretelle de sortie
l'uscita / a rampa de saída

freeway / die Autobahn
la autopista / l'autoroute
l'autostrada / a autoestrada

underpass / die Unterführung
el paso subterráneo
le passage souterrain
il sottopassaggio / o subviaduto

on-ramp / die Auffahrtsrampe
la rampa de entrada
la bretelle d'accès / la rampa
a rampa de acesso

divided highway / die geteilte
Autobahn / la carretera
dividida / la route à chaussées
séparées / l'autostrada divisa
a rodovia duplicada

two-lane highway
die zweispurige Autobahn
la carretera de dos carriles
la route à deux voies
l'autostrada a due corsie
a estrada com duas
faixas de rodagem

one-way street
die Einbahnstraße / la calle de
un solo sentido / la rue
en sens unique / la strada
a senso unico / a rua
de sentido único

traffic jam
der Verkehrsstau
el embotellamiento
l'embouteillage / l'ingorgo
stradale / o engarrafamento

traffic circle
der Kreisverkehr
la rotonda / le rond-point
la rotatoria / a rotunda

traffic light
die Ampel
el semáforo
le feu de
signalisation
il semaforo
o semáforo

traffic cop
der Verkehrspolizist
el policía de tráfico
l'agent de
la circulation
l'ausiliario
del traffico
o polícia de trânsito

roadwork / die Baustelle
las obras viales / les travaux
i lavori stradali
as obras na estrada

parking meter / die Parkuhr
el parquímetro
le parcmètre / il parchimetro
o parquímetro

tow-away zone / die Abschleppzone
la zona de remolque
le stationnement gênant / la zona
rimozione forzata / sujeito a reboque

disabled parking
die Behindertenparkplatz
el estacionamiento
para discapacitados
la place handicapé
il parcheggio per disabili
o estacionamento para
pessoas com deficiência

road signs / die Verkehrsschilder / las señales de tráfico / les panneaux de signalisation
i segnali stradali / os sinais de trânsito

speed limit
die Geschwindigkeitsbegrenzung
el límite de velocidad
la limitation de vitesse / il limite
di velocità / o limite de velocidade

hazard / die Gefahr
peligro / le danger
il pericolo / perigo

no right turn / das Rechtsabbiegen
verboten / no girar a la derecha
interdiction de tourner à droite
il divieto di svolta a destra
proibido virar à direita

no stopping
das Anhalten verboten
no parar / arrêt interdit
il divieto di fermata
proibido parar

TRUCKS / DER LASTWAGEN / LOS CAMOIONES / LES CAMIONS
IL CAMION / OS CAMIÕES

tractor-trailer / die Sattelzugmaschine
el tractor-remolque / la semi-remorque
l'autoarticolato / a carreta

box truck / der Kastenwagen
el camión de caja / le camion
fourgon / il camion a cassone
o camião de caixa

delivery van / der Lieferwagen
la camioneta de reparto
la camionette de livraison
il furgone per consegne
a carrinha de entregas

van / der Lieferwagen
la furgoneta / la camionette
il furgone / a carrinha

ice cream truck
der Eiscreme-LKW
el camión de helados
le camion de glace
il camioncino dei gelati
a carrinha de gelados

flatbed truck
der Pritschenwagen
el camión de plataforma
le camion plateau
il camion a pianale
o camião de plataforma

pick-up truck
der Kleintransporter
la camioneta pickup
le pick-up / il camioncino
a carrinha de caixa aberta

campervan / das Wohnmobil
el cámper / le camping-car
il camper / a caravana

car carrier / der Autotransporter
el transportador de autos / le porte-voitures
la bisarca / o reboque

tanker / der Tankwagen
el camión cisterna / la citerne
l'autocisterna / a cisterna

AUTOMOBILE / DAS AUTO / EL COCHE / LA VOITURE L'AUTOMOBILE / O AUTOMÓVEL

exterior / das Äußere / el exterior / l'extérieur / l'esterno / o exterior

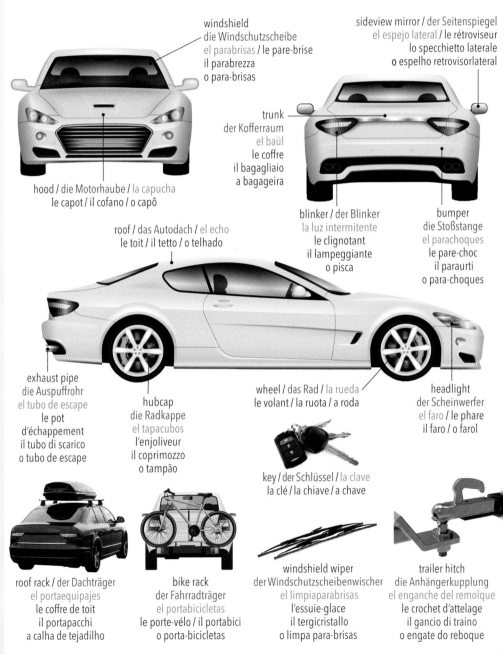

windshield
die Windschutzscheibe
el parabrisas / le pare-brise
il parabrezza
o para-brisas

sideview mirror / der Seitenspiegel
el espejo lateral / le rétroviseur
lo specchietto laterale
o espelho retrovisorlateral

trunk
der Kofferraum
el baúl
le coffre
il bagagliaio
a bagageira

hood / die Motorhaube / la capucha
le capot / il cofano / o capô

roof / das Autodach / el echo
le toit / il tetto / o telhado

blinker / der Blinker
la luz intermitente
le clignotant
il lampeggiante
o pisca

bumper
die Stoßstange
el parachoques
le pare-choc
il paraurti
o para-choques

exhaust pipe
die Auspuffrohr
el tubo de escape
le pot
d'échappement
il tubo di scarico
o tubo de escape

hubcap
die Radkappe
el tapacubos
l'enjoliveur
il coprimozzo
o tampão

wheel / das Rad / la rueda
le volant / la ruota / a roda

headlight
der Scheinwerfer
el faro / le phare
il faro / o farol

key / der Schlüssel / la clave
la clé / la chiave / a chave

roof rack / der Dachträger
el portaequipajes
le coffre de toit
il portapacchi
a calha de tejadilho

bike rack
der Fahrradträger
el portabicicletas
le porte-vélo / il portabici
o porta-bicicletas

windshield wiper
der Windschutzscheibenwischer
el limpiaparabrisas
l'essuie-glace
il tergicristallo
o limpa para-brisas

trailer hitch
die Anhängerkupplung
el enganche del remolque
le crochet d'attelage
il gancio di traino
o engate do reboque

types / die Typen / los tipos / les genres / i tipi / os tipos

four-door / viertürig / de cuatro
puertas / à quatre portes
a quattro porte / quatro portass

sedan / die Limousine
el sedán / la berline
la berlina / o sedan

coupe / das Coupé
el cupé / le coupé
la coupé / o coupé

hatchback / das Fließheck
el hatchback / la voiture
à hayon / l'utilitaria
o hatchback

station wagon / der Kombi
la camioneta / le break
la station wagon
a carrinha

convertible / der Cabrio
el convertible / le cabriolet
la decappottabile
o descapotável

minivan / der Minivan
la minivan / le minibus
il minivan / o monovolume

SUV / das SUV
la todoterreno / le SUV
il SUV / o SUV

four-wheel-drive
der Allradantrieb / la tracción
de cuatro ruedas / le 4x4
le quattro ruote motrici
a tração às quatro rodas

sports car / der Sportwagen
el coche deportivo
la voiture de sport
l'auto sportiva
o carro desportivo

limousine / die Limousine / la limusina
la limousine / la limousine / a limusina

vintage / der Oldtimer
el auto clásico / l'ancienne
il vintage / o vintage

electric car / das Elektroauto / el coche eléctrico
la voiture électrique / l'auto elettrica / o carro elétrico

| GB | UK PL8TE |

license plate / das Nummernschild
la matrícula / la plaque d'immatriculation
la targa / a matrícula

charging station
die Ladestation
la estación de carga
la borne de recharge
la stazione di ricarica
a estação de carga

interior / der Innenraum / el interior / l'intérieur / l'interno / o interior

sunshade / die Sonnenblende
el parasol / le pare-soleil
il parasole / o para-sol

light switch / der Lichtschalter
el interruptor de la luz / la commande
d'éclairage / l'interruttore delle luci
o interruptor de luz

rearview mirror / der Rückspiegel
el espejo retrovisor / le rétroviseur
lo specchietto retrovisore
o espelho retrovisor

steering wheel
das Lenkrad / el volante
le volant / il volante
o volante

doorlock / der Türschloss
la cerradura de la puerta
le verrou / il blocco porta
a fechadura da porta

air bag / das Airbag
la bolsa de aire / l'airbag
l'air bag / o airbag

armrest / die Armlehne
el apoyabrazos
l'accoudoir / il bracciolo
o apoio para o braço

right-hand drive / der Rechtslenker / el volante a la derecha
conduite à droite / la guida a destra / a condução à direita

dashboard
das Armaturenbrett
el tablero
le tableau de bord
il cruscotto / o tabliê

turn signal / der Blinker
la señal de giro
le clignotant / l'indicatore
di direzione / o sinal de
mudança de direção

ignition / die Zündung
el encendido
le contact / l'accensione
a ignição

horn / dieHupe
el cuerno / le klaxon
il clacson / a buzina

climate controls
die Klimasteuerung
los controles de clima
la commande
de la climatisation
i controlli del clima
o regulador
de temperatura

controls / die Steuerung / los controles
les commandes / i controlli / os comandos

tachometer / der Drehzahlmesser / el tacómetro
le compte-tours / il tachimetro / o conta-rotações

speedometer / der Tachometer / el velocímetro
le compteur de vitesse / il tachimetro / o velocímetro

temperature gauge
die Temperaturanzeige
el medidor de
temperatura
la jauge de
température
l'indicatore della
temperatura
o medidor de
temperatura

fuel gauge
die Kraftstoffanzeige
el indicador de
combustible
le niveau de
carburant
l'indicatore del
carburante
o medidor de
combustível

odometer / der Kilometerzähler / el odómetro
le compteur kilométrique / il contachilometri / o odómetro

satellite navigation / die Satellitennavigation / la navegación por satélite / le GPS / il navigatore / a navegação por satélite

gearshift / der Schalthebel
la palanca de cambios
le levier de vitesse / il cambio
a alavanca de mudanças

headrest / die Kopfstütze
el reposacabezas
l'appuie-tête
il poggiatesta
o apoio para a cabeça

handle / der Griff / la manija
a poignée / la maniglia
a maçaneta

window controls
der Fensterheber
los controles de la
ventana
les commandes
des vitres
i comandi dei finestrin
o interruptor de janela

front seat / der Vordersitz
el asiento delantero
le siège avant
il sedile anteriore
o banco da frente

console / die Konsole
la consola / la console
la console / o painel

back seat / der Rücksitz
el asiento trasero
le siège arrière
il sedile posteriore
o banco traseiro

brake pedal
das Bremspedal
el pedal del freno
la pédale de frein
il pedale del freno
o pedal do travão

stereo / die Stereoanlage
el estéreo
la stéréo / lo stereo
o sistema de som

touchscreen
das Touchscreen
la pantalla táctil
l'écran tactile / il touchscreen
o ecrã tátil

left-hand drive
der Linkslenker / le volante
a la izquierda / conduite à
gauche / la guida a sinistra
a condução à esquerda

accelerator
das Gaspedal
el acelerador
l'accélérateur
l'acceleratore / o acelerador

manual / manuell / el auto manual
une manuelle / manuale / manual

automatic / automatisch / el auto
automático / une automatique
automatico / automático

chassis / das Fahrgestell / el chasis
le chassis / il telaio / o chassis

car alarm / der Autoalarm / la alarma
del auto / l'alarme / l'antifurto
o alarme do carro

insurance / die Versicherung
el seguro / l'assurance
l'assicurazione / o seguro

registration / die Zulassung / el registro
la carte grise / la registrazione / o registo

tire pressure / der Reifendruck
la presión de los neumáticos
la pression / la pressione degli
pneumatici / a pressão dos pneus

fan belt / der Keilriemen / la correa
del ventilador / la courroie
de ventilateur / la cinghia / a correia
de ventoinha

timing / der Zahnriemen
la temporización / la synchronisation
la distribuzione / a cronometragem

parking brake
die Feststellbremse
el freno de estacionamiento
le frein à main
il freno di stazionamento
o travão de mão

alternator / die Lichtmaschine
el alternador / l'alternateur
l'alternatore / o alternador

turbocharger / der Turbolader
el turbocompresor / le turbo
il turbocompressore
o turbocompressor

mechanics / die Mechanik / los mecánicos / la mécanique / la meccanica / a mecânica

washer fluid reservoir / der Scheibenwaschflüssigkeitsvorrat
el depósito de líquido de parabrisas / le réservoir de lave-glace
il serbatoio del liquido lavavetri / o depósito do limpa-vidros

battery / die Batterie
la batería / la batterie
la batteria / a bateria

brake fluid reservoir / der
Bremsflüssigkeitsvorrat
el depósito de líquido de
frenos / le réservoir de
liquide de frein / la riserva
del liquido dei frenii
o depósito do líquido
dos travões

cylinder head
der Zylinderkopf
la culata / la culasse
la testa del cilindro
a cabeça do cilindro

dipstick / der Peilstab / la varilla / la jauge à huile / l'asta del livello / a vareta

muffler / der Schalldämpfer
el silenciador / le silencieux
la marmitta / o silenciador

brake / die Bremse / el freno
le frein / il freno / o travão

suspension / der Aufhängung
la suspensión / la suspension
la sospensione / a suspensão

air filter / derLuftfilter / el filtro de aire / le
filtre à air / il filtro dell'aria / o filtro de ar

driveshaft / die Antriebswelle / el eje de
transmisión / l'arbre de transmission
l'albero di trasmissione / o eixo de transmissão

sunroof / das Schiebedach
el techo corredizo / le toit ouvrant
il tettuccio apribile / o tejadilho

radiator / der Kühler
el radiador / le radiateur
il radiatore / o radiador

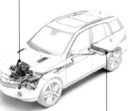

coolant reservoir
der Kühlmittelreserve
el depósito de
líquido refrigerante
le réservoir de liquide
de refroidissement
il serbatoio del liquido
di raffreddamento
o depósito de
líquido de refrigeração

tire
der Reifen
el neumático
le pneu
lo pneumatico
o pneu

transmission / das Getriebe
la transmisión / la transmission
la trasmissione / a transmissão

fan / der Lüfter
el ventilador / le ventilateur
il ventilatore / a ventoinha

gearbox / das Getriebe / la caja de cambios
la boite de vitesse / il cambio / a caixa de velocidades

repairs / die Reparaturen / las reparaciones / les réparations / le riparazioni / as reparações

mechanic
der Mechaniker
el mecanico
le mécanicien
il meccanico
o mecânico

garage / die Garage / el garaje
le garage / il garage / a garagem

flat tire / der platter Reifen / la llanta desinflada
le pneu crevé / lo pneumatico sgonfio / o pneu furado

spare tire / der Ersatzreifen
la llanta de repuesto
la roue de secours / la ruota
di scorta / o pneu sobressalente

tire iron / der Reifeneisen
la llanta de hierro / le démonte-
pneu / la chiave per pneumatici
a chave desmonta rodas

jack / der Wagenheber
la toma / le cric
il cric / o macaco

lug nut / die Radmutter / la tuerca / l'écrou de roue
il bullone della ruota / a porca de roda

tow truck / der Abschleppwagen
la grúa / la dépaneuse
il carro attrezzi / o reboque

car accident / der Autounfall
el accidente automovilístico / l'accident de
voiture / l'incidente d'auto / o acidente de carro

breakdown / die Panne / la avería
la panne / il guasto / o colapso

GAS STATION / TANKSTELLE / LA GASOLINERA
LA STATION SERVICE / LA STAZIONE DI SERVIZIO
A BOMBA DE GASOLINA

nozzle / die Zapfpistole
la boquilla / le pistolet
l'ugello / a pistola

price
der Preis
el precio
le prix
il prezzo
o preço

gas pump / die Zapfsäule / la bomba
de gas / la pompe / la pompa di
benzina / a bomba de gasolina

gas tank / der Benzintank
el tanque de gasolina
le réservoir / il serbatoio
della benzina
o depósito de combustível

gasoline / das Benzin / la gasolina
le gasoil / la benzina / a gasolina

leaded / verbleit / con plomo
au plomb / con piombo
com chumbo

unleaded / bleifrei / sin plomo
sans plomb / senza piombo / sem
chumbo

diesel / der Diesel / el diesel
le diesel / il diesel / o diesel

Fill it up, please. / Füll es bitte auf.
Llénelo, por favor. / À remplir, s'il
vous plait. / Il pieno, per favore.
Complete, por favor.

gas can
der Benzinkanister
la lata de gas
le jerricane
la tanica di gas
o jerricã

antifreeze
das Frostschutzmittel
el anticongelante
l'antigel
l'antigelo
o anticongelante

MOTORCYCLE / DAS MOTORRAD / LA MOTOCICLETA
LA MOTO / LA MOTO / A MOTA

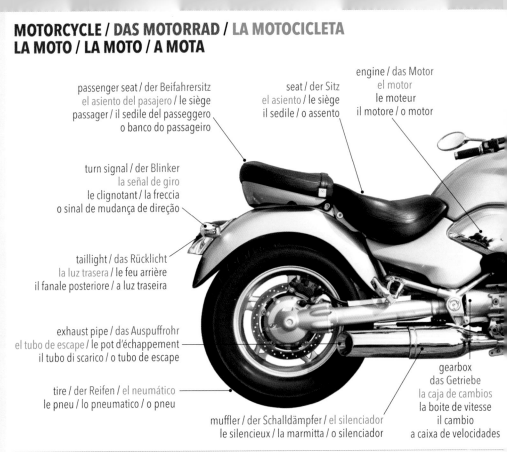

passenger seat / der Beifahrersitz
el asiento del pasajero / le siège
passager / il sedile del passeggero
o banco do passageiro

seat / der Sitz
el asiento / le siège
il sedile / o assento

engine / das Motor
el motor
le moteur
il motore / o motor

turn signal / der Blinker
la señal de giro
le clignotant / la freccia
o sinal de mudança de direção

taillight / das Rücklicht
la luz trasera / le feu arrière
il fanale posteriore / a luz traseira

exhaust pipe / das Auspuffrohr
el tubo de escape / le pot d'échappement
il tubo di scarico / o tubo de escape

gearbox
das Getriebe
la caja de cambios
la boite de vitesse
il cambio
a caixa de velocidades

tire / der Reifen / el neumático
le pneu / lo pneumatico / o pneu

muffler / der Schalldämpfer / el silenciador
le silencieux / la marmitta / o silenciador

types / die Typen / los tipos / les genres
i tipi / os tipos

windshield
die Windschutzscheibe
el parabrisas / la bulle
il parabrezza / o para-brisas

reflector / der Rückstrahler
el reflector / le réflecteur
il catarinfrangente / o refletor

visor / das Visier / la visera
la visière / la visiera / a viseira

leathers / die Ledersachen
los cueros / le cuir
il cuoio / o fato de cabedal

tourer / der Tourer
la motocicleta de turismo / la routière
da turismo / o carro de turismo

racing bike / das Rennrad
la motocicleta de carreras / la moto de course
la moto da corsa / a mota de corrida

fuel tank / der Kraftstofftank
el tanque de combustible
le réservoir
il serbatoio del carburante
o tanque de combustível

headlight / der Scheinwerfer
el faro / le phare / il faro / o farol

suspension / die Aufhängung / la suspensión
la suspension / la sospensione / a suspensão

mudguard / der Kotflügel
el guardabarros / le garde-boue
il parafango / o guarda-lamas

axle / die Achse / el eje
l'essieu / l'asse / o eixo

brake pedal
das Bremspedal
el pedal de freno
la pédale de frein
il pedale del freno
o pedal do travão

oil tank / der Öltank
el tanque de aceite
le réservoir d'huile / il serbatoio
dell'olio / o depósito de óleo

accessories / das Zubehör
los accesorios / les accessoires
gli accessori / os acessórios

helmet / der Helm / el casco
le casque / il casco / o elmo

knee pads / der Knieschoner
las rodilleras / les genouillères
le ginocchiere / as joelheiras

saddle bags / die Satteltaschen
las alforjas / les sacs de selle
le borse da sella / o alforge

controls / die Bedienelemente / los controles
les commandes / i controlli / os comandos

dirt bike / das Dirtbike
la motocicleta todoterreno
la motocicleta todoterreno / la moto
da cross / a mota de motocross

scooter / der Motorroller / el scooter
le scooter / lo scooter / a vespa

brake / die Bremse / el freno
le frein / il freno / o travão

clutch
die Kupplung
el embrague
l'embrayage
la frizione
a embraiagem

speedometer
der Tachometer / el velocímetro
le compteur de vitesse
il tachimetro / o velocímetro

throttle
die Drosselklappe
el acelerador
l'accélérateur
l'acceleratore
o acelerador

BICYCLE / DAS FAHRRAD / LA BICICLETA / LE VELO
LA BICICLETTA / A BICICLETA

grip / Griff
el puño / la poignée
l'impugnatura / o punho

brake lever / der Bremshebel / la palanca de freno
le levier de frein / la leva del freno / a alavanca do travão

gear lever / der Schalthebel / la palanca de cambios
le levier de vitesse / la leva del cambio / a alavanca de mudanças

frame / der Rahmen / el marco
le cadre / il telaio / o quadro

crossbar / Querlenker
/ el tubo superior / la
transverse / la barra
trasversale / a trave

brake / die Bremse / el freno
le frein / il freno / o travão

fork / die Gabel
la horquilla / la fourche
la forcella / a suspensão

hub / die Nabe / el buje
le moyeu / il mozzo / o eixo

pedal
das Pedal
el pedal
la pédale
il pedale
o pedal

tread / die Lauffläche
la banda de rodamiento
la bande de roulement
il battistrada
o padrão da
banda de rodagem

rim / die Felge
el rin / la jante
il cerchio / o aro

valve / das Ventil
la válvula / la valve
la valvola / a válvula

kickstand / der Ständer
el pie de apoyo / la béquille
il cavalletto / o suporte

types / die Typen / los tipos / les genres / i tipi / os tipos

racing bike / das Rennrad
la bicicleta de carreras
le vélo de course
la bici da corsa
a bicicleta de corrida

tandem bike
das Tandemfahrrad
la bicicleta tándem
le tandem / la bicicletta tandem
a bicicleta tandem

touring bike / das Reiserad
la bicicleta de turismo
le vélo de voyage
la bici da turismo
a bicicleta de passeio

mountain bike
das Mountainbike
la bicicleta de montaña
le VTT / la mountain bike
a bicicleta de montanha

saddle / der Sattel
el sillín / la selle
la sella / o selim

pedal (v) / Pedal / pedalear
pédaler / pedalare / pedalar

change gears (v) /
Gangschaltung
cambiar marcha / changer
de vitesse / cambiare marcia
meter a mudança

brake (v) / Bremse / frenar
freiner / frenare / travar

cycle (v) / Fahrrad / montar en
bicicleta / Faire du vélo
pedalare / andar de bicicleta

accessories / das Zubehör
los accesorios / les accessoires
gli accessori / os acessórios

helmet
der Helm
el casco
le casque
il casco
o elmo

child seat / der Kindersitz / el asiento para
niños / le siège enfant / il seggiolino per
bambini / o assento de criança

key / der Schlüssel
la llave / la clé
la chiave / a chave

lock / das Schloss / el candado
le verrou / la serratura / o cadeado

seat post
die Sattelstütze
la tija del sillín
le support de selle
il reggisella
o selim

inner tube / der Schlauch
el tubo interior
la chambre à air
la camera d'aria
a câmara de ar

tire
der Reifen
el neumático
le pneu
lo pneumatico
o pneu

gears
die Schaltung
los engranajes
les vitesses
gli ingranaggi
as mudanças

pump / die Pumpe / la bomba
la pompe / la pompa / a bomba

chain / die Kette
la cadena / la chaine
la catena / a corrente

spokes / die Speichen / los radios
les rayons / i raggi / os raios

repair kit / das Reparaturset / el kit
de reparación / le kit de réparation
il kit di riparazione / o kit de reparação

bell / die Klingel / el timbre
la sonnette / il campanello / o sino

handlebars / der Lenker / el manillar
le guidon / il manubrio / o guidão

basket
der Korb
la cesta
le panier
il cestino
a cesta

road bike / das Straßenrad
la bicicleta de carretera
le vélo de ville
la bici da strada
a bicicleta de estrada

tricycle / das Dreirad / el triciclo
le tricycle / il triciclo / o triciclo

training wheels / die Stützräder
la rueda de entrenamiento
le roulette / la ruota da allenamento
as rodinhas de apoio

PUBLIC TRANSPORT / ÖFFENTLICHE VERKEHRSMITTEL
EL TRANSPORTE PÚBLICO / LES TRANSPORTS PUBLICS
I TRASPORTI PUBBLICI / OS TRANSPORTES PÚBLICOS

BUS / DER BUS / EL BUS / LE BUS / IL BUS / O AUTOCARRO

automatic door
die automatische Tür
la puerta automatica
la porte automatique
il porta automatica
a porta automática

driver's seat
der Fahrersitz
el asiento del conductor
le siège conducteur
il sedile del conducente
o lugar do condutor

luggage hold
der Gepäckraum
la bodega de equipaje
la soute à bagages
il deposito bagagli
o porão

long-distance bus / der Langstreckenbus / el bus de larga distancia
le car longue distance / l'autobus a lunga percorrenza / o autocarro de longa distância

wheelchair access / der Zugang für Rollstuhlfahrer / el acceso
para sillas de ruedas / l'accès handicapé / l'accesso per sedia
rotelle / a rampa de acesso para cadeira de rodas

Do you stop at …? / Halten Sie in …? / ¿Este autobús
para en…? / Vous arrêtez-vous à …? / Si ferma a …? / Para em…?

Which bus goes to …? / Welcher Bus fährt nach …?
¿Cuál autobús va a…? / Quel bus se rend à …?
Quale autobus va a …? / Que autocarro vai para…?

stop button / die
Haltestellentaste / el botón
de parada / le bouton
d'arrêt / il pulsante di
fermata / o botão de parar

bus ticket
die Busfahrkarte
el boleto de bus
le ticket de bus
il biglietto
dell'autobus
o bilhete de autocarro

types / die Typen / los tipos / les genres / i tipi / os tipos

double-decker / der Doppeldeckerr
el bus de dos pisos / le bus
à deux étages / a due piani
o autocarro de dois andares

sight-seeing bus / der Sightseeing-Bus
el bus de recorridos históricos / le bus
pour touristes / l'autobus panoramico
o autocarro de visitas guiadas

tour bus / der Reisebus
el bus turístico / le bus de tourisme
l'autobus da turismo
o autocarro turístico

shuttle bus / Shuttle-Bus
el bus transbordador / la navette
il bus navetta / o autocarro

school bus / der Schulbus
el bus escolar / le bus d'école
lo scuolabus / o autocarro escolar

minibus / der Kleinbus
el microbús / le minibus
il minibus / o miniautocarro

bus stop / die Bushaltestelle
la parada / l'arrêt de bus
la fermata dell'autobus
o ponto de ônibus

bus shelter
das Buswartehäuschen
la parada del autobús / l'abribus
la pensilina dell'autobus
o abrigo de autocarro

bus station / der Busbahnhof / la estacion de bus / l'arrêt de bus / la stazione degli autobus / a estação de autocarros

SUBWAY / DIE U-BAHN / EL METRO / LE MÉTRO / LA METROPOLITANA / O METRÔ

subway car / U-Bahn-Wagen / el vagón del metro
la rame de métro / il vagone della metropolitana / a carruagem

route map
der Liniennetzplan
el mapa de ruta
l'itinéraire
la mappa del percorso
o mapa

handrail
der Handlauf
la barandilla
la rampe
il corrimano
o corrimão

sliding doors
die Schiebetüren
las puertas corredizas
les portes coulissantes
le porte scorrevoli
as portas deslizantes

turnstile / das Drehkreuz
el torniquete / le tourniquet
il tornello / o torniquete

fare cards / die Fahrkarten / las tarjetas de tarifa
la carte de métro / la tessera / o cartão de viagens

subway station / die U-Bahn-Station / la estación de metro
la station de métro / la stazione della metropolitana
a estação de metro

platform / der Bahnsteig
la plataforma / le quai
la piattaforma
a plataforma

subway stop / die U-Bahn-Haltestelle / la parada
del metro / l'arrêt de métro / la fermata della metropolitana / a paragem

emergency lever / der Nothebel
la palanca de emergencia
la manette d'arrêt d'urgence
la leva di emergenza
a alavanca de emergência

OTHER TRANSPORT / ANDERE VERKEHRSMITTEL / OTROS TRANSPORTES
LES AUTRES TRANSPORTS / GLI ALTRI TRASPORTI / OUTROS TRANSPORTES

tram / die Straßenbahn
el tranvía / le tram
il tram / o elétrico

monorail
die Einschienenbahn
el monorriel / le monorail
la monorotaia / o monocarril

cable car / die Seilbahn
el teleférico / le tramway
la funivia / o teleférico

funicular
die Standseilbahn
el funicular / le funiculaire
la funicolare / o funicular

TRAIN / DER ZUG / EL TREN / LE TRAIN / IL TRENO / O COMBOIO

engineer's cab / der Führerstand
la cabina del maquinista
le poste de conduite
la cabina del macchinista
a cabine do maquinista

engine / die Lokomotive
el motor / le moteur
il motore / o motor

railcar / der Triebwagen
el vagón / la voiture
l'automotrice / a carruagem

commuter train / der Pendlerzug / el tren de cercanías / le train de banlieue / il treno pendolare / o comboio pendular

tracks / die Gleise / las vías del tren
les voies / i binari / os carris

railroad crossing
der Bahnübergang
el cruce del
ferrocarril
le passage à niveau
l'incrocio ferroviario
a passagem de nível

types / die Typen / los tipos / les genres / i tipi / os tipos

steam train / der Dampfzug
el tren de vapor / le train à vapeur
la locomotiva a vapore / o trem a vapor

electric train / die Elektrischer Zug
el tren eléctrico / le train électrique
il treno elettrico / o comboio elétrico

high-speed train
der Hochgeschwindigkeitszug
el tren de alta velocidad
le train à grande vitesse
il treno ad alta velocità
o comboio de alta velocidade

freight train / der Güterzug / el tren
de carga / le train de fret / il treno
merci / o comboio de mercadorias

diesel train / der Dieselzug
el tren de diésel / le train diesel
il treno a diesel / o comboio a diesel

railroad / die Eisenbahn
el ferrocarril / les rails / la ferrovia
a ferrovia

express train / der Schnellzug
el tren expreso / le train express
il treno espresso
o comboio rápido

train station / der Bahnhof / la estación de tren / la gare
la stazione ferroviaria / a estação de comboio

track number / die Gleisnummer
el número de carril
le numéro de voie
il numero del binario
o número

ticket machine
der Fahrkartenautomat
la máquina de boletos
le distributeur
automatique de tickets
la macchina per i biglietti
a bilheteira automática

platform / der Bahnsteig / la plataforma / le quai / la piattaforma / a plataforma

schedule / der Fahrplan / el horario
les horaires / l'orario / o horário

ticket office
der Fahrkartenschalterr
la taquilla
l'espace de vente
la biglietteria
a bilheteira

commuter
der Nahverkehr
el viajero
le banlieusard
il pendolare
o viajante

sleeping compartment / der
Schlafwagenabteil / el compartimento
para dormir / le wagon couchette
lo scompartimento notte
o compartimento para dormir

concourse / die Schalterhalle / la terminal / le hall / l'atrio / o saguão

compartment / der Abteil
el compartimento / le compartiment
lo scompartimento
o compartimento

conductor / der Schaffner
el conductor / le chauffeur
il conduttore / o maquinista

ticket inspector
der Fahrkartenkontrolleur
el inspector de boletos / le contrôleur
il controllore / o revisor

dining car / der Speisewagen
el vagón comedor / le wagon bar
il vagone ristorante
o vagão-restaurante

delay / die Verspätung / el retraso
le retard / il ritardo / o atraso

fare / der Fahrpreis / la tarifa
le tarif / il tariffa / a tarifa

transfer (v) / umsteigen
transferirse / changer de train
trasferire / transferir

signal / das Signal / la señal
le signal / il segnale / o sinal

PA system / die Lautsprecheranlage
el sistema de megafonía
le système de sonorisation
il sistema annunci pubblici
o sistema de AP

AIRCRAFT / DAS FLUGZEUG / EL AVIÓN / L'AVION / L'AEREO / O AVIÃO

airliner / das Verkehrsflugzeug / el avión de pasajeros / l'avion de ligne / l'aereo di linea / o avião comercial

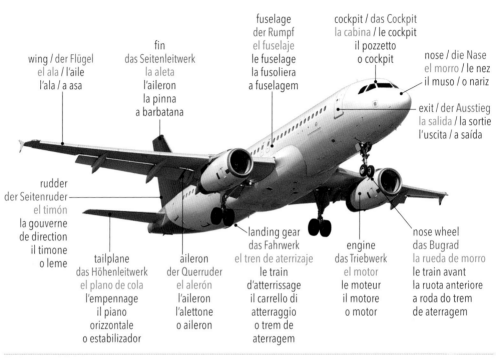

fuselage
der Rumpf
el fuselaje
le fuselage
la fusoliera
a fuselagem

cockpit / das Cockpit
la cabina / le cockpit
il pozzetto
o cockpit

nose / die Nase
el morro / le nez
il muso / o nariz

wing / der Flügel
el ala / l'aile
l'ala / a asa

fin
das Seitenleitwerk
la aleta
l'aileron
la pinna
a barbatana

exit / der Ausstieg
la salida / la sortie
l'uscita / a saída

rudder
der Seitenruder
el timón
la gouverne
de direction
il timone
o leme

tailplane
das Höhenleitwerk
el plano de cola
l'empennage
il piano
orizzontale
o estabilizador

aileron
der Querruder
el alerón
l'aileron
l'alettone
o aileron

landing gear
das Fahrwerk
el tren de aterrizaje
le train
d'atterrissage
il carrello di
atterraggio
o trem de
aterragem

engine
das Triebwerk
el motor
le moteur
il motore
o motor

nose wheel
das Bugrad
la rueda de morro
le train avant
la ruota anteriore
a roda do trem
de aterragem

types / die Typen / los tipos / les genres / i tipi / os tipos

helicopter / der Hubschrauber
el helicóptero / l'hélicoptère
l'elicottero / o helicóptero

prop plane / das Propellerflugzeug
el avión de hélice / l'avion à hélices
l'aereo a elica / a avioneta

private jet / das Privatjet
el jet privado / le jet privé
il jet privato / o jato privado

ultralight / das Ultraleichtflugzeug
el avión ultraligero / l'ultraléger
l'ultraleggero / o ultraleve

glider / das Segelflugzeug
el avión planeador / le planeur
l'aliante / o planador

biplane / der Doppeldecker
el avión biplano / le biplan
il biplano / o biplano

cabin / die Kabine / la cabina / la cabine / la cabina / a cabine

overhead bin / die Gepäckablage
el compartimento superior
le coffre à bagages / lo scomparto
sopraelevato / o compartimento superior

flight attendant / der Flugbegleiter
la azafata / le membre d'équipage
la assistente di volo
a hospedeira de bordo

reading light / das Leselicht
la luz de lectura / la liseuse
la luce per leggere / a luz de leitura

emergency exit
der Notausgang
la salida de emergencia
la sortie de secours
l'uscita di emergenza
a saída de emergência

call button / Ruftaste
el botón de llamada
le bouton d'appel
il pulsante di chiamata
o botão de chamar

air vent
die Belüftungsdüse
la salida de aire
l'aération
la bocchetta dell'aria
a saída de ar

seat / der Sitz
el asiento / le siège
il sedile / o lugar

seat back
die Rückenlehne
el respaldo del
asiento
le dossier
lo schienale
o encosto

aisle / der Gang
el pasillo / l'allée
il corridoio
o corredor

service trolley / der Servicewagen
el carro de servicio / le chariot de boissons
il carrello di servizio / o carrinho de serviço

row / die Reihe / la fila
la rangée / la fila / a fila

seatbelt
der Sicherheitsgurt
el cinturón
de seguridad
la ceinture
la cintura
di sicurezza
o cinto de segurança

window
das Fenster
la ventana
la fenêtre
la finestra
a janela

tray-table
der Tablett-Tisch
la bandeja-mesa
la tablette
il vassoio-tavolo
a mesa de bandeja

business class / der Business Class
la clase ejecutiva / la classe business
la prima classe / a classe executiva

fighter jet / das Kampfjet / el avión de
combate / l'avion de chasse / il jet da
combattimento / o caça

bomber / der Bomber / el avión
bombardero / le bombardier
il bombardiere / o bombardeiro

pilot / der Pilot / el piloto
le pilote / il pilota / o piloto

copilot / der Kopilot / el copiloto
le copilote / il copilota / o copiloto

fly (v) / fliegen / volar
piloter un avion / volare / voar

take-off (v) / abheben / despegar
décoller / decollare / descolar

land (v) / landen / aterrizar / atterrir
atterrare / aterrar

altitude / die Höhe / la altitud
l'altitude / l'altitudine / a altitude

economy / die Wirtschaft
la clase económica / la classe
économie / la seconda classe
a classe económica

board (v) / einsteigen / el tablero
embarquer / imbarcare / embarcar

drone / die Drohne / el dron
le drone / il drone / o drone

AIRPORT / DER FLUGHAFEN / EL AEROPUERTO / L'AÉROPORT
L'AEROPORTO / O AEROPORTO

apron / das Vorfeld
la plataforma
l'emplacement
de parking
il piazzale
o avental

jetway / die Fluggastbrücke
la pasarela / la passerelle
la passerella
a ponte telescópica

service vehicle
das Servicefahrzeug
el vehículo de servicio
le véhicule de service
il veicolo di servizio
o veículo de serviço

runway
die Landebahn
la pista / la piste
la pista / a pista

terminal
das Terminal
la terminal
le terminal
il terminal
o terminal

baggage trailer
der Gepäckträger
el vagón de equipaje
le chariot à bagages
il rimorchio
dei bagagli
o porta-malas

control tower / der Kontrollturm / la torre de control
la tour de contrôle / la torre di controllo / a torre de controlo

terminal / das Terminal / la terminal / le terminal / il terminal / o terminal

luggage
das Gepäckel
el equipaje
le bagage
il bagaglio
a bagagem

carry-on baggage
das Handgepäck
el equipaje de mano
le bagage à main
il bagaglio a mano
a bagagem de mão

arrivals
die Ankünfte
las llegadas
les arrivées
gli arrivi
as chegadas

departures
die Abflüge
las salidas
les départs
le partenze
as partidas

destination
das Zielort
el destino
la destination
la destinazione
o destino

flight number
die Flugnummer
el numero de vuelo
le numéro de vol
il numero del volo
o número do vôo

check-in desk / der Check-in-Schalter
el mostrador de facturación
le comptoir d'enregistrement
il banco del check-in / o balcão de check-in

information board / die Informationstafel
el tablero de información / le panneau d'affichage
la bacheca informazioni / o painel de informações

boarding pass / die Einsteigekarte
el pasaje de embarque
la carte d'embarquement
la carta d'imbarco
o cartão de embarque

gate number
die Flugsteignummer
el número de puerta
le numéro de porte
il numero del gate
o número da porta de embarque

mobile boarding pass
die mobile Bordkarte
el pasaje digital
de embarque
la carte d'embarquement
sur smartphone
la carta d'imbarco mobile
o cartão de
embarque móvel

passport control
die Passkontrolle
el control de pasaportes
le contrôle des passeports
il controllo del passaporto
o controlo de passaporte

visa / das Visum
la visa / le visa
il visto / o visto

passport
der Reisepass
el pasaporte
le passeport
il passaporto
o passaporte

gate / der Flugsteig / la puerta
la porte / il gate / a porta de embarque

baggage carousel / das Gepäckband
la cinta de equipaje / le tapis roulant
il nastro bagagli
a passadeira de bagagens

baggage claim / die Gepäckausgabe
el reclamo de equipaje
la récupération des bagages
il reclamo bagagli
a coleta de bagagem

departure lounge / die Abflughalle
la sala de embarque / la salle
d'embarquement / la sala partenze
a área de embarque

customs / der Zoll
las costumbres / les douanes
la dogana / a alfândega

duty-free shop / der Duty-Free-Shop
la tienda libre de impuestos
le magasin duty-free / il negozio
duty-free / a duty-free shop

car rental / die Autovermietung
el alquiler de autos / la location
de voitures / il noleggio auto
o aluguer de carros

taxi stand / der Taxistand
la parada de taxis / la station de taxi
la postazione taxi / a praça de táxis

ground transportation / der
Bodentransport / el transporte terrestre
le transport terrestre / il trasporto
a terra / o transporte terrestre

international flight
der internationale Flug
el vuelo internacional
le vol international / il volo
internazionale / o voo internacional

connection / die Verbindung
la conexión / la correspondance
il collegamento / a ligação

immigration / die Einwanderung
la inmigración / l'immigration
l'immigrazione / a imigração

security / die Sicherheit
la seguridad / la sécurité
la sicurezza / a segurança

vacation / der Urlaub
las vacaciones / les vacances
la vacanza / as férias

book a flight (v) / einen Flug
buchen / *reservar un vuelo*
réserver un vol / prenotare un volo
reservar um voo

SHIP / DAS SCHIFF / EL BARCO / LE BATEAU / LA NAVE / O NAVIO

cruise ship / das Kreuzfahrtschiff / el crucero / le bateau de croisière
la nave da crociera / o cruzeiro

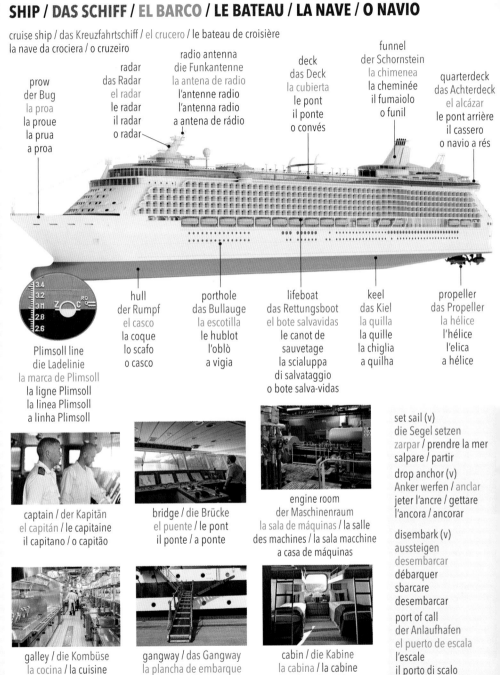

prow
der Bug
la proa
la proue
la prua
a proa

radar
das Radar
el radar
le radar
il radar
o radar

radio antenna
die Funkantenne
la antena de radio
l'antenne radio
l'antenna radio
a antena de rádio

deck
das Deck
la cubierta
le pont
il ponte
o convés

funnel
der Schornstein
la chimenea
la cheminée
il fumaiolo
o funil

quarterdeck
das Achterdeck
el alcázar
le pont arrière
il cassero
o navio a rés

Plimsoll line
die Ladelinie
la marca de Plimsoll
la ligne Plimsoll
la linea Plimsoll
a linha Plimsoll

hull
der Rumpf
el casco
la coque
lo scafo
o casco

porthole
das Bullauge
la escotilla
le hublot
l'oblò
a vigia

lifeboat
das Rettungsboot
el bote salvavidas
le canot de
sauvetage
la scialuppa
di salvataggio
o bote salva-vidas

keel
das Kiel
la quilla
la quille
la chiglia
a quilha

propeller
das Propeller
la hélice
l'hélice
l'elica
a hélice

captain / der Kapitän
el capitán / le capitaine
il capitano / o capitão

bridge / die Brücke
el puente / le pont
il ponte / a ponte

engine room
der Maschinenraum
la sala de máquinas / la salle
des machines / la sala macchine
a casa de máquinas

galley / die Kombüse
la cocina / la cuisine
la cucina / a galera

gangway / das Gangway
la plancha de embarque
la passerelle / la passerella
o corredor

cabin / die Kabine
la cabina / la cabine
la cabina / a cabine

set sail (v)
die Segel setzen
zarpar / prendre la mer
salpare / partir

drop anchor (v)
Anker werfen / anclar
jeter l'ancre / gettare
l'ancora / ancorar

disembark (v)
aussteigen
desembarcar
débarquer
sbarcare
desembarcar

port of call
der Anlaufhafen
el puerto de escala
l'escale
il porto di scalo
o porto de escala

types / die Typen / los tipos / les genres / i tipi / os tipos

tall ship / das Großsegler
el buque alto
le grand voilier
la nave alta / o navio alto

hovercraft
das Luftkissenfahrzeug
el aerodeslizador / l'aéroglisseur
l'hovercraft / o aerodeslizador

hydrofoil
das Tragflügelboot
el hidroala / l'hydroptère
l'aliscafo / o hidrofólio

tugboat / der Schlepper
el remolcador
le remorqueur
il rimorchiatore
o rebocador

aircraft carrier
der Flugzeugträger
el portaaviones
le porte-avions
la portaerei / o porta-aviões

freighter / der Frachter
el carguero / le cargo
la nave da carico
o cargueiro

oil tanker / das Öltankschiff
el petrolero / le pétrolier
la petroliera
o navio petroleiro

fishing boat
das Fischereiboot / el barco
de pesca / le bateau de
pêche / la barca da pesca
o barco de pesca

submarine / das U-Boot / el submarino
le sous-marin / il sottomarino / o submarino

port / der Hafen / el puerto / le port / il porto / o porto

gantry crane / der Brückenkran / la grúa pórtico
la grue à portique / la gru a cavalletto / o guindaste de pórtico

shipyard / die Werft / el astillero
le chantier naval / il cantiere navale / o estaleiro

cargo / die Fracht
el buque de carga
la cargaison
il carico
a carga

container ship
das Containerschiff
el barco
de contenedores
le porte-conteneurs
la nave container
o navio
porta-contentores

coast guard / die Küstenwache
la guardia costera / le garde-
côtes / la guardia costiera
a guarda costeira

harbor master / der Hafenmeister
el capitán del puerto
le capitaine de port
la capitaneria di porto
o capitão de porto

dry dock / der Trockendock
el dique seco / la cale sèche
il bacino di carenaggio
a doca seca

lighthouse / der Leuchtturm
el faro / le phare
il faro / o farol

ferry / die Fähre / el ferry
le ferry / il traghetto / o ferry

passenger
der Passagierschiff
el pasajero / le passager
il passeggero
o passageiro

ferry terminal / das Fährterminal / la terminal del ferry
la gare maritime / il terminal dei traghetti / o cais

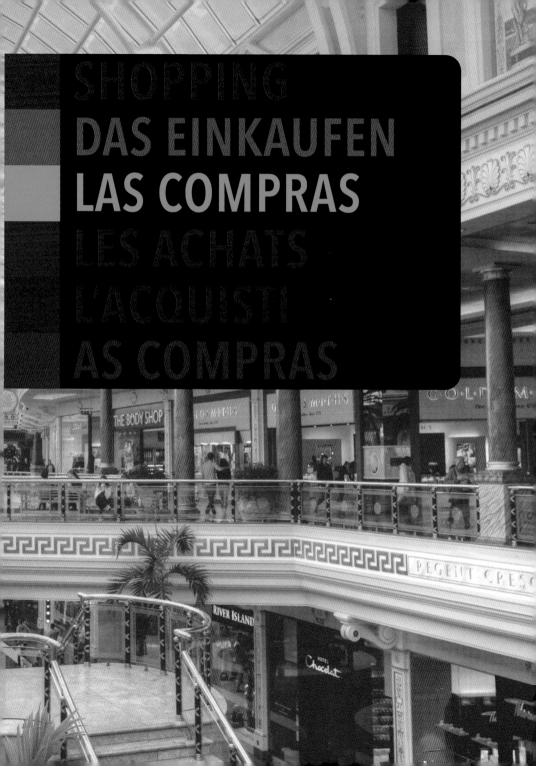

SHOPPING
DAS EINKAUFEN
LAS COMPRAS
LES ACHATS
L'ACQUISTI
AS COMPRAS

SUPERMARKET / DER SUPERMARKT / EL SUPERMERCADO
LE SUPERMARCHÉ / IL SUPERMERCATO / O SUPERMERCADO

checkout / die Kasse / la caja / le paiement / la caisses / a caixa

shopping basket
Einkaufskorb / la cesta de compras
le panier / il carrello della spesa
o cesto de compras

receipt / der Kassenbon
el recibo / le reçu
il scontrino / la ricevuta

cash register
die Registrierkasse
a caja registradora
la caisse
il registratore
di cassa
a caixa registradora

conveyer belt
das Fließband
la correa
transportadora
le tapis roulant
il nastro trasportatore
a correia
transportadora

scanner
der Scanner
el escáner
le scanner
lo scanner
o leitor

customers
die Kunden
los clientes
les clients
i clienti
os clientes

groceries
der Lebensmittel
los comestibles
l'épiceries / la drogheria
os mantimentos

bar code
der Strichcode
el código
de barras
le code barre
il codice a barre
o código
de barras

887549 059636

shopping bag
die Einkaufstasche
la bolsa
le sac
la sportina
a sacola

portable
shopping cart
der tragbarer
Einkaufswagen
el carrito
de compra portátil
le chariot
de courses
il carrello della
spesa portatile
o carrinho de
compras portátil

signs / die Schilder / las señales
les pancartes / i cartelli / os sinais

paying / Bezahlen / el pago / le payant
il pagamento / o pagamento

CLOSED
GESCHLOSSEN
CERRADO
FERMÉ
CHIUSO
FECHADO

OPEN
GEÖFFNET
ABIERTO
OUVERT
APERTO
ABERTO

pay with credit or debit card
Bezahlen mit Kredit- oder Debitkarte
el pago con tarjeta de crédito o débito
payer par carte bancaire
il pagamento con carta di credito o di debito
pagar com cartão de crédito ou débito

pay cash / bar bezahlen
el pago en efectivo
payer en liquide
il pagamento in contant
pagar em dinheiro

contactless payment
das Kontaktlos bezahlen
el pago sin contacto
le paiement sans contact
il pagamento contactless
o pagamento contactless

freezer case / die Tiefkühltruhe / la caja del congelador
le congélateur / la cella frigo / a caixa frigorífica

shelf / die Regal
el estante
l'étagère / il scaffale
a prateleira

shopping cart
der Einkaufswagene
el carrito de compras
lle chariot de courses
il carrello della spesa
o carrinho de compras

shopping list
die Einkaufsliste
la lista de compras
la liste de courses
la lista della spesa
a lista de compras

aisle / der Gang
el pasillo / l'allée
la corsia / o corredor

Bread
Milk
Eggs
Fruit
Rice
Pasta
Butter

SHOPPING CENTER / DAS EINKAUFSZENTRUM / EL CENTRO COMERCIAL
LE CENTRE COMMERCIAL / IL CENTRO COMMERCIALE / O CENTRO COMERCIAL

sign / das Schild
la señal / la pancarte
l'insegna / o sinal

atrium / das Atrium / el atrio / l'atrium / l'atrio / o átrio

department store
das Kaufhaus
los grandes almacenes
le grand magasin
il grande magazzino
o hipermercado

stand-alone shop
das Alleinstehendes
Geschäft
las tiendas
independientes
la boutique
indépendante
il negozio indipendente
a loja independente

escalator / die Rolltreppe
la escalera mecánica / l'escalier mécanique
la scala mobile / as escadas rolantes

food court / der Food Court
el patio de comidas
l'espace restauration
l'area ristoro
a praça de alimentação

directory
das Wegweiser
el directorio
l'annuaire
il direttivo
o diretório

other shopping centers / die andere Einkaufszentren / otros centros comerciales / les autres centres commerciaux / gli altri centri commerciali / os outros centros comerciais

strip mall / das Einkaufszentrum
el centro comercial / le complexe
commercial / la striscia di negozi
o pequeno centro comercial

open-air market / der Freiluftmarkt
el mercado al aire libre / le marché
en plein air / il mercato all'aperto
o mercado ao ar livre

shopping district / das Einkaufsviertel
el distrito comercial / le quartier
commerçant / il quartiere dello
shopping / o bairro comercial

fitting room / die Umkleidekabine
el probador / la cabine d'essayage
il camerino / o provador

restroom / die Toilette
el baño publico / les toilettes
la toilette / a casa de banho

bargain / das Schnäppchen
la ganga / la réduction / l'affare
a pechincha

on sale / im Verkauf / a la venta
en soldes / in vendita / à venda

customer service / die
Kundenbetreuung
el servicio al cliente / le service
client / il servizio clienti / o apoio
ao cliente

returns / die Rückgaben
las devoluciones / les retours
il reso / as devoluções

salesperson / der Verkäufer
el vendedor / le vendeur
il commesso / o vendedor

How much is this? / Wie viel kostet
das? / ¿Cuánto cuesta esto?
Combien cela coute-t-il ? / Quanto
costa questo? / Quanto custa?

May I exchange this? / Kann ich
es umtauschen? / ¿Puedo cambiar
esto? / Pourrais-je échanger ceci ?
Posso cambiarlo? / Posso trocar isto?

Where can I find…? / Wo finde ich…?
¿Dónde puedo encontrar…?
Où puis-je trouver…? / Dove posso
trovare…? / Onde posso encontrar…?

department store / das Kaufhaus / los grandes almacenes
le grand magasin / il grande magazzino / o hipermercado

menswear / die Herrenmode
la ropa de hombre
les vêtements pour hommes
l'abbigliamento da uomo
a roupa de homem

womenswear
die Damenmode
la ropa de mujer
les vêtements pour femmes
l'abbigliamento da donna
a roupa de mulher

children's wear
die Kindermode
la ropa de niños
les vêtements des enfants
l'abbigliamento per bambini
a secção de criança

sportswear / die
Sportbekleidung / la ropa
deportiva / les vêtements
de sport / l'abbigliamento
sportivo / os artigos
de desporto

price tag / das Preisschild
la etiqueta de precio
l'étiquette de prix
il cartellino del prezzo
a etiqueta de preço

lingerie / die Unterwäsche
/ la ropa interior
la lingerie / la lingeria
a lingerie

perfumes / die Parfüms
los perfumes / les parfums
i profumi / os perfumes

cosmetics / die Kosmetik
los cosméticos
les produits cosmétiques
i cosmetici / os cosméticos

toys / die Spielwaren
los juguetes / les jouets
i giocattoli / os brinquedos

appliances / die Geräte
los electrodomésticos
les appareils électro-
ménagers
gli elettrodomestici
os eletrodomésticos

home furnishings / die
Einrichtungsgegenstände
los muebles para el hogar
l'ameublement
l'arredamento per la casa
o mobiliário

housewares
die Haushaltswaren
los artículos para el hogar
les articles de cuisine
gli articoli per la casa
os artigos para a casa

shoes / die Schuhe
los zapatos / les chaussures
le scarpe / o calçado

linens / die Wäsche
la ropa de cama / le linge
de maison / la biancheria
a roupa de cama e de mesa

electronics / die Elektronik
los electrónicos
les appareil électroniques
l'elettronica
os aparelhos eletrónicos

lighting / die Beleuchtung
la iluminación / l'éclairage
l'illuminazione
a iluminação

accessories / das Zubehör
los accesorios
les accessoires
gli accessori / os acessórios

FLORIST / DER FLORIST / LA FLORISTERÍA / LE FLEURISTE
IL FIORISTA / A FLORISTA

floral cooler
der blumen Kühler
los refrigeradores florales
le réfrigérateur floral
la cella frigo
o armário frigorífico
para flores

florist
der Florist
la floristería
le fleuriste
il fiorista
a florista

wrapping / die Verpackung
el envoltorio / l'emballage
la confezione / o embrulho

bouquet / der Blumenstrauß
el ramo / le bouquet
il bouquet / o buquê

baby's breath / das Schleierkraut
la gipsófila / la gypsophile
la gipsofila / a gipsófila

flower market / der Blumenmarkt
el mercado de flores / le marché aux fleurs
il mercato dei fiori / o mercado de flores

flower stall / der Blumenstand
el puesto de flores / l'étal de fleurs
la bancarella di fiori / a banca de flores

equipment / die Ausrüstung / las herramientas / l'équipement / l'attrezzatura / o equipamento

stem cutter
der Stielschneider
el cortador de tallos
le sécateur
il tagliasiepi
o cortador de caules

floral tape
das Blumenband
la cinta floral
le ruban à fleurs
il nastro floreale
a fita adesiva
para flores

twine / der Bindfaden
el cordel / la ficelle
lo spago / o fio

wire cutter / der
Drahtschneider
el cortador
de alambre
la pince coupante
la taglierina
per filo metallico
o cortador
de arame

hot glue gun
die Heißklebepistole
la pistola de pegamento caliente
le pistolet à colle
la pistola per la colla a caldo
a pistola de cola quente

wire
der Draht
el alambre
le fil
il filo
o arame

floral foam
das Blumenschaum
la espuma floral
la mousse florale
la schiuma floreale
a esponja

floral arrangements / die Blumenarrangements / los arreglos florales
les arrangements floraux / le composizioni floreali / os arranjos de flores

tulip / die Tulpe
el tulipán / la tulipe
il tulipano / a tulipa

lily / die Lilie / el lirio / le lys / il giglio / o lírio

hydrangea
die Hortensie
la hortensia
l'hortensia
l'ortensia
a hortênsia

bunch / der Strauß
el racimo / le bouquet
il mazzo / o ramo

basket / der Korb / la cesta
le panier / il cestino / o cesto

vase / die Vase / el jarrón
le vase / il vaso / o vaso

dried flower / die Trockenblume
/ la flor seca / la fleur séchée
il fiore secco / a flor seca

garland / die Girlande
la guirnalda / le collier de fleurs
la ghirlanda / a grinalda

wreath / der Kranz / la corona
la couronne de fleurs / la ghirlanda
a coroa de flores

rose / die Rose
la rosa / la rose
la rosa / a rosa

corsage / die Korsage
el ramillete / le petit bouquet
il corsage / o ramalhete

head wreath / der Kopfkranz
la corona de flores
la couronne de fleurs
la coroncina / a coroa de flores

boutonnière / die Boutonnière
el botonier / la boutonnière
la boutonnière / a botoeira

iris
die Schwertlilie
l'iris
l'iris / a íris

satin ribbon
das Satinband
la cinta de raso
le ruban de satin
il nastro di raso
a fita de cetim

funeral flowers / die Beerdigungsblumen / las flores para funeral
les fleurs funéraires / i fiori funebri / as flores para funeral

bridal bouquet / der Brautstrauß
el ramo de novia
le bouquet de la mariée
il bouquet da sposa / o buquê de noiva

coffin / der Sarg
el ataúd / le cercueil
la bara / o caixão

NEWSSTAND / DER ZEITUNGSSTÄNDER / EL QUIOSCO
LE KIOSQUE A JOURNAUX / L'EDICOLA / O QUIOSQUE

magazine
die Zeitschrift
la revista
le magazine
la rivista
a revista

comic book
das Comic-Heft
el cómic
la bande dessinée
il fumetto
a banda desenhada

kiosk
der Kiosk
el quiosco
le kiosque
il chiosco
o quiosque

puzzle book
das Rätselheft
el libro de
rompecabezas
le recueil de
casse-têtes
il libro puzzle
o livro de puzzles

newspaper / die Zeitung / el periódico
le journal / il giornale / o jornal

newspaper box / die Zeitungsbox
la caja del periódico / le distributeur
automatique de journaux / la cassetta
dei giornali / a caixa de jornais

tobacconist / die Trafik / el estanco
le bureau de tabac / la tabaccheria / a tabacaria

smoking / das Rauchen / fumar / fumer / fumare / fumar

smoking area
der Raucherbereich
la zona de fumadores
l'espace fumeurs
l'area fumatori
o espaço para fumadores

stem / der Stiel
la boquilla / le tuyau
lo stelo / o tubo

e-cigarette
die E-Zigarette
el cigarrillo
electrónico
la cigarette
électronique
la sigaretta
elettronica
o cigarro eletrónico

pipe
die Pfeife
la pipa
la pipe
la pipa
o cachimbo

bowl
der Kopf
el cuenco
le fourneau
la ciotola
o fornilho

lighter / das Feuerzeug
el encendedor / le briquet
l'accendino / o isqueiro

ashtray / der Aschenbecher
el cenicero / le cendrier
il posacenere / o cinzeiro

cigarette
die Zigarette
el cigarrillo
la cigarette
la sigaretta
o cigarro

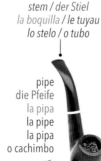

cigar / die Zigarre / el puro
le cigare / il sigaro / o charuto

tobacco / der Tabak
el tabaco / le tabac
il tabacco / o tabaco

pack / die Packung / el paquete
le paquet / il pacchetto / o maço

CANDY STORE / DER SÜSSWARENLADEN / LA TIENDA DE DULCES
LE MAGASIN DE BON-BONS / IL NEGOZIO DI CARAMELLE / A LOJA DE DOCES

pick and mix / die bunte Mischung / las golosinas a granel
les bonbons assortis / le caramelle assortite / o sortido de gomas

chocolate bar / der Schokoriegel / la barra
de chocolate / la barre chocolatée / la barretta
di cioccolato / a tablete de chocolate

scoop
die Schaufel
la cucharada
la pelle
il misurino
a colher

truffle / der Trüffel
la trufa / la truffe
il tartufo / a trufa

marshmallow / der Marshmallow
el malvavisco / le marshmallow
il marshmallow / o marshmallow

gummies / die Gummibärchen
las gomitas / les bonbons gomme
le caramelle gommose / as gomas

white chocolate / die weiße Schokolade
el chocolate blanco / le chocolat blanc
il cioccolato bianco / o chocolate branco

dark chocolate / die Zartbitterschokolade
el chocolate negro / le chocolat noir
il cioccolato fondente / o chocolate negro

milk chocolate / die Vollmilchschokolade
el chocolate con leche / le chocolat au lait
il cioccolato al latte
o chocolate de leite

mint / die Minze / la menta
la menthe / la menta
o rebuçado de menta

lollipop / der Lutscher
la piruleta / la sucette
il lecca-lecca
o chupa-chupa

hard candy / das Bonbon
el caramelo duro
le bonbon à croquer
la caramella / os rebuçados

licorice / das Lakritz
el regaliz / la réglisse
la liquirizia / o alcaçuz

caramel / die Karamelle
el caramelo / le caramel
il caramello / o caramelo

toffee / das Toffee
la melcocha
le caramel mou
il mou / o toffee

jellybean / das Geleebonbon
el gominola / le bonbon
à la gelée / la gelatina
os rebuçados

nougat / der Nougat
el turrón / le nougat
il torrone / o torrão

CONVENIENCE STORE / DER TANTE-EMMA-LADEN / LA TIENDA DE CONVENIENCIA / LA SUPERETTE / IL MINIMARKET / A LOJA DE CONVENIÊNCIA

cashier / die Kassiererin
la cajera / la caissière
la cassiera / o caixa

scratch-off
das Rubbellos
el raspadito
le jeu à gratter
il gratta e vinci
a raspadinha

chewing gum
das Kaugummi
la goma de mascar
le chewing-gum
la gomma da masticare
a pastilha elástica

lottery ticket
das Lotterielos
el boleto de lotería
le ticket de loterie
il biglietto della lotteria
o bilhete da lotaria

snacks / die Knabberzeug
los bocadillos / les en-cas
lo snack / os snacks

potato chips / die Kartoffelchips
las papas fritas / les chips
le patatine fritte
as batatas fritas

OTHER STORES / DIE ANDERE LÄDCHEN / OTRAS TIENDAS
LES AUTRES MAGASINS / GLI ALTRI NEGOZI / OUTRAS LOJAS

bookstore / die Buchhandlung
la librería / la librairie
la libreria / a livraria

antique store / der Antiquitätenladen
la tienda de antigüedades
l'antiquaire / il negozio di
antiquariato / o antiquário

gift shop / der Geschenkeladen
la tienda de regalos / la boutique
de souvenirs / il negozio di souvenir
a loja de presentes

jewelry store / das Juweliergeschäft
la tienda de joyas / le bijoutier
il negozio di gioielli / a joalharia

hardware store / das
Eisenwarengeschäft / la ferretería
le magasin de bricolage / il negozio
di ferramenta / a loja de ferragens

garden center / das Gartencenter
el centro de jardinería / le magasin
de jardinage / il vivaio / o centro
de jardinagem

liquor store / das
Spirituosengeschäft
la licorería / le débit
de boisson / il negozio di
liquori / a loja de bebidas

camera store / das Fotogeschäft
la tienda de cámaras
le vendeur d'appareils photos
il negozio di fotografia
a loja de fotografia

boutique / das Boutique
la boutique / la boutique
la boutique / a butique

tailor / die Schneiderei
el sastre / le tailleur
il sarto / o alfaiate

health food store / der
Naturkostladen / la tienda de
alimentos naturales / le magasin bio
il negozio di alimenti naturali
a loja de comida saudável

art supply store / das
Künstlerbedarfshändler / la tienda de
suministros de arte / le magasin d'art
il negozio di beni artistici
a loja de artigos de arte

bridal shop / das
Brautmodengeschäft / la tienda
de novias / la boutique de mariage
il negozio di abiti da sposa
a loja de noivas

pet store / die Zoohandlung
la tienda de mascotas / l'animalerie
il negozio di animali
a loja de animais

sporting goods / die Sportartikel
los artículos deportivos / le magasin
de sport / gli articoli sportivi
a loja de artigos desportivos

thrift shop / der Secondhandladen
la tienda de segunda mano
la friperie / il negozio di articoli usati
a loja em segunda mão

laundromat / der Waschsalon
la lavandería / le lavomatique
la lavanderia a gettoni
a lavandaria self-service

dry cleaner / die chemische
Reinigung / la tintorería
le pressing / il lavasecco
a lavandaria

farmer's market / der Bauernmarkt
el mercado de agricultores
le marché fermier / il mercato agricolo
o mercado agrícola

FOOD
DAS LEBENSMITTEL
LA COMIDA
LA NOURRITURE
IL CIBO
A COMIDA

FRUITS / DIE FRÜCHTE / LAS FRUTAS / LES FRUITS / LA FRUTTA / AS FRUTAS
BERRIES / DIE BEEREN / LAS BAYAS / LES BAIES / LE BACCHE / AS BAGAS

blackberry / die Brombeere
la mora / la mûre
la mora / a amora

cranberry / die Moosbeere
el arándano / la canneberge
il mirtillo rosso / o arando

mulberry / die Maulbeere / la morera
la mûre sauvage / il gelso / a amora

black currant / die schwarze
Johannisbeere / la grosella negra
le cassis / il ribes nero
a groselha negra

currant / die Johannisbeere
la grosella / la groseille
il ribes / a groselha

raspberry / die Himbeere
la frambuesa / la framboise
il lampone / a framboesa

blueberry / die Heidelbeere
el arándano / la myrtille
la mirtillo / o mirtilo

gooseberry / die Stachelbeere
la grosella espinosa / la groseille à
maquereau / l'uva spina / a groselha verde

strawberry / die Erdbeere / la fresa
la fraise / la fragola / o morango

MELONS / DIE MELONEN / LOS MELONES
LES MELONS / I MELONI / OS MELÕES

rind / die Schale
la cáscara
la peau
la crosta
a casca

pulp / das
Fruchtfleisch
la pulpa
la pulpe
la polpa
a polpa

watermelon / die Wassermelone
la sandia / la pastèque
l'anguria / a melancia

cantaloupe / die Warzenmelone
el melón / le cantaloup
il cantalupo / a meloa

grapes
die Trauben
las uvas
les raisins
l'uva / as uvas

honeydew / der Honigtau
el melón dulce / le melon miel
il melone / a melada

sweet / süß / dulce / doux
dolce / doce

sour / sauer / agrio / amer
aspro / azedo

fresh / frisch / fresco / frais
fresco / fresco

ripe / reif / maduro / mûr
maduro / maduro

rotten / faul / podrido
pourri / marcio / podre

juicy / saftig / jugoso / juteux
succoso / sumarento

acidic / sauer / ácido / acide
acido / ácido

tangy / spritzig / acre / acidulé
piccante / picante

POME FRUIT / DAS KERNOBST
LAS POMÁCEAS / LES FRUITS À PÉPINS
LE POMACEE / AS FRUTAS POMÓIDEAS

apple core
der Apfelbutzen
el corazón de manzana
le trognon de pomme
il torsolo di mela
o caroço da maçã

seed
der Samen
la semilla
la graine
il seme
a semente

apple / der Apfel / la manzana
la pomme / la mela / a maçã

kiwi / die Kiwi / el kiwi / le kiwi / il kiwi / o kiwi

stem / der Stiel
el tallo / la queue
il gambo / o caule

pear / die Birne / la pera / la poire / la pera / a pera

CITRUS FRUIT / DIE ZITRUSFRÜCHTE
LOS CÍTRICOS / LES AGRUMES
GLI AGRUMI / OS CITRINOS

clementine
die Clementine
la clementina
la clémentine
la clementina
a clementina

peel
die Schale
la cáscara
la peau
la buccia
a casca

pith
die weiße Haut
la médula
la moelle
il midollo
a medula

grapefruit / die Grapefruit
la toronja
le pamplemousse
il pompelmo / a toranja

kumquat / die Kumquat
el kumquat / le kumquat
il mandarino cinese
o kumquat

lemon / die Zitrone
el limón / le citron
il limone / o limão

lime / die Limette
la lima / le citron vert
il lime / a lima

orange / die Orange
la naranja / l'orange
l'arancia / a laranja

tangelo / der Tangelo
el tangelo / le tangelo
il mapo / o tangelo

segment
das Segment
el gajo
le quartier
il segmento
o gomo

tangerine / die Mandarine
la mandarina
la mandarine / il mandarino
a tangerina

STONE FRUITS / DIE STEINFRÜCHTE
LOS FRUTAS DE CAROZO / LES FRUITS A NOYAUX
LA DRUPA / AS FRUTAS DE CAROÇO

TROPICAL FRUITS / DIE TROPISCHE FRÜCHTE
LAS FRUTAS TROPICALES / LES FRUITS
TROPICAUX / I FRUTTI TROPICALI
AS FRUTAS TROPICAIS

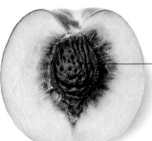

peach pit
die Pfirsichkern
el hueso
de durazno
le noyau
de pêche
la pescanoce
o caroço
de pêssego

banana / die Banane
el plátano / la banane
la banana / a banana

fig / die Feige / el higo
la figue / il fico / o figo

apricot / die Aprikose
el albaricoque / l'abricot
l'albicocca / o alperce

cherry / die Kirsche
la cereza / la cerise
la ciliegia / a cereja

date / die Dattel
el dátil / la datte
il dattero / a tâmara

papaya / die Papaya
la papaya / la papaye
la papaia / a papaia

nectarine / die Nektarine
la nectarina / la nectarine
la nettarina / a nectarina

peach / der Pfirsich
el durazno / la pêche
la pesca / o pêssego

mango / die Mango
el mango / la mangue
il mango / a manga

pomegranate
der Granatapfel
la granada / la grenade
il melograno / a romã

plum / die Pflaume
la ciruela / la prune
la prugna / a ameixa

pina colada
die Pina Colada
la piña colada
la pina colada
la pina colada
o abacaxi

coconut / die Kokosnuss
el coco / a noix de coco
il cocco / o coco

pineapple
die Ananas
la piña
l'ananas
l'ananas
o ananás

dried fruit / die Trockenfrüchte
los frutos secos
les fruits secs / la fruta secca
as frutas secas

nuts / die Nüsse
las nueces
les noix
le noci
os frutos secos

currant
die Johannisbeere
la grosella roja
le raisin de
Corinthe
il ribes
a groselha seca

raisin / die Rosine
la uva pasa
le raisin sec
il'uveta / a passa

sultana
die Sultanine
la sultana
le raisin de
Smyrne
l'uva sultanina
a sultana

prune
die Pflaume
la ciruela
le pruneau
la prugne secca
a ameixa seca

salted / gezalten / salado / salé
salato / com sal

unsalted / die Deutsche / sin sal
non salé / non salato / sem sal

roasted / geröstet / asado
grillé / tostato / torrado

shelled / geschält / sin cáscara
décortiqué / sgusciate
descascado

nutcracker / der Nussknacker
el cascanueces / le casse-noix
il schiaccianoci / o quebra-nozes

almond / die Mandel
la almendra / l'amande
la mandorla
a amêndoa

brazil nut
die Paranuss
la nuez de Brasil
la noix du Brésil
la noce brasiliana
a castanha-do-pará

cashew
die Cashew
el marañón
la noix de cajou
il anacardo / o caju

shell / die Schale
la cáscara / la coquille
il guscio / a casca

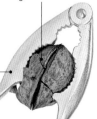

pecan
die Pekannuss
el pecán
la noix de pécan
il pecan
a noz-pecã

chestnut
die Kastanie
la castaña
le marron
la castagna
a castanha

hazelnut
die Haselnuss
la avellana
la noisette
la nocciola / a avelã

pine nut
der Pinienkern
el piñón
le pignon de pin
il pinolo
o pinhão

macadamia
die Macadamia
la macadamia
la macadamia
la macadamia
a macadâmia

pistachio
die Pistazie
el pistacho
la pistache
il pistacchio
o pistácio

peanut
die Erdnuss
el maní
la cacahuète
l'arachide
o amendoim

walnut
die Walnuss
la nuez de nogal
la noix
la noce
a noz

VEGETABLES / DAS GEMÜSE / LOS VEGETALES / LES LÉGUMES
LE VERDURE / OS VEGETAIS

CRUCIFEROUS VEGETABLES / DER KREUZBLÜTLER / LAS CRUCÍFERAS
LE CRUCIFÉRAIRE / LA CRUCIFERA / A CRUCÍFERAS

cauliflower / der Blumenkohl / la coliflor
le chou-fleur / il cavolfiore / a couve-flor

red cabbage
der Rotkohl
el repollo morado
le chou rouge
il cavolo rosso
o couve-roxa

cabbage / der Kohl
el repollo / le chou
il cavolo / o repolho

brussels sprouts
der Rosenkohl
los coles de bruselas
les choux de Bruxelles
i cavolini di bruxelles
as couves de Bruxelas

broccoli / der Brokoli
el brócoli / le brocoli
il broccoli / o brócolo

kohlrabi / das Kohlrabi
el clolirrábano / le chou-rave
il cavolo rapa
a couve-rábano

radish / der Rettich
el rábano / le radis
il ravanello / o rabanete

Swiss chard / der Mangold
la acelga / la blette
la bietola / a acelga

bok choy / der Bok Choy
el bok choy / le pak-choï
il cavolo cinese
a couve bok choy

floret / das Blümchen
el florete / le fleuron
la cimetta / o florete

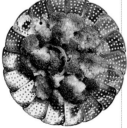

vegetable steamer
der Gemüsedämpfer
la vaporera de verduras
le cuiseur vapeur
la vaporiera per verdure
o vaporizador de vegetais

NIGHTSHADE FAMILY / DIE NACHTSCHATTENGEWÄCHSE
LAS SOLANÁCEAS / LA FAMILLE DES SOLANACEES
LA FAMIGLIA DELLA BELLADONNA / AS SOLANÁCEAS

tomato / die Tomate
el tomate / la tomate
il pomodoro / o tomate

eggplant / die Aubergine
la berenjena / l'aubergine
le melanzane
a beringela

bell pepper / die Paprika
el pimiento / le poivron
il peperone / o pimento

ROOT VEGETABLES / DAS WURZELGEMÜSE / LOS TUBÉRCULOS / LES LEGUME-RACINES
GLI ORTAGGI A RADICE / OS TUBÉRCULOS

yam / die Jamswurzel
el ñame / l'igname
il igname / o inhame

sweet potato
die Süßkartoffel
la batata / la patate douce
la patata dolce / a batata-doce

turnip / die Steckrübe
el nabo / le navet
la rapa / o nabo

potato
die Kartoffel / la papa
la pomme de terre
la patata / a batata

beetroot
die Rote Bete
la remolacha
la betterave
la barbabietola
a beterraba

carrot
die Karotte
la zanahoria
la carotte
la carota
a cenoura

parsnip / die Pastinake
la chirivía / le panais
la pastinaca / a pastinaca

rutabaga / die Steckrübe
el colinabo / le rutabaga
la rutabaga / a rutabaga

celeriac
der Knollensellerie
el apio / le céleri
il sedano rapa / o aipo

fennel / der Fenchel
el hinojo / le fenouil
il finocchio / o funcho

water chestnut
die Wasserkastanie
la castaña de agua
la châtaigne d'eau
la castagna d'acqua
a castanha d'água

bamboo shoot
die Bambussprosse
el brote de bambú
la pousse de bambou
il germoglio di bambù
o rebento de bambu

SQUASHES / DIE KÜRBISSE / LAS CALABAZAS / LES COURGES / LE ZUCCHE / AS ABÓBORAS

acorn squash / der Eichelkürbis
la calabaza bellota / la courge poivrée
la zucca a ghianda / a abóbora-bolota

butternut squash / der Butternusskürbis / el zapallo
la courge butternut / la zucca butternut / a abóbora manteiga

zucchini / das Zucchini / el calabacín
la courgette / la zucchina / a curgete

cucumber / die Gurke
el pepino / le concombre
il cetriolo / o pepino

squash blossoms
die Kürbisblüten
las flores de calabaza
les fleurs de courge
i fiori di zucca
as flores da abóbora

pumpkin / der Kürbis
la calabaza / la citrouille
la zucca / a abóbora

LEAFY VEGETABLES / DAS BLATTGEMÜSE
LAS HORTALIZAS / LES LEGUMES A FEUILLES
LE VERDURE A FOGLIA LARGA / OS VEGETAIS FOLHOSOS

tossed salad / der gemischter Salat
la ensalada mixta
la salade assaisonnée
l'insalata / a salada

lettuce / die Kopfsalate
las lechugas / la laitue
le lattughe / as alfaces

spinach / der Spinat
la espinaca / les épinards
gli spinaci / o espinafre

arugula / die Rucola / la rúgula
la roquette / la rucola / a rúcula

kale / der Grünkohl / la col rizada
le chou kale / il cavolo / a couve frisada

endive / die Endivie / la endivia
l'endive / l'indivia / a endívia

watercress / die Brunnenkresse
el berro / le cresson
il crescione / o agrião

dandelion / der Löwenzahn
el diente de león / le pissenlit
il dente di leone / o dente-de-leão

mustard greens / der Senfkohl
las hojas de mostaza
la moutarde brune / la senape
as folhas de mostarda

leaf / das Blatt / la hoja
la feuille / la foglia / a folha

raw / roh / crudo / cru
crudo / cru

frozen / gefroren / congelado
surgelé / congelato / congelado

organic / Bio / orgánico
biologique / biologico
organico

croutons / die Croûtons
los picatostes / les croûtons
i crostini / os croutons

rapini / die Rapini / el rapini
le rapini / i rapini / o grelo

salad dressing / das Salatdressing
el aderezo para ensala-das
l'assaisonnement
il condimento per in-salata
o molho para salada

BULB AND STEM VEGETABLES / DAS ZWIEBEL- UND STÄNGELGE-MÜSE
LAS VERDURAS DE BULBO Y TALLO / LES LEGUMES A BULBES ET A QUEUES
LE VERDURE A BULBO E A STELO / OS LEGUMES DE TALO E BULBO

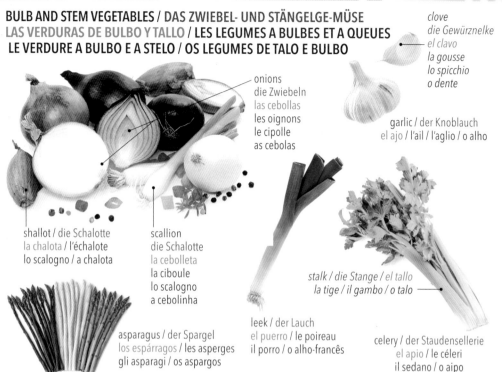

clove
die Gewürznelke
el clavo
la gousse
lo spicchio
o dente

onions
die Zwiebeln
las cebollas
les oignons
le cipolle
as cebolas

garlic / der Knoblauch
el ajo / l'ail / l'aglio / o alho

shallot / die Schalotte
la chalota / l'échalote
lo scalogno / a chalota

scallion
die Schalotte
la cebolleta
la ciboule
lo scalogno
a cebolinha

stalk / die Stange / el tallo
la tige / il gambo / o talo

asparagus / der Spargel
los espárragos / les asperges
gli asparagi / os aspargos

leek / der Lauch
el puerro / le poireau
il porro / o alho-francês

celery / der Staudensellerie
el apio / le céleri
il sedano / o aipo

OTHER VEGETABLES / DIE ANDERES GEMÜSE / OTRAS VERDURAS / LES AUTRES LEGUMES
LE ALTRE VERDURE / OUTROS LEGUMES

kernel / das Kerngehäuse / el kernel
l'épi / il nocciolo / o grão

artichoke / die Artischocke / la alcachofa
l'artichaud / il carciofo / a alcachofra

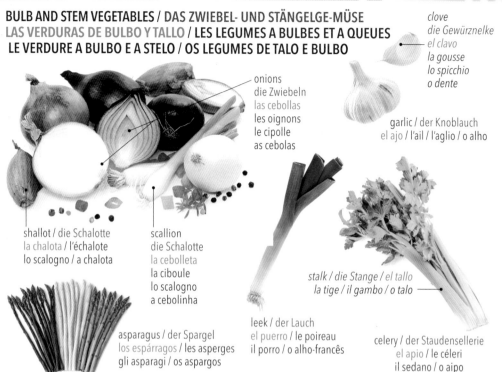

avocado / die Avocado / el aguacate
l'avocat / l'avocado / o abacate

heart / das Herz / el corazón
le coeur / il cuore / o coração

husk / die Schale
la cáscara / la feuille
la buccia / a casca

mushrooms / die Champignons
los champiñones
les champignons / i funghi
os cogumelos

corn / der Mais / el maíz
le maïs / il mais / o milho

truffle / der Trüffel / la trufa
la truffe / il tartufo / a trufa

HERBS / DIE KRÄUTER / LAS HIERBAS
LES HERBES / LE ERBE / AS ERVAS

bouquet garni
das Bouquet garni
el ramillete de hierbas
le bouquet garni
il fascio di erbe
o maço de ervas

parsley / die Petersilie
el perejil / le persil
il prezzemolo / a salsa

sage / der Salbei / la savia
la sauge / la salvia / a salva

rosemary / der Rosmarin
el romero / le romarin
il rosmarino / o alecrim

thyme / der Thymian
el tomillo / le thym
il timo / o tomilho

marjoram / der Majoran
la mejorana / la marjolaine
la maggiorana
a manjerona

dried herbs
die getrocknete Kräuter
las hierbas secas
les herbes séchées
le erbe secche
as ervas secas

bay leaf / das Lorbeerblatt
la hoja de laurel / la feuille
de laurier / l'alloro
a folha de louro

basil / das Basilikum
la albahaca / le basilic
il basilico / o manjericão

tarragon / der Estragon
el estragón / l'estragon
il dragoncello / o estragão

mint / die Minze
la menta / la menthe
la menta / a hortelã

dill / der Dill / el eneldo
l'aneth / l'aneto / o endro

chervil / der Kerbel
el perifollo / le cerfeuil
il cerfoglio / o cerefólio

cilantro / der Koriander
el cilantro / la coriandre
il coriandolo / o coentro

lemongrass
das Zitronengras
la citronela / la citronnelle
la citronella
a erva-príncipe

oregano / der Oregano
el orégano / l'origan
l'origano / o orégão

sorrel / der Sauerampfer
la acedera / l'oseille
l'acetosa / a azeda

savory / die Bohnenkraut
la ajedrea / la sarriette
la salvia / a segurelha

chives
die Schnittlauch
las cebolletas
la ciboulette / l'erba
cipollina / o cebolinho

SPICES / DIE GEWÜRZE / LAS ESPECIAS
LES ÉPICES / LE SPEZIE / AS ESPECIARIAS

chili pepper / der Chili-Pfeffer
el chile / le piment
il peperoncino
a malagueta

salt and pepper mills / die Salz- und Pfeffermühlen
los molinillos de sal y pimienta / les moulins à sel et à poivre
il macina sale e pepe / os moinhos de sal e pimenta

salt
das Salz
la sal
le sel
il sale
o sal

peppercorns
die Pfefferkörner
los granos
de pimienta
les grains
de poivre
i grani di pepe
os grãos
de pimenta

cumin / der Kreuzkümmel
el comino / le cumin
il cumino / os cominhos

flakes / die Flocken
las hojuelas / les flocons
i fiocchi / os flocos

cloves / die Nelken / los clavos
le clou de girofle / i chiodi
di garofano / os cravos

aniseed / die Anissamen
la semilla de anís / l'anis
i semi di anice / o anis

cardamom / der Kardamom
el cardamomo
la cardamone
il cardamomo / o
cardamomo

star anise / der Sternanis
el anís estrellado
la badiane / l'anice stellato
o anis estrelado

nutmeg / die Muskatnuss
la nuez moscada / la noix
de muscade / la noce
moscata / a noz-moscada

mace / die Muskatblüte
la maza / le macis
il macis / o macis

curry powder / das
Currypulver / el curry en polvo
/ le curry en poudre / il curry
in polvere / o caril em pó

turmeric / die Kurkuma
la cúrcuma / le curcuma
la curcuma / a curcuma

allspice / der Piment
la pimienta de Jamaica
le piment de la Jamaïque
il pimento / a pimenta
da Jamaica

coriander / der Koriander
el cilantro / la coriandre
il coriandolo / o coentro

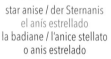

whole / ganz / completo
entier / integrale / inteiro

extract
der Auszug
el extracto
l'extrait
l'estratto
o extrato

saffron / der Safran
el azafrán / le safran
lo zafferano / o açafrão

ginger / der Ingwer
el jengibre / le gingembre
lo zenzero / o gengibre

vanilla / die Vanille
la vainilla / la vanille
la vaniglia / a baunilha

stick / die Stange / el palo
le bâton / il bastone / o pau

pod / die Schote
la vaina / la gousse
il baccello / a vagem

cinnamon / der Zimt
la canela / la cannelle
la cannella / a canela

ground / gemahlen / molido
la terre / il macinato / moído

BEANS AND GRAINS / DIE BOHNEN UND KÖRNER / LOS FRIJOLES Y CEREALES
LES POIS ET LES GRAINES / FAGIOLI E I CEREALI / OS FEIJÕES E GRÃOS

LEGUMES / DIE LEGUMENEN / LAS LEGUMINOSAS / LES LEGUMES / I LEGUMI / OS LEGUMES

haricot beans
die Stangenbohnen
las alubias / le haricot blanc
i fagioli bianchi
o feijão-verde

red kidney beans / die rote
Kidneybohnen / los frijoles
rojos / le haricot rouge
i fagioli rossi
o feijão vermelho

flageolet beans
die Flageolettbohnen
los frijoles flageolet
les flageolets / i fagioli verdi
o feijão branco

adzuki beans
die Adzukibohnen
los frijoles adzuki
le haricot azuki / i fagioli
adzuki / o feijão azuki

chickpeas / die Kichererbsen
los garbanzos
le pois chiche / i ceci
os grãos-de-bico

soybeans / die Sojabohnen
la soja / le germe de soja
i fagioli di soia / a soja

pinto beans / die Pinto-
Bohnen / los frijoles pintos
le haricot pinto / i fagioli
pinto / o feijão-rajado

fava beans / die Favabohnen
las habas / les fèves
i fagioli fava / as favas

black beans / die Schwarze
Bohnen / los frijoles negros
le haricot noir / i fagioli neri
o feijão preto

green peas
die grüne Erbsen
los guisantes verdes
les petits pois / i piselli verdi
as ervilhas verdes

mung beans
die Mungobohnen
los frijoles mungo
le haricot mungo / i fagioli
mung / o feijão mungo

lima beans
die Limabohnen / las habas
de lima / le haricot de Lima
i fagioli di lima
os feijões-de-lima

brown lentils
die braune Linsen
las lentejas marrones
les lentilles brunes
le lenticchie marroni
as lentilhas castanhas

red lentils
die rote Linsen
las lentejas rojas
les lentilles rouges
le lenticchie rosse
as lentilhas vermelhas

black-eyed peas
die schwarzäugige Erbsen
los frijoles de ojo negro
le pois à vache
i piselli dall'occhio nero
o feijão-frade

split peas / die Spalterbsen
los guisantes partidos
les pois cassés
i piselli spezzati
as ervilhas partidas

RICE / DER REIS / EL ARROZ / LE RIZ / IL RISO / O ARROZ

white rice
der weißer Reis
el arroz blanco
le riz blanc
il riso bianco
o arroz branco

brown rice
der brauner Reis
el arroz integral
le riz brun
il riso integrale
o arroz integral

arborio rice
der Arborio-Reis
el arroz arborio
le riz arborio
il riso arborio
o arroz arborio

wild rice
der Wildreis
el arroz salvaje
le riz sauvage
il riso selvatico
o arroz selvagem

GRAINS / DIE GETREIDE / LOS GRANOS
LES CEREALES / I CEREALI / OS CEREAIS

wheat / der Weizen
el trigo / le blé
il grano / o trigo

barley / die Gerste
la cebada / l'orge
l'orzo / a cevada

oats / der Hafer
la avena / l'avoine
l'avena / a aveia

millet / die Hirse
el mijo / le millet
il miglio / o milhete

corn / der Mais
el maíz / le maïs
il mais / o milho

quinoa / das Quinoa
la quinua / le quinoa
la quinoa / a quinoa

PROCESSED GRAINS / DIE VERARBEITETE
KÖRNER / LOS GRANOS PROCESSADOS
LES CEREALES TRANS-FORMEES / I CEREALI
LAVORATI / OS CEREAIS PROCESSADOS

bran / die Kleie
el salvado / le son de blé
la crusca / o farelo

cracked wheat
der Weizenschrot / el trigo
partido / le blé concassé
il farro / o trigo partido

semolina / das Grieß
la sémola / la semoule
la semola / a semolina

couscous / der Couscous
el cuscús / le couscous
il couscous / o cuscuz

SEEDS / DIE SAMEN / LAS SEMILLAS / LES GRAINES / I SEMI / AS SEMENTES

pumpkin seed
der Kürbiskern
la semilla de calabaza
la graine de citrouille
i semi di zucca
a semente
de abóbora

sesame seed
die Sesamsaat
la semilla de sésamo
la graine de sésame
i semi di sesamo
a semente de sésamo

poppy seed
der Mohn
la semilla
de amapola
la graine de pavot
il seme di papavero
a semente de papoila

caraway / der Kümmel
la alcaravea / le carvi
il cumino / a alcaravia

sunflower seed /die Sonnenblumenkerne
la semilla de girasol / la graine de tournesol
o semi di girasole / a semente de girassol

soak (v) / einweichen / remojar
faire tremper / ammollo / demolhar

short-grain rice / der Kurzkornreis
el arroz de grano corto / le riz à
petits grains/ il riso a grana corta
o arroz de grão pequeno

whole-grain rice / der Vollkornreis
el arroz integral / le riz complet
il riso integrale / o arroz integral

quick-cooking / Schnellkochende
la cocción rápida / la cuisson rapide
la cottura rapida / a cozedura rápida

long-grain rice / der Langkornreis
el arroz de grano / le riz long grain
il riso a grano largo / o arroz de grão
longo

MEAT AND POULTRY / DAS FLEISCH UND GEFLÜGEL / LA CARNE Y LAS AVES
LA VIANDE ET LES VOLAILLES / LA CARNE E IL POLLAME / A CARNE E AS AVES

butcher / der Fleischer
el carnicero / le boucher
il macellaio / o açougueiro

BEEF / DAS RINDFLEISCH / LA RES / LE BŒUF
A CARNE / A CARNE DE VACA

filet / das Filet / el filete
le filet / il filetto / o filete

beef cubes
der Rindfleischwürfel
los cubos de carne
des cubes de boeuf
i cubetti di manzo
os cubos de carne

ground / das Hackfleisch
la carne molida
la viande hachée
il macinato
a carne picada

veal / das Kalbfleisch / la ternera
le veau / il vitello / a vitela

sirloin steak
das Lendensteak
el solomillo / la bavette
d'aloyau / la bistecca di
controfiletto / o bife do
lombo de vaca

round roast / der runder
Braten / el medallón
le rôti / l'arrosto rotondo
o pojadouro

T-bone / die T-Bone
el T-bone / le bifteck
d'aloyau / la bistecca alla
fiorentina / a costeleta
de novilho

red meat / das rotes Fleisch
la carne roja / la viande
rouge / la carne rossa
a carne vermelha

lean meat / das mageres
Fleisch / la carne magra
la viande maigre / la carne
magra / a carne magra

flank steak
das Flankensteak
el bistec de falda / la bavette
la bistecca di manzo
o bife da vazia

ribs / die Rippen
las costillas / les cotes
le costolette / a costeleta

ORGAN MEAT / DAS ORGANFLEISCH / LA CARNE
DE ÓRGANOS / LES ABATS / LA CARNE BIOLOGICA
OS ÓRGÃOS

heart / das Herz / el corazón
le coeur / il cuore / o coração

liver
die Leber
el hígado
le foie
il fegato
o fígado

kidney
die Niere
el riñón
le rognon
il rene
o rim

tongue / die Zunge / la lengua
la langue / la lingua / a língua

GAME / DAS WILDBRET
LA CAZA / LE GIBIER
LA SELVAGGINA / A CARNE DE CAÇA

rabbit / das Kaninchen / el conejo
le lapin / il coniglio / o coelho

venison / das Wildbret / el venado
le chevreuil / il cervo / o veado

fat / das fett
la grasa / le gras
il grasso / a gordura

pork tenderloin / das Schweinefilet
el lomo de cerdo / le rôti de porc
il filetto di maiale / o lombo de porco

crown roast / der Kronenbraten
la corona asada / le carré d'agneau
il carré arrosto / a coroa de costeletas

ham / der Schinken / el jamón
le jambon / il prosciutto / o presunto

chop
das Kotelett
la chuleta
la côtelette
la braciola
a costeleta

leg of mutton / die Hammelkeule
la pierna de cordero / le gigot
d'agneau / la coscia di montone
a perna de carneiro

bacon
der Speck
el tocino
le bacon
la pancetta
o bacon

lamb / das Lammfleisch / el cordero
l'agneau / l'agnello / o borrego

sausages / die Würstchen
las salchichas / les saucisses
le salsicce / as salsichas

POULTRY / DAS GEFLÜGEL / LAS AVES / LA VOLAILLE / IL POLLO / AS AVES

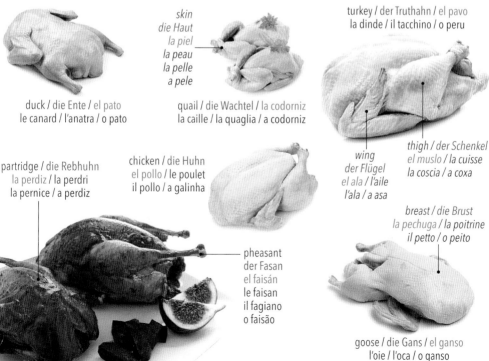

skin
die Haut
la piel
la peau
la pelle
a pele

turkey / der Truthahn / el pavo
la dinde / il tacchino / o peru

duck / die Ente / el pato
le canard / l'anatra / o pato

quail / die Wachtel / la codorniz
la caille / la quaglia / a codorniz

thigh / der Schenkel
el muslo / la cuisse
la coscia / a coxa

wing
der Flügel
el ala / l'aile
l'ala / a asa

partridge / die Rebhuhn
la perdiz / la perdri
la pernice / a perdiz

chicken / die Huhn
el pollo / le poulet
il pollo / a galinha

breast / die Brust
la pechuga / la poitrine
il petto / o peito

pheasant
der Fasan
el faisán
le faisan
il fagiano
o faisão

goose / die Gans / el ganso
l'oie / l'oca / o ganso

FISH / DER FISCH / EL PEZ / LE POISSON / IL PESCE / O PEIXE

fish counter / die Fischtheke / el mostrador de pescado / le rayon poissonnerie
il banco del pesce / a bancada de peixe

Dover sole / die Seezunge
la suela de Dover / la sole
la sogliola di Dover
o linguado

lemon sole / die Seezunge
el lenguado de limón
la limande-sole / la sogliola
al limone / a solha-limão

salmon / der Lachs
el salmón / la saumon
il salmone / o salmão

halibut / der Heilbutt
el rodaballo / le flétan
l'halibut / o alabote

tuna / der Thunfisch
el atún / le thon
il tonno / o atum

skate / der Rochen
la manta raya / la raie
la razza / a raia

sea bass / der Wolfsbarsch
la lubina / le bar
il branzino / o robalo

haddock / der Schellfisch
la merluza / le haddock
l'eglefino / a arinca

cod / der Kabeljau
el bacalao / le cabillaud
il merluzzo / o bacalhau

mackerel / die Makrele
la macarela / le maquereau
lo sgombro / a cavala

sardine / die Sardine
la sardina / la sardine
la sardina / a sardinha

smelt / der Stint
el esperlano / l'éperlan
l'osmeride / o eperlano

whiting / der Wittling
la pescadilla / le merlan
il merlano / o badejo

rainbow trout
die Regenbogenforelle
la trucha arcoíris / la truite arc-en-ciel
la trota iridea / a truta arco-íris

swordfish / der Schwertfisch / el pez espada
l'espadon / il pesce spada / o peixe-espada

seafood / die Meeresfrüchte / los mariscos / les fruits de mer / i frutti di mare / o marisco

lobster tail
der Hummerschwanz
la cola de langosta
la queue de homard
la coda dell'aragosta
a cauda de lagosta

crab / die Krabbe
el cangrejo / le crabe
il granchio / o caranguejo

shrimp
die Garnele
el camarón
la crevette
il gambero
o camarão

claw
die Klaue
la pinza de
cangrejo
la pince
la chela
a pinça

scallop
die Jakobsmuschel
la vieira / la noix de
Saint-Jacques / la capasanta
a vieira

prawn / die Garnele
la gamba / la crevette
il gambero / a gamba

langoustine
die Languste / la langosta
la langoustine / lo scampo
/ o lagostim

lobster / der Hummer
la langosta / le homard
l'aragosta / a lagosta

clam / die Venusmuschel
la almeja / la palourde
la vongola / a amêijoa

oyster / die Auster / la ostra
l'huitre / l'ostrica / a ostra

mussel / die Muschel
el mejillón / la moule
la cozza / o mexilhão

crayfish / der Flusskrebs
el cangrejo de río
la langouste
il gambero di fiume
o lagostim-de-água-doce

cockle / die Herzmuschel
el berberecho / la coque
la cariide / o berbigão

octopus / der Oktopus / el pulpo
la pieuvre / il polpo / o polvo

squid / der Tintenfisch / el calamar
le calamar / il calamaro / a lula

---

cleaned / gereinigt / limpio
nettoyé / pulito / limpo

smoked / geräuchert / ahumado
fumé / affumicato / fumado

salted / gesalzen / salado / salé
salato / salgado

boned / entbeint / deshuesado
désossé / disossato / desossado

skinned / gehäutet / sin piel
sans la peau / spellato / esfolado

peeled / geschält / pelado / pelé
pelato / descascado

fileted / filetiert / fileteado
en filets / filettato / em filetes

whole / ganz / completo / entier
intero / inteiro

jumbo / Jumbo / jumbo / géant
gigante / grande

DAIRY PRODUCTS / DIE MILCHPRODUKTE / LOS PRODUCTOS LÁCTEOS
LES PRODUITS LAITIERS / I PRODOTTI CASEARI / OS LATICÍNIOS

heavy cream
die Schlagsahne
la crema de leche
la crème épaisse
la panna / as natas

pitcher of milk / der Krug mit Milch
la jarra de leche / le pichet de lait
la brocca di latte / o jarro de leite

cottage cheese
der Hüttenkäse
el requesón
le fromage blanc
la ricotta
o requeijão

butter / die Butter
la mantequilla / le beurre
il burro / a manteiga

MILK / DIE MILCH / LA LECHE / LE LAIT / IL LATTE / O LEITE

cow's milk / die Kuhmilch / la leche de vaca / le lait de vache
il latte di mucca / o leite de vaca

whole milk / die Vollmilch
la leche entera / le lait entier
il latte intero / o leite gordo

skim milk / die Magermilch
la leche desnatada / le lait écrémé
latte scremato / o leite desnatado

reduced-fat milk
die fettreduzierte Milch
la leche descremada
le lait allégé
il latte ridotto
o leite magro

buttermilk / die Buttermilch
el suero de leche / le babeurre
il latticello / o soro de leite coalhado

condensed milk
die Kondensmilch
la leche condensada
le lait concentré
il latte condensato
o leite condensado

powdered milk
das Milchpulver
la leche en polvo
le lait en poudre
il latte in polvere
o leite em pó

evaporated milk
die evaporierte Milch
el leche evaporada
le lait évaporé
il latte evaporato
o leite evaporado

soy milk
die Sojamilch
la leche de soja
le lait de soja
il latte di soia
o leite de soja

coconut milk
die Kokosnussmilch
la leche de coco
le lait de coco
il latte di cocco
o leite de coco

whipped cream / die
Schlagsahne / la crema
batida / la crème fouettée
la panna montata
o chantilly

sour cream / die saure
Sahne / la crema agria
la crème aigre / la panna
acida / as natas ácidas

yogurt / der Joghurt
el yogurt / le yaourt
lo yogurt / o iogurte

free-range
Freilandhaltung / de corral
fermier / ruspante / criado
no campo

pasteurized / pasteurisiert
pasteurizado / pasteurisé
pastorizzato / pasteurizado

homogenized
homogenisiert
homogeneizado
homogénéisé
omogeneizzato
homogeneizado

low-fat / fettarm
baja en grasa / faible en
matières grasses / a basso
contenuto di grassi / baixo
teor de gordura

margarine / die Margarine
la margarina / la margarine
la margarina / a margarina

ice cream / die Eiscreme
el helado / la glace
il gelato / o gelado

pat of butter / ein
Stück Butter / la porción
de mantequilla
la plaquette de beurre
il panetto di burro
o pedaço de manteiga

CHEESE / DER KÄSE / EL QUESO
LE FROMAGE / IL FORMAGGIO
O QUEIJO

soft cheese / der Weichkäse
el queso suave / le fromage
à pâte molle / il formaggio
morbido / o queijo mole

hard cheese
der Hartkäse
el queso duro
le fromage à pâte dure
il formaggio duro
o queijo duro

blue cheese / der Blauschimmelkäse
el queso azul / le bleu
il formaggio blu / o queijo azul

goat cheese
der Ziegenkäse
el queso de cabra
le fromage de chèvre
il formaggio di capra
o queijo de cabra

cream cheese / der Frischkäse
el queso crema / le fromage frais à tartiner
il formaggio cremoso / o queijo creme

EGGS
DIE EIER
LOS HUEVOS
LES ŒUFS
LE UOVA
OS OVOS

goose egg
das Gänseei
el huevo de ganso
l'oeuf d'oie
l'uovo d'oca
o ovo de ganso

egg white / das Eiweiß
la clara / le blanc d'oeuf
l'albume d'uovo
a clara de ovo

yolk / das Eigelb
la yema / le jaune
d'oeuf / il tuorlo
a gema

duck egg
das Entenei
el huevo de pato
l'oeuf de canard
l'uovo d'anatra
o ovo de pato

hen's egg
das Hühnerei
el huevo de gallina
l'oeuf de poule
l'uovo di gallina
o ovo de galinha

quail egg / das Wachtelei
el huevo de codorniz / l'oeuf de caille
l'uovo di quaglia / o ovo de codorniz

PANTRY ITEMS / DIE PANTRY-ITEMEN / LOS ARTÍCULOS DE DESPENSA
LES ELEMENTS DU GARDE-MANGER / I PRODOTTI DA DISPENSA
OS ITENS DA DESPENSA

vinegars / die Essige / los vinagres / les vinaigres
gli aceti / os vinagres

malt vinegar / der Malzessig
el vinagre de malta
le vinaigre de malt
l'aceto di malto / o vinagre de malte

white vinegar / der Weißweinessig
el vinagre blanco
le vinaigre blanc / l'aceto bianco
o vinagre branco

cider vinegar
der Apfelessig
el vinagre de sidra
le vinaigre de cidre
l'aceto di sidro
o vinagre de sidra

balsamic vinegar
der Balsamico-Essig
el vinagre balsámico
le vinaigre balsamique
l'aceto balsamico
o vinagre balsâmico

red wine vinegar
der Rotweinessig
el vinagre de vino tinto
le vinaigre de vin
l'aceto di vino rosso
o vinagre de vinho tinto

oils / die Öle / los aceites / les huiles / gli oli / os óleos

grapeseed oil/ das
Traubenkernöl / el aceite de
semilla de uva / l'huile de pépin
de raisin / l'olio di vinaccioli
o óleo de grainha de uva

walnut oil / das
Walnussöl / el aceite
de nuez / l'huile de
noix / l'olio di noce
o óleo de noz

olive oil / das Olivenöl
el aceite de oliva
l'huile d'olive
l'olio d'oliva
o azeite

sesame oil / das Sesamöl
el aceite de sésamo
l'huile de sésame
l'olio di sesamo
o óleo de sésamo

sunflower oil
das Sonnenblumenöl
el aceite de girasol
l'huile de tournesol / l'olio di
girasole / o óleo de girassol

extra-virgin / das Natives Öl extra
el aceite extra virgen / extra-vierge
extravergine / o extravirgem

cold-pressed / kaltgepresst
el prensado en frío / pressée à froid
spremuto a freddo / o extraído a frio

box / die Dose
la caja / la boîte
la scatola / a caixa

dried pasta / die getrocknete Nudeln
la pasta seca / les pâtes sèches
la pasta secca / a massa seca

tomato sauce
die Tomatensoße
la salsa de tomate
la sauce tomate
la salsa di pomodoro
o molho de tomate

canned foods / die Lebensmittel in
Dosen / los alimentos enlatados
la nourriture en conserve / i cibi in
scatola / os alimentos enlatados

can opener / der Dosenöffner
el abrelatas / l'ouvre-boite
l'apriscatole / o abre-latas

sweet spreads / die süßen Aufstriche / el dulce para untar
les douceurs à tartiner / le creme dolci da spalmare / as pastas doces

mason jar / das Einmachglas
el frasco / le bocal
il vasetto / o frasco de vidro

honey / der Honig / la miel
le miel / il miele / o mel

jam / die Marmelade
la jalea / la confiture
la marmellata / a compota

marmalade
die Marmelade
la mermelada
la marmelade
la marmellata / a marmelada

preserves / das Eingemachtes
las conservas / la confiture
le conserve / as conservas

honeycomb / die Honigwabe
el panal / le rayon de miel
il favo / o favo de mel

peanut butter
die Erdnussbutter
la mantequilla de maní
le beurre de cacahuète
il burro di arachidi
a manteiga de amendoim

hazelnut spread
der Haselnussaufstrich
la crema de avellana
la pâte à tartiner aux noisettes
la crema di nocciole
o creme de avelã

maple syrup
der Ahornsirup
el jarabe de arce
le sirop d'érable-
lo sciroppo d'acero
o xarope de ácer

bottle / die Flasche
la botella / la bouteille
la bottiglia / a garrafa

---

condiments / die Gewürze / los condimentos / les condiments / i condimenti / os condimentos

chutney
das Chutney
el chutney
le chutney
il chutney
o chutney

English mustard
der Englischer Senf
la mostaza inglesa
la moutarde anglaise
la senape inglese
a mostarda inglesa

French mustard
der Französischer Senf
la mostaza francesa
la moutarde française
la senape francese
a mostarda francesa

whole-grain mustard
der Vollkornsenf
la mostaza a la antigua
la moutarde
à l'ancienne
la senape integrale
a mostarda com grãos

mayonnaise
die Mayonnaise
la mayonesa
la mayonnaise
la maionese
a maionese

pickle relish
das Essiggurken-Relish
el pepinillo encurtido
le pickle relish
i sottaceti
os pickles agridoces

brown sauce
die braune Soße
la salsa marrón
la sauce brune
la salsa barbecue
o molho de carne

steak sauce
die Steaksauce
la salsa de bistec
la sauce barbecue
la salsa per bistecche
o molho para bife

hot sauce
die scharfe Sauce
la salsa picante
la sauce piquante
la salsa piccante
o molho picante

ketchup
der Ketchup
la cátsup
le ketchup
il ketchup
o ketchup

BREAD / DAS BROT / EL PAN / LE PAIN / IL PANE / O PÃO

bakery
die Bäckerei
la pastelería
la boulangerie
la panetteria
a padaria

boule
das Boule
la miche
la boule
la boule
a bola

crust / die Kruste
la corteza
la croûte
la crosta
a côdea

baguette
das Baguette
la baguette
la baguette
la baguette
a baguete

slice / die Scheibe / la rebanada
la tranche / la fetta / a fatia

loaf of bread / der Laib Brot
la hogaza / la mie de pain
la pagnotta di pane
o pão de forma

---

breadmaking / das Brotbacken / la panadería / la panification / la panificazione / o fabrico de pão

white flour	whole-wheat flour	brown flour	yeast
das Weißmehl	das Weizenvollkornmehl	das Schwarzmehl	das Hefe
la harina blanca	la harina de trigo integral	la harina integral	la levadura
la farine blanche	la farine de blé complet	la farine brune	la levure
la farina bianca	la farina integrale	la farina marrone	il lievito
a farinha de trigo	a farinha integral	a farinha castanha	o fermento

rise (v) / aufgehen
reposar / lever
lievitare / crescer

self-rising
selbstbackend
la harina preparada
auto-levant
a lievitazione
istantanea
com fermento

all-purpose flour
das Allzweckmehl
la harina común
la farine tout usage
la farina universale
a farinha para todos
os fins

breadcrumbs
die Semmelbrösel
las migas de pan
les miettes de pain
il pangrattato
as migalhas

sifter / der Sieben / el tamiz
le tamis / il setaccio / a peneira

sift (v)	knead (v)	prove (v)	bake (v)
sichten / tamizar	kneten / amasar	prüfen / fermentar	backen / hornear
tamiser / setacciare	pétrir / impastare	faire lever / provare	cuire / cuocere
peneirar	amassar	levedar	cozer

white bread
das Weißbrot
el pan blanco
le pain blanc
il pane bianco
o pão branco

rye bread
das Roggenbrot
el pan de centeno
le pain de seigle
il pane di segale
o pão de centeio

whole-wheat bread
das Vollkornbrot
el pan de trigo entero
le pain au blé complet
il pane integrale
o pão integral

multigrain bread
das Mehrkornbrot
el pan multigrano
le pain multi-céréales
il pane multicereali
o pão de cereais

pumpernickel
der Pumpernickel
el pan integral
le pain noir
il pumpernickel
o pumpernickel

soda bread / das Sodabrot
el pan de soda
le pain au bicarbonate de soude
il pane di soda
o pão irlandês

corn bread
das Maisbrot
el pan de maíz
le pain de maïs
il pane di mais
o pão de milho

pita / das Fladenbrot
la pita / le pain pita
la pita / o pão pita

naan / das Naan
el naan / le naan
il naan / o pão naan

bagel / der Bagel
el bagel / le bagel
il bagel / a rosca

bun / das Brötchen
el bollo / le petit pain
il panino / o pão

roll / das Brötchen
el rollo / le petite pain
il rotolo / o rolo

crisp bread / das Knäckebrot
el pan crujiente / la biscotte
il pane croccante / o pão fresco

sourdough bread
das Sauerteigbrot
el pan de masa madre
le pain au levain
il pane con lievito naturale
o pão de fermentação

flat bread / das Fladenbrot
el pan plano / le pain sans
levain / la focaccia
o pão plano

challah / das Challah
la challah / le pain challah
il challah / o pão challah

nut bread / das Nussbrot
el pan de nueces
le pain aux noix
il pane alle noci
o pão de nozes

DESSERTS / DIE DESSERTS / LOS POSTRES / LES DESSERTS
IL DESSERT / AS SOBREMESAS

pastry shop / die Konditorei / la pastelería / la pâtisserie / la pasticceria / a pastelaria

pastry cream
die Konditorei-Creme
la crema pastelera
la crème pâtissière
la crema pasticcera
o creme de pasteleiro

eclair / das Eclair
el eclair / l'éclair
l'eclair / o éclair

choux pastry / der Brandteig
la pasta choux / la pâte à choux
la pasta choux / a massa choux

icing / der Zuckerguss
el glaseado / le glaçage
la glassa / a cobertura

layer cake / der Schichtkuchen
el pastel de capas
le gâteau à étages / la torta
a strati / o bolo em camadas

meringue / der Baiser
el merengue / la meringue
la meringa / o merengue

cinnamon bun / die
Zimtschnecke / el rollo de
canela / le roulé à la cannelle
il panino alla cannella
o rolo de canela

phyllo / der Phyllo
la pasta filo / la pâte phyllo
il phyllo / a massa filo

mousse / die Mousse
la mousse / la mousse
la mousse / a mousse

rice pudding
das Reispudding
el arroz con leche
le riz au lait
il budino di riso
o arroz-doce

filling / die Füllung
el relleno / le fourrage
il ripieno / o recheio

puff pastry / der Blätterteig
el hojaldre / la pâte feuilletée
la pasta sfoglia
a massa folhada

crème caramel / das Crème Caramel
la crema de caramelo / la crème
caramel / la crème caramel / o pudim

ladyfinger / das Löffelbiskuit
el bizcocho de soletilla / le boudoir
il savoiardo / os palitos de champanhe

cookie / der Keks
la galleta / le cookie
il biscotto / a bolacha

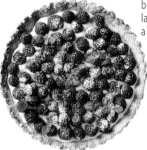

berry tart / der Beerenkuchen / la tarta de bayas
la tarte aux fruits rouges / la crostata ai frutti di bosco
a tarte de frutos silvestres

frosting
der Zuckerguss
el glaseado
le glaçage
la glassa
a cobertura

fruit pie / der Obstkuchen
el pastel de frutas / la tarte aux fruits
la torta di frutta / a tarte de fruta

cupcake / der Muffin / el bizcochito
le cupcake / il pasticcino / o queque

cream pie / die Sahnetorte / el pastel
de crema / la tarte à la crème
la torta alla crema / a tarte de natas

fruitcake / der Obstkuchen / la tarta de frutas
le gâteau aux fruits / la torta di frutta / o bolo de frutas

trifle / das Trifle
la bagatela / le diplomate
il tartufo / o trifle

brownie / das Brownie / el brownie
le brownie / il brownie / o brownie

chocolate cake / der Schokoladenkuchen
el pastel de chocolate / le gâteau au
chocolat / la torta al cioccolato
o bolo de chocolate

---

celebration cakes / die Festtagstorten / los pasteles de celebración / les gâteaux de fête le torte per le celebrazioni / os bolos de festa

top tier
die oberste Etage
la capa superior
l'étape supérieur
il livello superiore
a primeira camada

fondant / das Fondant
el fondant / la pâte à sucre
il fondente / o fondant

blow out (v) / ausblasen
soplar / souffler
soffiare / soprar

marzipan / das Marzipan
el mazapán / la pâte d'amandes
il marzapane/ o maçapão

bottom tier
die unterste Etage
la capa inferior
l'étape inférieu
il livello inferiore
a última camada

candles
die Kerzen
las velas
les bougies
le candele
as velas

wedding cake / die Hochzeitstorte / el pastel de bodas
le gâteau de mariage / la torta nuziale / o bolo de casamento

birthday cake / die Geburtstagstorte
el pastel de cumpleaños
le gâteau d'anniversaire / la torta di
compleanno / o bolo de aniversário

DRINKS / DIE GETRÄNKE / LAS BEBIDAS / LES BOISSONS LE BEVANDE / AS BEBIDAS

mineral water
das Mineralwasser
el agua mineral / l'eau
minérale / l'acqua
minerale / a água mineral

sparkling water
das Sprudelwasser
el agua con gas
l'eau pétillante
l'acqua frizzante
a água com gás

tonic
der Tonic
la tónica
le tonic
l'acqua tonica
a água tónica

still water / das
stilles Wasser
el agua sin gas
l'eau plate
l'acqua naturale
a água sem gás

club soda
das Sodawasser
la soda
l'eau gazeuse
l'acqua gassata
a água
gaseificada

tap water
das Leitungswasser
el agua de grifo
l'eau du robinet
l'acqua di rubinetto
a água da torneira

water goblet
der Wasserkelch
la copa de agua
le gobelet à eau
il calice d'acqua
o cálice de água

bottled water / das Wasser in Flaschen
el agua embotellada / l'eau en bouteille
l'acqua in bottiglia / a água engarrafada

soft drinks / die Erfrischungsgetränke / los refrescos / les sodas / le bevande analcoliche os refrigerantes

fruit juice / der Fruchtsaft
el jugo de fruta
le jus de fruit
il succo di frutta
o sumo de fruta

vegetable juice
der Gemüsesaft
el jugo de vegetales
le jus de légume
il succo di verdura
o sumo de vegetais

tomato juice
der Tomatensaft
el jugo de tomate
le jus de tomate
il succo di pomodoro
o suco de tomate

cola / das Cola / la cola
le coca / la cola / a coca-cola

orangeade / die
Orangenlimonade
la naranjada / l'orangeade
l'aranciata / a laranjada

lemonade / die Limonade
la limonada / la limonade
l'acqua limonata / a limonadas

milkshake
der Milchshake / el batido
le milk-shake / il frappè
o batido

smoothie / der Smoothie
el batido / le smoothie
il frullato / o batido

alcoholic beverages / die Alkoholische Getränke / las bebidas alcohólicas
les boissons alcoolisées / le bevande alcoliche / as bebidas alcoólicas

whiskey
der Whiskey
el whisky
le whisky
il whisky
o whisky

vodka
der Wodka
el vodka
la vodka
la vodka
a vodka

bourbon
der Bourbon
el bourbon
le bourbon
il bourbon
o bourbon

brandy
der Weinbrand
el brandy
l'eau-de-vie
il brandy
o conhaque

rum
der Rum
el ron
le rhum
il rum
o rum

gin
der Gin
la ginebra
le gin
il gin
o gin

rye
das Roggen
el whisky de centeno
le rye
la segale
o whisky

Scotch
der schottische Whisky
el Whisky escocés
le whisky écossais
lo scotch whisky
o escocês

tequila
der Tequila
el tequila
la tequila
la tequila
a tequila

liqueur
der Likör
el licor
la liqueur
il liquore
o licor

beer
das Bier
la cerveza
la bière
la birra
a cerveja

stout
das Starkbier
la cerveza negra
la bière brune
la stout
a cerveja preta

hard cider
der Apfelwein
la sidra
fermentada
le cidre
il sidro
a sidra

port
der Portwein
el oporto
le porto
il vino di porto
o vinho
do porto

sherry
der Sherry
el jerez
le sherry
lo sherry
o xerez

champagne
der Champagner
la champaña
le champagne
lo champagne
o champanhe

wine
der Wein
el vino
le vin
il vino
o vinho

BAR / DIE BAR / EL BAR / LE BAR / IL BAR / O BAR

beer tap
der Bierzapfhahn
el grifo de cerveza
la tireuse à bière
lo spillatore di birra
a torneira rápida

glasses
die Gläser
los vasos
les verres
i bicchieri
os copos

bartender
der Barkeeper
el barman
le barman
il barista
o barman

bottle
die Flasche
la botella
la bouteille
la bottiglia
a garrafa

dispenser
der Spender
el dispensador
le distributeur
il dispenser
o dispensador

bar counter / die Theke
la barra del bar / le bar
il bancone del bar / o balcão de bar

barstool / der Barhocker
el taburete / le tabouret de bar
lo sgabello / o banco alto

patron / der Gast
el cliente / le gérant
l'avventore / o cliente habitual

coaster
der Untersetzer
el portavasos
le dessous de verre
il sottobicchiere
a base para copos

cocktail shaker / der Cocktail Shaker
la coctelera / le shaker à cocktail
lo shaker da cocktail / a coqueteleira

stirrer / der Rührer
el agitador / le mélangeu
l'agitatore / o agitador

garnish
die Garnitur
la guarnición
la garniture
la guarnizione
a guarnição

measure / das Maß
la medida / le verre mesureur
la misura / a medida

tongs
die Zange
las tenazas
les pinces
le pinze
as pinças

cocktail / das Cocktail
el coctel / le cocktail
il cocktail / o cocktail

ice bucket / der Eiskübel
el cubo de hielo / le seau à glaçons
il secchiello per il ghiaccio
o balde de gelo

strainer / das Sieb
el colador / la passoire
il colino / o coador

rum and coke / der Rum
und das Cola / el cuba libre
le rhum coca / il rum
e coca / o Cuba Libre

scotch and water / der Scotch
und das Wasser
el whisky con agua
le whisky soda / lo scotch
e acqua / o whisky de malte

martini / der Martini
el martini / le martini
il martini / o martini

gin and tonic
der Gin und Tonic
el gin tonic / le gin tonic
il gin tonic / o gin tônico

white wine / der Weißwein
el vino blanco / le vin blanc
/ il vino bianco
o vinho branco

ale / das Ale / la cerveza
la bière / la birra / a cerveja

screwdriver
der Schraubenzieher
el destornillador
le vodka-orange
lo screwdriver / a vodka
com sumo de laranja

champagne
der Champagner
la champaña
le champagne
lo champagne
o champanhe

six-pack / das Sechserpack
el paquete de seis
le pack de bière
la confezione da sei
o six-pack

red wine / der Rotwein
el vino tinto / le vin rouge
il vino rosso / o vinho tinto

---

glassware / die Glaswaren / la cristalería / la verrerie / la cristalleria / os copos

rocks glass / die Steinglas
el vaso de tubo / le verre
à whisky / il bicchiere
da aperitivo
o copo de whisky

snifter / das Messbecher
la copa de brandy / le verre
à cognac / il bicchierino
o copo de balão

shot glass / das
Schnapsglas / el vaso de
chupito / le verre à shot
il bicchiere da shot
o copo de shot

cordial glass / das
Schnapsglas / el vaso de
grapa / le verre à cordial
il bicchiere da cordial
o copo cordial

pint glass
das Pintglas
el vaso de pinta
la pinte
il bicchiere da pinta
o copo de cerveja

wine glass
das Weinglas
la copa de vino
le verre à vin
il bicchiere da vino
o copo de vinho

flute / die Flöte
la copa flauta
la flute / il flute
o copo de
champanhe

cocktail glass
das Cocktailglas
la copa de coctel
le verre à cocktail
il bicchiere da cocktail
o copo de cocktail

highball glass
das Highball-Glas
el vaso alto
le grand verre
il bicchiere highball
o copo alto

CAFÉ / DAS CAFÉ / EL CAFÉ / LE CAFÉ / IL BAR / O CAFÉ

coffee / der Kaffee / el café / le café / il caffè / o café

sidewalk café / das Straßencafé / la terraza del café / la terrasse d'un café / il baretto / a esplanada

awning / die Markise / el toldo
le store / la tettoia / o toldo

waiter / der Kellner
el camarero / le serveur
il cameriere
o empregado de mesa

menu board / die Menütafel
el tablero del menú / le menu
il menu / a ementa

black coffee
der schwarze Kaffee
el cafe negro
le café noir
il caffè nero
o café preto

coffee with milk
der Kaffee mit Milch
el café con leche
le café au lait
il caffè macchiato
o café com leite

coffee shop / das Kaffeehaus / la cafetería
le café / il coffee shop / o café

coffee machine
die Kaffeemaschine
la máquina de café
la machine à café
la macchina da caffè
a máquina de café

steamed milk
die gedämpfte Milch
la leche al vapor
le lait mousseux
il latte caldo
o leite vaporizado

foam / der Schaum
la espuma / la mousse
la schiuma / a espuma

cappuccino / der Cappuccino
el cappuccino / le cappuccino
il cappuccino / o cappuccino

barista / die Barista / el barista
la barista / il barista / o barman

French press
die französische Presse
la prensa francesa
la cafetière à piston
la pressa francese
a prensa francesa

to-go cup / das Becher zum
Mitnehmen / la taza para llevar
le café à emporter / la tazza da asporto
o copo para levar

espresso / der Espresso
el espresso / l'espresso
l'espresso / o expresso

filtered coffee / der gefilterte
Kaffee / el café filtrado
le café filtre / il caffè filtrato
o café filtrado

iced coffee
der Eiskaffee
el café frío
le café glacé
il caffè freddo
o café gelado

carrier / der Träger
el portador / le porte-gobelet
il contenitore / a bandeja

sugar / der Zucker
el azúcar / le sucre
lo zucchero / o açúcar

artificial sweetener
der künstlicher Süßstoff
el edulcorante artificial
l'édulcorant artificiel / il dolcificante
artificiale / o adoçante

tea bag / der Teebeutel
la bolsita de té
le sachet de thé
la bustina di tè
a saqueta de chá

cocoa powder
das Kakaopulver / el cacao
en polvo / le cacao en
poudre / il cacao in polvere
o cacau em pó

TEA ROOM / DAS TEEZIMMER / LA SALA DE TÉ / LE SALON DE THE
LA SALA DEL TÈ / O SALÃO DE CHÁ

tea with lemon / der Tee mit Zitrone
el té con limón
le thé avec du citron
il tè con limone / o chá com limão

tea with milk / der Tee mit Milch
el té con leche / le thé avec du lait
il tè con latte / o chá com leite

black tea / der schwarze Tee
el té negro / le thé noir
il tè nero / o chá preto

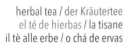

herbal tea / der Kräutertee
el té de hierbas / la tisane
il tè alle erbe / o chá de ervas

afternoon tea / der Nachmittagstee
el té de la tarde/ le thé de l'après-midi
il tè del pomeriggio / o chá das cinco

green tea / der grüne Tee
el té verde / le thé vert
il tè verde / o chá verde

macaron
die Macaron
el macarrón
le macaron
il macaron
o macaron

scone
das Gebäck
el bollo
le scone
la focaccina
o scone

chai / der Chai / el chai
le thé chaï / il chai / o chai

hot chocolate / die Heiße
Schokolade / el chocolate
caliente / le chocolat chaud
il cioccolato caldo
o chocolate quente

iced tea / der Eistee
el té frío / le thé glacé
il tè freddo / o chá gelado

finger sandwiches / die Finger-Sandwiches
los sándwiches mini / les petits sandwich
i tramezzini / as minissanduíches

RESTAURANT / DAS RESTAURANT / EL RESTAURANTE / LE RESTAURANT
IL RISTORANTE / O RESTAURANTE

seating
die Sitzgelegenheiten
los asientos
les places assises
i posti a sedere
os assentos

chef / der Chefkoch
el cocinero / le chef
lo chef / o chef

table setting
das Tischgedeck / la mesa
le dressage de table
l'apparecchiatura
as mesas

sous chef / der Sous-Chef
el sous chef / le sous-chef
il sous chef / o subchefe

wine list / die Weinkarte
la carta de vinos
la carte des vins
i carta dei vini
a carta de vinhos

maître d' / der Maître d'
el maitre / le maître d'hôtel
il maître / o mestre de

server / der Kellner
el mesero
le serveur
il cameriere
o empregado
de mesa

busser / der Kellner
el busser / l'aide-serveur
il cameriere / o ajudante

dishwasher
der Geschirrspüler
el lavavajillas
le lave-vaisselle
il lavapiatti
o lava-louças

menu
die Speisekarte
el menú
le menu
il menu
a ementa

tray / das Tablett
la bandeja
le plateau
il vassoio
o tabuleiro

order (v) / bestellen / pedir
commander / ordinare / pedir

receipt / der Beleg / el recibo
le reçu / la ricevuta / o recibo

dine (v) / speisen / cenar
diner / cenare / jantar

pay (v) / bezahlen / pagar
payer / pagare / pagar

tip / das Trinkgeld / la propina
le pourboire / la mancia / a gorjeta

buffet / das Buffet / el buffet
le buffet / il buffet / o bufê

child's meal / die Mahlzeit für Kinder
la comida para niños / le menu
enfant / il piatto per bambini
a refeição infantil

dessert cart / der Dessertwagen
el carrito de postres / le chariot
des desserts / il carrello dei dolci
o carrinho de sobremesas

courses / die Gänge / los platos / les plats / le portate / os pratos

apéritif / die Aperitif
el aperitivo / l'apéritif
l'aperitivo / o aperitivo

appetizer / die Vorspeise
la entrada / la mise
en bouche / l'antipasto
o aperitivo

soup / die Suppe / la sopa
la soupe / la zuppa / a sopa

side order / das
Nebengericht
el acompañamiento
l'accompagnement
il contorno
o acompanhamento

entrée / das Hauptgericht / el plato
fuerte / l'entrée / l'entrée / a entrada

salad / der Salat / la ensalada
la salade / l'insalata / a salada

dessert / die Nachspeise / el postre
le dessert / il dessert / a sobremesa

price / der Preis / el precio / le prix
il prezzo / o preço

specials / die Sonderangebote
los especiales / les spécialités
le offerte speciali / os especiais

family-style / das Familiengericht
al estilo familiar / à partager
familiare / familiar

service charge included / Inklusive
Servicegebühr / con propina
incluida / service inclus / il servizio
incluso / taxa de serviço incluída

service charge not included
Servicegebühr nicht inbe-griffen
sin propina incluida / service non
inclus / il servizio non incluso / taxa
de serviço não incluída

check / die Rechnung / la cuenta
l'addition / l'assegno / a conta

A table for two, please. / Einen Tisch
für zwei Perso-nen, bitte. / Una
mesa para dos, por favor. / Une
table pour deux, s'il vous plait. / Un
tavolo per due, per favore. / Queria
uma mesa para duas pessoas.

May I see the menu, please?
Darf ich bitte die Speisekar-te sehen?
¿Puedo ver el menú, por favor?
Pourrais-je vois le menu s'il vous
plait ? / Posso avere il menu, per
favore? / Poderia ver a ementa?

May I have the check, please?
Kann ich bitte die Rech-nung
haben? / ¿Me puede traer la
cuenta, por favor? / Pourrais-je avoir
l'addition s'il vous plait ?
Posso avere il conto, per favore?
A conta, por favor.

DELICATESSEN / DIE DELICATESSEN / LA CHARCUTERÍA / LA CHARCUTERIE LA GASTRONOMIA / A CHARCUTARIA

sandwich counter / die Sandwich-Theke / el mostrador de sándwiches
le bar à sandwich / il banco dei panini / o balcão de sanduíches

pickle
die Essiggurken
el pepinillo
le cornichon
il sottaceto
o pickle

pastrami sandwich
das Pastrami-Sandwich
el sándwich de pastrami
le sandwich au pastrami
il panino al pastrami
a sanduíche de pastrami

bologna / die Bologna
la mortadela / le saucisson italien
la mortadella / a mortadela

submarine sandwich / das Submarine-Sandwich
el sándwich submarino / le sandwich baguette
il panino macinino / a sanduíche submarino

caper / die Kapern
la alcaparra / les câpres
il cappero / a alcaparra

lox and bagel / der Lachs und
Bagel / el bagel con salmón
ahumado / du saumon fumé
dans un bagel / il salmone
affumicato e bagel / o bagel
de salmão e queijo creme

cold cuts / der Aufschnitt / los embutidos
la charcuterie / i salumi / os frios

dry sausage / die trockene Wurst
la salchicha seca / la saucisse sèche
la salsiccia secca / a chouriça

prosciutto
der Prosciutto
el prosciutto
le prosciutto
il prosciutto
o presunto

chorizo / die Chorizo / el chorizo
le chorizo / il chorizo / o chouriço

salami / die Salami / el salami / le salami / il salame / o salame

per pound / pro Pfund / por libra
au poids / per libbra / ao quilo

in brine / in Salzlake / en salmuera
en morceaux / in salamoia
em salmoura

marinated / mariniert / marinado
mariné / marinato / marinado

cured / gepökelt / curado / salé
stagionato / curado

smoked / geräuchert / ahumado
fumé / affumicato / fumado

in oil / in Öl / en aceite / conservé
dans l'huile / in olio / em óleo

caterer / der Caterer / el camarero
le traiteur / il ristoratore / o caterer

Please take a number. / Bitte
wählen Sie eine Zahl. / Por favor,
tome un número. / Veuillez prendre
un numéro. / Per favore, prenda un
numero. / Por favor, tire uma senha.

meat slicer / die Aufschnittmaschine
la cortadora de carne / la trancheuse à jambon
l'affettatrice / a fiambreira

smoked fish
der geräucherte Fisch
el pescado ahumado
le poisson fumé
il pesce affumicato
o peixe defumado

olives / die Oliven / las aceitunas
les olives / le olive / as azeitonas

pâté / die Pastete
el paté / le pâté
il paté / o paté

Manchego / der Manchego
el queso manchego / le Manchego
il Manchego / o Manchego

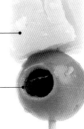

stuffed olive / die gefüllte Olive
la aceituna rellena / l'olive farcie
l'oliva ripiena / a azeitona recheada

Cheddar / der Cheddar
el queso cheddar
le cheddar / il cheddar
o cheddar

mozzarella
der Mozzarella
el queso mozzarella
la mozzarella
la mozzarella
o mozzarella

Camembert
der Camembert
el queso camembert
le Camembert
il Camembert
o Camembert

hors d'oeuvres
das Hors d'oeuvre
los entremeses
le hors d'oeuvre
gli antipasti / os canapés

Parmesan / der Parmesan
el queso parmesano
le Parmesan
il Parmigiano / o Parmesão

Brie / der Brie
el queso brie / le Brie
il Brie / o Brie

Edam / der Edamer
el queso edam / l'Edam
l'Edam / o Edam

Gouda / der Gouda
el queso gouda / le Gouda
il Gouda / o Gouda

FAST FOOD RESTAURANT / DAS SCHNELLRESTAURANT
EL RESTAURANTE DE COMIDA RÁPIDA / LE FAST-FOOD
IL RISTORANTE FAST FOOD / O RESTAURANTE DE FAST FOOD

soft drink
das Erfrischungsgetränk
el refresco / le soda
la bevanda analcolica
o refrigerante

straw / der Strohhalm
la pajita / la paille
la cannuccia / a palhinha

cheeseburger
der Cheeseburger
la hamburguesa
con queso
le cheeseburger
il cheeseburger
o cheeseburger

bun / das Brötchen / el bollo
le pain / il panino / o pão

french fries
die Pommes frites
las papas a la francesa
les frites / le patatine fritte
as batatas fritas

take-out
zum Mitnehmen
para llevar / à emporter
l'asporto / para levar

fish and chips / das Fish and Chips
el pescado y las papas fritas / le fish
and chips / il fish and chips / os filetes
de peixe com batatas fritas

delivery / die Lieferung
la entrega / la livraison
la consegna / a entrega

pizza / die Pizza
la pizza / la pizza
la pizza / a piza

pizzeria / die Pizzeria / la pizzería
la pizzeria / la pizzeria / a pizaria

topping / der Belag
el ingrediente / la garniture
il topping / o topping

eat-in / hier essen / la cocina
comedor / sur place / mangiare
sul posto / comer em casa

reheat / aufwärmen / recalentar
réchauffé / riscaldare / reaquecer

chicken nuggets
die Chicken Nuggets
los nuggets de pollo
les nuggets de poulet
le crocchette di pollo
os nuggets de frango

fried chicken
das Brathähnchen
el pollo frito / le poulet frit
il pollo fritto / o frango frito

hamburger / der Hamburger
la hamburguesa / le hamburger
l'hamburger / o hambúrguer

chicken sandwich
das Hähnchen-Sandwich
el sándwich de pollo / le hamburger au
poulet / il sandwich di pollo
o sanduíche de frango

veggie burger / der Veggie-Burger
la hamburguesa vegetariana
le hamburger végétarien
l'hamburger vegetariano
o hambúrguer vegetariano

street food / das Straßenessen / la comida callejera / la street food / lo street food a comida de rua

falafel pita / die Falafel-Pita
la pita de falafel / les falafel
il falafel pita
o falafel com pão pita

hot dog / das Hotdog
el perro caliente
le hot-dog / l'hot dog
o cachorro-quente

pretzel / die Brezel
el pretzel / le bretzel
il pretzel / o pretzel

taco / der Taco / el taco
le taco / il taco / o taco

crepe / der Krepp
el crepé / la crêpe
la crepe / o crepe

döner kebab / der Döner
Kebab / el döner kebab
le kebab / il döner kebab
o döner kebab

fried squid / gebratener
Tintenfisch / el calamar frito
le calamar frit / il calamaro
fritto / o choco frito

bratwurst / die Bratwurst
la salchicha / la bratwurst
il bratwurst / a bratwurst

ketchup
der Ketchup
la cátsup
le ketchup
il ketchup
o ketchup

mayonnaise
die Mayonnaise
la mayonesa
la mayonnaise
la maionese
a maionese

mustard
der Senf
la mostaza
la moutarde
la senape
a mostarda

street vendor / der Straßenhändler / el vendedor
ambulante / le vendeur ambulant
il venditore ambulante / o vendedor de rua

MEALS / DIE ESSEN / LAS COMIDAS / LES REPAS / I PASTI / AS REFEIÇÕES

BREAKFAST / DAS FRÜHSTÜCK / EL DESAYUNO / LE PETIT-DÉJEUNER
LA COLAZIONE / O PEQUENO-ALMOÇO

beans / die Bohnen / los frijoles
les haricots / i fagioli / os feijões

egg / das Ei / el huevo
l'oeuf / l'uovo / o ovo

fried tomato
die gebratene Tomate
el tomate frito
la tomate cuite
il pomodoro fritto
o tomate frito

bacon / der Speck
el tocino / le bacon
la pancetta / o bacon

mushroom
der Champignon
el hongo
les champignons
i funghi / o cogumelo

sausage / die Wurst
la salchicha / la saucisse
la salsiccia / a salsicha

black pudding / die Blutwurst
la morcilla / le boudin noir
il sanguinaccio / a morcela

English breakfast / das englisches Frühstück / el desayuno inglés
le petit-déjeuner anglais / la colazione all'inglese / o pequeno-almoço inglês

cooking methods / die Kochmethoden / los métodos de cocción / les méthodes de cuisson
i metodi di cottura / as técnicas de cozinha

fried egg / das Spiegele
el huevo frito / l'oeuf au plat
l'uovo fritto / o ovo estrelado

poached egg / dem pochiertem Ei
el huevo escalfado / l'œuf poché
l'uovo in camicia / o ovo escalfado

soft-boiled egg
das weichgekochtes Ei
el huevo pasado por agua
l'oeuf mollet
l'uovo alla coque
o ovo escaldado

hard-boiled egg
das hartgekochtes Ei
el huevo duro
l'oeuf dur
l'uovo sodo
o ovo cozido

omelet / das Omelett
la tortilla / l'omelette
l'omelette / a omelete

baked eggs / die gebackene Eier
los huevos horneados / l'oeuf cuit au four
le uova al forno / os ovos assados

scrambled egg / das Rührei
el huevo revuelto / les oeufs brouillés
l'uovo strapazzato / o ovo mexido

cereal / das Müsli / el cereal
les céréales / i cereali / os cereais

pancakes / der Pfannkuchen
los panqueques / les pancakes
le frittelle / as panquecas

waffle / die Waffel / el gofre
la gaufre / il waffle / o waffle

oatmeal / die Haferflocken
la avena / les flocons d'avoine
la farina d'avena / as papas de aveia

kippers / die Bücklinge
los arenques / le hareng fumé
l'aringa / o arenque defumado

brioche / die Brioche
el brioche / la brioche
la brioche / o brioche

yogurt / der Joghurt / el yogurt
la yaourt / lo yogurt / o iogurte

croissant / das Croissant / el cruasán
le croissant / il croissant / o croissant

donut / das Donut / la rosquilla
le donut / la ciambella / o donut

fresh fruit / das frische Obst
la fruta fresca / le fruit frais
la frutta fresca / a fruta fresca

muffin / der Muffin / el muffin
le muffin / il muffin / o queque

toast / der Toast / la tostada
le toast / il toast / a torrada

danish pastry / das dänisches Gebäck
la pastelería danesa / le pain aux raisins
la brioche danese / os bolos

LUNCH / DAS MITTAGESSEN / LA COMIDA / LE DÉJEUNER / IL PRANZO / O ALMOÇO

sandwich / das Sandwich
el sándwich / le sandwich
il panino / a sanduíche

club sandwich
das Club-Sandwich
el club sándwich
le club sandwich
il club sandwich
a sanduíche club

open-face sandwich
das Sandwich
mit offenem Gesicht
el sándwich abierto
la tartine
la tartina
a sanduíche aberta

wrap / der Wrap
el burrito / le wrap
il wrap / o wrap

soufflé / das Soufflé
el soufflé / le soufflé
il soufflé / o suflê

meat pie / die Fleischpastete
el pastel de carne / la tourte
à la viande / il pasticcio di
carne / a tarte de carne

panini / die Panini
el panini / le panini
i panini / a panini

quiche / die Quiche
el quiche / la quiche
la quiche / a quiche

PREPARATION METHODS / DIE ZUBEREITUNGSMETHODEN
LOS MÉTODOS DE PREPARACIÓN / LES METHODES DE PREPARATION
I METODI DI PREPARAZIONE / OS MÉTODOS DE PREPARAÇÃO

grilled / gegrillt
a la parrilla / grillé
grigliato / grelhado

mashed / püriert
en puré / écrasé
purè / esmagado

pan-fried
/ in der Pfanne gebraten
frito en sartén / poêlé
in padella / frito na frigideira

deep-fried / frittiert
frito / frit
fritto / frito

in sauce / in Sauce
en salsa / en sauce
in salsa / com molho

stuffed / Gefüllt
con relleno / farci
ripieno / recheado

roasted /gebraten
asado / rôti
arrostito / assado

steamed / gedünstet
al vapor / cuit à la vapeur
al vapore / cozido

DINNER / DAS DINNER / LA CENA / LE DÎNER / LA CENA / O JANTAR

broth / die Brühe / el caldo
le bouillon / il brodo / o caldo

soup / die Suppe / la sopa
la soupe / la zuppa / a sopa

pasta / die Nudeln / la pasta
les pâtes / la pasta / a massa

stew / der Eintopf / el guiso
la ragoût / lo stufato / o estufado

curry / der Curry / el curry
le curry / il curry / o caril

roast / der Braten / el asado
le rôti / l'arrosto / o assado

pot pie / der Topfkuchen
el pastel de olla / la tourte
la torta salata / o empadão

meatballs / die Frikadellen
las albóndigas / les boulettes de
viande / le polpette / as almôndegas

cutlet / das Schnitzel / la chuleta
la côtelette / la cotoletta / a costeleta

stir-fry / der Rührbraten
el salteado / la poêlée
saltato in padella / o salteado

casserole / der Auflauf
la cazuela / la casserole
la casseruola / o guisado

pizza / die Pizza
la pizza / la pizza
la pizza / a piza

SCHOOL AND WORK

DIE SCHULE UND ARBEIT

LA ESCUELA Y EL TRABAJO

L'ÉCOLE ET LE TRAVAIL

LA SCUOLA E IL LAVORO

A ESCOLA E O TRABALHO

SCHOOL / DIE SCHULE / LA ESCUELA / L'ÉCOLE / LA SCUOLA / A ESCOLA

teacher / der Lehrer
el maestro / le professeur
l'insegnante / o professor

student / der Schüler
el estudiante / l'élève
lo studente / o estudante

white board
die weiße Tafel
la pizarra blanca
le tableau blanc
la lavagna bianca
o quadro branco

raise hand (v)
Hand heben
alzar la mano
lever la main
alzare la mano
levantar a mão

classroom / das Klassenzimmer / el salón de clases / la salle de classe / l'aula / a sala de aula

nursery school
die Kinderkrippe
la guardería / l'école
maternelle / l'asilo nido
o infantário

kindergarten / der
Kindergarten / el jardín
de niños / la crèche
la scuola materna
o jardim de infância

primary school
die Primarschule
la escuela primaria
l'école primaire
la scuola primaria
o ensino primário

secondary school / die
weiterführende Schule
la escuela secundaria
le lycée / la scuola secondaria
o ensino secundário

schoolgirl
die Schülerin
la alumna
l'écolière
la studentessa
a estudante

schoolboy
der Schuljunge
el alumno
l'écolier
lo scolaro
o estudante

uniform
die Uniform
el uniforme
l'uniforme
l'uniforme
o uniforme

education / die Bildung
la educación / l'éducation
l'educazione / a educação

preschool / die Vorschule
el preescolar / l'école
maternelle / la scuola
materna / a pré-primária

homeschooling
das Homeschooling
la educación en casa
l'enseignement à domicile
l'istruzione domestica
o ensino doméstico

special education
die Sonderpädagogik
la educación especial
l'éducation spécialisée
l'educazione di sostegno
a educação especial

schoolchildren / die Schulkinder
los escolares / l'écolier
gli scolari / os alunos

crossing guard / der Schülerlotse / el guardia
de cruce / l'agent municipal / l'assistente
all'attraversamento / o guarda de trânsito

cafeteria / das Cafeteria
la cafetería / la cafétéria
la mensa / a cantina

school lunch
die Schulspeisung
el almuerzo escolar
la cantine
il pranzo scolastico
o almoço

school nurse
die Schulkrankenschwester
la enfermera de la escuela
l'infirmière scolaire
l'infermiera della scuola
o enfermeiro

principal / der Schulleiter
el director / le principal
il preside / o diretor

subjects / die Fächer / las materias / les matières / le materie / as disciplinas

reading / das Lesen
la lectura / la lecture
la lettura / a leitura

spelling
die Rechtschreibung
la ortografía
l'orthographe / l'ortografia
a ortografia

writing / das Schreiben
la escritura / l'écriture
la scrittura / a escrita

arithmetic / das Rechnen
la aritmética
l'arithmétique
l'aritmetica / a aritmética

history / die Geschichte
la historia / l'histoire
la storia / a história

geography / die Erdkunde
la geografía
la géographie
a geografia / a geografia

sciences
die Naturwissenschaften
las ciencias / les sciences
le scienze / as ciênciaa

literature / die Literatur
la literatura / la littérature
la letteratura / a literatura

music / die Musik
la música / la musique
la musica / a música

art / die Kunst
el arte / l'art
l'arte / a arte

modern languages
die modernen Sprachen
las lenguas modernas
les langues modernes
le lingue moderne
as línguas modernas

physical education
die Leibeserziehung
la educación física
l'éducation physique
l'educazione fisica
a educação física

activities / die Aktivitäten / las actividades / les activités / le attività / as atividades

read (v) / lesen / leer
lire / leggere / ler

write (v) / schreiben
escribir / écrire
scrivere / escrever

question (v) / fragen
preguntar / poser une
question / domandare
perguntar

answer (v) / antworten
responder / répondre
rispondere / responder

discuss (v) / diskutieren
discutir / discuter
discutere / discutir

spell (v) / die Deutsche
el español / la française
l'italiano / o portugues

draw (v) / zeichnen
dibujar / dessiner
disegnare / desenhar

study (v) / lernen
estudiar / étudier
studiare / estudar

lesson / die Lektion
la lección / la leçon
la lezione / a aula

curriculum / der Lehrplan
el programa
le programme
il curriculum / a curriculum

learn (v) / lernen
aprender / apprendre
imparare / aprender

essay / der Aufsatz
el ensayo / la rédaction
il saggio / a composição

homework / die
Hausarbeit / la tarea
les devoirs / i compiti
os trabalhos para casa

semester / das Semester
el semestre / le semestre
il semestre / o semestre

school term / das
Schulhalbjahr / el término
escolar / le trimestre scolaire
il periodo scolastico
o período escolar

test / prüfen / el examen
le test / il test / o teste

grade / benoten
la calificación / la note
il voto / a nota

take notes (v)
Notizen machen
tomar apuntes
prendre des notes
prendere appunti
tirar apontamentos

supplies / das Zubehör / los útiles / les équipements / i materiali / o material escolar

blackboard / die Wandtafel
la pizarra / le tableau noir
la lavagna
o quadro-negro

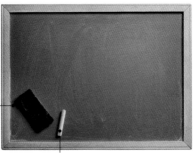

erase
das Radiergummi
el borrador
la brosse
la gomma
a borracha

chalk / die Kreide / la tiza
la craie / il gesso / o giz

textbook / das Lehrbuch
el libro de texto
le manuel scolaire
il libro di testo
o manual escolar

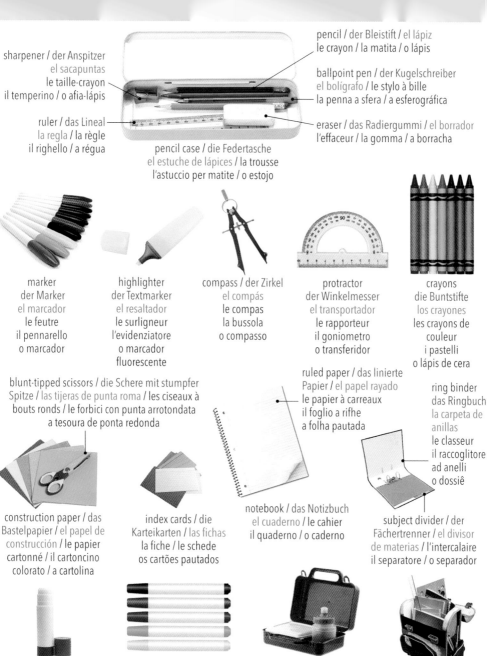

sharpener / der Anspitzer
el sacapuntas
le taille-crayon
il temperino / o afia-lápis

pencil / der Bleistift / el lápiz
le crayon / la matita / o lápis

ballpoint pen / der Kugelschreiber
el bolígrafo / le stylo à bille
la penna a sfera / a esferográfica

ruler / das Lineal
la regla / la règle
il righello / a régua

eraser / das Radiergummi / el borrador
l'effaceur / la gomma / a borracha

pencil case / die Federtasche
el estuche de lápices / la trousse
l'astuccio per matite / o estojo

marker
der Marker
el marcador
le feutre
il pennarello
o marcador

highlighter
der Textmarker
el resaltador
le surligneur
l'evidenziatore
o marcador
fluorescente

compass / der Zirkel
el compás
le compas
la bussola
o compasso

protractor
der Winkelmesser
el transportador
le rapporteur
il goniometro
o transferidor

crayons
die Buntstifte
los crayones
les crayons de
couleur
i pastelli
o lápis de cera

blunt-tipped scissors / die Schere mit stumpfer
Spitze / las tijeras de punta roma / les ciseaux à
bouts ronds / le forbici con punta arrotondata
a tesoura de ponta redonda

ruled paper / das linierte
Papier / el papel rayado
le papier à carreaux
il foglio a rifhe
a folha pautada

ring binder
das Ringbuch
la carpeta de
anillas
le classeur
il raccoglitore
ad anelli
o dossiê

construction paper / das
Bastelpapier / el papel de
construcción / le papier
cartonné / il cartoncino
colorato / a cartolina

index cards / die
Karteikarten / las fichas
la fiche / le schede
os cartões pautados

notebook / das Notizbuch
el cuaderno / le cahier
il quaderno / o caderno

subject divider / der
Fächertrenner / el divisor
de materias / l'intercalaire
il separatore / o separador

glue stick / der Klebestift
la barra de pegamento
le bâton de colle
la colla stick
a cola em bastão

dry-erase marker / der
Trockenlöschstift / el marcador
de borrado en seco / le feutre
effaçable à sec / il pennarello
o marcador para o quadro branco

lunchbox / die Brotdose
la lonchera
la boîte à repas
il cestino del pranzo
a lancheira

bookbag
die Büchertasche
la mochila / le cartable
la cartella / a mochila

UNIVERSITY / DIE UNIVERSITÄT / LA UNIVERSIDAD / L'UNIVERSITÉ / L'UNIVERSITÀ / A UNIVERSIDADE

lecture hall / der Hörsaal / la sala de conferencias
l'amphithéâtre / l'aula magna / o anfiteatro

professor / der Professor
el profesor / le professeur
il professore
o professor universitário

bachelor's degree
der Bachelorgrad
la licenciatura
la licence
la laurea di primo livello
a licenciatura

master's degree
der Master-Abschluss
la maestría
le master
la laurea magistrale
o mestrado

undergraduate / der Student / el estudiante
l'étudiant / lo studente universitario
o estudante universitário

tassel / die Quaste
a borla / le pompon
la nappa / a borla

doctorate
das Doktorat
el doctorado
le doctorat
il dottorato
o doutoramento

cap and gown
der Hut und Talar
la toga y el birrete
le costume
universitaire
il cappello
e la tunica
a toga e o capelo

diploma / das Diplom / el diploma
le diplôme / il diploma / o diploma

campus / der Campus / el campus / le campus / il campus / o campus

admissions office
die Zulassungsstelle
la oficina de admisiones
le bureau des inscriptions
l'ufficio accettazione
o gabinete de admissões

residence hall
das Studentenwohnheim
la residencia
la résidence universitaire
la residenza
a residência de estudantes

dorm room
das Wohnheimzimmer
el dormitorio / le dortoir
il dormitorio / o dormitório

dining hall / der Speisesaal
el comedor / le réfectoire
la sala da pranzo
a cantina

playing field / der Sportplatz
el campo de juego
le terrain de sport / il campo da gioco
o campo de jogos

health center / das
Gesundheitszentrum / el centro de
salud / le centre médical / il centro
benessere / o centro de saúde

student center / das
Studentenzentrum / el centro de
estudiantes / le foyer étudiant
lo studentato / o centro do estudante

schools / die Schulen / las escuelas / les écoles / le scuole / as escolas

art school / die Kunstschule
la escuela de arte / l'école
d'art / la scuola d'arte
a escola de artes

music school / die
Musikschule / la escuela
de música / l'école de
musique / la scuola di
musica / a escola de música

dramatic arts
die Schauspielkuns
las artes dramáticas
les arts dramatiques
le arti drammatiche
a escola de teatro

dance school
die Tanzschule / la escuela
de baile / l'école de danse
la scuola di danza
a escola de dança

departments / die Abteilungen / los departamentos / les départements
i dipartimenti / os departamentos

physics / die Physik
la física / la physique
la fisica / a física

economics / die Wirtschaft
la economía / l'économie
l'economia / a economia

political science
die Politikwissenschaft
la ciencia política / les sciences
politiques / le scienze politiche
a ciências políticas

philosophy
die Philosophie
la filosofía / la philosophie
la filosofia / a filosofia

engineering / die Technik
la ingeniería
l'ingénierie / l'ingegneria
a engenharia

adult education / die Erwachsenenbildung
la formación para adultos / la formation continue
la scuola serale / a educação de adultos

humanities / die
Geisteswissenschaften
las humanidades / les lettres
le scienze umane / as humanidades

college / die Hochschule
la universidad / l'université
il college / a universidade

fellowship / das
Stipendium / la beca de
investigación / la confrérie
la borsa di studio
a bolsa de estudo

scholarship / das
Stipendium / la beca
la bourse d'étude
la borsa di studio
a bolsa de mérito

student loan / das
Studentendarlehen
el préstamo estudiantil
le prêt étudiant
il prestito per studenti
o empréstimo para
estudantes

grant / das Stipendium
la subvención / la bourse
la borsa di studio / a bolsa

academic / akademisch
el académico / universitaire
l'accademico / académico

higher education
die Hochschulbildung
la educación superior
l'enseignement supérieur
l'istruzione superiore
o ensino superior

thesis / die Diplomarbeit
la tesis / la thèse / la tesi
a tese

dissertation / die
Dissertation / la disertación
le mémoire / la tesi di
laurea / a dissertação

graduation
die Graduierung
la graduación
la remise des diplômes
la laurea
a graduação

dean / der Dekan
el decano / le doyen
il rettore / o reitor

exam / die Prüfung
el examen / l'examen
l'esame / o exame

LIBRARY / DIE BIBLIOTHEK / LA BIBLIOTECA / LA BIBLIOTHÈQUE
LA BIBLIOTECA / A BIBLIOTECA

stacks
der Stapel
las pilas
les piles
le pile
a pilha

library card / der Bibliotheksausweis
la tarjeta de la biblioteca
la carte de bibliothèque
la tessera della biblioteca
o cartão da biblioteca

bookshelf
das Bücherregal
la estantería
l'étagère
lo scaffale
a estante

spine
die Wirbelsäule
el lomo
le dos
lo scaffale
a lombada

encyclopedia / die Enzyklopädie
la enciclopedia / l'encyclopédie
l'enciclopedia / a enciclopédia

ebook
das ebook
el libro
electrónico
le livre
électronique
l'ebook
o ebook

dictionary / das Wörterbuch
el diccionario / le dictionnaire
il dizionario / o dicionário

call number
die Rufnummer
el número de llamada
la cote / il codice
identificativo libro
o número de
referência

970.4
STO

library book / das Bibliotheksbuch
el libro de la biblioteca
le livre de bibliothèque
il libro della biblioteca
o livro da biblioteca

librarian
der Bibliothekar
el bibliotecario
la bibliothécaire
il bibliotecario
o bibliotecário

scan (v)
einscannen
escanear
scanner
scansionare
fazer o scan

check out (v)
ausleihen
sacar libros
emprunter
ritirare
fazer o
check out

book return / die Buchrückgabe
la devolución de libros / la boîte de retour
la restituzione del libro / a devolução do livro

circulation desk / die Ausleihtheke
el mostrador de circulación
le comptoir de prêt / lo sportello del
prestito / o balcão de atendimento

reading room / der Lesesaal / la sala de lectura
la salle de lecture / la sala di lettura / a sala de leitura

school library / die Schulbibliothek / la biblioteca
de la escuela / la bibliothèque scolaire
la biblioteca scolastica / a biblioteca escolar

book club / der Buchklub
el club de lectura / le club de lecture
il club del libro / o clube do livro

database / die Datenbank
la base de datos / la base de données
il database / a base de dados

story time / die Märchenstunde
la hora del cuento / l'heure de la lecture
l'ora della fiaba / a hora do conto

children's section / die
Kinderabteilung / la sección infantil
la section pour enfants / la sezione
bambini / a secção de criança

mobile library
die mobile Bibliothek
la biblioteca móvil
la bibliothèque mobile
la biblioteca mobile
a biblioteca móvel

reading list / die Leseliste / la lista de
lectura / la liste de lecture / la lista di
lettura / a lista de leitura

title / der Titel / el título / le titre
il titolo / o título

loan (v) / ausleihen / prestar / prêter
prestare / requisitar

reserve (v) / reservieren / reservar
réserver / prenotare / reservar

borrow (v) / ausleihen / pedir
prestado / emprunter / prendere
in prestito / pedir emprestado

renew (v) / erneuern / renovar
renouveler / rinnovare / renovar

due date / das Fälligkeitsdatum
la fecha de vencimiento / la date
limite / la data di scadenza
a data-limite

journal / die Zeitschrift
la revista / le journal
la rivista / a revista

periodical / die Zeitschrift
el periódico / le périodique
il periodico / a publicação periódica

reference / das Nachschlagewerk
la referencia / la référence
il riferimento / a referência

OCCUPATIONS / DIE BERUFE / LAS OCUPACIONES
LES METIERS / I LAVORI / AS PROFISSÕES

accountant
der Buchhalter
el contador / le comptable
il ragioniere
o contabilista

graphic designer
der Grafikdesigner
el diseñador gráfico
le graphiste
il graphic designer
o designer gráfico

editor / der Redakteur
el editor
le rédacteur en chef
l'editore / o editor

jeweler / der Juwelier
el joyero / le bijoutier
il gioielliere / o joalheiro

salesperson / der Verkäufer
el vendedor / le vendeur
il commesso / o vendedor

cleaner / die Reinigungskraft
el limpiador
l'agent d'entretien
l'addetto alle pulizie
o empregado de limpeza

gardener / der Gärtner
el jardinero / le jardinier
il giardiniere / o jardineiro

landscaper
der Landschaftsgärtner
el paisajista / le paysagiste
il paesaggista
o paisagista

electrician / der Elektriker
el electricista / l'électricien
l'elettricista / o eletricista

carpenter / der Schreiner
el carpintero
le charpentier
il falegname / o carpinteiro

plumber / der Klempner
el fontanero / le plombier
l'idraulico / o canalizador

repairperson
der Immobilienmakler
el agente inmobiliario
l'agent immobilier
l'agente immobiliare
o agente imobiliário

veterinarian / der Tierarzt
el veterinario
le vétérinaire
il veterinario / o veterinário

dog groomer / der
Hundefriseur / el peluquero
de perros / le toiletteur pour
chiens / il toelettatore
o cabeleireiro canino

dog walker / der
Hundeausführer / el paseador
de perros / le promeneur
de chiens / il passeggiatore
di cani / o passeador de cães

hairdresser / der Friseur
el estilista / le coiffeur
il parrucchiere
o cabeleireiro

soldier / der Soldat
el soldado / le soldat
il soldato / o soldado

sailor / der Matrose
el marinero / le marin
il marinaio / o marinheiros

pilot / der Pilot
el piloto / le pilote
il pilota / o piloto

security guard / der
Wachmann / el guardia
de seguridad / l'agent de
sécurité / la guardia di
sicurezza / o segurança

fishmonger
der Fischhändler
el pescadero
le poissonnier
il pescivendolo / o peixeiro

fisher / der Fischer
el pescador
le pêcheur
il pescatore
o pescador

computer programmer / der
Computerprogrammierer
el programador de computadoras
le programmeur
il programmatore
o programador informático

IT technician
der IT-Techniker
el técnico de TI
le technicien informatique
il tecnico informatico
o técnico de TI

realtor / der
Immobilienmakler
el agente inmobiliario
l'agent immobilier
l'agente immobiliare
o corretor

insurance
die Versicherung
el seguro
l'agent d'assurance
l'assicuratore
a seguradora

web developer
der Webentwickler
el desarrollador web
le développeur web
lo sviluppatore web
o desenvolvedor web

engineer / der Ingenieur
el ingeniero / l'ingénieur
l'ingegnere / o engenheiro

nanny
das Kindermädchen
el niñero / la nourrice
la tata / a ama

bus driver / der Busfahrer
el conductor de bus
le conducteur de bus
l'autista di autobus
o motorista de autocarro

taxi driver / der Taxifahrer
el taxista / le conducteur
de taxi / il tassista
o taxista

truck driver / der Lkw-
Fahrer / el camionero
le conducteur de camion
l'autista di camion
o camionista

OFFICE / DAS BÜRO / LA OFICINA / LE BUREAU / L'UFFICIO / O ESCRITÓRIO

office building / das Bürogebäude / el edificio de oficina
l'immeuble de bureaux / l'edificio per uffici / o edifício de escritórios

cubicle / die Kabine
el cubículo / le box
il cubicolo / o cubículo

conference room
der Konferenzraum
la sala de conferencias
la salle de conférence
la sala conferenze
a sala de conferências

water cooler
der Wasserspender
el enfriador de agua
la fontaine à eau
il dispenser
o dispensador de água

security / die Sicherheit
la seguridad / la sécurité
la sicurezza / a segurança

reception / der Empfang
la recepción / la réception
la reception / a receção

business lunch
das Geschäftsessen
el almuerzo de negocios
le déjeuner d'affaires
il pranzo d'affari
o almoço de negócios

business trip
die Geschäftsreise
el viaje de negocios
le voyage d'affaires
il viaggio d'affari
a viagem de negócios

business deal
der Geschäftsabschluss
el trato comercial
l'affaire
l'accordo d'affari
o acordo de negócios

meeting
die Sitzung
la reunión
la réunion
la riunione
a reunião

departments / die Abteilungen / los departamentos / les services / i dipartimenti
os departamentos

CEO / der CEO / el CEO
le PDG / il CEO / o CEO

sales department / die Verkaufsabteilung / el departamento de ventas / le service commercial il reparto vendite / o departamento de vendas

legal department die Rechtsabteilung el departamento legal / le service juridique / il dipartimento legale o departamento jurídico

accounting / die Buchhaltung la contabilidad / la comptabilité la contabilità / a contabilidade

marketing / das Marketing el marketing / le marketing il marketing / o marketing

receptionist
die Empfangsdame
la recepcionista
la réceptionniste
la centralinista
a recepcionista

customer service die Kundenbetreuung el servicio al cliente le service client il servizio clienti o apoio ao cliente

human resources das Personalwesen los recursos humanos les ressources humaines le risorse umane os recursos humanos

presentation
die Präsentation
la presentación
la présentation
la presentazione
a apresentação

minutes / das Protokoll las minutas / le compte-rendu / il verbale os minutos

report / der Bericht el informe / le rapporteur il rapporto / o relatório

agenda
die Tagesordnung
la agenda / l'agenda
l'agenda / a ordem
de trabalhos

payroll / die Gehaltsabrechnung la nómina / la masse salariale / il libro paga a folha de salários

salary / das Gehalt el salario / le salaire lo stipendio / o salário

company / das Unternehmen la empresa / l'entreprise l'azienda / a empresa

head office / der Hauptsitz la oficina central le siège social / la sede centrale / a sede social

regional office / das Regionalbüro / la oficina regional / la succursale l'ufficio regionale a sede regional

staff / das Personal el personal / le personnel / il personale / o staff

OFFICE FURNITURE / DIE BÜROMÖBEL / LOS MUEBLES DE LA OFICINA
LES FOURNITURES DE BUREAU / L'ARREDAMENTO PER UFFICIO
O MOBILIÁRIO DE ESCRITÓRIO

in-out tray / das Ein-/Ausgabefach
la bandeja de entrada y salida / la corbeille à
documents / il vassoio / o organizador de papéis

wall clock / die Wanduhr / el reloj de pared
l'horloge murale / l'orologio da parete
o relógio de parede

binder
der Aktenordner
la carpeta
le classeur
il raccoglitore
o dossiê

desk
der
Schreibtisch
el escritorio
le bureau
la scrivania
a secretária

personal organizer / der persönliche Organizer
el organizador personal / l'agenda personnel
l'organizer personale / a agenda pessoal

filing cabinet / der Aktenschrank
el archivador / le classeur à tiroirs
lo schedario / o arquivador

swivel chair / der Drehstuhl
la silla giratoria / le fauteuil de bureau
la sedia girevole / a cadeira giratória

kitchen area
der Küchenbereich
el área de cocina
l'espace cuisine
la zona cucina
a área de cozinha

drawer
die Schublade
el cajón
le tiroir
il cassetto
a gaveta

open plan / das Großraumbüro / el plan abierto
l'open space / il piano aperto / o plano aberto

home office / das Heimbüro / la oficina en casa
le bureau à la maison / l'ufficio domestico
o teletrabalho

remote meeting / die Fernbesprechung
la reunión remota / la réunion à distance
la riunione a distanza / a reunião à distância

supplies and equipment / das Material und die Ausrüstung / los suministros y el equipo
les fournitures et l'équipement / i materiali e le attrezzature / os materiais e o equipamento

shredder / der Schredder
la trituradora / le broyeur
il tritadocumenti
a trituradora

desktop organizer
der Schreibtisch-Organizer
el organizador de
escritorio
l'organisateur de bureau
l'organizer da tavolo
o organizador de secretária

wastebasket
der Papierkorb
la papelera / la corbeille
il cestino dei rifiuti
o caixote do lixo

staples / die Heftklammern / las grapas
les agrafes / le graffette / os agrafos

stapler / der Hefter
la engrapadora / l'agrafeuse
la cucitrice / o agrafador

letterhead
das Briefpapier
el membrete / le papier à
en-tête / la carta intestata
o cabeçalho impresso

clipboard / das Klemmbrett
el portapapeles
le porte-bloc / la cartellina
o bloco de notas com mola

sticky note / die Haftnotiz
la nota adhesiva / la note
collante / la nota adesiva
as nota adesiva

tape / das Klebeband
la cinta / le ruban adhésif
il nastro adesivo / a fita-cola

tape dispenser / der
Klebebandabroller
el dispensador de cinta
le dévidoir à ruban adhésif
il distributore di nastro adesivo
o dispensador de fita-cola

hanging file
die Hängemappe
los ficheros colgados
le dossier suspendu
il raccoglitore
o arquivo suspenso

box file / der Kastenordner
el archivo de caja / la boîte
à archives / la scatola dei
documenti / o arquivador

expanding file
der Schnellhefter
las carpetas clasificadoras
le trieur à soufflets
la cartella espandibile
o arquivo expansível

hole punch
der Locher / la perforadora
la perforatrice
la perforatrice / o furador

bulldog clip
die Bulldogklemme
el clip grande / la pince à dessin
la clip / o clipe dobrável

rubber band / das
Gummiband / la goma
elástica / l'élastique
l'elastico / o elástico

paper clip
die Büroklammer
el clip / le trombone
la graffetta / o clipe

thumbtack
die Reißnagel
la chincheta
la punaise
la puntina
o pionés

bulletin board / die Pinnwand / el tablero de anuncios
le panneau d'affichage / la bacheca / o quadro de avisos

COMPUTER / DER COMPUTER / LA COMPUTADORA / L'ORDINATEUR
IL COMPUTER / O COMPUTADOR

desktop computer / der Desktop-Computer
la computadora de escritorio
l'ordinateur de bureau / il computer fisso
o computador desktop

monitor / der Bildschirm
el monitor / l'écran
il monitor / o monitor

mouse / die Maus / el ratón
la souris / il mouse / o rato

tower / der Turm
la torre / la tour
la torre / a torre

mousepad / das Mauspad
la almohadilla / le tapis
de souris / il tappetino del
mouse / o tapete de rato

smartphone
das Smartphone
el celular inteligente
le smartphone
lo smartphone
o smartphone

USB cable / das USB-Kabel
el cable USB / la câble USB
il cavo USB / o cabo USB

keyboard / die Tastatur
el teclado / le clavier
la tastiera / o teclado

external hard drive
die externe Festplatte
el disco duro externo
le disque dur externe
l'hard disk esterno
o disco externo o portugues

thumb drive / der USB-Stick
la memoria USB / la clé USB
la chiavetta USB / a pen USB

social media / die sozialen Medien
las redes sociales / les réseaux sociaux
il social media / a rede social

scanner / der Scanner
el escáner / le scanner
lo scanner / o scanner

ink cartridge
die Tintenpatrone
el cartucho de tinta
la cartouche d'encre
la cartuccia d'inchiostro / o tinteiro

selfie
das Selfie
la selfie
le selfie
il selfie
a selfie

paper tray / das Papierfach
la bandeja de papel
le bac à papier / il cassetto della
carta / a bandeja do papel

hashtag
das Hashtag
el hashtag
le hashtag
l'hashtag
a hashtag

printer / der Drucker / la impresora
l'imprimante / la stampante / a impressora

tablet / die Tablette
la tablet / la tablette
il tablet / o tablet

Internet / das Internet / la Internet / l'Internet
Internet / a Internet

laptop / der Laptop / el portátil
l'ordinateur portable / il portatile / o portátil

menubar
die Menüleiste
la barra de menú
la barre de menu
la barra dei menu
a barra de menu

wallpaper
das Hintergrundbild
el fondo de pantalla
le fond d'écran
lo sfondo
o fundo de ecrã

toolbar / die Symbolleiste / la barra de herramientas
la barre d'outils / la barra degli strumenti / a barra de tarefas

text message / die Textnachricht
el mensaje de texto / le SMS
l'SMS / a mensagem de texto

emoji / die Emoji / el emoji
l'emoji / l'emoji / o emoji

tab / die Registerkarte / la pestaña
l'onglet / la scheda / o separador

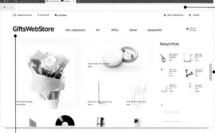

website / die Webseite
el sitio web / le site internet
il sito web / o website

online shopping
die Online-Shopping
las compras en línea
les achats en ligne
lo shopping online
as compras online

browser
der Browser
el navegador
le navigateur
il browser
o navegador

scrollbar
die Bildlaufleiste
la barra de desplazamiento
la barre de défilement
la barra di scorrimento
a barra de deslocamento

icons / die Symbole / los iconos
les icônes / le icone / os ícones

file / die Datei / el archivo
le fichier / il file / o ficheiro

folder / der Ordner
la carpeta / le dossier
a cartella / a pasta

trash / der Papierkorb
la basura / la corbeille
il cestino / o lixo

email / die E-Mail / el correo electrónico
l'email / l'email / o email

email address / die E-Mail-Adresse
la dirección de correo electrónico
l'adresse e-mail
l'indirizzo email / o endereço de e-mail

Wi-Fi / das WiFi / el wifi / le WiFi
il WiFi / o wi-fi

inbox / der Posteingang / la bandeja de entrada / la boite de réception
la casella di posta / a caixa de entrada

browse (v) / blättern / navegar
naviguer / navigare / navegar

connect (v) / verbinden / conectarse
se connecter / connettere / conectar

install (v) / installieren / instalar
installer / installare / instalar

service provider / der Dienstanbieter
el proveedor de servicios / le fournisseur
d'accès à internet / il provider di servizi
o fornecedor de serviços

log on (v) / anmelden / iniciar sesión
se connecter à / accedere / iniciar sessão

attachment / der Anhang / el archivo
adjunto / la pièce jointe / l'allegato
o anexo

download (v) / herunterladen / descargar
télécharger / scaricare / descarregar

MEDIA / DIE MEDIEN / LOS MEDIOS DE COMUNICACIÓN / LES MEDIAS I MEDIA / OS MEIOS DE COMUNICAÇÃO

TELEVISION / DAS FERNSEHEN / LA TELEVISIÓN / LA TELEVISION / LA TELEVISIONE / A TELEVISÃO

TV studio / das TV-Studio / el estudio de televisión / le studio de télévision / lo studio televisivo / o estúdio de TV

teleprompter
der Teleprompter
el teleprompter
le prompteur
il teleprompter
o teleponto

light
das Licht
la luz
la lumière
la luce
a luz

camera crane
der Kamerakran
la grúa para cámara
la grue de la caméra
la macchina da presa
o suporte de câmara

camera / die Kamera
la cámara / la caméra
la telecamera / a câmara

sound boom / der Tonarm / el boom del sonido
la perche / l'asta del microfono / o estrondo sónico

talk show / die Talkshow
el programa de entrevistas
le talk-show / il talk show
o talk show

host / der Moderator
el anfitrión
le présentateur
il conduttore
o apresentador

guest / der Gast
el invitado / l'invité
l'ospite / o convidado

programming / die Programmierung / la programación la programmation la programmazione / a programação

studio audience / das Studiopublikum / el público en estudio / le public sur le plateau pil ubblico in studio / a plateia de estúdio

series / die Reihe / las series la série / la serie / a série

repeat / die Wiederholung la repetición / la rediffusion la replica / a repetição

prerecorded / die Voraufzeichnung pregrabado / préenregistré preregistrato / pré-gravado

live / live / en vivo / en direct dal vivo / ao vivo

broadcast (v) / übertragen transmitir / diffuser / trasmettere transmitir

commentator / der Kommentator el comentarista / le commentateur il commentatore / o comentador

TV news / die TV-Nachrichten / las noticias de televisión / le journal télévisé
il telegiornale / as notícias da TV

reporter
der Reporter
el reportero
le reporter
il reporter
o jornalista

cameraman / der Kameramann / el camarógrafo
le caméraman / il cameraman / o operador de câmara

anchor / der Moderator
el presentador / le présentateur
il conduttore / o pivô

weather / das Wetter
el clima / la météo
il tempo / o clima

cable news / die Kabelnachrichten / las noticias por cable
la chaine d'informations du câble / il telegiornale
as notícias por cabo

interviewer
der Interviewer
el entrevistador
l'interviewer
l'intervistatore
o entrevistador

news van
der Nachrichtenwagen
la camioneta de noticias
le camion de télévision
il furgone delle notizie
o carro de reportagem

breaking news / die Eilmeldung
las noticias de última hora
le flash info
le notizie straordinarie
as notícias de última hora

chyron / das Chyron
el rótulo
le bandeau
il sovraimpressione
o chyron

JOURNALISM / DER JOURNALISMUS / EL PERIODISMO / LE JOURNALISME
IL GIORNALISMO / O JORNALISMO

magazine / das Magazin
la revista / le magazine
la rivista / a revista

newspaper / die Zeitung
el periódico / le journal
il giornale / o jornal

newsroom / der Redaktion / el cuarto de noticias
la salle de rédaction / la sala stampa / a sala de redação

press / die Presse / la prensa
la presse / la stampa / a imprensa

editorial / der Leitartikel / el artículo
de fondo / l'éditorial / l'editoriale
o editorial

column / die Rubrik / la columna
la rubrique / la colonna / a coluna

edition / die Auflage / la edición
l'édition / l'edizione / a edição

op-ed / die Meinungsseite
el artículo de opinión / la tribune
libre / l'op-ed / o editorial

masthead / das Impressum / la
cabecera / l'ours / la testata / o título

headline / die Schlagzeile
el encabezado / le gros titre
il titolo / a manchete

byline / die Schlagzeile / la firma
la signature / il sottotitolo
a assinatura

PUBLISHING / DAS VERLAG / EL MUNDO EDITORIAL / LA PUBLICATION L'EDITORIA / A INDÚSTRIA EDITORIAL

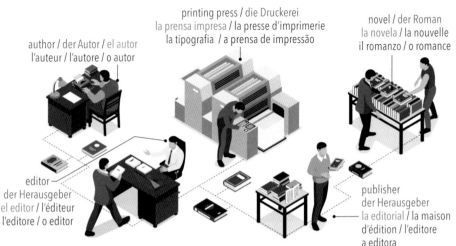

author / der Autor / el autor
l'auteur / l'autore / o autor

printing press / die Druckerei
la prensa impresa / la presse d'imprimerie
la tipografia / a prensa de impressão

novel / der Roman
la novela / la nouvelle
il romanzo / o romance

editor
der Herausgeber
el editor / l'éditeur
l'editore / o editor

publisher
der Herausgeber
la editorial / la maison
d'édition / l'editore
a editora

genres / die Genres / los géneros / les genres / i generi / os gêneros

fantasy / das Fantasy
la fantasía / le fantastique
il fantasy / a fantasia

sci-fi / die Science-Fiction
la ciencia ficción
la science-fiction
la fantascienza
a ficção científica

romance
der Liebesroman
el romance / le roman
d'amour / il romanzo
o romance

graphic novel
das Graphic Novel
la novela gráfica / la bande
dessinée / il fumetto
o romance gráfico

fiction / die Belletristik
la ficción / la fiction
la narrativa / a ficção

nonfiction / das Sachbuch
la no ficción
le documentaire
la saggistica / a não ficção

paperback
das Taschenbuch
el libro en rústica
le livre de poche
il libro in brossura
o livro de bolso

mystery / der Krimi
el misterio / le roman
policier / il mistero
o mistério

crime / der Krimi
el crimen / le polar
il poliziesco / o crime

classic / der Klassiker
el clásico / le classique
il classico / o clássico

RADIO / DAS RADIO / LA RADIO / LA RADIO / LA RADIO / A RÁDIO

radio station / der Radiosender / la estación de radio / la station de radio
la stazione radio / a estação de rádio

studio / das Studio / el estudio
le studio / lo studio / o estúdio

DJ / der DJ / el DJ / le DJ / il DJ / o DJ

control room
der Regieraum
la sala de control
la régie
la sala di controllo
o sala de controlo

headphones
die Kopfhörer
los auriculares
le casque
le cuffie
os auscultadores

microphone
das Mikrofon
el micrófono
le micro
il microfono
o microfone

mixer / der Mischpult / el mezclador / la table de mixage
il mixer / a mesa de mistura

on air / auf Sendung
al aire / à l'antenne
in onda / no ar

play list / das Playlist
la lista de reproducción
la liste de lecture
la lista di riproduzione
a lista de reprodução

station / der Sender
la estación / la station
la stazione / a estação

radio / das Radio / la radio
la radio / la radio / o rádio

recording studio
das Tonstudio
el estudio de
grabación / le studio
d'enregistrement
lo studio di registrazione
o estúdio de gravação

sound technician
der Tontechniker
el técnico de sonido
le preneur de son
il tecnico del suono
o técnico de som

podcast / der Podcast
el podcast / le podcast
il podcast / o podcast

frequency / die Frequenz
la frecuencia / la fréquence
la frequenza / a frequência

analog / analog / análogo
analogique / l'analogico
analógico

digital / digital / digital
numérique / il digitale
digital

wavelength
die Wellenlänge
la longitud de onda
la longueur d'onde
la lunghezza d'onda
o comprimento de onda

short wave / die Kurzwelle
de onda corta / les ondes
courtes / l'onda corta
a onda curta

long wave / die Langwelle
de onda corta / les grandes
ondes / l'onda lunga
a onda longa

soundproof / schalldicht
el cuarto insonorizado
insonorisé / insonorizzato
à prova de som

volume / die Lautstärke
el volumen / le volume
il volume / o volume

tune (v) / einstellen
sintonizar / être à l'écoute
sintonizzare / sincronizar

LAW / DAS GESETZ / LA LEY / LA JUSTICE / LA LEGGE / O DIREITO

courtroom / der Gerichtssaal / la sala del tribunal / la salle d'audience / l'aula di tribunale a sala de audiências

bailiff / der Gerichtsvollzieher
el alguacil / l'huissier de justice
l'ufficiale giudiziario / o oficial de diligências

stenographer / der Stenograf
el taquígrafo / le sténodactylo
la stenografa / o estenógrafo

judge / der Richter / el juez
le juge / il giudice / o juiz

jury box/ die
Geschworenenbank / la tribuna
del jurado / le banc des jurés
il banco della giuria
o banco dos jurados

judge's bench / die Richterbank
el banco del juez / les juges
il banco del giudice / o lugar do juiz

witness / der Zeuge
el testigo / le témoin
il testimone / a testemunha

witness stand
der Zeugenstand
el estrado de los testigos
la barre des témoins
il banco dei testimoni
o banco da testemunha

jury
die Jury
el jurado
le jury
la giuria
o júri

defendant / der Angeklagte
el acusado / l'accusé
l'imputato / o réu

spectator / die Zuschauer
el espectador / l'audience
lo spettatore / o espetador

lawyer / der Anwalt / el abogado
l'avocat / l'avvocato / o advogado

attorney's table / der Tisch des Anwalts / la mesa del abogado
la table de l'avocat / il tavolo dell'avvocato / a mesa do advogado

gavel / der Hammer
el martillo / le marteau
il martelletto / o martelo

court clerk / der
Gerichtsschreiber
el secretario de la corte
le greffier / il cancelliere
o escrivão

prosecution / die
Staatsanwaltschaft
el enjuiciamiento
les poursuites / l'accusa
a acusação

defense / die Verteidigung
la defensa / la défense
a difesa / a defesa

verdict / das Urteil
el veredicto / le verdict
il verdetto / o veredicto

law office / die Anwaltskanzlei
la oficina de abogados
le cabinet d'avocat / l'ufficio legale
o escritório de advogados

client
der Klient
el cliente
le client
il cliente
o cliente

legal advice / die Rechtsberatung
el asesoramiento legal / le conseil juridique
la consulenza legale / a consultoria jurídica

suspect / der Verdächtige / el sospechoso
le suspect / il sospetto / o suspeito

criminal record / der Strafregister / los antecedentes penales
le casier judiciaire / il casellario giudiziale / o cadastro

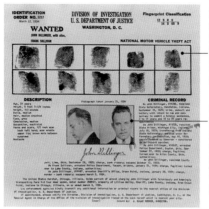

fingerprints
die Fingerabdrücke
las huellas dactilares
les empreintes digitales
le impronte digitali
as impressões digitais

mug shot
das Fahndungsfoto
la foto policial
la photo d'identité judiciaire
la foto segnaletica
o retrato

composite sketch / das Phantombild
el boceto compuesto / le portrait-robot
l'identikit / o retrato facial

cell
die Zelle
la celda
la cellule
la cella
a cela

arrest / die Verhaftung
el arresto / l'arrestation
l'arresto / a detenção

prison / das Gefängnis
la prisión / la prison
la prigione / a prisão

prison guard / der Gefängniswärter
el guardia de la prisión / le gardien de prison
la guardia carceraria / o guarda prisional

summons / die Vorladung
la citación / la convocation
la citazione
a convocatória

statement / die Aussage
la declaración
la déclaration
la deposizione
a declaração

warrant / das Haftbefehl
la orden / le mandat
il mandato / o mandado

writ / das Schriftstück
el mandato / le décret
il mandato / o decreto

plea / das Plädoyer
la súplica / le plaidoyer
l'appello / a alegação

court date / der Gerichtstermin
la cita en la corte
la date d'audience
la data del processo
a data de tribunal

case / der Fall / el caso
l'affaire / il caso / o caso

charge / die Anklage
los cargos / l'accusation
l'accusa / a acusação

accused / der Angeklagte
el acusado / accusé
l'accusato / o acusado

subpoena / die Vorladung
la citación / la citation à comparaître / la citazione in giudizio / a intimação

evidence / die Beweise
la evidencia / la preuve
la prova / a evidência

innocent / unschuldig
inocente / innocent
l'innocente / o inocente

guilty / schuldig
culpable / coupable
il colpevole / o culpado

acquittal / der Freispruch
la absolución
l'acquittement
l'assoluzione
a absolvição

sentence / das Urteil
la sentencia / la sentence
la sentenza / a sentença

bail / die Kaution
la fianza / la caution
la cauzione / a fiança

appeal / die Berufung
la apelación / l'appel
l'appello / o recurso

parole / die Bewährung
la libertad condicional
la liberté conditionnelle
la condizionale
a liberdade condicional

I want to see a lawyer.
Ich möchte einen Anwalt sprechen. / Quiero ver a un abogado. / Je veux voir mon avocat. / Voglio un avvocato. / Quero falar com um advogado.

POLICE / DIE POLIZEI / LA POLICÍA / LA POLICE / LA POLIZIA / A POLÍCIA

police officer
der Polizeibeamte
el oficial de policía / le policier
l'agente di polizia / o polícia

badge
die Dienstmarke
la insignia
le badge
il distintivo
o distintivo

bike cop
der Fahrradpolizist
el policía motorista
le policier à vélo
il poliziotto
in bicicletta
a bicicleta
de policía

police station / die Polizeiwache / la estación de policía
le commissariat / la stazione di polizia / a esquadra

radio / das Radio / la radio
la radio / la radio / o walkie-talkie

siren / die Sirene
la sirena / la sirène
la sirena / a sirene

handcuffs / die Handschellen
las esposas / les menottes
le manette / as algemas

police car / das Polizeiauto / el coche de la policía
la voiture de police / l'auto della polizia
o carro da polícia

crime / das Verbrechen
el crimen / le crime
il crimine / o crime

mugging / der Raubüberfall
el atraco / l'agression
lo scippo / el roubo

assault / die
Körperverletzung
el asalto / l'agression
l'aggressione / a agressão

burglary / der Einbruch
el robo / le cambriolage
il furto con scasso
o assalto

robbery / der Raubüberfall
el robo / le vol / la rapina
o roubo

complaint / die Beschwerde
la queja / la plainte
la denuncia / a queixa

captain / der Hauptmann
el capitán / le capitaine
il capitano / o comandante

detective / der Detektiv
el detective / l'inspecteur
il detective / o detetive

investigation
die Untersuchung
la investigación / l'enquête
l'indagine / a investigação

jail / das Gefängnis
la cárcel / la prison
la prigione / a prisão

riot gear / die Einsatzkleidung
el equipo antidisturbios
l'équipement anti-émeute
la tenuta antisommossa
o equipamento antimotim

shield
der Schild
el escudo
le bouclier
lo scudo
o escudo

gun
die Waffe
el arma
le pistolet
la pistola
a arma

baton
der Schlagstock
la batuta
la matraque
il manganello
o cassetete

FIRE DEPARTMENT / DIE FEUERWEHR / EL DEPARTAMENTO DE BOMBEROS
LES POMPIERS / I VIGILI DEL FUOCO / OS BOMBEIROS

hose
der Schlauch
la manguera
la lance
incendie
la manichetta
a mangueira

smoke / der Rauch
el humo / la fumée
il fumo / o fumo

fire / das Feuer
el fuego / le feu
il fuoco / o incêndio

boom
das Ausleger
el boom
la flèche
il braccio
a lança

water jet
der Wasserstrahl
el chorro de agua
le jet d'eau
il getto d'acqua
o jato de água

fire station / die Feuerwache
la estación de bomberos
la caserne
la caserma dei pompieri
o quartel dos bombeiros

basket / der Korb / la cesta
la nacelle / il cesto / o cesto

fire alarm
der Feuermelder
la alarma
de incendio
l'alarme incendie
l'allarme
antincendio
o alarme
de incêndio

helmet / der Helm / el casco
le casque / il casco / o capacete

fire extinguisher
der Feuerlöscher
el extintor / l'extincteur
l'estintore
o extintor de incêndio

hydrant
der Hydrant
el hidrante
la borne incendie
l'idrante
a boca de incêndio

ax
die Axt
el hacha
la hache
l'ascia
o machado

fire escape / die Feuertreppe
la escalera de incendios / l'issue
de secours / la scala antincendio
a saída de emergência

flashing lights / der
Blinklichter / las luces
intermitentes / les gyrophares
le luci lampeggianti
as luzes intermitenteso

ladder / die Leiter / la escalera
l'échelle / la scala / a escada

fire fighter
der Feuerwehrmann
el bombero / le pompier
il vigile del fuoco
o bombeiro

fire engine / das Feuerwehrauto / el camión de bomberos
le camion de pompiers / l'autopompa / o camião dos bombeiros

FARM / DER BAUERNHOF / LA GRANJA / LA FERME / LA FATTORIA / A QUINTA

outbuilding / das Nebengebäude
la dependencia / la dépendance
la dependance / o anexo

barn / die Scheune
el granero / la grange
il fienile / o celeiro

silo / das Silo / el silo
le silo / il silo / o silo

farmland
das Ackerland
la tierra de cultivo
les terres cultivées
il terreno agricolo
a terra de cultivo

field / das Feld
el campo / le champs
il campo / o campo

farmhouse
das Bauernhaus
la finca
la ferme
la cascina
a casa da quinta

farmyard
der Bauernhof
el corral
la cour de ferme
l'aia
o pátio da quinta

---

types / die Typen / los tipos / les types / i tipi / os tipos

dairy farm
der Milchviehbetrieb
la granja lechera
l'exploitation laitière
la fattoria del latte
a exploração leiteira

poultry farm
der Geflügelzuchtbetrieb
la granja avícola
l'élevage de volailles
l'allevamento di polli
a exploração avícola

crop farm
der Ackerbauernhof
la granja de cultivos
l'exploitation céréalière
l'azienda agricola
a exploração agrícola

sheep farm
die Schäferei
la granja de ovejas
l'élevage de moutons
l'allevamento di pecore
a exploração ovina

farmer / der Landwirt
el granjero / le fermier
l'agricoltore / o agricultor

pig farm
die Schweinefarm
la granja de cerdos
la porcherie
l'allevamento di maiali
a exploração suína

fruit farm
der Obstbauernhof
la granja de frutas
l'exploitation fruitière
l'azienda agricola della frutta
a fruticultura

vineyard / der Weinberg
el viñedo / le vignoble
il vigneto / a vinha

fish farm / die Fischfarm
la piscifactoría
la ferme piscicole
l'allevamento di pesci
o viveiro de peixes

crops / die Feldfrüchte / los cultivos / les cultures / le coltivazioni / as plantações

wheat / der Weizen
el trigo / le blé
il grano / o trigo

alfalfa / die Alfalfa
la alfalfa / la luzerne
l'erba medica / a alfalfa

barley / die Gerste
la cebada / l'orge
l'orzo / a cevada

scarecrow
die Vogelscheuche
el espantapájaros
l'épouvantail
lo spaventapasseri
o espantalho

bale / die Ballen / la paca / la balle / la balla / o fardo

hay / das Heu
el heno / le foin
il fieno / o feno

tobacco / der Tabak
el tabaco / le tabac
il tabacco / o tabaco

sunflower
die Sonnenblume
el girasol / le tournesol
il girasole / o girassol

corn / der Mais / el maíz
le maïs / il mais / o milho

tea / der Tee
el té / le thé
il tè / o chá

coffee / der Kaffee
el café / le café
il caffè / o café

cotton / die Baumwolle
el algodón / le coton
il cotone / o algodão

flax / der Flachs
el lino / le lin
il lino / o linho

sugarcane / das Zuckerrohr
la caña de azucar
la canne à sucre
la canna da zucchero
a cana-de-açúcar

rapeseed / der Raps
la canola / le colza
la colza / a colza

rice / der Reis
el arroz / le riz
il riso / o arroz

soy / die Soja
la soja / le soja
la soia / a soja

tractor / der Traktor / el tractor
le tracteur / il trattore / o trator

combine / der Mähdrescher / la cosechadora
la moissonneuse-batteuse / la mietitrebbia
a ceifeira-debulhadora

activities / die Aktivitäten / las actividades / les activités / le attività / as atividades

furrow
die Furche
el surco
le sillon
il solco
a leira

plow (v) / pflügen / arar
labourer / arare / aradar

plant (v) / pflanzen
plantar / planter
piantare / plantar

sow (v) / säen / sembrar
semer / seminare / semear

irrigate (v) / bewässern / irrigar
irriguer / irrigare / regar

harvest (v) / ernten / cosechar
récolter / raccogliere / colher

feed (v) / füttern / alimentar
nourrir / nutrire / alimentar

pesticide
das Pestizid
el pesticida
le pesticide
il pesticida
o pesticida

spray (v) / spritzen / rociar
pulvériser / spruzzare / pulverizar

milk (v) / melken / ordeñar
traire / mungere / ordenhar

livestock / der Viehbestand / el ganado / le bétail / il bestiame / o gado

lamb
der Lamm
el cordero
l'agneau
l'agnello
o borrego

foal
das Fohlen
el potro
le poulain
il puledro
o potro

sheep / das Schaf / la oveja
le mouton / la pecora / a ovelha

donkey / der Esel / el burro
l'âne / l'asino / o burro

horse / das Pferd / el caballo
le cheval / il cavallo / o cavalo

calf
das Kalb
el becerro
le veau
il vitello
o bezerro

pig / das Schwein / el cerdo
le cochon / il maiale / o porco

kid
das Zicklein
el cabrito
le chevreau
il capretto
o cabrito

cow / die Kuh / la vaca
la vache / la mucca / a vaca

bull / der Stier / el toro
le taureau / il toro / o touro

piglet / das Ferkel
el lechón / le porcelet
il maialino / o leitão

goat / die Ziege
la cabra / la chèvre
la capra / a cabra

chick
das Küken
el pollito
le poussin
il pulcino
o pintainho

duckling
das Entenküken
el patito
le caneton
l'anatroccolo
o patinho

rooster / der Hahn / el gallo
le coq / il gallo / o galo

chicken / die Huhn
el pollo / la poule
il pollo / a galinha

duck / die Ente
el pato / le canard
l'anatra / o pato

turkey / der Truthahn
el pavo / la dinde
il tacchino / o peru

trough / der Trog
el comedero / l'auge
la mangiatoia / a gamela

chicken coop / der
Hühnerstall / el gallinero
le poulailler / il pollaio
o galinheiro

sty / der Stall
la pocilga / la porcherie
il porcile / a pocilga

pen / der Stall / el corral
l'enclos / la penna / o cerco

stable / der Stall
el establo / l'écurie
la stalla / o estábulo

CONSTRUCTION / DAS BAUWERK / LA CONSTRUCCIÓN / LA CONSTRUCTION LA COSTRUZIONE / A CONSTRUÇÃO

construction site / die Baustelle / el sitio de construcción
le chantier / il cantiere / a obra

rafter / der Sparren / la viga
le chevron / la trave / o caibro

scaffolding / das Gerüst
el andamio / l'échafaudage
l'impalcatura / o andaime

lumber / das Bauholz
la madera
le bois de construction
il legname / a tábua

ladder / die Leiter
la escalera / l'échelle
la scala / a escada

lintel / der Sturz
el dintel / le linteau
l'architrave / o lintel

dumpster
der Müllcontainer
el contenedor de basura
la benne
il cassonetto
o contentor do lixo

pallet / die Palette / la plataforma
la palette / il pallet / a palete

brick / der Ziegelstein
el ladrillo / la brique
il mattone / o tijolo

frame (v) / rahmen / enmarcar
bâtir / incorniciare / projetar

girder / der Balken / la viga
la poutre / la trave / a viga

hard hat
der Schutzhelm
el casco
le casque de chantier
l'elmetto
o capacete de segurança

construction worker
der Bauarbeiter
el obrero de la construcción
l'ouvrier du bâtiment
l'operaio edile / o trolha

build (v) / bauen / construir
construire / costruire / construir

beam / der Balken / la viga
la poutre / la trave / a viga mestra

saw (v) / sägen / serruchar
scier / segare / serrar

materials / die Werkstoffe / los materiales / les matériaux / i materiali / os materiais

cement / der Zement
el cemento / le ciment
il cemento / o cimento

roof tile / der Dachziegel
la teja del techo / la tuile
la tegola / a telha

mortar / der Mörtel
el mortero / le mortier
la malta / a argamassa

cinder block / der
Schlackenstein / el bloque
de cemento / le parpaing
il blocco di cemento
o bloco de cimento

---

machinery / die Maschinen / la maquinaria / les machines / il macchinario / as máquinas

dump truck / der Kippwagen
el camión volquete / le tombereau
l'autocarro con cassone ribaltabile
o camião de descargas

bulldozer / der Bulldozer
el bulldozer / le bulldozer
il bulldozer / buldôzer

excavator / der Bagger
la excavadora / la pelleteuse
l'escavatore / a escavadora

cement mixer / der Zementmischer
la hormigonera / la bétonnière
la betoniera / a betoneira

roadwork / der Straßenbau / las obras viales / les travaux i lavori stradali / a obra na estrada

road roller
die Straßenwalze
el rodillo de camino
le rouleau
compresseur
il rullo compressore
o rolo compressor

asphalt
der Asphalt
el asfalto
l'asphalte
l'asfalto
o asfalto

resurfacing / die Erneuerung des Straßenbelags / la repavimentación
le resurfaçage / il rifacimento / o repavimentação

jackhammer
der Presslufthammer
el martillo neumático
le marteau-piqueur
il martello pneumatico
o martelo pneumático

cone
der Kegel
el cono
le cône
il cono
o cone

crane / der Kran / la grúa
la grue / la gru / a grua

LEISURE
DIE FREIZEIT
EL OCIO
LES LOISIRS
SVAGO
O LAZER

FILM / DER FILM / LA PELÍCULA / LES FILMS / IL CINEMA / O CINEMA

movie theater / das Kino / el cine / le cinéma / il cinema / o cinema

box office
die Kinokasse
la taquilla
le box office
il botteghino
a bilheteira

marquee
das Zelt
la marquesina
le fronton
il tendone
a tenda

poster / das Plakat
el póster / l'affiche
il poster / o cartaz

snack bar
die Snackbar
el snack bar
le snack
lo snack bar
o snack bar

popcorn / das Popcorn
las palomitas
e popcorn / il popcorn
as pipocas

lobby / das Foyer / el lobby / le hall d'entrée / l'atrio / a entrada

projectionist / der Filmvorführer
el proyeccionista
le projectionniste
il proiezionista / o projecionista

movie-goers / die Kinobesucher
los cinéfilos / le cinéphile
gli spettatori
o espetador de cinema

screen / die Leinwand / la pantalla / l'écran / lo schermo / o ecrã

genres / die Genres / los géneros / les genres / i generi / os géneros

comedy / die Komödie
la película de comedia
la comédie / la commedia
a comédia

drama / das Drama
la película de drama
le drame / il dramma
o drama

action / die Action
la película de acción
le film d'action / il film
d'azione / o filme de ação

adventure / das Abenteuer
la película de aventuras
le film d'aventure
l'avventura / a aventura

fantasy / das Fantasy
la película de fantasía
le film fantastique
la fantasia / a fantasia

horror / der Horror
la película de terror
le film d'horreur / il film
dell'orrore / o filme de terror

war / der Krieg / la película
de guerra / le film de
guerre / il film di guerra
o filme de guerra

romance / die Romanze
la película romántica
le film romantique
il film romantico / o romance

sci-fi / die Sci-Fi
la película de ciencia ficción
le film de science-fiction
la sci-fi / a ficção científica

thriller / der Thriller
la película de suspenso
le thriller / il thriller
o suspense

anime / das Anime
la película de anime
l'animé / l'anime
o anime

animated / der
Zeichentrickfilm / la película
animada / le film d'animation
il film d'animazione
o filme de animação

mystery / der Krimi
el misterio / le roman
policier / il mistero
o mistério

documentary
der Dokumentarfilm
el documental / le documentaire
il documentario / documentário

western / der Western
la película western
le western / il western
a western

soundtrack / das
Soundtrack / la banda
sonora / la bande son
la colonna sonora
a banda sonora

musical score / die Partitur
la partitura musical
la bande originale
la colonna sonora
a partitura do filme

THEATER / DAS THEATER / EL TEATRO / LE THÉÂTRE / IL TEATRO / O TEATRO

balcony
der Balkon
el balcón
le balcon
la balconata
o segundo balcão

box / die Loge
la taquilla / la loge
il box / o camarote

orchestra seats
die Orchesterplätze
los asientos
de la orquesta
les sièges
de l'orchestre
le sedie
per l'orchestra
os bancos
da orquestra

mezzanine
die Hochparterre
el entrepiso
la mezzanine
il mezzanino
o mezanino

seating / die Sitzplätze / los asientos / les sièges
le poltrone / os lugares sentados

row / die Reihe
la fila / la rangée
la fila / a fila

aisle / der Gang
el pasillo / l'allée
il corridoio / o corredor

curtain / der Vorhang / la cortina
les rideaux / il sipario / a cortina

stage / die Bühne / el escenario
la scène / il palco / o palco

wings / der Flügel
las alas / les coulisses
le ali / a coxia

set / das Bühnenbild
el set / le décor
il set / o cenário

backstage
Hinter der Bühne
el backstage
les coulisses
il dietro le quinte
os bastidores

spotlight
der Scheinwerfer
el foco
le projecteur
i riflettori
o holofote

stage door / die Bühnentür
la puerta del escenario
l'entrée des artistes
l'ingresso di scena
a porta privativa
dos artistas

orchestra pit
der Orchestergraben
el foso de la orquesta
la fosse d'orchestre
la buca dell'orchestra
o fosso da orquestra

actress
die Schauspielerin
la actriz
l'actrice
l'attrice
a atriz

actor
der Schauspieler
el actor
l'acteur
l'attore
o ator

script / das Drehbuch / el guion
le script / il copione / o guião

costume /das Kostüm / el disfraz
le costume / il costume / o traje

cast rehearsal / die Probe der Besetzung / el ensayo del
elenco / la répétition des comédiens / le prove / o elenco

director / der Regisseur
el director / le metteur en
scène / il regista
o realizador

stage hand / der Bühnenarbeiter
el utilero / le machiniste
il macchinista
o ajudante de teatro

ticket stub
der Kartenabriss
el boleto / le talon
la matrice del biglietto
o bilhete

opening night / der
Eröffnungsabend / la noche
de apertura / la première
la prima / a noite de abertura

producer / der Produzent
el productor / le producteur
il produttore / o produtor

I'd like two tickets for
tonight's performance,
please. / Ich hätte gerne
zwei Karten für die heutige
Vorstellung, bitte.
Me gustaría dos entradas
para la función de esta
noche, por favor. / Pourrais-
je avoir deux billets pour
la représentation de ce soir
s'il vous plait. / Vorrei due
biglietti per lo spettacolo di
stasera, per favore. / Gostaria
de comprar dois bilhetes
para a sessão de hoje.

intermission / die
Unterbrechung
el intermedio / l'entracte
l'intervallo / a interrupção

applaud (v) / applaudieren
aplaudir / applaudir
applaudire / aplaudir

audience / die das
Publikum / el público
le public / il pubblico
o público

program
das Programm
el programa
la programmation
il programma
o programa

performances / die Aufführungen / las actuaciones / les représentations
gli spettacoli / as sessões

sing (v) / singen
cantar / chanter
cantare / cantar

ballet / das Ballett
el ballet / le ballet
il balletto / o ballet

musical / das Musical
el musical / la comédie
musicale / il musical
o musical

opera / die Oper
la ópera / l'opéra
l'opera / a ópera

play / das Theaterstück
la obra de teatro / la pièce
de théâtre / lo spettacolo
teatrale / a peça de teatro

CONCERT / DAS KONZERT / EL CONCIERTO / LE CONCERT
IL CONCERTO / O CONCERTO

concert hall / der Konzertsaal / la sala de conciertos / la salle de concert / la sala da concerto / a sala de concertos

symphony orchestra / das Sinfonieorchester / la orquesta sinfónica
l'orchestre symphonique / l'orchestra sinfonica / a orquestra sinfónica

treble clef / der Violinschlüssel
la clave de sol / la clé de so
la chiave di violino
a clave de sol

bass clef / der Bass-Schlüssel
la clave de fa / la clé de fa
la chiave di basso
a clave de fá

staff / das Notensystem
el personal / la portée
il pentagramma / o staff

note / die Note
la nota / la note
la nota / a nota

notation / die Notation / la notación / la notation
la notazione / a notação

MUSICAL INSTRUMENTS / DIE MUSIKINSTRUMENTE / LOS INSTRUMENTOS MUSICALES
LES INSTRUMENTS DE MUSIQUE / GLI STRUMENTI MUSICALI / OS INSTRUMENTOS MUSICAIS

woodwind / die Holzblasinstrumente / los instrumentos de viento de madera / les bois
gli strumenti a fiato / os instrumentos de sopro de madeira

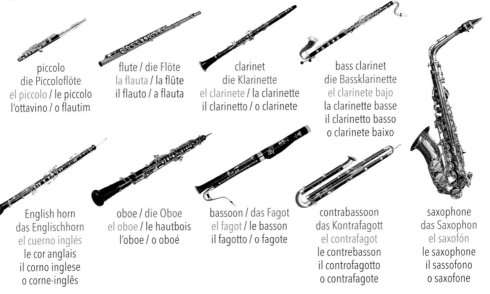

piccolo
die Piccoloflöte
el piccolo / le piccolo
l'ottavino / o flautim

flute / die Flöte
la flauta / la flûte
il flauto / a flauta

clarinet
die Klarinette
el clarinete / la clarinette
il clarinetto / o clarinete

bass clarinet
die Bassklarinette
el clarinete bajo
la clarinette basse
il clarinetto basso
o clarinete baixo

English horn
das Englischhorn
el cuerno inglés
le cor anglais
il corno inglese
o corne-inglês

oboe / die Oboe
el oboe / le hautbois
l'oboe / o oboé

bassoon / das Fagot
el fagot / le basson
il fagotto / o fagote

contrabassoon
das Kontrafagott
el contrafagot
le contrebasson
il controfagotto
o contrafagote

saxophone
das Saxophon
el saxofón
le saxophone
il sassofono
o saxofone

brass / der Blechbläse / los instrumentos de viento de metal / les cuivres l'ottone / os instrumentos de metal

trombone / die Posaune
el trombón / le trombone
il trombone / o trombone

trumpet / die Trompete
la trompeta / la trompette
la tromba / o trompete

French horn / das Waldhorn
el cuerno francés / le cor d'harmonie
il corno francese / a trompa

tuba / die Tuba
la tuba / le tuba
la tuba / a tuba

---

percussion / das Schlagzeug / la percusión / les percussions / le percussioni os instrumentos de percussão

kettledrum
die Pauke / el timbal
la timbale
il timpano / o timbale

cymbals
die Zimbeln
los platillos
les cymbales
i piatti / o címbalo

vibraphone
das Vibraphon
el vibráfono
le vibraphone
il vibrafono
o vibrafone

tambourine
das Tamburin
la pandereta
le tambourin
il tamburello
a pandeireta

gong / der Gong
el gong / le gong
il gong / o gongo

bongos
die Bongos
el bongó / les bongos
i bonghi / o bongó

snare drum
die kleine Trommel
el tambor / la caisse
claire / il rullante
o tambor de parada

maracas / die Maracas
las maracas
les maracas
le maracas
as maracas

keyboard
die Keyboard
el teclado
le clavier / la tastiera
o teclado

triangle / der Triangel
el triángulo
le triangle
il triangolo
o triângulo

fan / die Fächer
los fanáticos / les fans
il fan / os fãs

concert / das Konzert
el concierto / le concert
il concerto / o concerto

encore / die Zugabe / el bis
le rappel / il bis / o bis

overture / die Ouvertüre
la obertura / l'ouverture
l'ouverture / a abertura

sonata / die Sonate
la sonata / la sonate
la sonata / a sonata

pitch / die Tonhöhe / el tono
le ton / l'altezza / o tom

sharp / scharf / sostenido
perçant / il diesis / agudo

flat / flach / bemol / plat
il piatto / bemol

natural / natürlich / natural
naturel / naturale / natural

scale / die Skala
la escala / la gamme
la scala / a escala

conductor / der
Orchesterdirigent
el director de orquesta
le chef d'orchestre
il direttore di orchestra
o maestro

baton / der Taktstock
la batuta / la baguette
la bacchetta / a batuta

piano / das Klavier
el piano / le piano
il pianoforte / o piano

strings / die Streicher / las cuerdas / les cordes / le corde / os instrumentos de corda

bow / der Bogen
el arco / l'archet
l'arco / o arco

violin / die Geige
el violín / le violon
il violino / o violino

viola / die Bratsche / la viola
l'alto / la viola / a viola

cello / das Cello
el violonchelo / le violoncelle
il violoncello / o violoncelo

harp / die Harfe
el arpa / la harpe
l'arpa / a harpa

double bass
der Kontrabass
el contrabajo / la contrebasse
il contrabbasso / o contrabaixo

string / der Streicher
la cuerda / la corde
la corda / a corda

banjo / das Banjo / el banjo
le banjo / il banjo / o banjo

mandoline
die Mandoline
la mandolina
la mandoline
il mandolino
o bandolim

acoustic guitar / die Akustikgitarre
la guitarra acustica / la guitare
acoustique / la chitarra acustica
a guitarra acústica

amplifier / der Verstärker
el amplificador / l'amplificateur
l'amplificatore / o amplificador

tuning peg
der Stimmwirbel
la clavija de afinación
la cheville
la chiave
a cravelha

neck / das Hals
el mástil
le manche
il manico
o braço

pick / das Plektrum
la uñeta / le médiator
il plettro / a palheta

fret / das Bundstäbchen
el traste / la frette
il tasto / o traste

pickup / der Tonabnehmer
la pastilla / le micro
il pickup / o captador

bridge / der Steg
el puente / le chevalet
il ponte / a ponte

electric guitar / die E-Gitarre
la guitarra eléctrica / la guitare
électrique / la chitarra elettrica
a guitarra elétrica

bass guitar / die Bassgitarre / el bajo
la basse / il basso elettrico / o baixo elétrico

rock concert / das Rockkonzert / el concierto de rock / le concert de rock / il concerto rock / o concerto de rock

bassist / der Bassis
el bajista / le bassiste
il bassista / o baixista

drummer / der Schlagzeuger
el baterista / le batteur
il batterista / o baterista

guitarist
der Gitarrist
el guitarrista
le guitariste
il chitarrista
o guitarrista

lead singer / der Leadsänger
el cantante principal / le chanteur
il cantante / o vocalista

drum kit
das Schlagzeug
la batería / la batterie
la batteria / o kit
de bateria

musical styles / die Musikstile / los estilos musicales / les styles musicaux gli stili musicali / os estilos musicais

jazz / der Jazz
el jazz / le jazz
jazz / jazz

blues / der Blues
el blues / le blues
blues / blues

pop / der Pop
el pop / la pop
pop / pop

rap / der Rap
el rap / le rap
rap / rap

punk / der Punk
el punk / le punk
punk / punk

dance / der Tanz
el dance / la dance
dance / dance

folk / der Folk
el folk / la folk
folk / folk

country / der Country
el country / la country
country / country

choir / der Cho
el coro / le choeur
coro / coro

reggae / der Reggae
el reggae / le reggae
reggae / reggae

classical / die Klassik
la música clásica
le classique / la classica
a música clássica

song / das Lied
la canción / la chanson
la canzone / a música

lyrics / der Text / la letra
les paroles / il testo
a letra

melody / die Melodie
la melodía / la mélodie
la melodia / a melodia

OUTDOOR ACTIVITIES / DIE AKTIVITÄTEN IM FREIEN
LAS ACTIVIDADES AL AIRE LIBRE / LES ACTIVITES EN EXTERIEUR
LE ATTIVITÀ ALL'APERTO / AS ATIVIDADES AO AR LIVRE

park / der Park
el parque / le parc
il parco / o parque

street lamp / die Straßenlaterne
la farola / le lampadaire
il lampione / o poste de
iluminação pública

bench / die Bank / el banco
le banc / la panchina / o banco

footpath / der Fußweg / el sendero
le sentier / il sentiero pedonale / o passeio

band shell
die Konzertmuschel
la concha acústica
la scène en plein air
l'anfiteatro / a concha
acústica

pond / der Teich
el estanque / l'étang
lo stagno / o lago

fountain
der Springbrunnen
la fuente / la fontaine
la fontana / a fonte

footbridge
die Fußgängerbrücke
el puente peatonal
la passerelle / la passerella
a passarela

amusement park / der Vergnügungspark / el parque de atracciones
le parc d'attraction / il parco divertimenti / o parque de diversões

roller coaster / die Achterbahn
la montaña rusa / les montagnes
russes / le montagne russe
a montanha-russa

carousel / das Karussell
el carrusel / le manège
la giostra / o carrossel

Ferris wheel / das Riesenrad
la rueda de chicago / la grande roue
la ruota panoramica / a roda-gigante

theme park / der
Themenpark / el parque
temático / le parc
d'attraction / il parco a
tema / o parque temático

water park / der Wasserpark
el parque acuático
le parc aquatique
il parco acquatico
o parque aquático

zoo / der Tierpark
el zoológico / le zoo
lo zoo / o jardim zoológico

aquarium / das Aquarium
el acuario / l'aquarium
l'acquario / o aquário

activities / die Aktivitäten / las actividades / les activités / le attività / as atividades

ramp / die Rampe / la rampa
la rampe / la rampa
a rampa

skateboarding
das Skateboarden
el monopatinaje
le skateboard / lo skateboarding
o skateboarding

rollerblading
das Rollschuhlaufen
el patinaje / le roller
il rollerblading
os patins em linha

rollerskating / das
Rollschuhlaufen / el patinaje
le patin à roulettes
il pattinaggio a rotelle
os patins de quatro rodas

jogging / das Joggen
el jogging / le jogging
il jogging / o jogging

hiking / das Wandern
el senderismo
la promenade
l'escursionismo
o pedestrianismo

horseback riding
das Reiten / la equitación
la promenade à cheval
l'equitazione / a equitação

picnic / das Picknick
el pícnic / le pique-nique
il picnic / o piquenique

bird-watching
die Vogelbeobachtung
la observación de aves
l'observation des oiseaux
il bird-watching
a observação de pássaros

playground / der Spielplatz / el patio de juegos / l'aire de jeu
il parco giochi / o parque infantil

climber / der Kletterer
la escaladora / le mur d'escalade
il muro da arrampicata / o trepador

seesaw / die Wippe
el balancín
la balançoire à bascule
l'altalena / o balancé

wading pool
das Planschbecken
la piscina para niños
la pataugeoire
la piscina per bambini
a piscina para crianças

swings / das Schaukeln
los columpios
les balançoires
le altalene
os baloiços

sandbox / der Sandkasten
la caja de arena
le bac à sable / la sabbiera
a caixa de areia

spring rider / die Federwippe
el balancín / le cheval à ressort
il cavallo a dondolo
o cavalo de balanço

slide / die Rutsche / la diapositiva
le toboggan / lo scivolo / o escorrega

CAMPING / DAS CAMPING / EL CAMPING / LE CAMPING
IL CAMPEGGIO / O CAMPISMO

campground / der Campingplatz / la zona de campamento / le camping / il campeggio / o parque de campismo

waste disposal
die Müllentsorgung
la disposición de residuos
le traitement des déchets
lo smaltimento dei rifiuti
a eliminação de resíduos

site manager's office / das Büro des Platzleiters
la oficina del administrador
le bureau du gestionnaire du terrain
l'ufficio del direttore del campeggio
o gabinete do gestor do lugar

picnic table/ der Picknick-Tisch / la mesa
de picnic / le table de pique-nique
il tavolo di picnic / a mesa de piquenique

campsite / der Zeltplatz
el campamento / le terrain de camping
il campeggio / o parque de campismo

trailer / der Wohnwagen
la caravana / la caravane
la roulotte / a caravana

RV / das Wohnmobil / la casa rodante
le camping-car / il camper / a autocaravana

camper / das Wohnmobil / el campista
le campeur / il camper / a caravana de campismo

electric hookup / der Stromanschluss
la conexión eléctrica
le branchement électrique
l'allacciamento elettrico
o engate elétrico

campfire / das Lagerfeuer / la fogata
le feu de camp / il falò / a fogueira

tentpole
die Zeltstangen
los postes de carpa
le piquet de tente
il palo della tenda
a estaca

guy rope
das Abspannseil
la cuerda
le tendeur
il tirante
a corda de firmar

fly sheet
die Überzeltplane
el doble techo
le prospecteur
il sovratelo / a lona

full / voll / lleno
entier / il completo
completo

camp (v) / lager
acampar / camper
accampare
acampar

tent / das Zelt / la carpa / la tente / la tenda / a tenda

flap / die Klappe / la solapa
le rabat / la patta / a aba

ground sheet
die Bodenplane
la hoja de tierra
le tapis de sol
il telo di terra
a tela impermeável

mosquito net
das Moskitonetz
la mosquitera
la moustiquaire
la zanzariera
a rede mosquiteira

frame / das Gestell
el marco / le cadre
il telaio / a armação

sleeping bag
der Schlafsack
el saco de dormir
le sac de couchage
il sacco a pelo / o saco-cama

air mattress
die Luftmatratze
el colchón de aire
le matelas gonflable
il materasso ad aria
o colchão insuflável

camp bed / das Feldbett
la cama de campamento
le lit de camp
il materassino
a cama portátil

hammock
die Hängematte
la hamaca / le hamac
l'amaca / a rede

camp stove
der Campingkocher
la estufa de campamento
le réchaud
il fornello da campo
o fogão de campismo

grill / der Grill
la parrilla / le grill
la griglia / o grelhador

charcoal / die Holzkohle
el carbón / le charbon
la carbonella / o carvão

thermos
die Thermoskanne
el termo / le thermos
il thermos
a garrafa térmica

light a fire (v) / ein Feuer
anzünden / prender una
fogata / allumer un feu
accendere un fuoco
acender o lume

pitch a tent (v) / ein Zelt
aufschlagen / armar la
carpa / installer une tente
montare una tenda
montar a tenda

thermal underwear
die Thermounterwäsche
la ropa interior térmica
le sous-vêtement technique
la biancheria intima termica
a roupa interior térmica

insect repellant
das Insektenschutzmittel
el repelente contra insectos
le produit anti-insectes
il repellente per insetti
o repelente de insetos

BEACH / DER STRAND / LA PLAYA / LA PLAGE / LA SPIAGGIA / A PRAIA

hotel / das Hotel
el hotel / l'hôtel
l'hotel / o hotel

sand / der Sand
la arena / le sable
la sabbia / a areia

wave / die Welle
la ola / la vague
l'onda / a onda

sea / das Meer
el mar / la mer
il mare / o mar

beach hut / die Strandhütte
la casa de playa / la paillote
la capanna sulla spiaggia / a barraca

boardwalk / die Strandpromenade
el malecón / la passerelle
la passerella / o passadiço

lifeguard tower
der Rettungsschwimmer-Turm
la torre de salvavidas
le poste de secours
la torre del bagnino
a torre do nadador-salvador

beach umbrella / der Sonnenschirm
la sombrilla de playa / le parasol
l'ombrellone da spiaggia / o guarda-sol

windbreak / der Windschutz
el cortavientos / le coupe-vent
il frangivento / o paravento

lifeguard / der Rettungsschwimmer
el salvavidas / le sauveteur
il bagnino / o nadador-salvador

sunbathe (v) / sonnenbaden / asolearse / bronzer / prendere il sole / apanhar sol

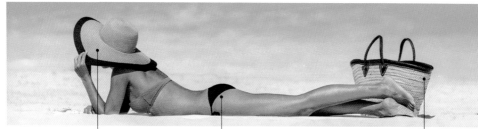

sunhat / der Sonnenhut
el sombrero para el sol
le bob / il cappello da sole
o chapéu de abas largas

bikini / das Bikini
el bikini / le bikini
il bikini / o biquíni

beach bag / die Strandtasche / la bolsa de playa
le sac de plage / la borsa da spiaggia
o saco de praia

beach ball / der Strandball
la pelota de playa / le ballon de plage
il pallone da spiaggia / a bola de praia

beach towel
das Strandhandtuch
la toalla de playa
la serviette de plage
il telo da spiaggia
a toalha de praia

pail and shovel
der Eimer und
die Schaufel
el cubo y la pala
le seau et la pelle
il secchio ela paletta
o balde e a pá

sandcastle / die Sandburg
el castillo de arena / le château de sable
il castello di sabbia / o castelo de areia

deck chair / der Liegestuhl
la tumbona / le transa
la sedia a sdraio
a espreguiçadeira

sunblock
die Sonnencreme
el bloqueador solar
la crème solaire
la crema solare
o protetor solar

inflatable tube / der aufblasbare Schlauch
el tubo inflable / le tube gonflable
il tubo gonfiabile / a boia insuflável

suntan lotion / das Sonnenschutzmittel
la loción bronceadora / la crème solaire
la lozione abbronzante / o bronzeador

surfboard / das Surfbrett
la tabla de surf / la planche de surf
la tavola da surf / a prancha de surf

windsurf (v) / windsurfen
hacer windsurf / faire de
la planche à voile / fare windsurf
fazer windsurf

paddleboard (v) / paddeln
hacer paddle surf / faire du paddle
fare paddleboard
fazer stand up paddle

surfer
der Wellenreiter
el surfista
le surfer
il surfista
o surfista

surf (v) / surfen / surfear
surfer / fare surf / surfar

PHOTOGRAPHY / DIE FOTOGRAFIE / LA FOTOGRAFÍA / LA PHOTOGRAPHIE LA FOTOGRAFIA / A FOTOGRAFIA

DSLR camera / die DSLR-Kamera / la cámara réflex digital
l'appareil reflex numérique / fola tocamera reflex / a câmara DSLR

shutter release
der Auslöser / el disparador
la vitesse d'obturation
lo scatto dell'otturatore
o disparador do obturador

aperature dial
das Blendenwahlrad
el dial de abertura
le réglage de l'ouverture
la ghiera del diaframma
a abertura de diafragma

filter
der Filter
el filtro
le filtre
il filtro
o filtro

lens cap / das Objektivdecke
la tapa de la lente
le cache d'objectif
il tappo dell'obiettivo
a tampa da lente

strap / der Riemen / la correa
la lanière / la cinghia / a correia

lens / das Objektiv / la lente
la lentille / la lente / as lentes

camera case
die Kameratasche
la caja de la cámara
l'étui d'appareil photo
la custodia per macchina
fotografica
o estojo da câmara

light meter
der Belichtungsmesser
el medidor de luz
le posemètre / il misuratore
di luce / o exposímetro

zoom lens
das Zoomobjektiv / la lente
de zoom / le zoom optique
l'obiettivo zoom
as lentes de zoom

flash gun / das Blitzgerät
el flash / le flash
il flash esterno / o flash

film camera / die Filmkamera
la cámara de cine / la caméra
la macchina fotografica a pellicola
a câmara de filmar

compact camera
die Kompaktkamera / la cámara
compacta / l'appareil compact
la macchina fotografica compatta
a câmara compacta

disposable camera / die Wegwerfkamera
la cámara desechable
l'appareil photo jetable
la macchina fotografica usa e getta
a câmara descartável

matte / matt / el papel mate
mat / opaco / mate

gloss / glänzend / el papel brillante
brillant / lucido / gloss

exposure / die Belichtung / la exposición
l'exposition / l'esposizione / a fotografia

print / das Drucken / la impresión
l'impression / la stampa
a cópia fotográfica

enlargement / die Vergrößerung
la ampliación / l'agrandissement
l'ingrandimento / a ampliação

camera phone / das Fotohandy
la cámara telefónica / la caméra
de smartphone / il telefono
con fotocamera / a câmara
do telemóvel

photography studio / das Fotostudio / el estudio de fotografía
le studio de photographie / lo studio fotografico / o estúdio fotográfico

photo shoot / das Fotoshooting
la sesión de fotos / le shooting photo
il servizio fotografico
a sessão fotográfica

backdrop / die Kulisse / el telón de fondo
le fond / il fondale / o cenário

photographer / der Fotograf
el fotógrafo / le photographe
il fotografo / o fotógrafo

light / das Licht / la luz
la lumière / la luce / a luz

models / die Modelle
los modelos / les modèles
le modelle / os modelos

tripod / das Stativ
el trípode / le trépied
il treppiede / o tripé

---

photograph (v) / fotografieren / fotografía / photographier / fotografare / fotografar

focus (v) / fokussieren
enfocar / faire la mise
au point / mettere a fuoco
focar

film
der Film
la película
la pellicule
la pellicola
o rolo

memory card / die Speicherkarte
la tarjeta de memoria / la carte
mémoire / il scheda di memoria
o cartão de memória

negative / das Negativ
el negativo / le négatif
il negativo / o negativo

develop (v) / entwickeln
revelar / développer
sviluppare / revelar

photograph
die Fotografie
la fotografía
le photographe
la fotografia
a fotografia

portrait / das Porträt / el retrato
le portrait / il ritratto / o retrato

underexposed / unterbelichtet
subexpuesta / sous-exposé
sottoesposto / pouco exposto

overexposed / überbelichtet
sobreexpuesta / surexposé
sovraesposto / demasiado exposto

landscape / die Landschaft
el paisaje / le paysage
il paesaggio / o panorama

out of focus / unscharf
desenfocado / flou
fuori fuoco / desfocado

red eye / die roten Augen
el ojo rojo / les yeux
rouges / gli occhi rossi
olhos vermelhos

HOME ENTERTAINMENT / *DAS HOME ENTERTAINMENT*
EL ENTRETENIMIENTO EN CASA / **L'IMAGE ET LE SON**
L'INTRATTENIMENTO DOMESTICO / ENTRETENIMENTO EM CASA

television / **das Fernsehen** / la televisión / la télévision / la televisione / a televisão

home theater system / das Heimkino-System / el sistema de cine en casa
le système home cinema / il sistema home theater / o sistema de cinema em casa

smart TV / das Smart-TV / la televisión inteligente
la smart TV / lo smart TV / a smart TV

speaker / der Lautsprecher / el altavoz
le haut-parleur / l'altoparlante / a coluna

AV receiver / der AV-Receiver / el receptor de AV
le récepteur audio/vidéo / il sintolettore / o recetor AV

watch TV (v) / TV schauen
ver televisión / regarder la télévision
guardare la TV / ver TV

cable box / die Kabelbox
la caja de cable / la cable box
il decoder via cavo / a caixa de TV a cabo

remote control / die Fernbedienung
el control remoto / la télécommande
il telecomando / o telecomando

power / der Strom
el botón de encendido
l'alimentation
l'alimentazione / a energia

Wi-Fi router
der Wi-Fi-Router
el enrutador Wi-Fi
le routeur Wi-Fi
il router Wi-Fi
o router wi-fi

modem / das Modem
el modem / le modem
il modem / o modem

volume
die Lautstärke
el botón de
volumen
le volume
il volume
o volume

channel / der Kanal
el botón de canales
la chaine / il canale / o canal

fast-foward / der Schnellvorlauf
el botón de avance rápido
avance rapide
l'avanzamento veloce / avançar

rewind
der Rücklauf
el botón de
rebobinado
rembobiner
il riavvolgimento
rebobinar

record / das Aufnehmen
el botón de grabar
enregistrer / registra / gravar

DVD / das DVD
el DVD / le DVD
il DVD / o DVD

DVD player / der DVD-Spieler
el reproductor de DVD
le lecteur DVD / il lettore DVD
o leitor de DVD

pause / die Pause
el botón de pausa
mettre sur pause
la pausa / pausar

gaming / das Spiel / el juego / les jeux / videogiochi / os videojogos

game console
die Spielkonsole
la consola de juegos
la console de jeux
la console di gioco
a consola de jogos

controller / der Controller / el controlador
la manette / il controller / o comando

joystick / der Joystick
el joystick / le joystick
il joystick / o joystick

headset / das Headset
el auricular / le casque
le cuffie / os auscultadores

gaming chair
der Gaming-Stuhl
la silla de juego
le fauteuil gaming
la sedia da gaming
a cadeira gaming

video game
das Videospie
el videojuego
le jeu vidéo
il videogioco
o videojogo

game capture device
das Spiel-Erfassungsgerät
el dispositivo de captura del juego
la carte de capture du jeu
il dispositivo di registrazione del gioco
o dispositivo de captura de ecrã

charging station
die Ladestation
la estación de carga
la station de recharge
la base di ricarica
a base de carregamento

---

music systems / die Musiksysteme
los sistemas de música / les systèmes audio
i sistemi musicali / o sistema de música

CD player / der CD-Spieler
el reproductor de CD
le lecteur CD / il lettore CD
o leitor de CD

*CD / das CD / el CD
le CD / il CD / o CD*

streaming (v)
das Streaming
la transmisión
le streaming
lo streaming
a transmissão

Bluetooth speaker
der Bluetooth-Lautsprecher
el altavoz blue-tooth
l'enceinte bluetooth
l'altoparlante Blue-tooth
a coluna bluetooth

turn on the TV
einschalten des
Fernsehers / encender
la televisión / allumer la
télévision / accendi la TV
liga a TV

turn off the TV
ausschalten des
Fernsehers / apagar la
televisión / éteindre la
télévision / spegni la TV
desligar a TV

HD / das HD / alta
definición / HD
HD / o HD

digital / digital / digital
numérique / digitale
digital

program
das Programm
el programa
le programme
il programma
o programa

live feed
die Live-Übertragung
a transmisión en vivo
le flux en direct
a trasmissione in diretta
a transmissão ao vivo

livestream / das Livestream
la transmisión en vivo
l'émission en direct
il livestream
a transmissão ao vivo

stereo system / die
Stereoanlage / el sistema
estéreo / le système stéréo
il sistema stereo
a aparelhagem de som

GAMES / DIE SPIELE / LOS JUEGOS / LES JEUX / I GIOCHI / OS JOGOS

board game / das Brettspie
el juego de mesa / le jeu de plateau
il gioco da tavolo
o jogo de tabuleiro

Monopoly / die Monopoly
Monopolio / le Monopoly
Monopoly / o Monopólio

dice / der Würfel / el dado
le dé / i dadi / o dado

play money / das Geld spielen
el dinero ficticio / de l'argent factice
i soldi finti / o dinheiro fictício

token / die Spielsteine / la ficha
le jeton / il gettone / a peça

square / das Quadrat
la casilla / le carré
il quadrato/ o quadrado

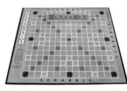

backgammon
das Backgammon
el backgammon
le backgammon
il backgammon / o gamão

dominos / der Domino
el dominó / les dominos
il domino / o dominó

Scrabble / das Scrabble
Scrabble / le Scrabble
Scarabeo / o Scrabble

checkers / die Dame
damas / les dames
dama / o jogo das damas

play (v) / spielen / jugar
jouer / giocare / jogar

player / der Spieler
el jugador / le joueur
il giocatore / o jogador

win (v) / gewinnen
ganar / gagner / vincere
ganhar

winner / der Gewinner
el ganador
le vainqueur
il vincitore / o vencedor

lose (v) / verlieren
perder / perdre
perdere / perder

loser / der Verlierer
el perdedor
le perdant / il perdente
o derrotado

bet / die Wette
la apuesta / le pari
la scommessa / a aposta

score / das Ergebnis
el marcador / le score
il punteggio
a pontuação

point / der Punkt
el punto / le point
il punto / o ponto

It's your move. / Du bist
am Zug. / Es tu turno.
C'est à toi de jouer.
Tocca a te / É a tua vez.

Whose turn is it?
Wer ist am Zug?
¿A quién le toca jugar?
C'est à qui de jouer ?
A chi tocca?
É a vez de quem?

Roll the dice. / Würfeln
Sie. / Lanza los dados.
Lance les dés. / Tira i
dadi. / Lança o dado.

jigsaw puzzle
das Jigsaw-Puzzle
el rompecabezas
le puzzle
il puzzle
o puzzle

dart / der Dart / el dardo
la fléchette / la freccetta / o dardo

bull's-eye / der Volltreffer
la diana / dans le mille
il centro / o centro do alvo

dartboard / die Dartscheibe
el tablero de dardos / la cible
de fléchettes / il bersaglio delle
freccette / o alvo

darts / die Darts / los dardos
les fléchettes / le freccette / os dardos

playing cards / die Spielkarten / las cartas
les cartes à jouer / le carte da gioco / as cartas de jogar

club / die Keule / la pica
carreau / fiori / paus

heart / das Herz
el corazón / coeur
cuiri / copas

diamond / das Karo
el diamante / pique
quadri / ouros

hand / das Blatt / la mano
la main / la mano / a mão

spade / das Pik / la pala
trèfle / picche / espadas

shuffle (v) / mischen
barajar / mélanger
mischiare / baralhar

deal (v) / austeilen
repartir / distribuer
distribuire / dar as cartas

deck / das Deck
el mazo / la pioche
il mazzo / o baralho

suit
die Farbe
el palo
la couleur
il seme
o naipe

chess / das Schach / el ajedrez
les échecs / gli scacchi / o xadrez

rook / der Turm / la torre
la tour / la torre / a torre

pawn / der Bauer / el alfil
le pion / il pedone / o peão

chessboard / das Schachbrett
el tablero de ajedrez
l'échiquier / la scacchiera
o tabuleiro de xadrez

knight / der Springer
el caballo / le cavalier
il cavallo / o cavalo

queen / die Königin
la reina / la reine
la regina / a rainha

king / der König
el rey / le roi
il re / o rei

bishop / der Läufer
el obispo / le fou
l'alfiere / o bispo

---

hobbies / die Hobbys / los pasatiempos / les hobbies / l'hobby / os passatempos

model-making / der Modellbau
el modelismo / le modélisme
il modellismo / o modelismo

coin-collecting / das Münzsammeln
la recolección de monedas
la numismatique / la numismatica
coleção de moedas

stamp-collecting / das Briefmarken-
Sammeln / la colección de sellos
la philatélie / la filatelia
a coleção de selos

ARTS AND CRAFTS / DAS KUNSTHANDWERK / ARTES Y OFICIOS
LES ARTS ET L'ARTISANAT / LE ARTI E MESTIERI / AS ARTES E O ARTESANATO

fine arts / die schönen Künste / las bellas artes / les beaux-arts / le belle arti / as belas artes

painting / das Malen / la pintura
la peinture / la pittura / a pintura

art studio / das Kunstatelier / el estudio de arte
l'atelier d'art / lo studio d'arte / o estúdio de arte

artist
der Künstler
el artista
l'artiste
l'artista
o artista

canvas
die Leinwand
el lienzo
la toile
la tela
a tela impermeável

sculptor
der Bildhauer
el escultor
le sculpteur
lo scultore
o escultor

palette
die Palette
la paleta
la palette
la tavolozza
a paleta

easel
die Staffelei
el caballete
le chevalet
il cavalletto
o cavalete de pintor

sculpture
die Bildhauerei
la escultura
la sculpture
la scultura
a escultura

mallet
der Schlägel
el mazo
le maillet
il martello
o maço

chisel
der Meißel
el cincel
le ciseau
lo scalpello
o cinzel

stone / der Stein
la piedra / la pierre
la pietra / a pedra

oil paint / die Ölfarbe
la pintura al óleo
la peinture à l'huile
la vernice ad olio
a pintura a óleo

acrylic paint / die Acrylfarbe
la pintura acrílica
la peinture acrylique
la vernice acrilica
a pintura em acrílico

drawing / die Zeichnung / el dibujo
le dessin / il disegno / desenhar

colored pencils / die Buntstifte
los lápices de colores
les crayons de couleur
le matite colorate
os lápis de cor

paintbrush / die Pinsel
el pincel / le pinceau
il pennello / o pincel

pencils / die Bleistifte / los lápices
les crayons / le matite / os lápis

watercolor paint / die Aquarellfarbe
la pintura de acuarela
la peinture à l'eau
la pittura ad acquerello
a pintura em aguarela

sketchbox / das Skizzenbuch
la caja de bocetos / la boite
à croquis / la cassetta degli
schizzi / o kit de desenho

charcoal / die Holzkohle
el carboncillo / le charbon
il carboncino / o carvão

sketch
die Skizze
el boceto
le brouillon
lo schizzo
o rascunho

sketchpad
der Skizzenblock
el bloc de dibujo
le carnet à croquis
il blocco da
disegno
o bloco de desenho

crayon / der Buntstift
el crayón / le crayon de
couleur / il pastello a cera
o lápis de desenho

pastel / das Pastell
el pastel / la pastel
il pastello / o pastel

collage / die Collage
el collage / le collage
il collage / a colagem

origami / das Origami
el origami / l'origami
l'origami / o origami

jewelry-making
die Schmuckherstellung
la joyería / la création
de bijoux / creare gioielli
o design de joias

papier mache / das
Pappmaché / el papel maché
le papier maché
la cartapesta / o papel machê

wood carving
die Holzschnitzerei
la talla de madera
la sculpture sur bois
l'intagliatura del legno
a escultura de madeira

decoupage / die Decoupage
el decoupage / le collage
il decoupage / a découpage

calligraphy / die Kalligrafie
la caligrafía / la calligraphie
la calligrafia / a caligrafia

linocut / der Linolschnitt
el linograbado / la linogravure
la linoleografia
a linoleogravuras

modeling tool / das Modellierwerkzeug
la herramienta de modelado / la mirette
lo strumento di modellazione
a ferramenta de modelagem

pottery
die Töpferei
la alfarería
la poterie
la ceramica
a cerâmica

clay / der Ton / la arcilla
l'argile / l'argilla / o barro

potter's wheel / die Töpferscheibe
el torno de alfarero / le tour
de potier / il tornio da vasaio
a roda de oleiro

screen-printing / der Siebdruck
la serigrafía / la sérigraphie
la serigrafia/ a serigrafia

etching / das Ätzen
el grabado / la gravure
à l'eau-forte / l'acquaforte
a água-forte

kiln / der Brennofen / el horno
le four à poterie / il forno
o forno

ink / die Tinte / la tinta / l'encre
l'inchiostro / a tinta

color wheel / das Farbkreis / la rueda de color
la roue des couleurs / la ruota dei colori / o círculo cromático

red / rot / rojo / rouge
rosso / vermelho

violet / violett / violeta
violet / viola / violeta

blue / blau
azul / bleu
blu / azul

yellow / gelbe
amarillo / jaune
giallo / amarela

orange / orange
naranja / orange
arancione / laranja

green / grün
verde / vert
verde / verde

primary colors / die Grundfarben
los colores primarios / les couleurs primaires
i colori primari / as cores primárias

secondary colors / die Sekundärfarben
los colores secundarios / les couleurs secondaires
i colori secondari / as cores secundárias

cyan / cyan / cian / cyan / ciano / ciano

magenta / magenta / magenta / magenta / magenta / magenta

SEWING / DAS NÄHEN / LA COSTURA / LA COUTURE / IL CUCITO / A COSTURA

thread guide / die Fadenführung
la guía del hilo / le guide
pour le fil / la guida per il filo
o guia de fio

takeup lever
der Aufwickelhebel
la palanca tensora
le levier tire-fil
la leva alzapiedino
a alavanca do calcador

presser foot / der Drückerfuß
el prensatelas / le pied presseur
il piedino premistoffa
o pé de pressão

needle plate / die Stichplatte
la placa de la aguja / la plaque
à aiguille / la piastra dell'ago
a placa da agulha

spool pin / der Spulenstift
el portacarrete / le porte-bobine
il perno della bobina / a bobina

bobbin winder / der Spulenkörper
la bobinadora / le dévidoir externe
l'avvolgitore della bobina / o pino
enrolador da bobina

balance wheel / das Ausgleichsrad
la rueda de equilibrio / la roue
d'équilibrage / la ruota di
bilanciamento / o volante

stitch selector / der Stichwähler
el selector de puntadas
le sélecteur de point
il selettore dei punti
o painel de controlo do ponto

sewing machine / die Nähmachine
la máquina de coser / la machine à coudre
la macchina da cucire / a máquina de costura

needle / die Nadel / la aguja
l'aiguille / l'ago / a agulha

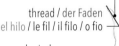

thread / der Faden
el hilo / le fil / il filo / o fio

scissors / die Schere
las tijeras / les ciseaux
le forbici / a tesoura

bobbin / der Spule
la canilla / la bobine
la bobina / a bobina

dressmaker's dummy
die Schneiderpuppe
el maniquí de
la modista
le mannequin
de tailleur
il manichino da sarto
o manequim da
costureira

thimble /der Fingerhut / el dedal
le dé à coudre / il ditale / o dedal

tailor's chalk
die Schneiderkreide
la tiza del sastre / la craie
du tailleur / il gesso da
sarto / o giz de costura

pin
die Stecknadel
el alfiler
l'épingle
lo spillo
o alfinete

pin cushion / das Nadelkissen
el cojín de alfileres / la pelote à épingles
il cuscino per spilli / a almofada
para alfinetes

tracing wheel
die das Pausierrad
la rueda marcadora
la roue de traçage
la rotella di ricalco
o marcador de tecido

pattern / das Schnittmuster / el patrón
le motif / il modello / o padrão

fabric / der Stoff
la tela / le tissu
il tessuto / o tecido

pinking shears / die Zickzackschere
las tijeras dentadas / les ciseaux à denteler
le cesoie / a tesoura dentada

measuring tape / die Maßband
la cinta métrica / le ruban mesureur
il nastro da sarto / a fita métrica

sewing basket / der Nähkorb
la canasta de coser / la boîte
à couture / il cestino da cucito
o cesto de costura

sew (v) / nähen
coser / coudre
cucire / costurar

darn (v) / stopfen
zurcir / raccommoder
rammendare / pontear

baste (v) / heften
hilvanar / faufiler
imbastire / alinhavar

thread (v) / einfädeln
enhebrar / enfiler
filare / passar fio

hem (v) / säumen / hacer
un dobladillo / faire un
ourlet / orlare / abainhar

pin (v) / stecken / fijar
épingler / appuntare
prender com alfinete

cut (v) / schneiden
cortar / découper
tagliare / cortar

seam / das Nähen
la costura / la couture
la cucitura / a costura

stitch / nähen
la puntada / le point
il punto / o ponto

alter (v) / ändern
alterar / faire des
retouches / alterare
ajustar

tack (v) / heften / poner
tachuelas / faufiler
imbastire / pregar

unpick (v) / aufreißen
descoser / défaire
disfare / descoser

material / das Material
el material / le tissu
il materiale / o material

loom / der Webstuhl
el telar / le métier à tisser
il telaio / o tear

quilting / das Quilten
el acolchado / la confection
de dessus-de-lit
la trapuntatura / o acolchoado

patchwork / das Patchwork / el mosaico
le patchwork / il patchwork / o patchwork

crochet hook
die Häkelnadel / el ganchillo
l'aiguille à crochet / l'uncinetto
a agulha de crochê

knitting / das Stricken / el tejido
le tricot / la maglieria / a malha

yarn
das Garn
el hilo
le fil
il filato
o fio

macrame
die Makramee
el macramé
le macramé
il macramè
o macramé

crochet / die Häkeln
el crochet / le crochet
l'uncinetto / o crochê

knitting needle / die Stricknadel
la aguja de tejer / l' aiguille à tricoter
l'ago per lavorare a maglia / a agulha de tricô

lace-making
das Klöppeln
la confección de encajes
la dentellerie / il merlettoa
a renda de bilros

weaving / das Weben
el tejido / le tissage
la tessitura / a tecelagem

embroidery / das Sticken
el bordado / la broderie
il ricamo / o bordado

cross-stitch / der Kreuzstich
el punto de cruz / le point
de croix / il punto croce
o ponto-cruz

SPORTS

DIE SPORTE

LOS DEPORTES

LES SPORTS

LO SPORT

OS DESPORTOS

SOCCER / DER FUßBALL / EL FÚTBOL / LE FOOTBALL / IL CALCIO / O FUTEBOL

soccer field / das Fußballfeld / el campo de fútbol / le terrain de football / il campo di calcio / o campo de futebol

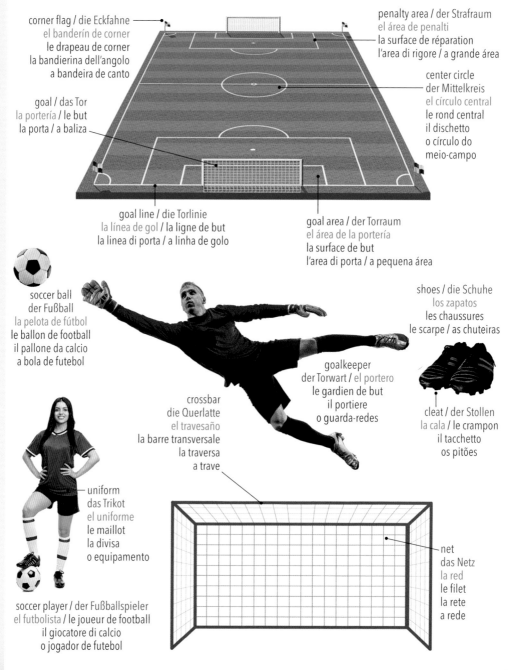

corner flag / die Eckfahne
el banderín de corner
le drapeau de corner
la bandierina dell'angolo
a bandeira de canto

penalty area / der Strafraum
el área de penalti
la surface de réparation
l'area di rigore / a grande área

center circle
der Mittelkreis
el círculo central
le rond central
il dischetto
o círculo do
meio-campo

goal / das Tor
la portería / le but
la porta / a baliza

goal line / die Torlinie
la línea de gol / la ligne de but
la linea di porta / a linha de golo

goal area / der Torraum
el área de la portería
la surface de but
l'area di porta / a pequena área

soccer ball
der Fußball
la pelota de fútbol
le ballon de football
il pallone da calcio
a bola de futebol

shoes / die Schuhe
los zapatos
les chaussures
le scarpe / as chuteiras

goalkeeper
der Torwart / el portero
le gardien de but
il portiere
o guarda-redes

cleat / der Stollen
la cala / le crampon
il tacchetto
os pitões

crossbar
die Querlatte
el travesaño
la barre transversale
la traversa
a trave

uniform
das Trikot
el uniforme
le maillot
la divisa
o equipamento

net
das Netz
la red
le filet
la rete
a rede

soccer player / der Fußballspieler
el futbolista / le joueur de football
il giocatore di calcio
o jogador de futebol

techniques / die Techniken / las técnicas / les techniques / le tecniche / as técnicas

free kick / der Freistoß
el tiro libre / le coup franc
il calcio di punizione
o pontapé livre

wall / die Mauer
la pared / le mur
il muro / a barreira

referee / der Schiedsrichter
el arbitro / l'arbitre
l'arbitro / o árbitro

red and yellow cards / die rote und gelbe
Karten / las tarjetas roja y amarilla
les cartons rouges et jaunes / i cartellini
rossi e gialli / os cartões
amarelo e vermelho

whistle / der Pfiff
el silbato / le sifflet
il fischietto / o apito

throw in (v) / einwurfen
hacer un saque lateral
faire la remis en jeu
lanciare / lançar

tackle (v) / Tackling
taclear / tacler
contrastare / atacar

head (v) / köpfen
dar un cabezazo
faire un tête
colpire di testa / cabecear

dribble (v) / dribbeln
driblar / dribbler
dribblare / driblar

pass (v) / passen
pasar / faire une passe
passare / passar

shoot (v) / schießen
lanzar / tirer
tirare / rematar

save (v) / redden
salvar la portería / faire un
arrêt / parare / defender

score (v) / punkten
anotar / marquer
segnare / marcar

---

forward / nach vorne / el delantero
l'attaquant / l'attaccante / o avançado

defender / der Verteidiger
el defensor / le défenseur
il difensore / o defesa

lineman / der Linienrichter
el defensa / l'arbitre de touche
il guardalinee / o lateral

offside / Abseits / fuera de juego
le hors-jeu / il fuorigioco
o fora de jogo

foul / das Foul / la falta / la faute
il fallo / a falta

penalty / der Elfmeter / el penalti
le penalty / il rigore / a grande
penalidade

send off / der Platzverweis
la expulsión / dégager
l'espulsione / a expulsão

extra time / die Nachspielzeit
el tiempo extra / le temps
additionnel / il tempo
supplementare / o prolongamento

substitute / die Auswechslung
el sustituto / le remplaçant
il sostituto / o suplente

stadium / das Stadion / el estadio
le stade / lo stadio / o estádio

substitution / die Auswechslung
la sustitución / Le changement
la sostituzione / a substituição

tie / das Unentschieden / el empate
le match-nul / il pareggio / o empate

halftime / die Halbzeit
el entretiempo / la mi-temps
l'intervallo / o intervalo

league / die Liga / la liga / la ligue
il campionato / o campeonato

BASKETBALL / DER BASKETBALL / EL BALONCESTO / LE BASKETBALL IL BASKET / O BASQUETEBOL

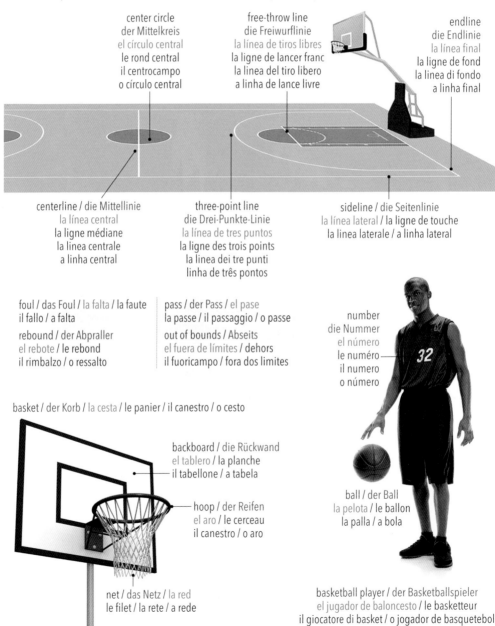

court / das Spielfeld / la cancha de baloncesto / le terrain / il campo / o campo

center circle
der Mittelkreis
el círculo central
le rond central
il centrocampo
o círculo central

free-throw line
die Freiwurflinie
la línea de tiros libres
la ligne de lancer franc
la linea del tiro libero
a linha de lance livre

endline
die Endlinie
la línea final
la ligne de fond
la linea di fondo
a linha final

centerline / die Mittellinie
la línea central
la ligne médiane
la linea centrale
a linha central

three-point line
die Drei-Punkte-Linie
la línea de tres puntos
la ligne des trois points
la linea dei tre punti
linha de três pontos

sideline / die Seitenlinie
la línea lateral / la ligne de touche
la linea laterale / a linha lateral

foul / das Foul / la falta / la faute
il fallo / a falta

pass / der Pass / el pase
la passe / il passaggio / o passe

number
die Nummer
el número
le numéro
il numero
o número

rebound / der Abpraller
el rebote / le rebond
il rimbalzo / o ressalto

out of bounds / Abseits
el fuera de límites / dehors
il fuoricampo / fora dos limites

basket / der Korb / la cesta / le panier / il canestro / o cesto

backboard / die Rückwand
el tablero / la planche
il tabellone / a tabela

hoop / der Reifen
el aro / le cerceau
il canestro / o aro

ball / der Ball
la pelota / le ballon
la palla / a bola

net / das Netz / la red
le filet / la rete / a rede

basketball player / der Basketballspieler
el jugador de baloncesto / le basketteur
il giocatore di basket / o jogador de basquetebol

actions / die Aktionen / las acciones / les actions / le azioni / as ações

guard (v) / bewachen
defender / conserver
le ballon / fare la guardia
defender

shoot (v) / schießen
lanzar / tirer / tirare / lançar

catch (v) / fangen
atrapar / attraper
prendere / apanhar

mark (v) / markieren
anotar / marquer
segnare / marcar

throw (v) / werfen
tirar / lancer
lanciare / lançar

dunk (v) / eintauchen
encestar / dunker
schiacciare / afundar

jump (v) / springen
saltar / sauter
saltare / saltar

dribble (v) / dribbeln
rebotar / dribbler
palleggiare / driblar

VOLLEYBALL / DER VOLLEYBALL / EL VOLEIBOL / LE VOLLEYBALL
IL VOLLEY / O VOLEIBOL

block (v) / Block
bloquear / bloquer
bloccare / bloquear

net / das Netz
la red / le filet
rete / a rede

knee support
die Kniestütze
el soporte de rodilla
la genouillère
la ginocchiera
a joelheira

referee
die Schiedsrichter
el árbitro
l'arbitre
l'arbitro
o árbitro

dig (v) / graben
hacer un dig
plonger / la tuffare
mergulhar

BASEBALL / DER BASEBALL / EL BÉISBOL / LE BASEBALL
IL BASEBALL / O BEISEBOL

field / das Feld / el campo / le terrain / il campo / o campo

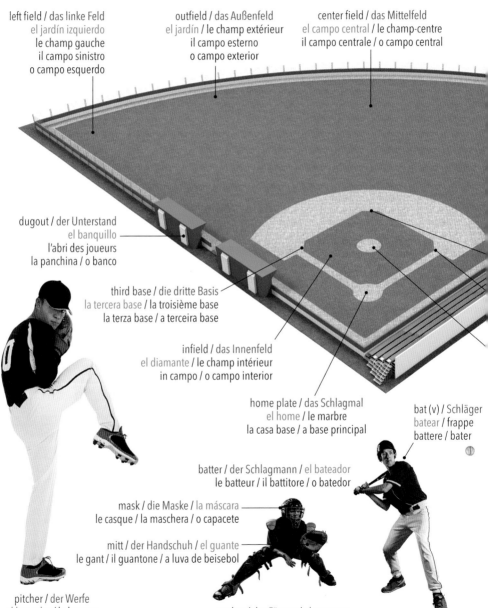

left field / das linke Feld
el jardín izquierdo
le champ gauche
il campo sinistro
o campo esquerdo

outfield / das Außenfeld
el jardín / le champ extérieur
il campo esterno
o campo exterior

center field / das Mittelfeld
el campo central / le champ-centre
il campo centrale / o campo central

dugout / der Unterstand
el banquillo
l'abri des joueurs
la panchina / o banco

third base / die dritte Basis
la tercera base / la troisième base
la terza base / a terceira base

infield / das Innenfeld
el diamante / le champ intérieur
in campo / o campo interior

home plate / das Schlagmal
el home / le marbre
la casa base / a base principal

bat (v) / Schläger
batear / frappe
battere / bater

batter / der Schlagmann / el bateador
le batteur / il battitore / o batedor

mask / die Maske / la máscara
le casque / la maschera / o capacete

mitt / der Handschuh / el guante
le gant / il guantone / a luva de beisebol

pitcher / der Werfe
el lanzador / le lanceur
il lanciatore / o lançador

catcher / der Fänger / el receptor
le receveur / il ricevitore / o recetor

out / Aus / fuera / faute / fuori
a eliminação

safe / sicher / safe / sauf / salvo
seguro

strike / der Strike / strike / le strike
lo strike / o strike

inning / das Inning / la entrada
la manche / l'inning / o turno

homerun / das Homerun
el homerun / le homerun
il fuoricampo / o home run

right field / das rechte Feld
el jardín derecho / le champ droit
/ il campo destro
o campo direito

foul line
die Foullinie
la línea de falta
la ligne de jeu
la linea di fallo
a linha lateral

actions / die Aktionen / las acciones
les actions / le azioni / as ações

throw (v) / werfen
lanzar / lancer
lanciare / atirar

catch (v) / fangen
atrapar / attraper
prendere / apanhar

field (v) / Feld
estar en el campo
tenir le champ / schierare
correr e apanhar a bola

bleachers / die Tribüne
las gradas / les gradins
la gradinata / as bancadas

second base / die zweite Basis
la segunda base / la deuxième base
la seconda base / a segunda base

tag (v)
markieren
hacer tag
marquer
acchiappare
marcar

first base / die erste Base
la primera base / la première base
la prima base / a primeira base

pitcher's mound / das Pitcher's Mound
el montículo del lanzador / le monticule du lanceur
la zona del lanciatore / a área do lançador

slide (v) / Rutschen / lanzar un slider
glisser / scivolare / deslizar

ball / der Ball / la pelota
la balle / la palla / a bola

umpire / der Schiedsrichter
el árbitro / l' arbitre
il arbitro / o árbitro

pitch (v) / werfen
lanzar / lance
lanciare / lançar

bat / der Schläger
el bate / la batte
la mazza / o taco

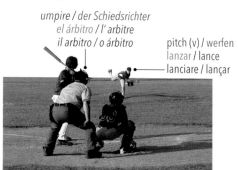

glove / der Handschuh / el guante
le gant / il guanto / a luva

play (v) / spielen / jugar / jouer / giocare / jogar

FOOTBALL / DER FOOTBALL / EL FÚTBOL AMERICANO / LE FOOT AMÉRICAIN
IL FOOTBALL / O FUTEBOL AMERICANO

field / das Spielfeld
el campo / le terrain
il campo / o campo

goal line / die Torlinie
la línea de gol / la ligne d'embut
la linea di porta / a linha de golo

goalpost / der Torpfosten
el poste de la portería
le poteau de but
il palo / a baliza

sideline / die Seitenlinie
la línea lateral
la ligne de touche
la linea laterale
a linha lateral

end zone / die Endzone
la zona de anotación
la zone d'embut
la zona di fondo
a end zone

hash marks
die Rautenmarkierungen
las marcas / le marquage
la linee di taglio
as marcas de hash

touchdown
das Touchdown
el touchdown
le touchdown
il touchdown
touchdown

cheerleader / der Cheerleader
la animadora / la pom-pom girl
la cheerleader / a chefe de claque

tackle (v) / Tackle
taclear / plaquer
placcare / placar

pass (v) / passen
pasar / faire une passe
passare / passar

helmet / der Helm
el casco / le casque
il casco / o capacete

ball / der Ball / la pelota
la balle / la palla / a bola

fumble / fummeln
soltar el balón
laisser échapper / fumble
perder a bola

catch (v) / fangen
atrapar / attraper
prendere / apanhar

field goal / das Feldtor
el gol de campo
le field goal / il gol sul
campo / o pontapé livre

quarterback
das Quarterback
el mariscal de campo
le quaterback
il quarterback
o quarterback

time out / die Auszeit
el tiempo fuera / le temps
mort / il time out / a pausa

halftime / die Halbzeit
el entretiempo / la mi-temps
l'intervallo / o intervalo

defense / die Verteidigung
la defensa / la défense
la difesa / a defesa

offense / die Offensive
la ofensa / l'attaque
l'attacco / o ataque

HOCKEY / DAS HOCKEY / EL HOCKEY / LE HOCKEY / IL HOCKEY / O HÓQUEI

ice hockey / das Eishockey / el hockey sobre hielo / le hockey sur glace l'hockey su ghiaccio / o hóquei no gelo

attacking zone / die Angriffszone
la zona de ataque / la zone d'attaque
la zona d'attacco / a zona de ataque

neutral zone / die neutrale Zone
la zona neutral / la zone neutre
la zona neutrale / a zona neutra

defending zone
die Verteidigungszone
la zona de defensa
la zone de défense
la zona di difesa
a zona de defesa

goal / das Tor / la portería
le but / il gol / a baliza

boards / die Bretter
las vallas / les panneaux
le tavole / os painéis

goal line / das Torlinie
la línea de gol
la ligne d'embut
la linea di porta
a linha de golo

center circle / der Mittelkreis
el círculo central / le rond central
il cerchio centrale / o círculo central

face-off circle
der Anspielkreis
el círculo de cara a cara
le rond de mise en jeu
il cerchio del face-off
o círculo de início do jogo

forward / der Stürmer / el delantero
la passe / l'attaccante / o atacante

pad / der Belag
la almohadilla / la protection
il cuscinetto / a caneleira

glove / der Handschuh
el guante / le gant
il guanto / a luva

ice skates
die Schlittschuhe
los patines de hielo
les patins à glace
i pattini da ghiaccio
os patins de gelo

puck / der Puck
el disco / le palet
il disco / o disco

penalty box / der Strafraum
el área penal / le banc de
pénalité / l'area di rigore
a caixa de penalidade

referee / der Schiedsrichter
el árbitro / l'arbitre
l'arbitro / o árbitro

player's bench / die Spielerbank
el banco de jugadores
le banc des joueurs
la panchina del giocatore
o banco dos jogadores

hit (v) / schlagen / golpear
frapper / colpire / chocar

goalie / der Torwart
el portero / le gardien
il portiere / o guarda-redes

shoot (v) / schießen
lanzar / tirer
tirare / rematar

field hockey / das Feldhockey / el hockey sobre césped / le hockey sur gazon l'hockey su prato / o campo de hóquei

hockey player / der Hockeyspieler
el jugador de hockey / la joueuse
de hockey / il giocatore di hockey
o jogador de hóquei

hockey stick / der Hockeyschläger
el palo de hockey / la crosse de hockey
il bastone da hockey
o taco de hóquei

TRACK AND FIELD / DIE LEICHTATHLETIK / EL ATLETISMO / L' ATHLÉTISME L'ATLETICA LEGGERA / O ATLETISMO

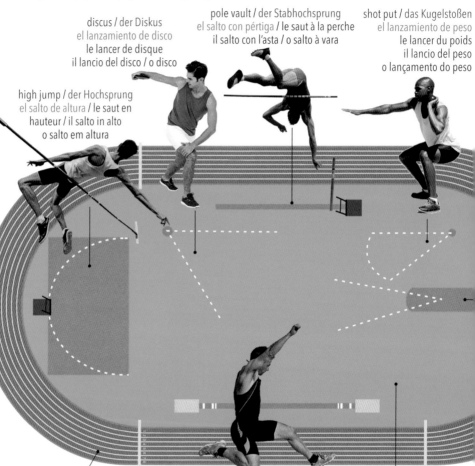

discus / der Diskus
el lanzamiento de disco
le lancer de disque
il lancio del disco / o disco

pole vault / der Stabhochsprung
el salto con pértiga / le saut à la perche
il salto con l'asta / o salto à vara

shot put / das Kugelstoßen
el lanzamiento de peso
le lancer du poids
il lancio del peso
o lançamento do peso

high jump / der Hochsprung
el salto de altura / le saut en
hauteur / il salto in alto
o salto em altura

track / die Leichtathletik
la pista / la piste
l'atletica / a pista

long jump / der Weitsprung
el salto de longitud / le saut en longueur
il salto in lungo / o salto em comprimento

field / das Feld
el campo / le terrain
il campo / o campo

hurdles / der Hürdenlauf
los obstáculos / les haies
gli ostacoli / a corrida de barreiras

baton / der Staffelstab
la batuta / le témoin
il bastone / o testemunho

relay race / der Staffellauf / la carrera de relevos
la course en relai / la staffetta / a corrida de estafetas

personal best / die
persönliche Bestleistung
la mejor marca personal
le record personnel / il record
personale / o recorde pessoal

record / der Rekord
el récord / le record
il record / o recorde

break a record (v) / einen
Rekord brechen / romper
un récord / établir un record
battere un record
bater um recorde

marathon / der Marathon
el maratón / le marathon
la maratona / a maratona

medal / die Medaille
la medalla / la médaille
la medaglia / a medalha

podium / das Podium
el podio / le podium
il podio / o pódio

starting line / die Startlinie
la línea de salida / la ligne de départ
la linea di partenza / a linha de partida

gymnastics / das Turnen / la gimnasia / la gymnastique la ginnastica / a ginástica

javelin
der Speerwurf
la jabalina
le javelot
il giavellotto
o dardo

pommel horse
das Pauschenpferd
el caballo con arcos
le cheval d'arçon
il cavallo con maniglie
o cavalo de arções

vault / das Voltigieren
el caballo / le saut de cheval
il volteggio / a mesa de salto

springboard
der Sprungbrett
el trampolín / le tremplin
il trampolino / o trampolim

lane / die Fahrspur
el carril / le couloir
la corsia
a pista individual

horizontal bar / das Reck
la barra horizontal
la barre fixe / la barra
orizzontale / a barra
horizontal

parallel bars
die Parallelbarren
las barras paralelas
les barres parallèles
le barre parallele
as barras paralelas

uneven bars
die Stufenbarren
las barras asimétricas
les barres asymétriques
le barre asimmetriche
as barras assimétricas

finish line / die Ziellinie
la meta / la ligne d'arrivée
il traguardo / a meta final

balance beam / der Schwebebalken
la barra de equilibrio / la poutre
il bilanciere / a trave olímpica

floor routine
die Bodenübung
la rutina de piso
la gymnastique au sol
la ginnastica artistica
a ginástica de solo

still rings
die stillen Ringe
las anillas
les anneaux
gli anelli
as argolas

rhythmic gymnastics
die rhythmischen
Sportgymnastik
la gimnasia rítmica
la gymnastique rythmique
la ginnastica ritmica
a ginástica rítmica

TENNIS / DAS TENNIS / EL TENIS / LE TENNIS / IL TENNIS / O TENNIS

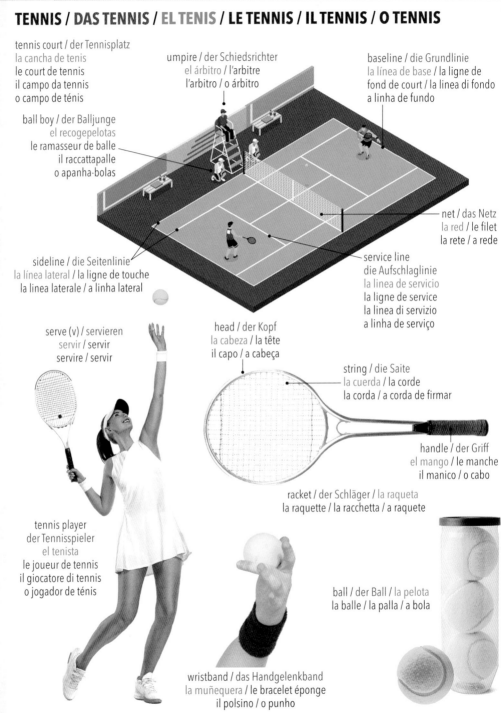

tennis court / der Tennisplatz
la cancha de tenis
le court de tennis
il campo da tennis
o campo de ténis

umpire / der Schiedsrichter
el árbitro / l'arbitre
l'arbitro / o árbitro

baseline / die Grundlinie
la línea de base / la ligne de
fond de court / la linea di fondo
a linha de fundo

ball boy / der Balljunge
el recogepelotas
le ramasseur de balle
il raccattapalle
o apanha-bolas

net / das Netz
la red / le filet
la rete / a rede

sideline / die Seitenlinie
la línea lateral / la ligne de touche
la linea laterale / a linha lateral

service line
die Aufschlaglinie
la línea de servicio
la ligne de service
la linea di servizio
a linha de serviço

serve (v) / servieren
servir / servir
servire / servir

head / der Kopf
la cabeza / la tête
il capo / a cabeça

string / die Saite
la cuerda / la corde
la corda / a corda de firmar

handle / der Griff
el mango / le manche
il manico / o cabo

racket / der Schläger / la raqueta
la raquette / la racchetta / a raquete

tennis player
der Tennisspieler
el tenista
le joueur de tennis
il giocatore di tennis
o jogador de ténis

ball / der Ball / la pelota
la balle / la palla / a bola

wristband / das Handgelenkband
la muñequera / le bracelet éponge
il polsino / o punho

singles / das Einzel
los individuales / les simples
singolo / singulares

doubles / das Doppelte
los dobles / les doubles
doppio / pares

set / der Satz / el set
le set / il set / o set

match / das Spiel
el partido / le match
partita / a partida

love / die Liebe / amor
zéro / la zero / zero a zero

deuce / der Einstand
deuce / égalité / pari
deuce

fault / der Fehler / falta
la faute / il fallo / a falta

spin / der Spin / el spin
la rotation / lo spin / o giro

ace / der Ass / el saque
directo / l'ace / l'ace / ace

Grand Slam
der Großschlemm
el grand slam
le grand chelem
il grande slam
o Grand Slam

tiebreaker / der Tiebreak
el desempate
le tiebreak / il tiebreak
o set decisivo

advantage / der Vorteil
la ventaja / l'avantage
il vantaggio / a vantagem

strokes / die Schläge / los golpes / les coups
i colpi / a raquetada

smash (v) / Schmetterball
rematar / smasher
schiacciare
fazer um smash

volley (v) / Volley
volear / reprendre de volée
volley / bater a bola no ar

return (v) / Rückschlag
devolver / renvoyer
rovesciare / retomar

lob / der Lob
el lanzamiento / le lob
il pallonetto / o lob

forehand / die Vorhand
el golpe de derecha
le coup droit / il dritto
forehand

backhand / die Rückhand
el revés / le revers
il rovescio / backhand

RACKET GAMES / DIE RACKET-SPIELE / LOS JUEGOS DE RAQUETA
LES JEUX DE RAQUETTE / I GIOCHI CON IL VOLANO / JOGOS DE RAQUETES

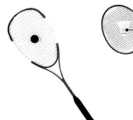

shuttlecock
der Federball
el volante
le volant
il volano
o volante

paddle / der Schläger
la paleta / la raquette
il paddle / o paddle

squash / das Squash
la calabaza / le squash
lo squash / o squash

badminton / das Badminton
el bádminton / le bádminton
il badminton / o badminton

table tennis / der Tischtennis
el tenis de mesa / le tennis
de table / il ping pong
o ténis de mesa

racquetball
das racquetball
el racquetball / le racquetball
il racquetball / o racquetball

GOLF / DAS GOLF / EL GOLF / LE GOLF / IL GOLF / O GOLF

golf course / der Golfplatz / el campo de golf / le parcours de golf / il campo da golf / o campo de golfe

flag / die Fahne / la bandera
le drapeau / la bandiera
a bandeira de canto

hole / das Loch
el hoyo / le trou
la buca / o buraco

bunker / sand trap
der Bunker / die Sandfalle
el búnker / la trampa de arena
le bunker / la fosse de sable
il bunker / trappola di sabbia
o obstáculo

rough / das Rough
el rough / le rough
il rough / o rough

teeing ground
der Abschlagplatz / el lugar
de salida / l'aire de départ
il campo da golf
o campo de tee

green / das Grün
el green / le green
il green / o green

water hazard
das Wasserhindernis
el obstáculo de agua
l'obstacle d'eau
l'acqua / o lago

fairway
das Fairway
el pasaje
le fairway
il fairway
a parte plana

clubhouse / das Clubhaus
la casa club / le club-house
il circolo / a sede do clube

golf swing
der Golfschwung
el swing de golf
le swing de golf
l'altalena da golf
o balanço do golf

caddy / das Caddy / el caddie
le caddy / il caddy / o caddie

stance / die Haltung
la postura / la position
la posizione / a postura

golfer / der Golfer / el golfista / le golfeur
il golfista / o jogador de golfe

golf cart / der Golfwagen / el carrito de golf
le chariot de golf / il golf cart / o carro de golfe

par / das Par / el golf par / le par
par / o par

handicap / das Handicap
la desventaja / le handicap
l'handicap / o handicap

hole in one / das Hole in One
el hoyo en uno / le trou en un
la buca in uno / de uma tacada só

tournament / der Turnier
el torneo / le tournoi / il torneo
o torneio

driving range / die Driving Range
el campo de prácticas / le practice
il campo pratica / o campo de gofle

spectators / die Zuschauer
los espectadores / les spectateurs
gli spettatori / os espetadores

stroke / der Schlaganfall / el golpe
le coup / il tiro / a tacada

line of play / die Spiellinie / la línea
de juego / la ligne de jeu / la linea
di gioco / a linha de jogo

championship / die Meisterschaft
el campeonato / le championnat
il campionato / o campeonato

equipment / die Ausrüstung / el equipo
l'équipement / l'attrezzatura / o equipamento

shoes / die Schuhe
los zapatos / les
chaussures / le scarpe
as sapatilhas

gloves / die Sandschuhe / los guantes
les gants / i guanti / as luvas

golf ball / der Golfball
la pelota de golf
la balle de golf / la pallina
da golf / a bola de golfe

putter / der Putter
el putter / le putter
il putter / o putter

wood / das Holz / la madera
le bois / il legno / madeira

tee / der Abschlag
el tee de golf / le tee
il tee / o tee

golf bag / die Golftasche
la bolsa de golf / le sac de
golf / la sacca da golf
a mochila de golfe

iron / das Eisen
el hierro / le fer
il ferro / ferro

wedge / das Wedge
la cuña / le wedge
il wedge / a cunha

actions / die Aktionen / las acciones / les actions / le azioni / as ações

tee off (v) / abschlagen
el golpe de salida
prendre le départ / tee-off
iniciar com a bola no tee

drive (v) / abschlagen
el drive / driver / drive
tacar de longa distância

putt (v) / putten
putt / putt
putt / putt

chip (v) / Chip
el chip / chiper
chip / tacar curto

BOATING / DAS SEGELN / EL BARCO
LES BATEAUX / LA BARCA / A NÁUTICA

sailing / das Segeln / la navegación / la voile
la vela / la navegação

rigging / die Takelage
el aparejo / le gréement
il sartiame / a enxárcia

mast / der Mast / el mástil
le mât / l'albero / o mastro

sailboat / das Segelboot / el velero
le bateau à voile / la barca a vela / o barco à vela

jib / die Fock
el foque / le foc
il fiocco / a bujarrona

mainsail / das Großsegel / la vela mayor
la grand-voile / la randa / a vela grande

boom / der Baum / la pluma
la bôme / la boma / o portaló

port side
die Backbordseite
la banda de babor
le côté bâbord
il lato sinistro
a margem do porto

stern / das Heck / la popa
la poupe / la poppa / a popa

rudder / der Ruder / el timón
le gouvernail / il timone / o leme

starboard / das Steuerbord
el estribor / tribord
la dritta / o estibordo

bow / der Bug
la proa / la proue
la prua / a proa

keel / der Kiel / la quilla
la quille / la chiglia / a quilha

hull / der Rumpf / el casco
la coque / lo scafo/ / o casco

capsize (v) / kentern
volcarse / chavirer
capovolgere / virar

tiller / die Pinne
el timón / la barre
la barra / a cana do leme

navigate (v) / navigieren
navegar / naviguer
navigare / navegar

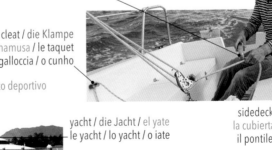

cleat / die Klampe
la cornamusa / le taquet
la galloccia / o cunho

marina / der Yachthafen / el puerto deportivo
la marina / la marina / a marina

sidedeck / das Seitendeck
la cubierta lateral / le rebord
il pontile / o convés lateral

yacht / die Jacht / el yate
le yacht / lo yacht / o iate

mooring / der Liegeplatz
el amarre / le mouillage
l'ormeggio / a ancoragem

slip / der Slip / el muelle
la cale / lo scivolo / o recuo

dock / der Steg / el puerto
le quai / il molo / a doca

anchor / der Anker
el ancla / l'ancre
l'ancora / a âncora

other boats / die andere Boote / otros barcos / les autres embarcations / le altre barche outros barcos

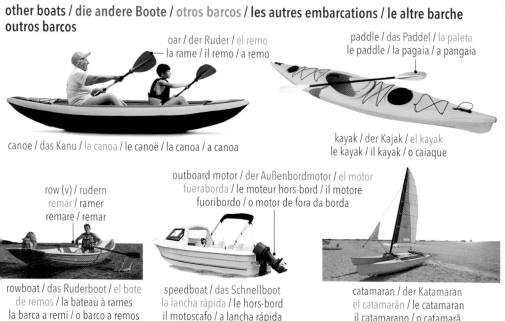

oar / der Ruder / el remo
la rame / il remo / a remo

paddle / das Paddel / la paleta
le paddle / la pagaia / a pangaia

canoe / das Kanu / la canoa / le canoë / la canoa / a canoa

kayak / der Kajak / el kayak
le kayak / il kayak / o caiaque

outboard motor / der Außenbordmotor / el motor
fueraborda / le moteur hors-bord / il motore
fuoribordo / o motor de fora da borda

row (v) / rudern
remar / ramer
remare / remar

rowboat / das Ruderboot / el bote
de remos / la bateau à rames
la barca a remi / o barco a remos

speedboat / das Schnellboot
la lancha rápida / le hors-bord
il motoscafo / a lancha rápida

catamaran / der Katamaran
el catamarán / le catamaran
il catamarano / o catamarã

water sports / der Wassersport / los deportes acuáticos / les sports aquatiques gli sport acquatici / os desportos aquáticos

rapids / die Stromschnellen / los rápidos
les rapides / le rapide / os botes

jet skiing / der Jetski
el jet esquñi / le jet-ski
il jet ski / o jet ski

waterskiing / das Wasserskifahren
el esquí acuático / le ski nautique
lo sci nautico / o esqui aquático

rafting / das Rafting / el rafting
le rafting / il rafting / o rafting

safety / die Sicherheit / la seguridad / la sécurité / la sicurezza / a segurança

life buoy / die
Rettungsboje / el
salvavidas / la bouée de
sauvetage / il salvagente
a boia de salvamento

life vest / die Rettungsweste
el chaleco salvavidas / le gilet
de sauvetage / il giubbotto
di salvataggio / o colete
salva-vidas

life raft / der Rettungsinsel
la balsa salvavidas
le radeau de sauvetage
la zattere di salvataggio
o salva-vidas

flare / die Fackel
la llamarada / la fusée
éclairante / il razzo
di segnalazione
o sinalizador

SWIMMING / DAS SCHWIMMEN / LA NATACIÓN / LA NAGE
IL NUOTO / A NATAÇÃO

starting block
der Startblock
el bloque de salida
le starting-block
il blocco di partenza
o bloco de partida

lane
die Bahn
el carril
la ligne d'eau
la corsia
a pista
individual

swimming cap
die Badekappe
el gorro de natación
le bonnet de bain
la cuffia
a touca de natação

ladder
die Leiter
la escalera
l'échelle
la scaletta
a escada

swimming pool / das Schwimmbecken
la piscina / la piscine / la piscina / a piscina

goggles
die Schwimmbrille
las gafas de natación
les lunettes
gli occhiali
os óculos

diving board / der Sprungbrett
el trampolín / le plongeoir
il trampolino / a prancha de mergulho

deep end / das tiefe Ende
la parte honda / le grand bain
il lato profondo / a parte funda

dive (v) / tauchen / zambullirse
plonger / tuffare / mergulhar

trunks / die Badehose
el bañador / le caleçon
de bain / il costume
os calções

swimmer / der Schwimmer / el nadador
le nageur / il nuotatore / o nadador

swim (v) / schwimmen
nadar / nager
nuotare / nadar

turn (v) / drehen
voltearse / faire un virage
girare / virar

---

accessories / das Zubehör / los accesorios / les accessoires / gli accessori / os acessórios

swimsuit
der Badeanzug
el traje de baño
le maillot de bain
il costume da bagno
o fato de banho

water wings
der Schwimmflüge
los flotadores
les brassards
i braccioli
as braçadeiras

kickboard / das Kickboard
la tabla / la planche
la tavola / a prancha de natação

nose clip / die Nasenklammer
el clip nasal / le pince-nez
la pinza stringinaso
a pinça nasal

styles / die Stile / los estilos / les styles / gli stili / os estilos

front crawl / das Kraulen vorne / el estilo crol / le crawl
lo stile libero / crawl

backstroke / das Rückenschwimmen
el estilo espalda / le dos crawlé / il dorso / costas

butterfly / der Schmetterling / el estilo mariposa
le papillon / la farfalla / mariposa

breaststroke / das Brustschwimmen / el estilo brazada
la brasse / la rana / bruços

SCUBA DIVING / DAS TAUCHEN / EL BUCEO / LA PLONGÉE SOUS-MARINE L'IMMERSIONE / O MERGULHO SUBMARINO

air cylinder / die Pressluftflasche / el cilindro de aire
la bouteille d'air / la bombola d'aria / o cilindro de ar

snorkel / das Schnorcheln
el esnórquel / le tuba
il boccaglio / mergulho
submarino com tubo

mask / die Maske
la máscara / le masque
la maschera / a máscara

regulator / der Atemregler
el regulador / le détendeur
l'erogatore / o regulador

swimfin / die Schwimmflosse
el nadador / la palme
le pinne / o pé de pato

wetsuit / der Neoprenanzug
el traje de neopreno
la combinaison de plongée
la muta / o fato de mergulho

weight belt / der Bleigürtel
el cinturón de lastre
la ceinture de plomb
la cintura coi pesi
o cinto de mergulho

dive / das Tauchen / el buceo
le plongeon / il tuffo / o mergulho

high dive / der Sturzflug / el buceo
profundo / le grand plongeon
il tuffo da grandi altezze
o mergulho em alto mar

tread water (v) / Wasser treten
mante / nager sur place
restare a galla / boiar

lockers / die Schließfächer
los casilleros / les casiers
gli armadietti / o balneário

water polo / der Wasserball
el waterpolo / le water-polo
la pallanuoto / o polo aquático

shallow end / das seichte Ende
la zona poco profunda / le petit
bassin / la parte bassa / a parte baixa

synchronized swimming
das Synchronschwimmen
la natación sincronizada / la natation
synchronisée / il nuoto sincronizzato
a natação sincronizada

drown (v) / ertrinken / ahogarse
couler / annegare / afogar

cramp / die Krämpfe / el calambre
la crampe / il crampo / a cãibra

FISHING / DIE FISCHEREI / LA PESCA / LA PÊCHE / LA PESCA / A PESCA

fly fishing / das Fliegenfischen
la pesca con mosca / la pêche à la mouche
la pesca a mosca / a pesca à pluma

angler / der Angler / el pescador
le pêcheur / il pescatore / o pescador à linha

waders / die Wathose / el traje de pesca
les cuissardes / gli scarponi per la pesca / o wader

tackle / das Angelgerät / el aparejo / le matériel de pêche / l'attrezzatura / os apetrechos

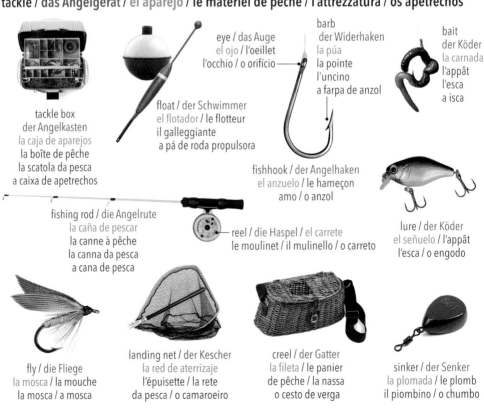

tackle box
der Angelkasten
la caja de aparejos
la boîte de pêche
la scatola da pesca
a caixa de apetrechos

float / der Schwimmer
el flotador / le flotteur
il galleggiante
a pá de roda propulsora

eye / das Auge
el ojo / l'oeillet
l'occhio / o orifício

barb
der Widerhaken
la púa
la pointe
l'uncino
a farpa de anzol

bait
der Köder
la carnada
l'appât
l'esca
a isca

fishhook / der Angelhaken
el anzuelo / le hameçon
amo / o anzol

fishing rod / die Angelrute
la caña de pescar
la canne à pêche
la canna da pesca
a cana de pesca

reel / die Haspel / el carrete
le moulinet / il mulinello / o carreto

lure / der Köder
el señuelo / l'appât
l'esca / o engodo

fly / die Fliege
la mosca / la mouche
la mosca / a mosca

landing net / der Kescher
la red de aterrizaje
l'épuisette / la rete
da pesca / o camaroeiro

creel / der Gatter
la fileta / le panier
de pêche / la nassa
o cesto de verga

sinker / der Senker
la plomada / le plomb
il piombino / o chumbo

types / die Arten / los tipos / les types / i tipi / os tipos

surfcasting / das Brandungsangeln
el surfcasting / la pêche dans la
vague / il surfcasting / o surfcasting

freshwater fishing / das
Süßwasserfischen / la pesca de agua
dulce / la pêche en eau douce
il pesca d'acqua dolce
a pesca em água doce

sport fishing / das Sportfischen
la pesca deportiva / la pêche sportive
pesca sportiva / a pesca desportiva

keep net / das Stellnetz
el guardador de red
le filet / il rezzaglio
a rede para peixes

spearfishing / das Speerfischen
la pesca submarina / la chasse sous-
marine / la pesca subacquea
a pesca com arpão

deep-sea fishing / das
Hochseefischen / la pesca de altura
la pêche en haute mer / la pesca
d'altura / a pesca em alto-mar

fishing pier / der Angelsteg
el muelle de pesca / le quai de pêche
il molo di pesca
a plataforma de pesca

line / die Leine
el sedal / la ligne
la lenza / a linha

fishing license / der Angelschein
la licencia de pesca / le permis
de pêche / la licenza di pesca
a licença de pesca

activities / die Aktivitäten / las actividades / les activités le attività / as atividades

cast (v) / werfen / tirar
la atarraya / lancer
lanciare / lançar

reel in (v) / einholen
enrollar / ramener
avvolgere / recolher

catch (v) / fangen
pescar / attraper
catturare / apanhar

release (v) / freilassen
desenganchar / relâcher
rilasciare / libertar

bait (v) / Köder
encarnar / appâter
attirare / iscar

net (v) / Netz
tirar la red / prendre
au filet / catturare
con la rete
apanhar na rede

SKIING / DAS SKIING / EL ESQUÍ / LE SKI / GLI SCI / O ESQUI

ski slope / die Skipiste / la pista de esquí
la piste / la pista da sci / a estância de esqui

chairlift / der Sessellift / el telesilla
le télésiège / la seggiovia / a telecadeira

safety barrier
die Sicherheitsschranke
la barrera de seguridad
le filet de sécurité / la barriera di
sicurezza / a barreira de segurança

ski run / die Piste
la pista de esquí
la piste de ski
la pista da sci
a pista de esqui

gondola lift / die Gondelbahn / la telecabina
le télécabine / la cabinovia / o teleférico

downhill skiing / die Skiabfahrt / el esquí alpino
le ski de descente / lo sci alpino / o esqui alpino

glove / der Handschuh
el guante / le gant
il guanto / a luva

skier / der Skifahrer
el esquiador / le skieur
lo sciatore / o esquiador

ski jacket / die Skijacke
la chaqueta de esquí
la veste de ski
la giacca da sci
o casaco de esqui

ski / der Ski
el esquí / le ski
gli sci / o esqui

ski pole
der Skistock
el bastón de esquí
le bâton de ski
il bastone da sci
o bastão de esqui

tip / die Spitze
la punta / la spatule
la punta
a ponta do esqui

edge/ / die Kante
el borde/ / la care
il bordo/ / a borda do esqui

ski boot / der Skischuh
la bota de esquí
la chaussure de ski
lo scarpone da sci
as botas de esqui

alpine skiing / der Ski
Alpin / el esquí alpino
le ski alpin / lo sci alpino
o esqui alpino

giant slalom / der
Riesenslalom / el eslalon
gigante / le slalom géant
lo slalom gigante
o slalom gigante

ski jump / der Skisprung
el salto de esquí / le saut
à ski / il salto con gli sci
o salto de esqui

off-piste / abseits der Piste
fuera de pista / le hors
piste / il fuori pista
o esqui fora de pista

slalom / der Slalom
el eslalon / le slalom
lo slalom / o slalom

biathlon / das Biathlon
el biatlón / le biathlon
il biathlon / o biathlon

cross-country skiing
der Skilanglauf / el esquí
de fondo / le ski de fond
lo sci di fondo
o esqui nórdico

winter sports / der Wintersport / los deportes de invierno / les sports d'hiver / gli sport invernali / os desportos de inverno

ice skating
das Schlittschuhlaufen
el patinaje sobre hielo
le patinage
il pattinaggio su ghiaccio
a patinagem no gelo

speed skating
der Eisschnelllauf
el patinaje de velocidad
le patinage de vitesse
il pattinaggio di velocità
a patinagem de velocidade

figure skating
der Eiskunstlauf
el patinaje artístico
le patinage artistique
il pattinaggio artistico
a patinagem artística

snowboarding
das Snowboarden
el snowboard
le snowboard
lo snowboard
o snowboard

snowmobile
das Motorschlitten
la moto de nieve
la motoneige
la motoslitta
a moto para a neve

dogsledding
das Hundeschlittenfahren
el trineo de perros
le traîneur à chien
lo sleddog
o trenó puxado por cães

ice climbing
das Eisklettern
la escalada en hielo
la cascade de glace
l'arrampicata su ghiaccio
escalada no gelo

luge / das Rodeln
el luge / la luge
lo slittino / o luge

bobsled / das Bobsport
el bobsleigh / le bobsleigh
il bob / o bobsled

sledding / das
Schlittenfahren / el trineo
la luge / slittino / trenó

curling
das Eisstockschießen
el curling / le curling
il curling / o curling

MARTIAL ARTS / DIE KUNSTSTOFFE / LAS ARTES MARCIALES
LES ARTS MARTIAUX / LE ARTI MARZIALI / AS ARTES MARCIAIS

kick (v) / kicken
patear / frapper
calciare / pontapear

black belt
der schwarze Gürtel
el cinturón negro
la ceinture noire
la cintura nera
o cinturão negro

judo / das Judo
el judo / le judo
il judo / o judo

kung fu / das Kung Fu
el kung fu / le kung fu
il kung fu / o kung fu

tae kwon do / das Tae kwon do / el taekwondo
le tae kwon do / il tae kwon do / o taekwondo

opponent / der Gegner
el oponente / l'adversaire
l'avversario / o oponente

aikodo / das Aikodo
el aikido / l'aïkido
l'aikodo / o aikido

karate / das Karate
el karate / le karaté
il karate / o karaté

kendo / das Kendo / el kendo
le kendo / il kendo / o kendo

jump (v) / Sprung / saltar
sauter / saltare / saltar

capoeira / das Capoeira
la capoeira / la capoeira
la capoeira / a capoeira

mouth guard
der Mundschutz
el protector bucal
le protège-dents
il paradenti
a proteção dentária

round / die Runde
la ronda / le round
il round / o assalto

bout / der Kampf/ el combate
le combat / l'incontro
o combate

knockout / K.O. / el nocaut
K.O. / il knockout / o K.O.

self-defense
die Selbstverteidigung
la autodefensa / la self-défense
l'autodifesa / a autodefesa

tai chi / das Thai-Chi
el tai chi / le tai chi
il tai chi / o tai-chi

boxing / das Boxen / el boxeo
la boxe / la boxe / o boxe

boxer / der Boxer
el boxeador / le boxeur
il pugile / o lutador de boxe

ropes / die Seile
las cuerdas / les cordes
le corde / as cordas

boxing ring / der Boxring / el ring de boxeo
le ring de boxe / il ring di pugilato
o ringue de boxe

punch (v) / schlagen
dar un puñetazo
donner un coup de poing
dare un pugno / socar

boxing glove
der Boxhandschuh
el guante de boxeo
le gant de boxe
il guantone da boxe
a luva de boxe

punching bag / der Sandsack
el saco de boxeo / le sac de frappe
il sacco da boxe / o saco de boxe

kickboxing / das Kickboxen
el kickboxing / le kickboxing
il kickboxing / o kickboxing

sumo wrestling / das Sumo-Ringen
la lucha de sumo / le sumo
il sumo / o sumo

wrestling / das Ringen
la lucha libre / la lutte
il wrestling / o wrestling

---

actions / die Aktionen / las acciones / les actions / le azioni / as ações

hold (v) / festhalten / mantener
faire une prise / tenere / segurar

spar (v) / sparren / entrenar
s'entraîner / fare sparring / lutar

throw (v)
werfen
lanzar
lancer
lanciare
atirar

fall (v) / fallen / caer
tomber / cadere / cair

strike (v) / schlagen
atacar / frapper
colpire / atacar

block (v) / Blocken
bloquear / bloquer
bloccare / bloquear

chop (v) / Schlagen
golpear / donner un coup
colpire / golpear

pin (v) / feststecken
sujetar / coincer
immobilizzare / imobilizar

EQUESTRIAN SPORTS / DER PFERDESPORT / LOS DEPORTES ECUESTRES LES SPORTS EQUESTRES / GLI SPORT EQUESTRI OS DESPORTOS EQUESTRES

horseback riding / das Reiten / la cabalgata / l'équitation / l'equitazione / a equitação

riding hat / die Reitkappe
el sombrero de montar
la bombe / il cappello da
equitazione / o capacete equestre

rider / der Reiter
el jinete / le cavalier
il cavaliere / o cavaleiro

mane / die Mähne
la melena / la crinière
la criniera / a crina

tail / der Schweif
la cola / la queue
la coda / o rabo

horse / das Pferd
el caballo
le cheval
il cavallo
o cavalo de arções

reins / der Zügel
las riendas / les rênes
le redini / as rédeas

jodhpurs / die Reithosen
los pantalones de montar
les jodhpurs
i pantaloni da equitazione
as calças de equitação

girth / der Sattelgurt
la cincha / la sangle
il sottopancia / a cilha

hoof / der Huf / la pezuña
le sabot / gli zoccoli / o casco

riding boot / der Reitstiefe
la bota de montar / le botte d'équitation
lo stivale da equitazione / a bota de equitação

horseshoe / das Hufeisen
la herradura / le fer à cheval
il ferro di cavallo / a ferradura

bridle
das Zaumzeug
la brida
la bride
la briglia
a brida

saddle / der Sattel
la silla de montar / la selle
la sella / a sela

browboard / das Stirnbrett
la frontalera / le frontal
la briglia / o cabresto

stirrup
der Steigbügel
el estribo
l'étrier
la staffa
o estribo

noseband
der Reithalfter
la muserola
la muserolle
la fascia per il naso
a focinheira

bit / das Gebiss
la testera / le mors
il morso / o freio

pony / das Pony / el pony
le poney / il pony / o pónei

events / die Veranstaltungen / los eventos / les événements / gli eventi / os eventos

steeplechase / die Steeplechase
la carrera de obstáculos / le steeple-chase
la steeplechase / a prova de corta-mato

horse race / das Pferderennen / la carrera de caballos
la course de chevaux / la corsa di cavalli / a corrida de cavalos

riding crop / die Reitgerte / la fusta
la cravache / il frustino / a chibata de corrida

jockey / der Jockey
el jockey / le jockey
il fantino / o jóquei

fence / der Zaun / la cerca
l'obstacle / il recinto / a cerca

racecourse / die Galopprennbahn / el hipódromo
l'hippodrome / l'ippodromo / o hipódromo

rodeo / das Rodeo / el rodeo
le rodeo / il rodeo / o rodeo

harness race / das Trabrennen
la carrera de arneses / la course attelée
la gara di trotto / a corria de arreios

carriage race / das Kutschenrennen
la carrera de carruajes / le trot attelé
la corsa in carrozza
a corrida de carruagens

dressage / das Dressurreiten
la doma / le dressage
il dressage / o adestramento

polo / das Polo / el polo
le polo / il polo / o polo

show jumping / das Springreiten
el espectáculo de saltos / le saut
d'obstacles / il salto ostacoli
o espetáculo de saltos

---

gaits / das Gangarten / los pasos / l'allure / le andature / a marcha

walk (v) / gehen
caminar / aller au pas
camminare / andar

trot (v) / traben
trotar / trotter
trottare / trotar

canter (v) / kantern
ir a medio galope / aller
au petit galop / andare al
canter / galopar brando

gallop (v) / galoppieren
galopar / galoper
galoppare / galopar

FITNESS / DIE FITNESS / EL FITNESS / LE FITNESS / IL FITNESS / O FITNESS

gym / das Fitnessstudio / el gimnasio / la salle de sport / la palestra / o ginásio

exercise (v) / trainieren / ejercitarse / faire de l'exercice / esercitare / exercitar

elliptical
der elliptischen Maschine
la elíptica
le vélo elliptique
l'ellittica
a elítica

treadmill / das Laufband
la caminadora / le tapis de course
il tapis roulant / a passadeira

weight bench / die Hantelbank
el banco de pesas
le banc de musculation / la panca
o banco de musculação

dumbbell / die Kurzhantel / la mancuerna
la dumbbell / il manubrio / o haltere

gym machines / die Fitnessgeräte / las máquinas del gimnasio
les machines de musculation / il macchinario da palestra / as máquinas do ginásio

stationary bike	stair climber	rowing machine	leg press
der Heimtrainer	der Treppenkletterer	das Rudergerät	die Beinpresse
la bicicleta estática	el escalador	la máquina de remo	la prensa de piernas
le vélo d'appartement	le simulateur d'escaliers	le rameur	la presse
la cyclette	lo scalatore	il vogatore / o aparelho	la leg press
a bicicleta estática	a escada elétrica	para exercícios de remo	o leg press

amenities / die Annehmlichkeiten / las comodidades / les équipements
i servizi / os serviços

personal trainer	swimming pool	sauna / die Sauna	showers / die Duschen
der Personal Trainer	das Schwimmbad	la sauna / le sauna	las duchas / les douches
el entrenador personal	la piscina / la piscine	la sauna / a sauna	le docce / os banhos
le coach privé / il personal	la piscina / a piscina		
trainer / o personal trainer			

exercises / die Übungen / los ejercicios / les exercices / gli esercizi / os exercícios

run in place (v) / das Laufen auf der Stelle
correr en el puesto / courir sur place
corere sul posto / correr sem sair do lugar

stretch / das Stretching
el estiramiento / l'étirement
il stretching / o exercício de alongamento

push-up / der Liegestütz / la lagartija
les pompes / il push-up / o push-up

jump rope
das Springseil
la cuerda de saltar
la corde à sauter
il salto con la corda
a corda de saltar

lunge / die Ausfallschritte / la estocada
la fente / l'affondo / a investida

squat / die Hocke / la cuclilla
le squat / lo squat / o agachamento

pull-up / der Klimmzug / la flexión
les tractions / il pull-up / a elevação

sit-up / das Sit-up / la sentadilla
les abdominaux / il sit-up
o abdominal

biceps curl / das Bizeps-Curl
la flexión de bíceps / le travail des
biceps / il curl bicipiti / a rosca bíceps

barbell / die Langhantel
— la barra / la barre
il bilanciere
o haltere comprido

weight training
das Krafttraining
el entrenamiento con pesas
la musculation
l'allenamento con i pesi
a musculação

circuit training / das
Zirkeltraining / el circuito
de entrenamiento
le parcours de santé
l'allenamento a circuito
o treino em circuito

Pilates / das Pilates
el pilates / le Pilate
il Pilates / pilates

aerobics / das Aerobic
los aeróbicos / l'aérobique
l'aerobica
a ginástica aeróbica

OTHER SPORTS / DIE ANDERE SPORTARTEN / OTROS DEPORTES
LES AUTRES SPORTS / GLI ALTRI SPORT / OUTROS ESPORTES

cricket / das Kricket / el grillo
le cricket / il cricket / o críquete

rugby / das Rugby / el rugby
le rugby / il rugby / o râguebi

lacrosse / das Lacrosse / el lacrosse
le lacrosse / la lacrosse / o lacrosse

alley / die Gasse / el callejón
la piste / il vicolo / a pista

billiards / das Billard
el billar / le billard
il biliardo / o bilhar

pin / die Pin
el pin / la quille
il pin / o pino

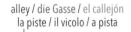

bowling ball
das Bowling
la bola de boliche
la boule de bowling
la palla da bowling
a bola de bowling

cue
das Queue
la señal
la queue
la stecca
o taco

bowling / das Bowling / el boliche
le bowling / il bowling / o bowling

pool / das Billard / el billar
le billard américain / il biliardo / a mesa de bilhar

bow / der Bogen
el arco / l'arc
l'arco / o arco

arrow
der Pfeil
la flecha
la flèche
le freccette
a flecha

sword / der Degen
la espada / l'épée
la spada / a espada

archery / das Bogenschießen / el tiro con arco
le tir à l'arc / il tiro con l'arco / o tiro com arco

fencing / das Fechten / la cerca
l'escrime / la scherma / a esgrima

hang-glider / das Drachenfliegen
el ala delta / le deltaplane
il deltaplano / a asa-delta

hang-gliding / das Drachenfliegen
volar en ala delta / faire du
deltaplane / il deltaplano
a modalidade asa-delta

parachute / der Fallschirm
el paracaídas / le parachute
il paracadute / o paraquedas

skydiving / das Fallschirmspringen
el paracaidismo / le parachutisme
il paracadutismo / o paraquedismo

paragliding / das Gleitschirmfliegen
el parapente / le parapente
il parapendio / o parapente

bungee jumping / das Bungee-
Jumping / el puenting / le saut à
l'élastique / il bungee jumping
o bungee jumping

rope / das Seil / la cuerda
la corde / la corda / a corda

rappelling / das Abseilen / el rappel
le rappel / il rappel / o rapel

rock climbing / das Klettern
la escalada en roca / l'escalade
arrampicata su roccia / a escalada

racecar driver
der Rennwagenfahrer
el piloto de carreras
le pilote de course
il pilota di auto da corsa
o piloto de corrida

auto racing
das Autorennen
las carreras de autos
la course automobile
l'auto da corsa
o automobilismo

motocross / das Motocross
el motocross / le motocross
la motocross / o motocrosse

motorcycle racing
das Motorradrennen
las carreras de motos
la course moto / le corse
di moto / o motociclismo

rally driving
das Rallyefahren
la conducción de rally
le rallye / il rally / o rally

SCIENCE

DIE WISSENSCHAFT

LAS CIENCIAS

LA SCIENCE

LA SCIENZA

A CIÊNCIA

SPACE / DIE RAUMFAHRT / EL ESPACIO / L'ESPACE / LO SPAZIO / O ESPAÇO

SOLAR SYSTEM / DAS SOLARSYSTEM / EL SISTEMA SOLAR / LE SYSTÈME SOLAIRE
IL SISTEMA SOLARE / O SISTEMA SOLAR

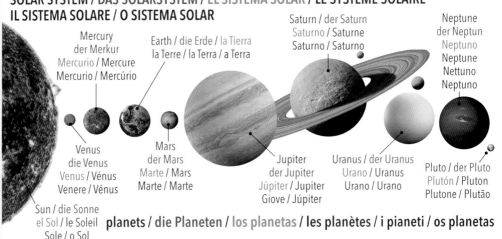

Mercury
der Merkur
Mercurio / Mercure
Mercurio / Mercúrio

Earth / die Erde / la Tierra
la Terre / la Terra / a Terra

Saturn / der Saturn
Saturno / Saturne
Saturno / Saturno

Neptune
der Neptun
Neptuno
Neptune
Nettuno
Neptuno

Venus
die Venus
Venus / Vénus
Venere / Vénus

Mars
der Mars
Marte / Mars
Marte / Marte

Jupiter
der Jupiter
Júpiter / Jupiter
Giove / Júpiter

Uranus / der Uranus
Urano / Uranus
Urano / Urano

Pluto / der Pluto
Plutón / Pluton
Plutone / Plutão

Sun / die Sonne
el Sol / le Soleil
Sole / o Sol

planets / die Planeten / los planetas / les planètes / i pianeti / os planetas

---

astronomy / die Astronomie / la astronomia / l'astronomie / l'astronomia / a astronomia

comet / der Komet
el cometa / la comète
la cometa / o cometa

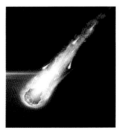

meteor / der Meteor
el meteoro / le météore
la meteora / o meteoro

asteroid / der Asteroid
el asteroide / l'astéroïde
l'asteroide / o asteroide

nebula / der Nebelfleck
la nebulosa / la nébuleuse
la nebulosa / a nebulosa

telescope / das Teleskop
el telescopio / le télescope
il telescopio / o telescópio

constellation / das Sternbild / la constelación
la constellation / la costellazione / a constelação

Milky Way / die Milchstraße
la vía Láctea / la Voie Lactée
la Via Lattea / a Via Láctea

star / der Stern
la estrella / l'étoile
la stella / a estrela

galaxy / die Galaxie / la galaxia
la galaxie / la galassia / a galáxia

full moon / der Vollmond / la luna llena
la pleine lune / la luna piena / a lua cheia

crescent moon / die Mondsichel
la luna creciente / le croissant de lune
la luna crescente / o quarto crescente

phases of the moon / die Mondphasen
las fases de la luna / les phases de la lune
le fasi della luna / as fases da lua

eclipse / die Sonnenfinsternis
el eclipse / l'éclipse
l'eclissi / o eclipse

---

space exploration / die Weltraumerkundung / la exploración espacial
l'exploration spatiale / l'esplorazione spaziale / o exploração espacial

rocket
die Rakete
el cohete
la fusée
il razzo
o foguetão

space suit
der Raumanzug
el traje espacial
la combinaison spatiale
la tuta spaziale
o fato espacial

launch pad / die Startrampe / la plataforma
de lanzamiento / la rampe de lancement
la rampa di lancio / a rampa de lançamento

astronaut / der Astronaut / el astronauta
l'astronaute / l'astronauta / o astronauta

satellite / der Satellit
el satélite / le satellite
il satellite / o satélite

space station / die Raumstation
la estación espacial / la station
spatiale / la stazione spaziale
a estação espacial

Mars rover / der Mars-Rover / el rover de Marte
le rover martien / il rover di Marte / o rover marciano

black hole / das schwarze
Loch / el agujero negro
le trou noir / il buco nero
o buraco negro

mission control
die Missionskontrolle
el centro de control
le centre de contrôle
il comando della missione
o controlo da missão

space flight
die Raumfahrt
el vuelo espacial
le vol spatial / il volo
spaziale / o voo espacial

booster rocket / die
Trägerrakete / el cohete
propulsor / le propulseur
auxiliaire / il razzo booster
o foguete auxiliar

orbit / die Umlaufbahn
la órbita / l'orbite
l'orbita / a órbita

space tourism / der
Weltraumtourismus
el turismo espacial
le tourisme spatial
il turismo spaziale
o turismo espacial

universe / das Weltall
el universo / l'univers
l'universo / o universo

space capsule
die Raumkapsel
la cápsula espacial
la capsule spatiale
la capsula spaziale
a cápsula espacial

EARTH / DIE ERDE / LA TIERRA / LA TERRE / LA TIERRA / A TERRA

North Pole / der Nordpol
el Polo Norte / le pôle Nord
il polo nord / o Polo Norte

pole / der Pol / el polo
le pôle / il polo / o polo

mountain range
der Gebirgszug
la cordillera
la chaine de montagne
la catena montuosa
a cordilheira

sea / das Meer
el mar / la mer
il mare / o mar

peninsula
die Halbinsel
la peninsula
la péninsule
la penisola
a península

land / das Land
la tierra / la terre
la terra / a terra

ocean / der Ozean
el océano / l'océan
l'oceano / o oceano

continent / der Kontinent
el continente / le continent
il continente / o continente

island / die Insel / la isla
l'île / l'isola / a ilha

South Pole / der Südpol / el Polo Sur
le pôle Sud / il Polo Sud / o Polo Sul

atmosphere / die Atmosphäre / la atmósfera
l'atmosphère / l'atmosfera / a atmosfera

mantle
der Erdmantel
el manto
le manteau
il mantello
o manto

crust
die Kruste
la corteza
la croûte
la crosta
a crosta

outer core
der äußere Kern
el núcleo externo
le coeur externe
il nucleo esterno
o núcleo externo

inner core / der innere Kern
el núcleo interno / le coeur interne
il nucleo interno / o núcleo interno

Earth's axis / die Erdachse / el eje de la Tierra
l'axe de rotation de la Terre / l'asse terrestre
o eixo da Terra

Earth's layers / die Schichten der Erde
las capas de la Tierra / les couches de la Terre
gli strati della Terra / as camadas da Terra

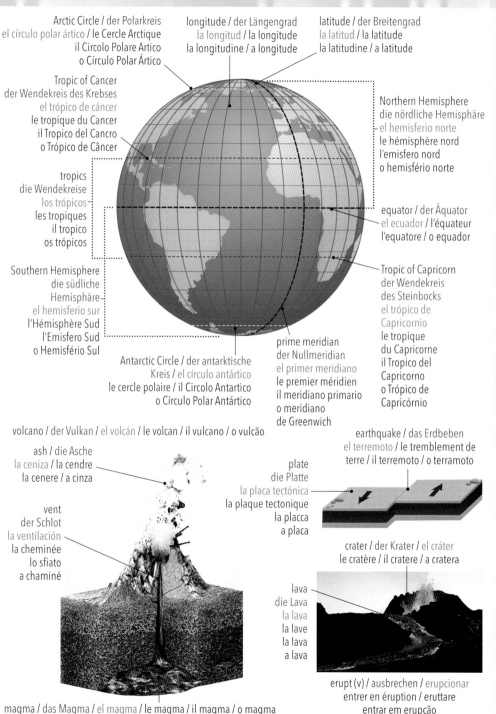

Arctic Circle / der Polarkreis
el círculo polar ártico / le Cercle Arctique
il Circolo Polare Artico
o Círculo Polar Ártico

longitude / der Längengrad
la longitud / la longitude
la longitudine / a longitude

latitude / der Breitengrad
la latitud / la latitude
la latitudine / a latitude

Tropic of Cancer
der Wendekreis des Krebses
el trópico de cáncer
le tropique du Cancer
il Tropico del Cancro
o Trópico de Câncer

Northern Hemisphere
die nördliche Hemisphäre
el hemisferio norte
le hémisphère nord
l'emisfero nord
o hemisfério norte

tropics
die Wendekreise
los trópicos
les tropiques
il tropico
os trópicos

equator / der Äquator
el ecuador / l'équateur
l'equatore / o equador

Southern Hemisphere
die südliche
Hemisphäre
el hemisferio sur
l'Hémisphère Sud
l'Emisfero Sud
o Hemisfério Sul

Tropic of Capricorn
der Wendekreis
des Steinbocks
el trópico de
Capricornio
le tropique
du Capricorne
il Tropico del
Capricorno
o Trópico de
Capricórnio

Antarctic Circle / der antarktische
Kreis / el círculo antártico
le cercle polaire / il Circolo Antartico
o Círculo Polar Antártico

prime meridian
der Nullmeridian
el primer meridiano
le premier méridien
il meridiano primario
o meridiano
de Greenwich

volcano / der Vulkan / el volcán / le volcan / il vulcano / o vulcão

ash / die Asche
la ceniza / la cendre
la cenere / a cinza

plate
die Platte
la placa tectónica
la plaque tectonique
la placca
a placa

earthquake / das Erdbeben
el terremoto / le tremblement de
terre / il terremoto / o terramoto

vent
der Schlot
la ventilación
la cheminée
lo sfiato
a chaminé

crater / der Krater / el cráter
le cratère / il cratere / a cratera

lava
die Lava
la lava
la lave
la lava
a lava

magma / das Magma / el magma / le magma / il magma / o magma

erupt (v) / ausbrechen / erupcionar
entrer en éruption / eruttare
entrar em erupção

WEATHER / DAS WETTER / EL CLIMA / LE CLIMAT / IL METEO / O CLIMA

Earth's atmosphere
die Erdatmosphäre
la atmósfera de la tierra
l'atmosphère terrestre
l'atmosfera terrestre
a atmosfera da Terra

exosphere / die Exosphäre / la exosfera
l'exosphère / l'esosfera / a exosfera

satellite / der Satellit / el satélite
le satellite / il satellite / o satélite

thermosphere / die Thermosphäre
la termosfera / la thermosphère
la termosfera / a termosfera

aurora / das Polarlicht / la aurora
l'aurore / l'aurora / a aurora

ionosphere
die Ionosphäre
la ionosfera
la ionosphère
la ionosfera
a ionosfera

mesosphere / die Mesosphäre
la mesosfera / la mésosphère
la mesosfera / a mesosfera

meteor / der Meteor / el meteoro
le météore / la meteora / o meteoro

ultraviolet rays
die ultravioletten
Strahlen
los rayos ultravioleta
les rayons ultraviolets
i raggi ultravioletti
os raios ultravioleta

stratosphere / die Stratosphäre
la estratosfera / la stratosphère
la stratosfera / a estratosfera

weather balloon
der Wetterballon / el globo
meteorológico / le ballon météo
il pallone meteorologico
o balão meteorológico

cloud / die Wolke
la nube / le nuage
la nuvola / a nuvem

ozone layer
die Ozonschicht
la capa de ozono
la couche d'ozone
lo strato di ozono
a camada de ozono

troposphere
die Troposphäre
la troposfera
la troposphère
la troposfera
a troposfera

sunshine / der Sonnenschein
la luz solar / le lever de soleil
le sole / a luz solar

lightning / der Blitzschlag
el relámpago / l'éclair
il fulmine / o relâmpago

thunderstorm / das Gewitter
la tormenta electrica / l'orage
il temporale / a trovoada

icicle / die Eiszapfen
el témpano de hielo
la stalactite / il ghiaccio
o sincelo

freeze / das Gefrieren
el congelamiento / le gel
la stalattite / o congelamento

---

windy / windig / el viento
venteux / ventoso / ventoso

humid / feucht / húmedo
humide / umido / húmido

hot / heiß / caliente / chaud
caldo / quente

warm / warm / cálido / chaud
caldo / ameno

cool / kühl / fresco / frais
fresco / fresco

cold / kalt / frío / froid
freddo / frio

thunder / das Gewitter / el trueno
l'éclair / il tuono / o trovão

meteorology / die Meteorologie
la meteorologia / la météorologie
la meteorologia / a meteorologia

wind / der Wind
el viento / le vent
il vento / o vento

fog / der Nebel
la niebla
le brouillard
la nebbia / o nevoeiro

cloudy / bewölkt
nublado / nuageux
nuvoloso / nublado

hail / der Hagel
el granizo / la grêle
la grandine
a saraiva

sleet / die Graupel
el aguanieve
le grésil / il nevischio
o granizo

rain / der Regen
la lluvia / la pluie
la pioggia / a chuva

rainbow / der Regenbogen
el arcoíris / l'arc-en-ciel
arcobaleno / o arco-íris

snow / der Schnee
la nieve / la neige
la neve / a neve

frost / der Frost
la escarcha / le gel
il gelo / a geada

flood / die Überschwemmung
la inundación / l'inondation
l'alluvione / a cheia

hurricane / der
Wirbelsturm
el huracán / la tornade
l'uragano / o furacão

monsoon / der Monsun
el monzón / la mousson
il monsone / a monção

tsunami / der Tsunami
el tsunami / le tsunami
lo tsunami / o tsunami

tidal wave / die Flutwelle
el maremoto
le raz-de-marée
il maremoto / o maremoto

tornado / der Wirbelsturm
el tornado / la tornade
il tornado / o tornado

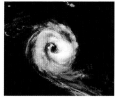

cyclone / der Wirbelsturm
el ciclón / le cyclone
il ciclone / o ciclone

typhoon / der Taifun
el tifón / le typhon
il tifone / o tufão

drought / die Dürre
la sequía / la sécheresse
la siccità / a seca

LANDSCAPE / DER LANDSCHAFT / EL PAISAJE / LES PAYSAGES
IL PAESAGGIO / A PAISAGEM

mist / der Nebel
la niebla / la brume
la nebbia / a névoa

mountains / die Berge
las montañas / les montagnes
le montagne / as montanhas

bank / der Ufer
la ladera / la rive
la banca / a margem

woodland / das Waldgebiet / el bosque
les bois / il bosco / o bosque

river / der Fluss / el río
la rivière / il fiume / o rio

hill / der Hügel / la colina
la colline / la collina / a colina

forest / der Wald
el bosque / la forêt
la foresta / a floresta

gorge / die Schlucht
el desfiladero / la gorge
la gola / a ravina

seashore / die Meeresküste
la orilla del mar / la côte
la riva del mare / o litoral

swamp / der Sumpf
el pantano / le marais
la palude / o pântano

cliff / die Klippe
el acantilado / la falaise
la scogliera / o penhasco

valley / das Tal
el valle / la vallée
la valle / o vale

rain forest / der Regenwald
el bosque lluvioso / la forêt tropicale
la foresta pluviale / a floresta tropical

desert / die Wüste
el desierto / le désert
il deserto / o deserto

plateau / die Hochebene
la meseta / le plateau
l'altopiano / o planalto

mesa / der Tafelberg
la mesa / la mesa
la mesa / a mesa

savannah / die Savanne
la sabana / la savane
la savana / a savana

meadowland
das Wiesenland
la pradera / la prairie
la prateria / o pasto

estuary
die Flussmündung
el estuario / l'estuaire
l'estuario / o estuário

waterfall
der Wasserfall
la cascada / la cascade
la cascata / a cascata

coral reef / der Korallenriff
el arrecife de coral
la barrière de corail
la barriera corallina
o recife de coral

tundra / die Tundra
la tundra / la toundra
la tundra / a tundra

glacier / der Gletscher
el glaciar / le glacier
il ghiacciaio / o glaciar

bog / das Moor
el pantano / la tourbière
la palude / o paul

steppe / die Steppe
la estepa / la steppe
la steppa / a estepe

plain / die Ebene
la planicie / la plaine
la pianura / a planície

stream / der Bach
la corriente / le ruisseau
il torrente / o riacho

coast / die Küste
la costa / la côte
la costa / a costa

lake / der See
el lago / le lac
il lago / o lago

ROCKS / DIE STEINE / LAS ROCAS / LES ROCHERS / LE ROCCE / AS ROCHAS

sedimentary / sedimentär / sedimentarias / sédimentaires / sedimentario / sedimentar

fossil / das Fossil
el fósil / le fossile
il fossile / o fóssil

rock hammer
der Steinhammer
el martillo de roca
le marteau à pierres
il martello da roccia
o martelo de rocha

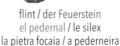

sandstone / der Sandstein
la piedra arenisca / le grès
l'arenaria / o arenito

shale / der Schiefer
la lutita / l'argile
lo shale / o xisto

conglomerate / das Konglomerat
el conglomerado / le conglomérat
il conglomerato / o conglomerado

limestone / der Kalkstein
la piedra caliza / le calcaire
il calcare / o calcário

chalk / die Kreide
la tiza / la craie
il gesso / o giz

flint / der Feuerstein
el pedernal / le silex
la pietra focaia / a pederneira

coal / die Kohle / el carbón
le charbon / il carbone
o carvão

---

igneous / vulkanisch / ígneas / ignées igneo / ígneo

pumice / der Bimsstein
la piedra pómez / la pierre ponce
la pomice / a pedra-pomes

granite / der Granit
el granito / le granit
il granito / o granito

obsidian / der Obsidian
la obsidiana / l'obsidienne
l'ossidiana / a obsidiana

basalt / der Basalt
el basalto / le basalte
il basalto / o basalto

metamorphic / metamorph / metamórficas métamorphiques / metamorfico / metamórfica

slate / der Schiefer
la pizarra / l'ardoise
l'ardesia / a ardósia

schist / der Schiefer
el esquisto / le schiste
lo scisto / o xistos

gneiss / der Gneis
el gneis / le gneiss
lo gneiss / a gnaisse

marble / der Marmor
el mármol / le marbre
il marmo / o mármore

---

gems / die Edelsteine / las gemas / les pierres précieuses / le gemme / as gemas

diamond
der Diamant
el diamante
le diamant
il diamante
o diamante

ruby
der Rubin
el rubí
le rubis
il rubino
o rubi

emerald
der Smaragd
la esmeralda
l'émeraude
lo smeraldo
a esmeralda

sapphire
der Saphir
el zafiro
le saphir
lo zaffiro
a safira

MINERALS / DIE MINERALIEN / LOS MINERALES / LES MINERAUX
I MINERALI / OS MINERAIS

malachite
der Malachit
la malaquita
la malachite
la malachite
a malaquita

quartz / der Quarz
el cuarzo / le quartz
il quarzo / o quartzo

turquoise
der Türkis
la turquesa
la turquoise
il turchese
a turquesa

graphite / der Graphit
el grafito / le graphite
la grafite / a grafite

mica / der Glimmer
la mica / le mica
la mica / a mica

sulfur / der Schwefel
el azufre / le soufre
lo zolfo / o enxofre

hematite
der Hämati
la hematita
l'hématite / l'ematite
a hematite

calcite / der Calcit
la calcita / la calcite
la calcite / a calcite

fluorite / der Fluorit
la fluorita / le fluor
la fluorite / a fluorite

agate / der Achat
el ágata / l'agate
l'agata / a ágata

metals / die Metalle / los metales / les métaux / i metalli / os metais

silver / das Silber
la plata / l'argent
l'argento / a prata

gold / das Gold
el oro / l'or
l'oro / o ouro

copper / das Kupfer
el cobre / le cuire
il rame / o cobre

aluminum
das Aluminium
el aluminio
l'aluminium
l'alluminio
o alumínio

nickel / das Nickel
el níquel / le nickel
il nichel / o níquel

lead / das Blei
el plomo / le plomb
il piombo / o chumbo

iron / das Eisen
el hierro / le fer
il ferro / o ferro

platinum
das Platin / el platino
le platine / il platino
a platina

zinc / das Zink
el zinc / le zinc
lo zinco / o zinco

tin / das Zinn
la lata / l'étain
lo stagno / o estanho

PLANTS / DIE PFLANZEN / LAS PLANTAS
LES PLANTES / LE PIANTE / AS PLANTAS

trees / die Bäume / los árboles / les arbres gli alberi / as árvores

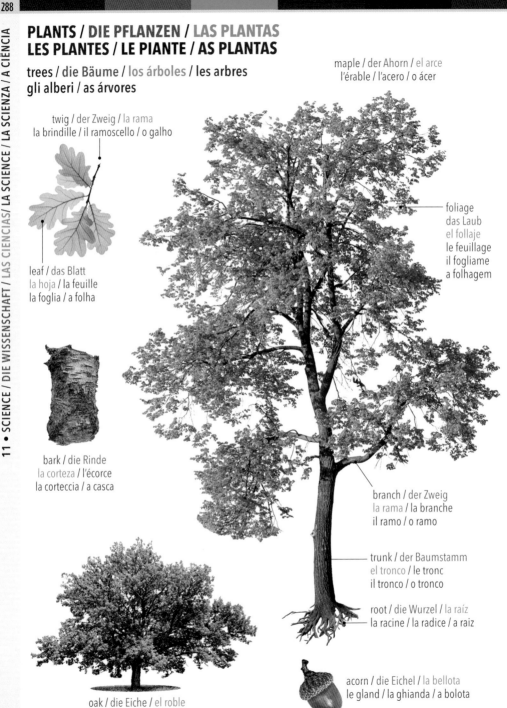

maple / der Ahorn / el arce
l'érable / l'acero / o ácer

twig / der Zweig / la rama
la brindille / il ramoscello / o galho

leaf / das Blatt
la hoja / la feuille
la foglia / a folha

foliage
das Laub
el follaje
le feuillage
il fogliame
a folhagem

bark / die Rinde
la corteza / l'écorce
la corteccia / a casca

branch / der Zweig
la rama / la branche
il ramo / o ramo

trunk / der Baumstamm
el tronco / le tronc
il tronco / o tronco

root / die Wurzel / la raíz
la racine / la radice / a raiz

oak / die Eiche / el roble
le chêne / la quercia / o carvalho

acorn / die Eichel / la bellota
le gland / la ghianda / a bolota

elm / die Ulme
el olmo / l'orme
l'olmo / o olmo

beech / die Buche
la haya / le hêtre
il faggio / a faia

willow / die Weide
el sauce / le saule
il salice / o salgueiro

palm / die Palme
la palma / le palmier
la palma / a palmeira

poplar / die Pappel
el álame / le peuplier
il pioppo / o choupo

holly / die Stechpalme
el acebo / le houx
l'agrifoglio /o azevinho

birch / die Birke
el abedul / le bouleau
la betulla / a bétula

eucalyptus / der Eukalyptus
el eucalipto
l'eucalyptus / l'eucalipto
o eucalipto

cedar / die Zeder
el cedro / le cèdre
il cedro / o cedro

pine / die Kiefer
el pino / le pin
il pino / o pinheiro

spruce / die Fichte
el abeto / l'épicéa
l'abete rosso / o abeto

flowering plants / die blühenden Pflanzen / las plantas florales
les plantes à fleurs / la piante da fiore / as plantas com flores

poppy / der Mohn / la amapola
le coquelicot / il papavero / a papoila

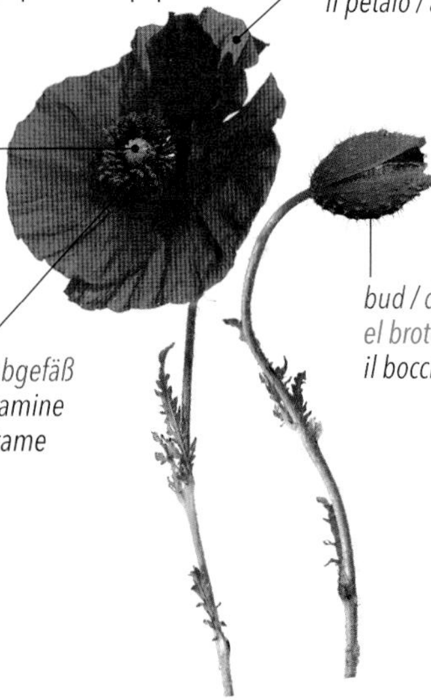

petal / das Blütenblatt
el pétalo / le pétale
il petalo / a pétala

pistil
der Griffel
el pistilo
le pistil
il pistillo
o pistilo

violet / das Veilchen
la violeta / la violette
la violetta / a violeta

bud / die Knospe
el brote / le bourgeon
il bocciolo / o botão

stamen / das Staubgefäß
el estambre / l'étamine
lo stame / o estame

honeysuckle
das Geißblatt
la madreselva
le chèvrefeuille
il caprifoglio
a madressilva

primrose
die Schlüsselblume
la onagra
la primevère
la primula
a prímula

lupine
die Lupine
el lupino
le lupin
il lupino
o lupino

buttercup
der Hahnenfuß
el botón de oro
le bouton d'or
il ranuncolo
o ranúnculo

lavender
der Lavendel
la lavanda
la lavande
la lavanda
a lavanda

daisy
das Gänseblümchen
la margarita
la marguerite
la margherita
a margarida

nettle
die Brennnessel
la ortiga / l'ortie
l'ortica / a urtiga

crocus
der Krokus
el azafrán / le crocus
il croco / o croco

jasmine
der Jasmin
el jazmín / le jasmin
il gelsomino
o jasmim

marigold
die Ringelblume
la caléndula / le souci
la calendula
a calêndula

clover / der Klee
el trébol / le trèfle
il trifoglio / o trevo

thistle / die Distel
el cardo / le chardon
il cardo / o cardo

dandelion
der Löwenzahn
el diente de león / le pissenlit
il dente di leone
o dente-de-leão

lily of the valley
das Maiglöckchen
el lirio de los valles
le muguet / il mughetto
o lírio do vale

orchid / die Orchidee
la orquídea / l'orchidée
l'orchidea / a orquídea

bluebells
die Glockenblumen
las campanillas
la jacinthe des bois
il mughetgo / a campainha

heather / die Heidekraut
el brezo / la bruyère
l'erica / a urze

daffodil / die Narzisse
el narciso / la jonquille
la giunchiglia / o narciso

foxglove / der Fingerhut
la dedalera / la digitale
il digitale / a dedaleira

geranium / die Geranie
el geranio / le géranium
il geranio / a sardinheira

dahlia / die Dahlie
la dalia / le dahlia
la dalia / a dália

zinnia / die Zinnie
el zinnia / la zinnia
la zinnia / a zínia

sunflower
die Sonnenblume
el girasol / le tournesol
il girasole / o girassol

ANIMALS / DIE TIERE / LOS ANIMALES / LES ANIMAUX GLI ANIMALI / OS ANIMAIS

amphibians / die Amphibien / los anfibios / les amphibiens / gli anfibi / os anfíbios

frog / der Frosch
la rana / la grenouille
la rana / a rã

tadpole
die Kaulquappe
el renacuajo
le têtard
il girino
o girino

toad / die Kröte
el sapo
le crapaud
il rospo / o sapo

salamander
der Salamander
la salamandra
la salamandre
la salamandra
a salamandra

newt / der Molch
el tritón / le triton
il tritone / o tritão

reptiles / die Reptilien / los reptiles / les reptiles / i rettili / os répteis

scales
der Schuppen
las escamas
les écailles
le squame
as escamas

snout / die Schnauze / el hocico
le museau / il muso / o focinho

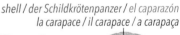

snake / die Schlange / la serpiente
le serpent / il serpente / a cobra

crocodile / das Krokodil / el cocodrilo
le crocodile / il coccodrillo
o crocodilo

alligator / der Alligator / el caimán
l'alligator / l'alligatore / o jacaré

shell / der Schildkrötenpanzer / el caparazón
la carapace / il carapace / a carapaça

iguana / der Leguan
la iguana / l'iguane
l'iguana / a iguana

lizard / die Eidechse
el lagarto / le lézard
la lucertola / o lagarto

turtle / die Schildkröte
la tortuga / la tortue
la tartaruga / a tartaruga

tortoise/ die Schildkröte
el galápago / la tortue
terrestre / la testuggine
a tartaruga terrestre

birds / die Vögel / las aves / les oiseaux / gli uccelli / os pássaros

swallow / die Schwalbe
la golondrina
la hirondelle
la rondine
a andorinha

crow / die Krähe
el cuervo / le corbeau
il corvo / o corvo

pigeon / die Taube
la paloma / le pigeon
il piccione
o pombo

woodpecker
der Specht / el pájaro
carpintero / le pic
il picchio / o pica-pau

hummingbird
der Kolibri / el colibrí
le colibri / il colibrì
o colibri

sparrow / der Sperling
el gorrión
le moineau
il passero / o pardal

wing / die Flügel
el ala / l'aile
l'ala / a asa

tail / der Schwanz
la cola / la queue
la coda / a cauda

feather / die Feder
la pluma / la plume
la piuma / a pena

falcon / der Falke
el halcón / le faucon
il falco / o falcão

hawk / der Habicht
el gavilán / l'aigle
il falco / o açor

owl / die Eule
el búho / le hibou
il gufo / a coruja

talon / die Kralle
la garra / la serre
l'artiglio / a garra

crane / der Kranich
la grulla / la grue
la gru / o grou

stork / der Storch
la cigüeña
la cigogne
la cicogna / a cegonha

gull / der Möwe
la gaviota
la mouette
il gabbiano
a gaivota

pelican / der Pelikan
el pelícano
le pélican / il pellicano
o pelicano

eagle / der Adler
el águila / l'aigle
l'aquila / a águia

penguin / der Pinguin
el pingüino
le pingouin
il pinguino / o pinguim

goose / die Gans
el ganso / l'oie
l'oca / o ganso

swan / der Schwan
el cisne / le cygne
il cigno / o cisne

duck / die Ente
el pato / le canard
l'anatra / o pato

ostrich / der Strauß
el avestruz
l'autruche / lo struzzo
a avestruz

peacock / der Pfau
el pavo real / le paon
il pavone / o pavão

pheasant / der Fasan
el faisán / le faisan
il fagiano / o faisão

turkey / der Truthahn
el pavo / la dinde
il tacchino / o peru

beak
der Schnabel
el pico / le bec
il becco / o bico

parrot / der Papagei
el loro / le perroquet
il pappagallo
o papagaio

cockatoo
der Kakadu
la cacatúa
le cacatoès
il cacatua / a catatua

parakeet
der Sittich
el perico / la perruche
il parrocchetto
o periquito

canary
der Kanarienvogel
el canario / le canari
il canarino / o canário

flamingo
der Flamingo
el flamenco
le flamand rose
il fenicottero
o flamingo

fishes / die Fische / los peces / les poissons / i pesci / os peixes

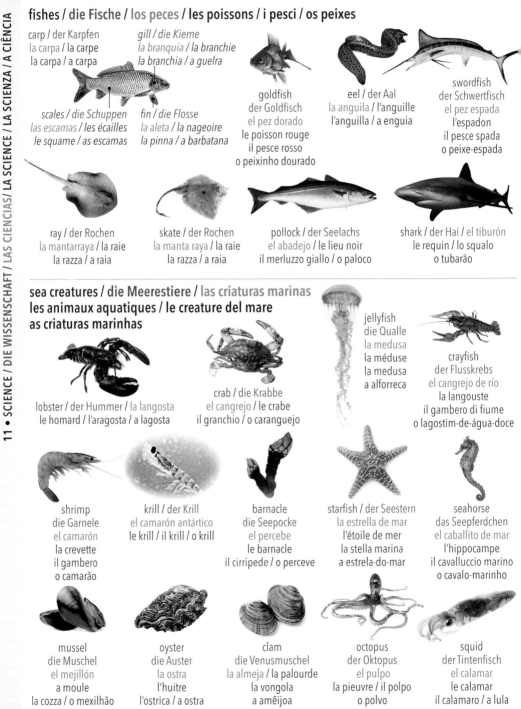

carp / der Karpfen
la carpa / la carpe
la carpa / a carpa

gill / die Kieme
la branquia / la branchie
la branchia / a guelra

scales / die Schuppen
las escamas / les écailles
le squame / as escamas

fin / die Flosse
la aleta / la nageoire
la pinna / a barbatana

goldfish
der Goldfisch
el pez dorado
le poisson rouge
il pesce rosso
o peixinho dourado

eel / der Aal
la anguila / l'anguille
l'anguilla / a enguia

swordfish
der Schwertfisch
el pez espada
l'espadon
il pesce spada
o peixe-espada

ray / der Rochen
la mantarraya / la raie
la razza / a raia

skate / der Rochen
la manta raya / la raie
la razza / a raia

pollock / der Seelachs
el abadejo / le lieu noir
il merluzzo giallo / o paloco

shark / der Hai / el tiburón
le requin / lo squalo
o tubarão

sea creatures / die Meerestiere / las criaturas marinas
les animaux aquatiques / le creature del mare
as criaturas marinhas

jellyfish
die Qualle
la medusa
la méduse
la medusa
a alforreca

crayfish
der Flusskrebs
el cangrejo de río
la langouste
il gambero di fiume
o lagostim-de-água-doce

lobster / der Hummer / la langosta
le homard / l'aragosta / a lagosta

crab / die Krabbe
el cangrejo / le crabe
il granchio / o caranguejo

shrimp
die Garnele
el camarón
la crevette
il gambero
o camarão

krill / der Krill
el camarón antártico
le krill / il krill / o krill

barnacle
die Seepocke
el percebe
le barnacle
il cirripede / o perceve

starfish / der Seestern
la estrella de mar
l'étoile de mer
la stella marina
a estrela-do-mar

seahorse
das Seepferdchen
el caballito de mar
l'hippocampe
il cavalluccio marino
o cavalo-marinho

mussel
die Muschel
el mejillón
a moule
la cozza / o mexilhão

oyster
die Auster
la ostra
l'huitre
l'ostrica / a ostra

clam
die Venusmuschel
la almeja / la palourde
la vongola
a amêijoa

octopus
der Oktopus
el pulpo
la pieuvre / il polpo
o polvo

squid
der Tintenfisch
el calamar
le calamar
il calamaro / a lula

insects / die Insekten / los insectos / les insectes / gli insetti / os insetos

ant / die Ameise
la hormiga
la fourmi / la formica
a formiga

beetle / der Käfer
el escarabajo
le scarabée
lo scarabeo
o escaravelho

bee / die Biene
la abeja / l'abeille
l'ape / a abelha

wasp / die Wespe
la avispa / la guêpe
la vespa / a vespa

hornet / die Hornisse
el avispón / le frelon
il calabrone
o vespão

cockroach
der Küchenschabe
la cucaracha
le cafard
lo scarafaggio
a barata

moth / die Motte
la polilla / le papillon
de nuit / la falena
a traça

*cocoon
der Kokon
el capullo
le cocon
il bozzolo
o casulo*

caterpillar / die Raupe / la oruga
la chenille / il bruco / a lagarta

*antenna / die Antenne
la antena / l'antenne
l'antenna / a antena*

butterfly / der Schmetterling
la mariposa / le papillon
la farfalla / a borboleta

cricket / die Grille
el grillo / le criquet
il grillo / o grilo

grasshopper
der Grashüpfer
el saltamontes
la sauterelle
la cavalletta
o gafanhoto

ladybug
der Marienkäfer
la mariquita
la coccinelle
la coccinella
a joaninha

scorpion
der Skorpion
el escorpión
le scorpion
lo scorpione
o escorpião

centipede
der Tausendfüßler
el ciempiés
le mille-pattes
il millepiedi
a centopeia

dragonfly / die Libelle / la libélula
la libellule / la libellula / a libélula

fly / die Fliege
la mosca / la mouche
la mosca / a mosca

mosquito / die Stechmück
el mosquito / le moustique
la zanzara / o mosquito

spider / die Spinne
la araña / l'araignée
il ragno / a aranha

slug / die Schnecke
la babosa / la limace
la lumaca / a lesma

snail / die Schnecke
el caracol / l'escargot
la coccinella
o caracol

worm / der Wurm
el gusano
le ver de terre
il verme
a minhoca

praying mantis / die Gottesanbeterin
la mantis religiosa / la mante religieuse
la mantide religiosa / a louva-a-deus

mammals / die Säugetiere / los mamíferos / les mammifères / i mammiferi / os mamíferos

mouse / die Maus
el ratón / la souris
il topo / o rato

hamster / der Hamtser
el hámster
le hamster / il criceto
o hamster

rat / die Ratte
la rata / le rat
il ratto / a ratazana

squirrel
das Eichhörnchen
la ardilla / l'écureuil
lo scoiattolo / o esquilo

rabbit
das Kaninchen
el conejo / le lapin
il coniglio / o coelho

hedgehog / der Igel
el erizo / le hérisson
il riccio
o ouriço-cacheiro

raccoon
der Waschbär
el mapache / le raton
laveur / il procione
o guaxinim

chipmunk / das
Streifenhörnchen
la ardilla / le tamia
lo scoiattolo
o esquilo norte-
americano

skunk / der Stinktier
la mofeta / le putois
la puzzola
a doninha

opossum
der Opossum
la zarigüeya
l'opossum
l'opussum
o gambá

dog / der Hund
el perro / le chien
il cane / o cachorro

*puppy / der Welpe
el cachorro / le chiot
il cucciolo
o cachorro*

fox / der Fuchs
el zorro / le renard
la volpe / a raposa

wolf / der Wolf
el lobo / le loup
il lupo / o lobo

coyote / der Kojote
el coyote / le coyote
il coyote / o coiote

*kitten / das Kätzchen / el gatito
le chaton / il gattino / o gatinho*

cat / die Katze
el gato / le chat
il gatto / o gato

leopard / der Leopard
el leopardo / le léopard
il leopardo / o leopardo

lion / der Löwe
el león / le lion
il leone / o leão

tiger / der Tiger
el tigre / le tigre
la tigre / o tigre

jaguar / der Jaguar
el jaguar / le jaguar
il giaguaro / o jaguar

zebra / das Zebra
la cebra / le zèbre
la zebra / a zebra

*tusk
der Stoßzahn
el colmillo
la défense
la zanna / o javali*

*trunk / der Rüssel
el tronco
la trompe
la proboscide
a tromba*

elephant / der Elefant
el elefante / l'éléphant
l'elefante / o elefante

rhinoceros
die Rhinozeros
el rinoceronte
le rhinocéros / il rinoceronte
o rinoceronte

hippopotamus
das Nilpferd
el hipopótamo
l'hippopotame
l'ippopotamo
o hipopótamo

hump / der Höcker / la joroba
la bosse / la gobba / a bossa

antlers / das Geweih / las astas
les bois / le corna / os chifres

camel / das Kamel
el camello / le chameau
il cammello / o camelo

llama / das Lama
la llama / le lama
il lama / o lama

giraffe / die Giraffe
la jirafa / la girafe
la giraffa / a girafa

sloth / das Faultier
el perezoso
le paresseux
il bradipo / a preguiça

deer / der Hirsch
el ciervo / le cerf
il cervo / o veado

orangutan
der Orang-Utan
el orangután
l'orang-outang
l'orango
o orangotango

monkey / der Affe
el mono / le singe
la scimmia / o macaco

chimpanzee / der Schimpanse
el chimpancé / le chimpanzé
lo scimpanzé / o chimpanzé

gorilla / der Gorilla
el gorila / le gorille
il gorilla / o gorila

pouch / der Beutel
la bolsa / la poche
il marsupio / a bolsa

kangaroo / der Känguru / el canguro
le kangourou / il canguro / o canguru

panda / der Panda
el panda / le panda
il panda / o panda

polar bear
der Eisbär
el oso polar
l'ours polaire
l'orso polare
o urso polar

bear / der Bär
el oso / l'ours
l'orso / o urso

sea lion / der Seelöwe
el león marino / l'otarie
il leone marino
o leão marinho

koala / der Koala
el koala / le koala
il koala / o coala

flipper / der Flipper
la aleta / la nageoire
la pinna / a barbatana

walrus / das Walross / la morsa
le morse / il tricheco / a morsa

blowhole / das Blasloch / el espiráculo
l'évent / lo sfiatatoio / o espiráculo

seal / der Seehund
la foca / le phoque
la foca / a foca

porpoise
der Schweinswal
la marsopa
le marsouin
la focena
o porco-do-mar

dolphin / der Delphin
el delfin / le dauphin
il delfino / o golfinho

whale / der Wal / la ballena
la baleine / la balena / a baleia

SCIENCE / DIE WISSENSCHAFT / LAS CIENCIAS / LES SCIENCES
LA SCIENZA / A CIÊNCIA

scientist / der Wissenschaftler / el científico
le scientifique / lo scienziato / o cientista

bunsen burner
der Bunsenbrenner
el mechero Bunsen / le bec Bunsen
il becco di Bunsen / o bico de Bunsen

laboratory / das Labor / el laboratorio
le laboratoire / il laboratorio / o laboratório

crucible / der Schmelztiegel
el crisol / le creuset
il crogiolo / o cadinho

experiment / das Experiment
el experimento / l'expérience
l'esperimento / a experiência

stopper / das Stopfen
el tapón / le bouchon
il tappo / o tampão

funnel / der Trichter
el embudo / l'entonnoir
l'imbuto / o funil

test tube / das Reagenzglas
el tubo de ensayo
le tube à essai / la provetta
o tubo de ensaio

stirring rod / der Rührstab
la varilla agitadora
le mélangeur
la bacchetta
a vareta

rack / das Gestell
el estante / le support
la rastrelliera / o suporte

beaker / das Becherglas
el vaso de precipitados
le bécher / il becher
o gobelé

flask / der Kolben / el matraz / la fiol
la boccetta / o balão de vidro

alligator clip
die Krokodilklemme
el clip cocodrilo
la pince crocodile
il morsetto
o clipe jacaré

spring balance
der Federwaage
la balanza de resorte
la balance à ressort
la bilancia a molla
o dinamómetro

dropper / der Tropfer
el gotero
le compte-gouttes
il contagocce / o conta-gotas

magnet / das Magnet
el imán / l'aimant
il magnete / o íman

microscope / das Mikroskop
el microscopio / le microscope
il microscopio / o microscópio

pestle / der Stößel
el pilón / le pilon
il pestello / o pilau

objective lens
die Objektivlinse
el lente objetivo
la lentille de focalisation
la lente obiettio / a objetiva

focusing knob
der Fokussierknopf
la perilla de enfoque
le bouton de mise au point
la manopola
della messa a fuoco
o botão de foco

stage / die Bühne
la placa / la platine
la piastrina / a platina

mortar / der Mörser
el mortero / le mortier
il mortaio / o almofariz

slide / der Objektträger
el portaobjetos / la lame
il vetrino / a lâmina

mirror / der Spiegel
el espejo / le miroir
lo specchio / o espelho

pipette / die Pipette
la pipeta / la pipette
la pipetta / a pipeta

positive electrode
die positive Elektrode
el electrodo positivo
le pôle plus
l'elettrodo positivo
o elétrodo positivo

negative electrode
die negative Elektrode
el electrodo negativo
le pôle moins
l'elettrodo negativo
o elétrodo negativo

petri dish / die Petrischale
la placa de petri
la boîte de Petri
la capsula di Petri
a placa de Petri

centrifuge / die Zentrifuge
la centrifugadora / la centrifugeuse
la centrifuga / a centrifugadora

battery / die Batterie
la batería / la batterie
la batteria / a pilha

MATHEMATICS / DIE MATHEMATIK / LAS MATEMÁTICAS
LES MATHEMATIQUES / LA MATEMATICA / A MATEMÁTICA

operations / die Operationen / las operaciones / les opérations / le operazioni / as operações

addition / die Addition
la suma / l'addition
l'addizione / a adição

$$1 + 2 = 3$$

add (v) / addieren
agregar / ajouter
aggiungere / somar

multiplication
die Multiplikation
la multiplicación
la multiplication
la moltiplicazione
a multiplicação

$$2 \times 3 = 6$$

multiply (v) / multiplizieren
multiplicar / multiplier
moltiplicare / multiplicar

subtraction / die Subtraktion
la resta / la soustraction
la sottrazione / a subtração

$$7 - 2 = 5$$

subtract (v) / subtrahieren
restar / soustraire
sottrarre / subtrair

division / die Division
la división / la division
la divisione / a divisão

$$9 \div 3 = 3$$

divide (v) / dividieren
dividir / diviser
dividere / dividir

+ plus / plus / el más
plus / più / mais

− minus / minus / el menos
moins / meno / menos

= equals / ist gleich / el igual
égale / uguale a / igual

fraction
der Bruch
la fracción
la fraction
la frazione
a fração

$\dfrac{3}{4}$ — numerator / der Zähler / el numerador
le numérateur / il numeratore / o numerador
— denominator / der Nenner
el denominador / le dénominateur
il denominatore / o denominador

equation
die Gleichung
la ecuación
l'équation
l'equazione
a equação

exponent / der Exponent
el exponente / l'exposant
l'esponente / o expoente

$$(x + 3)^2 = 16$$

lines / die Linien / las líneas / les lignes / le linee / as linhas

straight / gerade / recta
droite / retta / reta

curved / gekrümmt / la curva
courbe / le curve / a linha curva

parallel / parallel / paralela
parallèle / parallela / paralela

perpendicular / senkrecht / perpendicular
perpendiculaire / perpendicolare / perpendicular

solid figures / die festen Figuren / las figuras sólidas / les solides
le figure solide / as figuras

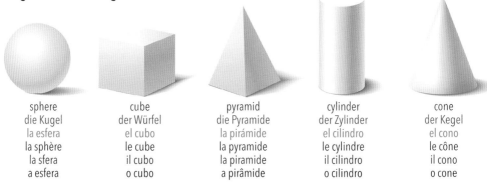

sphere	cube	pyramid	cylinder	cone
die Kugel	der Würfel	die Pyramide	der Zylinder	der Kegel
la esfera	el cubo	la pirámide	el cilindro	el cono
la sphère	le cube	la pyramide	le cylindre	le cône
la sfera	il cubo	la piramide	il cilindro	il cono
a esfera	o cubo	a pirâmide	o cilindro	o cone

shapes / die Formen / las formas / les formes / le forme / as formas

circle / der Kreis / el círculo / le cercle / il cerchio / o círculo

arc / der Bogen
el arco / l'arc de cercle
l'arco / o arco

circumference
der Kreisumfang
la circunferencia
la circonférence
la circonferenza
a circunferência

center
der Mittelpunkt
el centro / le centre
il centro / o centro

diameter / der Durchmesser
el diámetro / le diamètre
il diametro / o diâmetro

radius / der Radius
el radio / le rayon
il raggio / o raio

parallelogram / das Parallelogramm
el paralelogramo
le parallélogramme
il parallelogramma
o paralelogramo

square / das Quadrat / el cuadrado
le carré / il quadrato / o quadrado

diagonal / die Diagonale / la diagonal
la diagonale / la diagonale / a diagonal

rectangle / das Rechteck
el rectángulo
le rectangle / il rettangolo
o retângulo

trapezoid / das Trapez
el trapezoide
le trapèze / il trapezio
o trapézio

rhombus / der Rhombus
el rombo / le losange
il rombo / o losango

pentagon / das Fünfeck
el pentágono
le pentagone
il pentagono
o pentágono

hexagon / das Sechseck
el hexágono / l'hexagone
l'esagono / o hexágono

octagon / das Achteck
el octágono / l'octogone
l'ottagono / o octógono

angle
der Winkel
el ángulo
l'angle
l'angolo
o ângulo

hypotenuse / die Hypotenuse
la hipotenusa / l'hypoténuse
l'ipotenusa / a hipotenusa

triangle / das Dreieck / el triángulo
le triangle / il triangolo / o triângulo

---

measurements / die Maße / las medidas / les mesures / le misure / as medidas

dimensions
die Abmessungen
las dimensiones
les dimensions
le dimensioni
as dimensões

height / die Höhe / la altura
la hauteur / l'altezza / a altura

depth / die Tiefe
la profundidad
la profondeur
la profondità
a profundidade

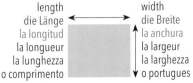

area / die Fläche / la zona / l'aire / l'area / a área

length
die Länge
la longitud
la longueur
la lunghezza
o comprimento

width
die Breite
la anchura
la largeur
la larghezza
o portugues

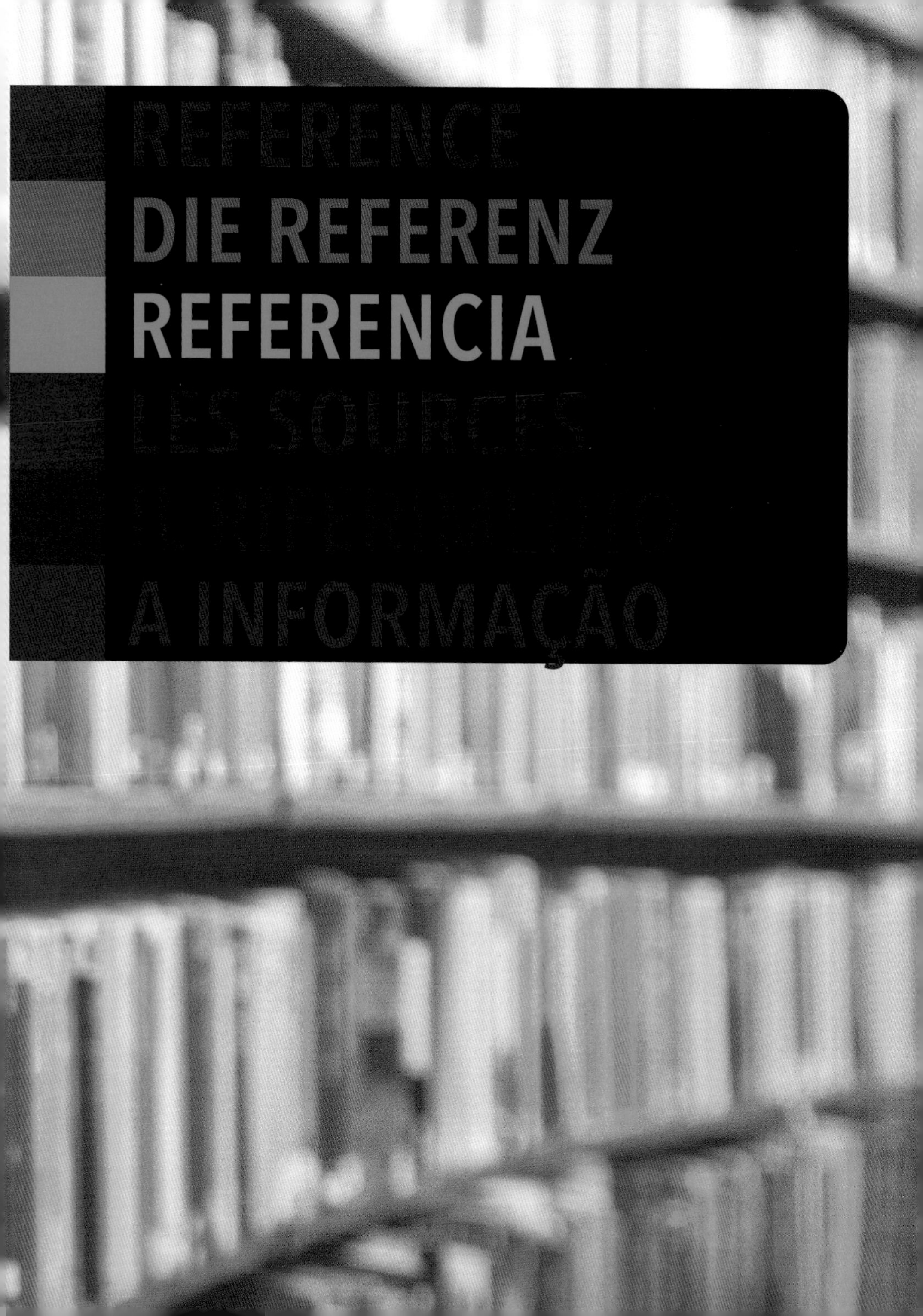

REFERENCE

DIE REFERENZ

REFERENCIA

LES SOURCES

DI RIFERIMENTO

A INFORMAÇÃO

GRAMMAR / DIE GRAMMATIK / LA GRAMÁTICA / LA GRAMMAIRE
LA GRAMMATICA / A GRAMÁTICA

ARTICLES / DIE ARTIKEL
LOS ARTÍCULOS / LES ARTICLES
GLI ARTICOLI / OS ARTIGOS

a / a / un/una / un/une / a / um/uma

an / ein / un/una / un/une
un / um/uma

the / die/der/das / el/la / le/la
il/la / o/a

on top of / über
encima de / sur
sopra a / em cima de

PRONOUNS / DIE PRONOMEN
LOS PRONOMBRES
LES PRONOMS / I PRONOMI
OS PRONOMES

him / er / él / lui / lui / ele

her / ihr / ella / elle / lei / ela

it / es / ese/esa / lui / esso / ele/ela

they / sie / ellos/ellas / ils / loro
eles/elas

them / sie / ellos/ellas / eux
loro / eles/elas

behind / hinter / detrás de
derrière / dietro / atrás

he / er / él / ils
lui / ele

she / sie / ella / elle / lei / ela

PREPOSITIONS / DIE
VORBEMERKUNGEN
LAS PREPOSICIONES
LES PREPOSITIONS
LE PREPOSIZIONI
AS PREPOSIÇÕES

at / unter / en / à / su / em

for / für / para / pour / per / para

to / zu / a / vers / a / para

by / von / por / par / da / por

in / in / dentro de / dans / in / em

of / von / de / de / di / de

out / aus / fuera de / hors de
out / fora

above / oben / encima / au-dessus
sopra / acima

below / unten / debajo / en-dessous
sotto / abaixo

over / über / sobre / par-dessus
sopra / sobre

under / unter / bajo / sous
sotto / sob

between / zwischen / entre
entre / tra / entre

in front of / vor / frente a
devant / davanti a / à frente de

up / auf / arriba de / dans / su / cima

down / unten / abajo / en bas de
giù / baixo

before / vor / antes / avant
prima di / antes

after / nach / después / après
dopo / após

from / von / desde / de / da / de

around / um / alrededor / autour
intorno a / à volta

beside / neben / al lado de / à côté de
accanto a / junto

through / durch / a través de
à travers / attraverso / através

toward / zu / hacia / vers / verso
em direção a

with / mit / con / avec / con / com

within / innerhalb / en / dans
dentro / dentro de

without / ohne / sin / sans
senza / sem

along / entlang / a lo largo de
le long de / con / adiante

PHRASES / DIE PHRASEN / LAS FRASES / LES PHRASES / LE FRASI / AS FRASES

essential phrases / die wesentliche Phrasen / las frases esenciales les phrases essentielles / le fasi essenziali as frases essenciais

Yes. / Ja. / Sí. / Oui. / Sì. / Sim.

No. / Nein. / No. / Non. / No. / Não.

Maybe. / Vielleicht. / Quizás. / Peut-être. / Forse. / Talvez.

Please. / Bitte. / Por favor. / S'il vous plait. / Per favore. Por favor.

Thank you. / Dankeschön. / Gracias. / Merci. / Grazie. Obrigado.

You're welcome. / Nichts zu danken. / De nada. Je vous en prie. / Non c'è di che. / De nada.

Excuse me. / Verzeihen Sie. / Disculpa. / Excusez-moi. Scusami. / Desculpa.

I'm sorry. / Es tut mir leid. / Lo siento. / Je suis désolé. Mi dispiace. / Peço desculpa.

Okay. / Schon gut. / Está bien. / D'accord. / Ok. / Está bem.

That's right. / Das ist richtig. / Así es. / C'est exact. È giusto. / Está certo.

That's wrong. / Das ist falsch. / Es incorrecto. / C'est faux. È sbagliato. / Está errado.

Help! / Hilfe! / ¡Ayuda! / A l'aide ! / Aiuto! / Socorro!

salutations / die Begrüßungen / los saludos les saluts / saluti / as saudações

Hello. / Guten Tag. / Hola. / Bonjour. / Salve. / Olá.

Good morning. / Guten Morgen. / Buenos días. / Bonjour. Buongiorno. / Bom dia.

Good day. / Guten Tag. / Buen día. / Bonne journée. Buona giornata. / Um bom dia.

Good afternoon. / Guten Tag. / Buenas tardes. / Bonjour. Buon pomeriggio. / Boa tarde.

Good night. / Gute Nacht. / Buenas noches. / Bonne nuit. Buona notte. / Boa noite.

Goodbye. / Auf Wiedersehen. / Adiós. / Au revoir. Arrivederci. / Adeus.

How are you? / Wie geht's dir denn? / ¿Cómo estás? Comment allez-vous ? / Come stai? / Como estás?

I am fine. / Sehr gut. / Estoy bien. / Je vais bien. Sto bene. / Estou bem.

Pleased to meet you. / Hat mich gefreut, Sie kennenzulernen. / Encantado de conocerte. Ravi de vous rencontrer. / Piacere di conoscerti. Prazer em conhecerte.

How do you do? / Wie geht es Ihnen? / ¿Cómo te va? Je suis ravi de faire votre connaissance. / Come stai? Como vais?

My name is . . . / Ich heiße . . . / Yo me llamo . . . Je m'appelle . . . / Il mio nome è . . . / Chamo-me . . .

What is your name? / Und wie heißen Sie? ¿Cómo te llamas? / Comment vous appelez-vous ? Come ti chiami? / Como te chamas?

shake hands / das Händeschütteln
apretón de manos / se serrer la main
stringere la mano / o aperto de mãos

May I introduce . . . / Darf ich vorstellen . . .
Quisiera presentar a . . . / Puis-je vous pré-senter . . .
Ti presento . . . / Posso apresentar . . .

This is . . . / Das ist . . . / Esto es . . . / Voici . . .
Questo è . . . / Este/Esta é . . .

See you later. / Wir sehen uns später. / Hasta luego.
A plus tard. / Ci vediamo più tardi. / Até logo.

Until tomorrow. / Bis morgen. / Hasta mañana.
A demain. / A domani. / Até amanhã.

Cheers! / Prost! / ¡Gracias! / Au revoir ! / Salute! / Saúde!

useful phrases / Nützliche Redewendungenl las frases útiles / les phrases utiles frasi utili / as frases úteis

Do you speak . . . ? / Sprechen Sie . . . ? / ¿Sabes hablar en . . . ?
Parlez-vous . . . ? / Parli . . . ? / Falas . . . ?

I speak . . . / Ich spreche . . . / Hablo el . . . / Je parle . . .
Io parlo . . . / Eu falo . . .

Please speak more slowly. / Bitte sprechen Sie langsamer.
Por favor, habla más despacio. / Veuillez parler plus
lentement. / Per favore parla più lentamente.
Podes falar mais devagar?

Where is . . . ? / Wo ist . . . ? / ¿Dónde es . . . ?
Où se trouve . . . ? / Dove si trova . . . ? / Onde é . . . ?

To the right / Auf der rechten Seite / A la derecha
A droite / A destra / À direita

To the left / Nach links / A la izquierda / A gauche
A sinistra / À esquerda

How far is . . . ? / Wie weit ist . . . ? / ¿Qué tan lejos está?
A quelle distance . . . ? / Quanto è lontano . . . ?
O quão longe é . . . ?

Please write it down for me. / Bitte notieren Sie es für mich.
¿Lo puedes escribir, por favor? / Veuillez me l'écrire s'il
vous plait. / Per favore, scrivime-lo. / Podes escrever?

I don't understand. / Ich verstehe nicht ganz.
No entiendo. / Je ne comprends pas. / Non capisco.
Não entendo.

See you later. / Wir sehen uns später. / Hasta luego.
A plus tard. / Ci vediamo dopo. / Até logo.

Where is the restroom? / Wo ist die Toilette?
¿Dónde está el baño? / Où sont les toilettes ?
Dov'è il bagno? / Onde é a casa de banho?

You're early. / Sie sind früh dran. / Llegas temprano.
Vous êtes en avance. / Sei in anticipo. / Chegaste cedo.

Sorry I am late. / Tut mir leid, ich bin zu spät.
Lamento llegar tarde. / Désolé, je suis en retard.
Mi dispiace, sono in ritardo. / Desculpa, estou atrasado.

What time does it start? / Wann geht's los? / ¿A qué hora
empieza? / A quelle heure est-ce que ça commence ?
A che ora comincia? / A que horas começa?

I'll see you later. / Wir sehen uns später. / Te veo luego.
Je vous dis à plus tard. / Ci vediamo dopo.
Vejo-te depois.

Can you help me? / Kannst du mir helfen?
¿Puedes ayudarme? / Pouvez-vous m'aider ?
Puoi aiutarmi? / Podes ajudar-me?

May I see the menu? / Darf ich die Speisekarte sehen?
¿Puedo ver el menú? / Pourrais-je voir le menu ?
Posso vedere il menù? / Posso ver a ementa?

May I have some more? / Kann ich noch etwas haben?
¿Me puedes dar un poco más? / Pourrais-je en avoir
davantage ? / Posso averne ancora un po'?
Posso comer mais?

How do I get to . . . ?
Wie komme ich . . . ?
¿Como llego a . . . ?
Comment puis-je
me rendre à . . . ?
Come si va a . . . ?
Como chego a. . . ?

Straight ahead.
Geradeaus.
Hacia adelante.
Tout droit.
Sempre dritto.
Em frente.

I am done. / Ich bin fertig. / Ya terminé. / J'ai terminé.
Ho finito. / Estou cheio.

I don't drink. / Ich trinke nicht. / No bebo.
Je ne bois pas. / Non bevo. / Não bebo.

May we have the check? / Können wir die Rech-nung
haben? / ¿Nos puedes traer la cuenta? / Pourrais-je avoir
l'addition ? / Possiamo avere il conto? / A conta, por favor.

Can I have a receipt? / Kann ich eine Quittung haben?
¿Me puedes dar un recibo? / Pourrais-je avoir un reçu ?
Posso avere una ricevuta? / Pode passar fatura?

signs / die Schilder / las señales
les pancartes / i cartelli / os sinais

Stop / Stopp / Pare / Arrêtez-vous / Stop / Parar

Go / Gehen / Siga / Avancez / Vai / Avançar

Entrance / der Eingang / Entrada / Entrée
Ingresso / Entrada

Exit / die Ausfahrt / Salida / Sortie / Uscita / Saída

Emergency exit only / Nur Notausgang
Salida de emergencia / Sortie de secours
Solo uscita di emergenza / Saída de Emergência

No admittance / der Zutritt verboten / No pase
Entrée interdite / Vietato l'ingresso / Entrada proibida

No trespassing / Unbefugtes Betreten verboten
Prohibido el paso / Défense d'entrer / Vietato l'accesso
Passagem proibida

Private property / das Privatgrundstück
Propiedad privada / Propriété privée
Proprietà privata / Propriedade privada

Please keep off the grass. / Bitte den Rasen nicht betreten.
Por favor, manténgase alejado del césped.
Interdiction de marcher sur la pelouse.
Non calpestare l'erba. / Não pisar a relva.

Keep out / Nicht betreten / No entrar
Défense d'entrer / Accesso vietato
Não entrar

No dogs allowed / Hunde sind
nicht erlaubt / No se permiten
perros / Chiens non admis
Non sono ammessi cani
Não são permitidos cães

Please curb your dog. / Bitte zügeln
Sie Ihren Hund. / Por favor, controle
su perro. / Veuillez tenir vo-tre chien
en laisse. / Per favore, tieni il tuo cane.
Por favor, supervisione o seu cão.

in case of emergency use stairs / in Notfällen die
Treppe benutzen / en caso de emer-gencia, utilice la escalera
en cas d'urgence, veuillez utiliser les escaliers
in caso di emergenza usare le scale
em caso de emergência, usar as escadas

Opening times / Die Öffnungszeiten / Horario
de atención / Horaires d'ouver-ture / Orari di apertura
Horário de abertura

Hours of business / die Geschäftszeiten / Horario
de trabajo / Heures ouvrables / Orari di apertura
Horário de funcionamento

Standing room only / Nur Stehplätze / Sala sin sillas
Places debout / Solo posti in piedi / Lugares de pé

Free admission / Freier Eintritt / Entrada libre
Entrée libre / Ingresso gratuito / Entrada livre

Sold out / Ausverkauft / Agotado / Epuisé
Tutto esaurito / Esgotado

Push / Stoßen / Empuje / Pousser / Spingi / Empurrar

Pull / Ziehen / Hale / Tirer / Tira / Puxar

Danger! / Gefahr! / ¡Peligro! / Danger !
Pericolo! / Perigo!

Out of order / Außer Betrieb / Fuera de servicio
Hors service / Fuori servizio / Fora de serviço

Tourist information / Touristische Informationen
la información turística / Informations touristiques
Informazioni per i turisti / Informação
para turistas

Smoking area / die Raucherzone
Zona de fumadores / Zone fumeur
Area fumatori / Zona para
fumadores

No smoking
das Rauchen verboten
No fumar
Interdiction de fumer
Vietato fumare
Proibido fumar

NUMBERS / DIE ZAHLEN / LOS NÚMEROS / LES NOMBRES
I NUMERI / OS NÚMEROS

1 one / eine / uno / un / uno / um

2 two / zwei / dos / deux / due / dois

3 three / drei / tres / trois / tre / três

4 four / vier / cuatro / quatre / quattro / quatro

5 five / fünf / cinco / cinq / cinque / cinco

6 six / sechs / seis / six / sei / seis

7 seven / sieben / siete / sept / sette / sete

8 eight / acht / ocho / huit / otto / oito

9 nine / neun / nueve / neuf / nove / nove

10 ten / zehn / diez / dix / dieci / dez

11 eleven / elf / once / onze / undici / onze

12 twelve / zwölf / doce / douze / dodici / doze

13 thirteen / dreizehn / trece / treize / tredici / treze

14 fourteen / vierzehn / catorce / quatorze / quattordici / catorze

15 fifteen / fünfzehn / quince / quinze / quindici / quinze

16 sixteen / sechzehn / dieciséis / seize / sedici / dezasseis

17 seventeen / siebzehn / diecisiete / dix-sept / diciassette / dezassete

18 eighteen / achtzehn / dieciocho / dix-huit / diciotto / dezoito

19 nineteen / neunzehn / diecinueve / dix-neuf / diciannove / dezanove

20 twenty / zwanzig / veinte / vingt / venti / vinte

30 thirty / dreißig / treinta / trente / trenta / trinta

40 forty / vierzig / cuarenta / quarante / quaranta / quarenta

50 fifty / fünfzig / cincuenta / cinquante / cinquanta / cinquenta

60 sixty / sechzig / sesenta / soixante / sessanta / sessenta

70 seventy / siebzig / setenta / soixante-dix / settanta / setenta

80 eighty / achtzig / ochenta / quatre-vingts / ottanta / oitenta

90 ninety / neunzig / noventa / quatre-vingt-dix / novanta / noventa

100 one hundred / einhundert / cien / cent / cento / cem

200 two hundred / zweihundert / doscientos / deux cents / duecento / duzentos

300 three hundred / dreihundert / trescientos / trois cents / trecento / trezentos

400 four hundred / vierhundert / cuatrocientos / quatre cents / quattrocento / quatrocentos

500 five hundred / fünfhundert / quinientos / cinq cents / cinquecento / quinhentos

600 six hundred / sechshundert / sescientos / six cents / seicento / seiscentos

700 seven hundred / siebenhundert / setecientos / sept cents / settecento / setecentos

800 eight hundred / achthundert / ochocientos / huit cents / ottocento / oitocentos

900 / nine hundred / neunhundert / novecientos / neuf cents / novecento / novecentos

1,000 one thousand / eintausend / mil / mille / mille / mil

10,000 ten thousand / zehntausend / diez mil / dix mille / diecimila / dez mil

100,000 one hundred thousand / einhunderttausend / cien mil / cent mille / centomila / cem mil

1,000,000 one million / eine Million / un millón / un million / un milione / um milhão

ordinals / die Ordnungszahlen / los números ordinales / les nombres ordinaux
i numeri ordinali / os números ordinais

first / erste / primero / premier / primo / primeiro

second / zweite / segundo
deuxième / secondo / segundo

third / dritte
tercero / troisième
terzo / terceiro

fourth / vierte
cuarto / quatrième
quarto / quarto

fifth / fünfte
quinto / cinquième
quinto / quinto

sixth / sechste / sexto
sixième / sesto / sexto

seventh / siebter
séptimo / septième
settimo / sétimo

eighth / achtens
octavo / huitième
ottavo / oitavo

ninth / neunte / noveno
neuvième / nono / nono

tenth / zehnte / décimo / dixième
decimo / décimo

eleventh / elfte / decimoprimero
onzième / undicesimo
décimo primeiro

twelfth / zwölfte / decimosegundo
douzième / dodicesimo
décimo segundo

thirteenth / dreizehnte
decimotercero / treizième
tredicesimo / décimo terceiro

fourteenth / vierzehnte
decimocuarto / quatorzième
quattordicesimo / décimo quarto

fifteenth / fünfzehnte
decimoquinto / quinzième
quindicesimo / décimo quinto

sixteenth / sechzehnte
decimosexto / seizième
sedicesimo / décimo sexto

seventeenth / siebzehnte
decimoséptimo / dix-septième
diciassettesimo / décimo sétimo

eighteenth / achtzehnte
decimoctavo / dix-huitième
diciottesimo / décimo oitavo

nineteenth / neunzehnte
decimonoveno / dix-neuvième
diciannovesimo / décimo nono

twentieth / zwanzigste / vigésimo
vingtième / ventesimo / vigésimo

thirtieth / dreißigste / trigésimo
trentième / trentesimo / trigésimo

fortieth / vierzigste / cuadragésimo
quarantième / quarantesimo
quadragésimo

fiftieth / fünfzigste / quincuagésimo
cinquantième / cinquantesimo
quinquagésimo

sixtieth / sechzigste / sexagésimo
soixantième / sessantesimo
sexagésimo

seventieth / siebzigste
septuagésimo / soixante-dixième
settantesimo / septuagésimo

eightieth / achtzigste / octogésimo
quatre-vingtième / ottantesimo
octogésimo

ninetieth / neunzigste / nonagésimo
quatre-vingt-dixième / novantesimo
nonagésimo

hundredth / hundertste / centésimo
centième / centesimo / centésimo

Roman numerals
die Römischen Ziffern
los números romanos
les chiffres romains
i numeri romani
os números romanos

WEIGHTS AND MEASURES / DIE GEWICHTE UND MAßE / LOS PESOS Y MEDIDAS LES POIDS ET MESURES / I PESI E LE MISURE / OS PESOS E MEDIDAS

LENGTH / DIE LÄNGE / LA LONGITUD / LA LONGUEUR / LA LUNGHEZZA / O COMPRIMENTO

foot / der Fuß / el pie / le pied / il piede / pé

inch / der Zoll / la pulgada / le pouce / il pollice / polegada

ruler / das Lineal / la regla
la règle / il righello / a régua

centimenter / das Zentimetermaß / el centímetro
le centimètre / il centimetro / centímetro

DISTANCE / DIE ENTFERNUNG LA DISTANCIA / LA DISTANCE LA DISTANZA / A DISTÂNCIA

kilometer / der Kilometer
el kilómetro / le kilomètre
il chilometro / quilómetro

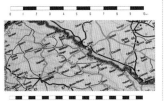

mile / die Meile / la milla
la mile / il miglio / milha

CIRCUMFERENCE DIE KREISZEIT LA CIRCUNFERENCIA LA CIRCONFÉRENCE LA CIRCONFERENZA A CIRCUNFERÊNCIA

millimeter
der Millimeter
el milímetro
le millimètre
il millimetro
milímetro

tape measure / das Bandmaß / la cinta métrica
le mètre ruban / il metro a nastro / a fita métrica

HEIGHT / DIE HÖHE / LA ALTURA / L'HAUTEUR / L'ALTEZZA A ALTURA

4 feet
4 Fuß
4 pies
4 pieds
4 piedi
4 pés

122 centimenters
122 Zentimeter
122 centímetros
122 centimètres
122 centimetri
122 centímetros

AREA / DIE FLÄCHE / EL ÁREA L'AIRE / L'AREA / A ÁREA

square foot / der Quadratfuß
el pie cuadrado / le pied carré
il piede quadrato / pé quadrado

square meter / der Quadratmeter
el metro cuadrado / le mètre carré
il metro quadrato / metro quadrado

WEIGHT / DAS GEWICHT / EL PESO / LE POIDS / IL PESO / O PESO

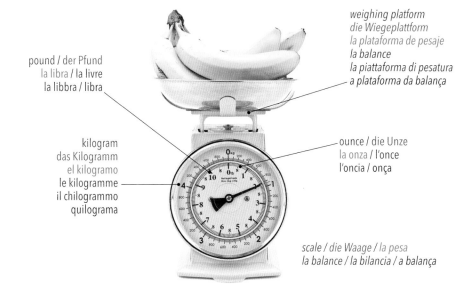

weighing platform
die Wiegeplattform
la plataforma de pesaje
la balance
la piattaforma di pesatura
a plataforma da balança

pound / der Pfund
la libra / la livre
la libbra / libra

kilogram
das Kilogramm
el kilogramo
le kilogramme
il chilogrammo
quilograma

ounce / die Unze
la onza / l'once
l'oncia / onça

scale / die Waage / la pesa
la balance / la bilancia / a balança

CAPACITY / DIE KAPAZITÄT / LA CAPACIDAD / LE VOLUME / LA CAPACITÀ / A CAPACIDADE

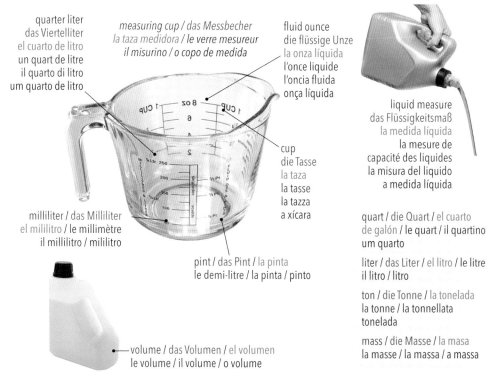

quarter liter
das Viertelliter
el cuarto de litro
un quart de litre
il quarto di litro
um quarto de litro

measuring cup / das Messbecher
la taza medidora / le verre mesureur
il misurino / o copo de medida

fluid ounce
die flüssige Unze
la onza líquida
l'once liquide
l'oncia fluida
onça líquida

liquid measure
das Flüssigkeitsmaß
la medida líquida
la mesure de
capacité des liquides
la misura del liquido
a medida líquida

cup
die Tasse
la taza
la tasse
la tazza
a xícara

milliliter / das Milliliter
el mililitro / le millimètre
il millilitro / mililitro

pint / das Pint / la pinta
le demi-litre / la pinta / pinto

quart / die Quart / el cuarto
de galón / le quart / il quartino
um quarto

liter / das Liter / el litro / le litre
il litro / litro

ton / die Tonne / la tonelada
la tonne / la tonnellata
tonelada

mass / die Masse / la masa
la masse / la massa / a massa

volume / das Volumen / el volumen
le volume / il volume / o volume

TIME / DIE UHRZEIT / EL TIEMPO / LE TEMPS / IL TEMPO / O TEMPO

one o'clock / ein Uhr
la una en punto / une heure
l'una / uma em ponto

quarter past one / Viertel nach eins
la una y cuarto / une heure et quart
l'una e un quarto / uma e um quarto

one thirty / eins dreißig
la una y media / une heure trente
l'una e trenta / uma e meia

quarter to two / Viertel vor zwei
el cuarto para las dos / deux heures
moins le quart / un quarto alle due
duas menos um quarto

What time is it?
Wie spät ist es?
¿Qué hora es?
Quelle heure est-il?
Che ore sono?
Que horas são?

It is seven-fifteen.
Es ist sieben Uhr fünfzehn.
Son las siete y cuarto.
Il est sept heures quinze.
Sono le sette e un quarto.
São sete e um quarto.

now / jetzt / ahora / maintenant
l'ora / agora

later / später / luego / plus tard
più tardi / mais tarde

soon / bald / pronto / bientôt
presto / em breve

early / früh / temprano / tôt
presto / cedo

late / spät / tarde / tard
tardi / tarde

on time / pünktlich / a tiempo
à l'heure / in orario / a tempo

alarm clock / der Wecker
el despertador / le réveil
la sveglia / o despertador

hour hand
der Uhrzeiger
la manecilla de las horas
'aiguille des heures
la lancetta delle ore
o ponteiro das horas

minute hand
der Minutenzeiger
la manecilla de los minutos
l'aiguille des minutes
la lancetta dei minuti
o ponteiro dos minutos

second hand
der Sekundenzeiger
la manecilla de los segundos
l'aiguille des secondes
la lancetta dei secondi
o ponteiro dos segundos

HOURS OF THE DAY / DIE STUNDEN DES TAGES / LAS HORAS DEL DIA
LES MOMENTS DE LA JOURNEE / LE ORE DEL GIORNO / AS ALTURAS DO DIA

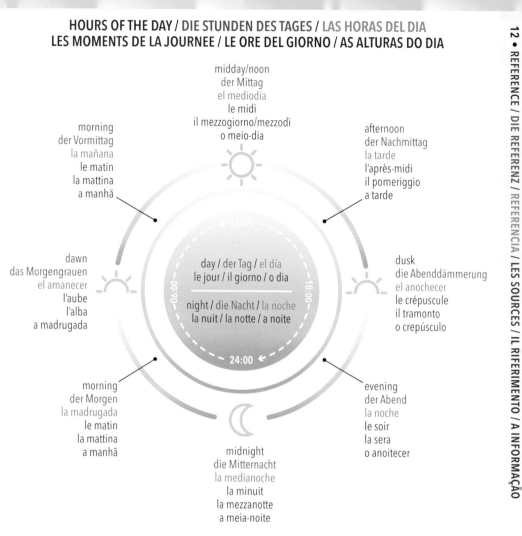

midday/noon
der Mittag
el mediodía
le midi
il mezzogiorno/mezzodì
o meio-dia

afternoon
der Nachmittag
la tarde
l'après-midi
il pomeriggio
a tarde

morning
der Vormittag
la mañana
le matin
la mattina
a manhã

dawn
das Morgengrauen
el amanecer
l'aube
l'alba
a madrugada

dusk
die Abenddämmerung
el anochecer
le crépuscule
il tramonto
o crepúsculo

day / der Tag / el día
le jour / il giorno / o dia

night / die Nacht / la noche
la nuit / la notte / a noite

12:00

06:00

18:00

24:00

morning
der Morgen
la madrugada
le matin
la mattina
a manhã

evening
der Abend
la noche
le soir
la sera
o anoitecer

midnight
die Mitternacht
la medianoche
la minuit
la mezzanotte
a meia-noite

sunrise
der Sonnenaufgang
el amanecer
le lever du soleil
l'alba
o nascer do sol

sunset
der Sonnenuntergang
el atardecer
le coucher du soleil
il tramonto
o pôr-do-sol

THE CALENDAR / DER KALENDER / EL CALENDARIO
LE CALENDRIER / IL CALENDARIO / O CALENDÁRIO

JANUARY —— month   year —— 2023

Monday	Tuesday	Wednesday	Thursday	Friday	Saturday	Sunday
1	2	3	4	5	6	7
8	9	10	11	12	13	14
15	16	17	18	19	20	21
22	23	24	25	26	27	28
29	30	(31)— date			weekend	

—days of the week

months

01 January	07 July
02 February	08 August
03 March	09 September
04 April	10 October
05 May	11 November
06 June	12 December

JANUAR —— der Monat   das Jahr —— 2023

Montag	Dienstag	Mittwoch	Donnerstag	Freitag	Samstag	Sonntag
1	2	3	4	5	6	7
8	9	10	11	12	13	14
15	16	17	18	19	20	21
22	23	24	25	26	27	28
29	30	(31)— das Datum			das Wochenende	

—Die Tage der Woche

die Monate

01 Januar	07 Juli
02 Februa	08 August
03 März	09 September
04 April	10 Oktober
05 Ma	11 November
06 Juni	12 Dezember

ENERO —— el mes   el año —— 2023

lunes	martes	miércoles	jueves	viernes	sábado	domingo
1	2	3	4	5	6	7
8	9	10	11	12	13	14
15	16	17	18	19	20	21
22	23	24	25	26	27	28
29	30	(31)— la fecha			el fin de semana	

—los días de la semana

los meses

01 enero	07 julio
02 febrero	08 agosto
03 marzo	09 septiembre
04 abril	10 octubre
05 mayo	11 noviembre
06 junio	12 diciembre

JANVIER —— le mois   l'année —— 2023

lundi	mardi	mercredi	jeudi	vendredi	samedi	dimanche
1	2	3	4	5	6	7
8	9	10	11	12	13	14
15	16	17	18	19	20	21
22	23	24	25	26	27	28
29	30	(31)— la date			le week-end	

—les jours de la semaine

les mois

01 janvier	07 juillet
02 février	08 aout
03 mars	09 septembre
04 avril	10 octobre
05 mai	11 novembre
06 juin	12 décembre

GENNAIO — il mese · gli anno — 2023

lunedì	martedì	mercoledì	giovedì	venerdì	sabato	domenica
1	2	3	4	5	6	7
8	9	10	11	12	13	14
15	16	17	18	19	20	21
22	23	24	25	26	27	28
29	30	(31) — l' appuntamento			il fine settimana	

— i giorni della settimana

i mesi

01 gennaio 07 luglio
02 febbraio 08 agosto
03 marzo 09 settembre
04 aprile 10 ottobre
05 maggio 11 novembre
06 giugno 12 dicembre

JANEIRO — o mês · o ano — 2023

segunda	terça	quarta	quinta	sexta	sábado	domingo
1	2	3	4	5	6	7
8	9	10	11	12	13	14
15	16	17	18	19	20	21
22	23	24	25	26	27	28
29	30	(31) — a data			o fim de semana	

— os dias da semana

os meses

01 janeiro 07 julho
02 fevereiro 08 agosto
03 março 09 setembro
04 abril 10 outubro
05 maio 11 novembro
06 junho 12 dezembro

---

yesterday / gestern / ayer / hier ieri / ontem

today / heute / hoy / aujourd'hui oggi / hoje

tomorrow / morgen / mañana demain / domani / amanhã

this week / diese Woche esta semana / cette semaine questa settimana / esta semana

daily / täglich / a diario / chaque jour / quotidiano / diariamente

weekly / wöchentlich / semanal chaque semaine / settimanale semanalmente

monthy / monatlich / mensual chaque mois / mensile mensualmente

yearly / jährlich / cada año / chaque année / annuale / anualmente

next week / nächste Woche la próxima semana / la semaine prochaine / la prossima settimana a próxima semana

last month / letzter Monat / el mes pasado / le mois dernier / il mese scorso / o mês passado

annual / jährlich / anual / annuel annuale / anual

decade / das Jahrzehnt / la década la décennie / il decennio / a década

century / das Jahrhundert / el siglo le siècle / il secolo / o século

millennium / das Jahrtausend el milenio / le millénaire il millennio / o milénio

---

SEASONS / DIE JAHRESZEITEN / LAS ESTACIONES / LES SAISONS / LE STAGIONI / AS ESTAÇÕES

spring / der Frühling la primavera / le printemps la primavera / a primavera

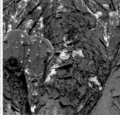

summer / der Sommer el verano / l'été l'estate / o verão

autumn / der Herbst el otoño / l'automne l'autunno / o outono

winter / der Winter el invierno / l'hiver l'inverno / o inverno

PHYSICAL MAP OF THE WORLD / DIE PHYSISCHE KARTE DER WELT
EL MAPA FÍSICO DEL MUNDO / LA CARTE PHYSIQUE DU MONDE
LA MAPPA FISICA DEL MONDO / O MAPA FÍSICO DO MUNDO

North America / das Nord-Amerika
América del Norte
l'Amérique du Nord
l'América del Nord
a América do Norte

Mississippi River
der Mississippi
el río Mississippi
la rivière Mississippi
il Fiume Mississippi
o Rio Mississípi

Arctic Ocean / der Arktische
Ozean / el océano Ártico / l'océan
Arctique / l'Oceano Artico
o Oceano Ártico

North Sea
die Nordsee
el mar del Norte
la mer du Nord
il Mare del Nord
o Mar do Norte

Bering Sea / das Beringmeer
el mar de Bering / la mer de Béring
il Mare di Bering / o Mar de Bering

Rocky Mountains
die Rocky Mountains
las montañas Rocosas
le montagne Rocciose
le Montagne Rocciose
as Montanhas Rochosas

Caribbean Sea
das Karibische Meer
el mar Caribe
la mer des Caraïbes
il Mar dei Caraibi
o Mar das Caraíbas

Amazon River
die Amazonas
el río Amazonas
la rivière Amazon
il Rio delle Amazzoni
o Rio Amazonas

Pacific Ocean
der Pazifische Ozean
el océano Pacífico
l'océan Pacifique
l'Oceano Pacifico
o Oceano Pacífico

The Andes / die Anden / los Andes
les Andes / le Ande / os Andes

South America / das Südamerika
América del Sur / l'Amérique du Sud
l'América del Sud / a América do Sul

Southern Ocean / der Südliche Ozean
el océano Austral / l'océan austral
l'Oceano del Sud / o Oceano Antártico

Antarctica / die Antarktis
la Antártida / l'Antarctique
l'Antartide / a Antártida

Atlantic Ocean
er Atlantische Ozean
el océano Atlántico
l'océan Atlantique
l'Oceano Atlantico
o Oceano Atlântico

Baltic Sea
das Baltische Meer
el mar báltico
la mer Baltique
il Mar Baltico
o Mar Báltico

Europe
das Europa
Europa
l'Europe
l'Europa
a Europa

Mediterranean Sea
das Mittelmeer
el mar Mediterráneo
la mer Méditerranée
il Mar Mediterraneo
o Mar Mediterrâneo

Black Sea / das Schwarze Meer
el mar Negro / la mer Noire
il Mar Nero / o Mar Negro

Caspian Sea / das Kaspische Meer
el mar Caspio / la mer Caspienne
il Mar Caspio / o Mar Cáspio

Asia / das Asien / Asia
l'Asie / l'Asia / a Ásia

The Himalayas / die Himalaya
el Himalaya / l'Himalaya
l'Himalaya / os Himalaias

Red Sea / das Rote Meer
el mar Rojo / la mer Rouge
il Mar Rosso
o Mar Vermelho

Arabian Sea
das Arabische Meer
el mar Arábigo
la mer d'Arabie
il Mar Arabico
o Mar Arábico

Coral Sea
das Korallenmeer
el mar del Coral
la mer de Corail
il Mar dei Coralli
o Mar de Coral

Australia / das Australien
Australia / l'Australie
l'Australia / a Austrália

compass / der Kompass / la brújula
la boussole / la bussola / a bússola

north / der Norden / el norte
le nord / il nord / o norte

west
der Westen
el oeste
l'ouest
l'ovest
o oeste

east
der Osten
el este
l'est
l'est
o este

south / der Süden / el sur
le sud / il sud / o sul

Africa / das Afrika
África / l'Afrique
l'Africa / a África

Indian Ocean
der Indische
Ozean
el océano Índico
l'océan Indien
l'Oceano Indiano
o Oceano Índico

Nile River / der Nil
el río Nilo / le Nil
il Fiume Nilo / o Rio Nilo

GERMAN INDEX

FRENCH INDEX

ITALIAN INDEX

PORTUGUESE INDEX